D1221269

Mathematical Theory of Economic Behavior

JOSEF HADAR

Case Western Reserve University

ADDISON-WESLEY PUBLISHING COMPANY

Reading, Massachusetts · Menlo Park, California · London · Don Mills, Ontario

330
H125m

155041

Copyright © 1971 by Addison-Wesley Publishing Company, Inc. Philippines copyright 1971 by Addison-Wesley Publishing Company, Inc.

All rights reserved. No part of this publication may be reproduced, stored in a retrieval system, or transmitted, in any form or by any means, electronic, mechanical, photocopying, recording, or otherwise, without the prior written permission of the publisher. Printed in the United States of America. Published simultaneously in Canada. Library of Congress Catalog Card No. 70-109513.

PREFACE

This book presents a mathematical exposition of the basic theories of the economic behavior of individual decision makers, and extensions of these theories to the workings of markets and general equilibrium systems. While it may possibly fulfill the occasional need of the professional economist for a reference work, the book is designed primarily to serve as a text for a graduate-level course (or sequence of courses) in microtheory. For this reason, the organization of the text has been determined mainly by pedagogical requirements; by and large, the material is presented in order of increasing difficulty, even in those instances where a different sequence would have been more logical from the point of view of the content.

The first few chapters of the text are essentially a review of undergraduate microtheory except, perhaps, for the fact that the formal analysis is carried out almost exclusively by means of mathematical tools. In other chapters the material is more advanced and of the type normally taught in graduate courses. Despite the formal character of the material, I have tried to be as informal as possible in the literary parts of the text, and have attempted to keep a fair balance between the derivation of formal results and the discussion of their meaning and implications. As is often done when writing a textbook, I have omitted from the general body of the text any references to source material; instead, at the end of each chapter, I have made a few comments on the relevant literature and listed selected references dealing with the subject matter of that chapter.

In writing this book I drew heavily on the existing literature, especially the items listed at the ends of chapters. I have also benefited from the comments and suggestions of several experts, each of whom read parts of the first draft. For this I am thankful to Lehman B. Fletcher, Rubin Saposnik, and Maurice Wilkinson, and also to Charles G. Cullen for his very precise comments on the mathematical review. Furthermore, while this book was in preparation, I enjoyed close associations with colleagues whom I was frequently able to consult, debate with, or exploit intellectually in one way or another. From the point of view of *my* needs, these exchanges were always most beneficial, and therefore I should like to express my gratitude to Claude

Hillinger, William Russell, and Thomas Saving. To identify a still earlier influence, I like to think of this work as the culmination of the development of my interest in mathematical economics. This interest was first aroused by Professor Leonid Hurwicz's lectures, which were in effect a most persuasive advocacy of the use of mathematics in economic analysis.

As any author knows, the conversion of a manuscript into a finished book can be a harrowing experience. Fortunately, thanks to the assistance of various kind people, I was spared the worst. The typing was expertly done by Mrs. Louise Kollar and Miss Susanne Preston; both deserve to be "mentioned in despatches" for having shown bravery and perseverance beyond the normal call of duty. In all other matters, my work was made as pleasant as possible by the complete co-operation of everyone at Addison-Wesley who was involved in the production of this book.

Cleveland, Ohio   J. H.
November 1970

CONTENTS

v

CHAPTER 1

INTRODUCTION

1.1 CONTENT AND STRUCTURE OF MICROTHEORY

The body of economic theory that deals with, or directly derives from, the behavior of economic decision units is commonly referred to as *microeconomic theory*, or for short, *microtheory*. Broadly speaking, microtheory consists of three levels which may be thought of as forming a pyramid. At the bottom of this pyramid are the theories of individual decision units, such as various theories of the firm, and theories of consumer behavior. Essentially, these theories of individual behavior form a part of the more general area of decision theory as it applies to choice problems in different economic contexts. The second level in this organizational structure consists of market theories for which the theories of individual behavior serve as building blocks. Market theories are concerned with the impact of the decisions of individual traders on the market price and on quantities exchanged. Thus, market theories deal with the allocation of resources and the distribution of goods among traders. Lastly, on the top of the pyramid, we have the theory of general equilibrium, in which all the markets in the economy are integrated into a whole for the purpose of studying the workings of the entire system.

The theories that make up the above pyramidal structure are the subject matter of this text. It may be appropriate to start this introductory discussion with some general comments about the nature of the material to be presented. First, we wish to draw the reader's attention to a certain distinction between economic theories (as well as those in other social sciences) and theories in the natural sciences. To be sure, this distinction is not of a fundamental nature inasmuch as the essential character and purpose of economic theories are the same as those of theories in the natural sciences (indeed, they are the same for all empirical sciences); rather, the distinction is one of achievement. Research in the natural sciences, as we all know, has resulted in the accumulation of a substantial body of knowledge about natural phenomena. To put it differently, many of the hypotheses that have been proposed in the natural sciences have repeatedly been confirmed through testing, and have consequently been accepted as laws. In economics, on the other hand, very few hypotheses have survived repeated testing (indeed, many have not been tested at all), as a result of which economics has, as of this time, only a handful of

1

laws to its credit. Furthermore, economic laws are mostly of a qualitative nature and do not always assume the form of a precise quantitative relationship; hence, in most cases these laws can be applied to specific problems only if additional quantitative information is available.

In view of this state of affairs, it is perhaps more correct to say that this text is not so much about economic *theories* as it is about economic *theorizing*. Roughly speaking, the latter term refers to the construction of economic theories, or models, and the derivation of conclusions from them. At this point, we shall briefly outline the main steps in this procedure, as it applies to microtheory.

Environment. As a first step in the construction of a model, one must describe the general framework of the problem under consideration. In the context of microtheory, this step refers to the specification of the environment in which the decision maker operates. For example, in the case of a firm, the environment encompasses such aspects as the structure of the market in which the firm operates and the technological conditions that govern its productive activities. Formally, the description of the environment involves the identification of the variables that affect the decision maker's actions, a choice of notation for these variables, and the specification of the relationships, if any, between the variables. The latter relationships may include identities (such as various accounting identities) as well as "behavioral" relationships (such as production, supply, and demand functions).

Objective. In microtheory it is generally assumed that the behavior of an economic unit is goal-oriented. This assumption means that the decisions taken by the economic unit (consumer or firm) are consistent with, or rather determined by, the desire to attain a certain objective. Therefore, a crucial step in the construction of a model is the specification of the decision maker's objective. In most microtheories this objective involves the maximization (or minimization) of an appropriate objective function.

Conclusions. Whereas the specifications of the environment and the objective can be chosen more or less freely by the model builder, the conclusions are not objects of choice since they are logical implications of the specifications; thus, choosing a set of specifications means "choosing" a set of conclusions. What remains for the model builder to do is to *derive* the conclusions from the chosen specifications. This is, of course, a purely deductive process which will be explained and illustrated in the text over and over again. Here we merely wish to point out that, by and large, the conclusions of micromodels fall into two classes. The conclusions in one of these classes are in the form of conditions that characterize the optimal decisions of the economic unit. These conditions can be interpreted as a set of rules which guide the economic unit in the making of its decisions. The second class of conclusions consists of the effects of changes in the environment: in the case of an individual model, these effects refer to changes in the optimal choices of the economic unit and, in the case of a market or general equilibrium model, the effects are changes in the equilibrium values of the endogenous variables (such as prices and quantities of goods). The conclusions in this class, to the extent that they are determinate, are in the nature of hypotheses about various economic phenomena, and, in principle, they may be tested and thus lead to the establishment of economic laws.

Optimality Conditions. The process of theorizing, whose principal steps we have outlined above, may be thought of as an intellectual, rather than physical, production process in which the assumptions about the environment and the objective serve as inputs, while the conclusions make up the output. Therefore, to appraise the potential usefulness of a model, we should look primarily at the conclusions. Let us briefly consider the first class of conclusions—the optimality conditions. Although these conditions are not hypotheses about general economic phenomena, they may nevertheless be of considerable use, especially to the economic practitioner (rather than the scientist). Essentially, these conditions are instructions for making optimal choices. For example, in the context of a firm, whose environment and objective are known, the optimality conditions determine the optimal choice of production process, input mix, output mix, output prices, and so on. Of course, it should be clear that the optimality rules will yield numerical results (decisions) only in situations in which the values of all environmental parameters are known. Even though such information may not always be available, the process of formulating the model and deriving the optimality conditions from it in itself serves to guide the firm with respect to the information it must collect and the manner in which this information is to be processed to yield the desired results. Thus, the formal model provides the decision maker with a rational basis for planning his action. In the broader framework of one or more markets, or an entire economic system, the optimality conditions may serve, at least in part, as a basis for the determination of public policies on such issues as taxation and subsidization, the distribution of government expenditures, price control, and economic regulation in general.

Hypotheses. The second class of conclusions, as we have already indicated, consists of the effects of changes in environmental parameters. These effects are usually called the *comparative static* properties of the model. The derivation of comparative static properties is one of the principal objectives of microtheory, since it is among these properties that we seek testable hypotheses. It is important to realize, however, that not every comparative static property constitutes a hypothesis, inasmuch as such a property may be of an indeterminate nature. For example, if a particular model implies that an increase in an excise tax will cause either an increase, a decrease, or no change in the price of the taxed commodity, then this particular comparative static property is of an indeterminate nature, and hence does not constitute a hypothesis. This is so because an essential feature of a hypothesis is that it must be *falsifiable*, i.e., capable of being shown to be false. In the present example, it is clear that the validity of the implication concerning the effect of a tax increase on the price of the commodity can be established without reference to any empirical observation; its truth being a logical necessity, the conclusion asserts nothing whatsoever about the effect of a tax increase on price, and hence it has no predictive content. On the other hand, if the model yields a determinate comparative static property, for example, the proposition that a tax increase causes a rise in the price of the good, then the latter proposition is a genuine hypothesis, since its validity may possibly be contradicted by empirical evidence.

Generality versus Empirical Content. The issue raised in the above section is an important one, and as our analysis will show, economic models, on the whole, yield relatively few determinate comparative static properties (i.e., hypotheses). It may be instructive to look briefly into the reason for this situation. As we have pointed out earlier, the conclusions of a model depend directly on the underlying assumptions, i.e., the specifications of the evironment and the objective. Since, by and large, we have almost no *a priori* quantitative information about the economic, technological, and psychological environments of a typical economic unit, we are necessarily forced to select for our models fairly general specifications. Unfortunately, it is almost invariably true that the greater the generality of the specifications (assumptions) of a model, the fewer are its hypotheses. Therefore, it seems that the only way of making it possible to extract more hypotheses from a model (i.e., to increase its predictive content) is by reducing the generality of the assumptions. But by strengthening the assumptions of the model, and thereby transforming it into a more specific (i.e., less general) one, we incur the risk of diminishing its relevance, inasmuch as when thus modified, it may not be applicable to large classes of phenomena. Consequently, in the construction of economic models we are confronted with a typical problem of choice under conditions of scarcity (not unlike practical problems in economics): namely, having more of one desirable thing can be achieved only by having less of another. In the present problem, we are concerned with two desirable traits of a theoretical model: empirical content and relevance (generality). As we have seen, the empirical content of a model can be increased by making the model more specific, but doing so is likely to make it less general; on the other hand, making the model more general, and thereby making it applicable to a wider range of phenomena, will tend to diminish its empirical content. This problem, by its very nature, cannot be solved by any rational method since there exists no rule by which one can determine the optimal mix of empirical content and generality. Consequently, the model builder must in each case use his own judgment in deciding how far he should go in tightening or loosening the specifications of his model.

Occasionally, of course, it may happen that quantitative data about environmental parameters become available, even if only with respect to such special cases as a particular product, market, or geographical area. In such a case, the data may be used for the construction of a specialized model which may possibly generate several hypotheses of interest. However, these hypotheses will be of limited scope since they will apply only to those classes of environments that satisfy the specification of the special model.

The process of theorizing, i.e., the construction and analysis of economic models, is the unifying theme of this book. Our purpose is to demonstrate how various problems in microtheory can be formulated and analyzed by means of formal models. Thus, our emphasis is on the *how* rather than the *what*. In particular, no attempt is made to consider all the possible problems that may arise in the context of microtheory, or to present all the different ways of modeling a particular problem. In choosing the models for inclusion in this text, we have tried to strike a balance between the two objectives of the text: (1) to familiarize the reader with the content of the important aspects of existing theories, and (2) to train him in the techniques of constructing and analyzing economic models. Many of the models included in the text have indeed gained fairly wide acceptance among economists, and thus constitute part of what is (currently) considered to be the standard body of microtheory. Others, on the other hand, have been included mainly for their pedagogical value.

1.2 THE MATHEMATICAL APPROACH

As the title of this work indicates, the exposition of the subject matter is carried out primarily by means of mathematical tools. While this introductory chapter is not the proper place for a lengthy discourse on the merits of the use of mathematics, a few comments on this issue are in order. One purpose of these comments is to dispel any notion the reader may entertain that mathematical economics is, somehow, a separate discipline from economics. Such an idea is, of course, a fundmental misconception. The mathematical approach is merely one of several possible approaches (such as the verbal and the diagrammatic approaches) to the analysis of economic problems. However, because of its highly formal character, the mathematical approach is quite distinct from the nonmathematical ones, and, indeed, it enjoys certain advantages over the others. First, there is the matter of precision. This is, of course, an absolute necessity when it comes to performing any kind of analytical work. In economic theory, the use of mathematics enables us, first of all, to state the specifications of the model in as precise a form as possible. Second, in deriving the various conclusions from the assumptions, the use of the mathematical method is most appropriate since, as we have already pointed out, the derivation of conclusions is a purely deductive process. Because of its well-defined rules of operation, the mathematical method has the advantage of providing us with a means of performing these derivations in an error-free manner. (True, we sometimes make errors by violating some mathematical rules, but in most instances the mathematical method also suggests ways of checking the results, thus making it possible to detect any errors.) Furthermore, if a model is of any complexity at all, then, for all practical purposes, the mathematical method is the only one capable of analyzing the problem under consideration. Third, the conclusions that are obtained as a result of the deductive process will also be stated in very precise terms, and this is of special importance for purposes of evaluating and testing the model. Generally speaking, the use of the mathematical method eliminates (or at least sharply reduces) any ambiguities that may arise with regard to the meaning of either the specifications or the conclusions of the model. This in itself is likely to increase our understanding of the problem under examination.

Another characteristic of the mathematical method is its economy. The implications of this feature are perhaps less apparent. When using the mathematical method, it is possible to express large and complex models by means of very compact notation. We are, therefore, able to consider and work with models which, because of their size and complexity, either cannot be analyzed at all by other methods or, at best, only with considerable difficulty. Moreover, the compactness of the mathematical notation greatly facilitates the typographical presentation of a model; often an entire model and its conclusions can be perceived visually at a glance. This aids in discovering the relationships between the various components of the model, so that we obtain a clearer picture of the structure of the entire model. Furthermore, the compact notation also facilitiates comparisons between different models, as a result of which we may discover differences and similarities between their structures and conclusions that might otherwise not be recognized as easily.

The last aspect that we wish to point out concerns the combined effect of the elements of precision and compactness. Not only does the mathematical method enable us to see the structure of a model with greater clarity, it also makes it possible to see things which under a different approach may remain hidden. It is often the case that, as a result of the compactness of the notation, and the ease with which the various parts of the model can be manipulated, conclusions are obtained which we would not have expected on the basis of our intuition about the problem, and which other methods may fail to reveal. The use of the mathematical method enables us to extract all the possible conclusions from any given set of specifications, and for this reason the mathematical method may be said to be more powerful than other methods. In summary, we may aptly describe the advantages of the mathematical method by saying that it deepens our insights into, and increases our understanding of, any economic model, while at the same time it may lead to the derivation of unsuspected hypotheses. Consequently, it seems that when applied to the construction and analysis of models, mathematics is more than just a language; since it enhances and extends our analytical facilities, it is truly an instrument of discovery.

1.3 ORGANIZATION OF THE TEXT

Finally, a few words about the organization of the text. Chapters 2 and 3 are devoted to the discussion of some concepts that play an important role in the construction of micromodels; these concepts are the cost and production functions that serve to describe the technological environment of a firm. In Chapters 4 through 8 we examine the behavior of a firm under a variety of different economic environments; these include pure competition, pure monopoly, and different forms of monopolistic competition. Chapter 9 deals with the decision making of a firm operating under conditions of a linear technology. The theory of consumer behaviour is taken up in Chapters 10 and 11; the former covers the basic theory, while the latter considers various aspects of intertemporal optimization. Chapter 12 considers behavior under uncertainty, with examples from both the theory of the consumer and the theory of the firm. The following two chapters deal with general equilibrium models: Chapter 13 is confined to positive aspects of general equilibrium theory, while Chapter 14 addresses itself to normative aspects. Last, in Chapter 15, we present a brief review of the mathematics used in the text.

BIBLIOGRAPHICAL NOTES

The selected items included in the following short list are designed to introduce the reader to the topic of scientific methodology. Familiarity with some basic aspects of methodology fulfills two objectives: (1) it provides a useful background and perspective for anyone about to embark on a theoretical endeavor, and (2) it constitutes a frame of reference for the evaluation of theoretical work. Consequently, the reader will do well to consult at least some of the general works on methodology *before* he starts studying the theories presented in the succeeding chapters, and to undertake additional reading in methodology after he has acquainted himself with several different models.

The following articles deal with various methodological aspects of economic theory: O. Lange, "The Scope and Method of Economics," *Review of Economic Studies*, **13**, 19–32 (1945), reprinted in D. R. Kamerschen (ed.), *Readings in Microeconomics*, Cleveland: World, 1967, pp. 3–22; P. Streeten, "Economics and Value Judgments," *Quarterly Journal of Economics*, **64**, 583–595 (1950); D. Novik, "Mathematics: Logic, Quantity and Method," *Review of Economics and Statistics*, **36**, 357–358 (1954), and the succeeding discussions of Novik's article by P. A. Samuelson, L. R. Klein, J. S. Duesenberry, J. S. Chipman, J. Tinbergen, D. G. Champernowne, R. Solow, R. Dorfman, and T. C. Koopmans; and last, T. C. Koopmans, "The Construction of Economic Knowledge," in *Three Essays on the*

State of Economic Science, New York: McGraw-Hill, 1957, Essay II, pp. 127–166.

Debate on some fairly technical aspects of methodology has recently taken place in the literature. This debate was stimulated to a large extent by M. Friedman's article "The Methodology of Positive Economics," in *Essays in Positive Economics*, Chicago: University of Chicago Press, 1953, pp. 3–43, reprinted in W. Breit and H. M. Hochman (eds.), *Readings in Microeconomics*, New York: Holt, Rinehart and Winston, 1968, pp. 23–47. Some of the ensuing discussions may be found in the following: E. Nagel, "Assumptions in Economic Theory," *American Economic Review* (Supplement), **53**, 211–219 (1963), reprinted in W. Breit and H. M. Hochman (eds.), *Readings in Microeconomics*, New York: Holt, Rinehart and Winston, 1968, pp. 60–66; F. Machlup, "Professor Samuelson on Theory and Realism," *American Economic Review*, **54**, 733–735 (1964); P. A. Samuelson, "Theory and Realism: A Reply," *American Economic Review*, **54**, 736–739 (1964); and J. Melitz, "Friedman and Machlup on the Significance of Testing Economic Assumptions," *Journal of Political Economy*, **73**, 37–60 (1965).

A recently published collection of original articles on methodology may be found in S. R. Krupp (ed.), *The Structure of Economic Science*, Englewood Cliffs, N.J.: Prentice-Hall, 1966. Readers who are willing to do additional reading on fundamental aspects of methodology of science are advised to consult the various monographs in the *Foundations of Philosophy Series* published by Prentice-Hall, and especially Carl Hempel, *Philosophy of Natural Science*, 1966, and Richard Rudner, *Philosophy of Social Science*, 1966.

CHAPTER 2

COST FUNCTIONS

2.1 THE SHORT RUN

2.1.1 Total Cost Functions

The first concepts to be introduced are three related cost concepts. The first of these is *total cost* (TC); it represents the sum of all the outlays in connection with producing a given level of output during some fixed period of time, and, whenever appropriate, the imputed cost of factors of production owned by the producer. The costs which make up TC are classified into two groups: *total variable cost* (TVC) and *total fixed cost* (TFC). The former comprises those costs which vary whenever the level of output is changed, and the latter represents costs which are independent of the level of output—so called overhead costs. Thus by definition

(2.1a) $$\mathrm{TC} = \mathrm{TVC} + \mathrm{TFC}.$$

It should be pointed out that overhead costs are not inherently fixed, but only relative to the length of the time period in question. Presumably, if the planning period is sufficiently long, all costs can be made variable. Therefore, whenever there exist fixed costs in the model, the latter is defined as a *short-run* model, and the respective cost functions are referred to as short-run cost functions. *Long-run* cost functions, on the other hand, are characterized by the absence of fixed costs. The latter are discussed in Section 2.2.

If we adopt the notation $\mathrm{TVC} = f(x)$, then the fundamental cost identity can be written as

(2.1b) $$\mathrm{TC} = f(x) + c,$$

where x denotes the rate, or level, of output during a given period of time, and c is some positive number. The function f is defined for finite and nonnegative values of x. Furthermore, the function f is assumed to possess certain fairly general properties which reflect the technological relationships underlying the productive process.

First of all, we assume

(2.2) $$f(0) = 0.$$

Equation (2.2) says simply that when the level of output is zero, the firm incurs no variable costs. Under these circumstances the firm incurs only the fixed costs which must be defrayed regardless of how much the firm chooses to produce.

Second, we should expect TVC to be a strictly increasing function since higher levels of output ordinarily require greater outlays. This assumption can be stated as follows:

$$f(x_1) > f(x_0) \quad \text{if and only if} \quad x_1 > x_0.$$

If f is differentiable everywhere in the domain of definition, as we shall assume, the above assumption can be translated into a restriction on the first derivative of the function f; that is,

(2.3) $f' > 0,$

where $f' = df/dx$. (First and second total derivatives will frequently be denoted by ' and " respectively.) Geometrically speaking, assumptions (2.2) and (2.3) state that the TVC function goes through the origin, and that it has a positive slope everywhere.

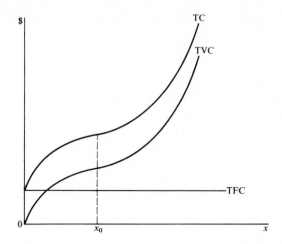

Figure 2.1

The above assumptions also imply that the TVC function takes only nonnegative values. The shape of the TVC function is illustrated in Fig. 2.1.

An additional assumption about TVC has to do with the curvature of the function. The assumption says, in effect, that the TVC function increases at a decreasing rate as output is increased from zero, but that beyond a certain level of output the TVC function increases at an increasing rate. Formally, this assumption can be stated as follows:

There exists some positive level of output x_0 such that

(2.4a) $\qquad\qquad\qquad f'' < 0 \qquad$ for $\qquad 0 \leqslant x < x_0,$

(2.4b) $\qquad\qquad\qquad f'' > 0 \qquad$ for $\qquad x > x_0,$

(2.4c) $\qquad\qquad\qquad f'' = 0 \qquad$ at $\qquad x = x_0.$

The TVC function, therefore, has an inflection point at x_0.

The assumptions about TVC immediately imply certain assumptions about TC through the definitional relationship (2.1). We have the following:

(2.5) $\qquad\qquad\qquad \text{TC}_0 \ (\text{TC at } x = 0) \ = c,$

(2.6) $\qquad\qquad\qquad \text{TC}' = f',$

(2.7) $\qquad\qquad\qquad \text{TC}'' = f''.$

According to conditions (2.5) through (2.7) the TC and TVC functions have identical shapes, with TC lying above TVC, and the distance between them at every point being equal to TFC. The graph of the TFC function is merely a horizontal line whose intercept coincides with that of TC. (See Fig. 2.1.)

2.1.2 Average and Marginal Cost Functions

Average cost refers to the cost of production *per unit of output*. For each of the three total cost functions there exists a corresponding average cost function which is obtained by dividing the corresponding total cost function by the level of output. Of course, since division by zero is an undefined operation, the average cost functions are not defined at the zero level of output.

According to these definitions we have

(2.8) $\qquad$ *Average total cost* (ATC) $= \dfrac{f(x) + c}{x},$

(2.9) $\qquad$ *Average variable cost* (AVC) $= \dfrac{f(x)}{x},$ $\qquad\qquad x \neq 0.$

(2.10) $\qquad$ *Average fixed cost* (AFC) $= \dfrac{c}{x},$

If we divide both sides of Eq. (2.1) by x, we obtain another cost identity, namely:

(2.11) $\qquad\qquad\qquad \text{ATC} = \text{AVC} + \text{AFC}.$

As the functional form shows, AFC is a rectangular hyperbola. ATC and AVC are both U-shaped, as will be proved in Section 2.1.3. ATC lies above AVC, and the vertical distance between the two is equal to the value of AFC at the corresponding level of x. Since AFC is a strictly decreasing function, it

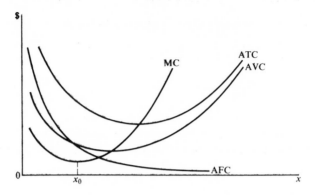

Figure 2.2

follows that AVC approaches ATC as x increases. These relationships are shown in Fig. 2.2.

Finally, we need the concept of *marginal cost* (MC). If the output x is increased by some small amount, say Δx, then TC, being a function of x, will also change by some amount, say ΔTC. We then define

(2.12a)
$$MC = \frac{\Delta TC}{\Delta x}.$$

However, in our analysis we usually allow x to change by infinitesimally small amounts. In that case, MC is defined as the limit of the ratio given in (2.12a) as Δx approaches zero. This limit (whose existence we have already assumed) is nothing but the first derivative of the TC function. Thus, when x is capable of continuous variation, MC may be thought of as the rate of change of TC at any given level of x. Formally,

(2.12b)
$$MC = TC' = f'.$$

Geometrically, MC represents the slope of the TC, as well as the TVC, function at any given level of x. From assumption (2.3) we see that MC is positive, and from (2.4) we see that MC decreases at outputs less than x_0, and increases at outputs greater than x_0. Thus, MC is also U-shaped.

It is quite easy to derive certain general and useful relationships between MC on the one hand, and ATC and AVC on the other. Suppose we differentiate ATC with respect to x. Then we get, making use of (2.8),

(2.13)
$$ATC' = \frac{xf' - f(x) - c}{x^2}.$$

Now, if in a certain range ATC is decreasing, i.e., if the above derivative is negative, then the numerator in the right-hand side (rhs) of (2.13) is also negative. That is,

if $ATC' < 0$, *then* $xf' - f(x) - c < 0$.

Rearranging the second inequality in the above statement, we have

$$\text{if } ATC' < 0, \quad \text{then } f' < \frac{f(x) + c}{x},$$

or in words,

> *if ATC is decreasing, then* MC < ATC.

In fact, the antecedent and conclusion in the above statement may be reversed, so that we are really entitled to say:

> ATC *is decreasing if and only if* MC < ATC.

Using the same derivations for the case in which ATC is either increasing or constant, we get two additional statements:

> ATC *is increasing if and only if* MC > ATC.
>
> ATC *is constant if and only if* MC = ATC.

It is easy to show that the truth of the above three statements is invariant to (i.e., unaffected by) a substitution of AVC for ATC.

Example 2.1 As an illustration consider the following TVC function:

$$TVC = (x - a)^3 + bx + a^3 = f(x), \qquad a, b > 0.$$

It is easy to verify that $f(0) = 0$, and furthermore that $f(x) > 0$ for $x > 0$. Differentiating the function f, we get

$$MC = 3(x - a)^2 + b = f',$$

which is always positive. In order to verify conditions (2.4), we differentiate once more to get

$$MC' = 6(x - a) = f''.$$

Hence

$$f'' < 0 \quad \text{for} \quad 0 \leqslant x < a,$$
$$f'' > 0 \quad \text{for} \quad x > a,$$
$$f'' = 0 \quad \text{at} \quad x = a.$$

The AVC function in this example takes the form

$$AVC = \frac{(x - a)^3 + bx + a^3}{x}.$$

Differentiating the above function, we obtain the slope of the AVC function. Thus

$$AVC' = 2x - 3a,$$

and hence the AVC function attains its minimum at the point $x = 3a/2$, at which point we also have MC = AVC. Note that the inflection point of the TVC function occurs at a level of output (that is, $x = a$) which is less than that at which AVC has its minimum.

2.1.3 The Shape of the AVC Function

In this section we shall prove formally that the assumptions about the shape of the TVC function imply that the AVC function is U-shaped. Among other things, this proof will illustrate the use of the Theorem of the Mean, and certain properties of continuous functions. We shall do this by proving the following proposition:

If conditions (2.2), (2.4a), *and* (2.4b) *of Section 2.1.1 hold, then there exists a level of output, say* x^*, *such that* $AVC' < 0$ *for* $0 < x < x^*$, $AVC' > 0$ *for* $x > x^*$, *and* $AVC' = 0$ *at* $x = x^*$.

The proof is divided into three parts.

a) We express the derivative of the AVC function in terms of the TVC function and its derivative by differentiating (2.9). This yields

$$(2.14) \qquad\qquad AVC' = \frac{xf'(x) - f(x)}{x^2}.$$

Since in the present problem we are concerned only with the sign of AVC', we need only consider the numerator of the expression on the rhs of (2.14). We now apply the Theorem of the Mean (see Proposition 15.6 in Chapter 15) to the function f in the interval $[0, x]$, and write

$$\frac{f(x) - f(0)}{x} = f'(\xi_1),$$

or

$$(2.15) \qquad\qquad xf'(\xi_1) - f(x) = -f(0),$$

where $0 < \xi_1 < x$. If we choose the point x such that $x \leqslant x_0$ [x_0 as defined in (2.4)], then it follows from (2.4a) that $f'(x) < f'(\xi_1)$. Therefore,

$$(2.16) \qquad\qquad xf'(x) - f(x) < xf'(\xi_1) - f(x) = 0,$$

where the equality follows from (2.15) and (2.2). Condition (2.16) implies, in conjunction with (2.14), that AVC' is negative for $0 < x \leqslant x_0$.

b) Rewriting (2.16) for $x = x_0$, we have

$$(2.17) \qquad\qquad x_0 f'(x_0) - f(x_0) < 0.$$

But since f' is an increasing function for $x > x_0$ by (2.4b), we can make f' as large as we wish by evaluating it at a sufficiently large value of x. Consequently, there exists a point $x > x_0$, say x_1, such that

$$(2.18) \qquad\qquad x_0 f'(x_1) - f(x_0) \geqslant 0.$$

Applying the Theorem of the Mean once more, this time to the interval $[x_0, x_1]$, we have

$$\frac{f(x_1) - f(x_0)}{x_1 - x_0} = f'(\xi_2),$$

or

(2.19) $(x_1 - x_0)f'(\xi_2) = f(x_1) - f(x_0),$

where $x_0 < \xi_2 < x_1$. But since $f'(x_1) > f'(\xi_2)$ by (2.4b), we have

(2.20) $(x_1 - x_0)f'(x_1) > (x_1 - x_0)f'(\xi_2) = f(x_1) - f(x_0).$

By suitably rearranging terms in (2.20), we can write

(2.21) $x_1 f'(x_1) - f(x_1) > x_0 f'(x_1) - f(x_0) \geqslant 0,$

where the second inequality follows from (2.18). This result obviously holds for any $x \geqslant x_1$. Thus, AVC' is positive for all $x \geqslant x_1$.

c) To summarize briefly, we have found two points, x_0 and x_1, $x_0 < x_1$, satisfying the following:

$$\text{AVC}' < 0 \quad \text{for} \quad 0 < x \leqslant x_0,$$
$$\text{AVC}' > 0 \quad \text{for} \quad x \geqslant x_1.$$

It remains to investigate the behavior of the AVC function in the interval $[x_0, x_1]$. Since the latter interval is a compact set, it follows (see Proposition 15.2) that AVC attains both an absolute minimum and an absolute maximum in the interval. But since the values of the derivative of AVC at the endpoints x_0 and x_1 have opposite signs, only one of these points can be an absolute extreme point (i.e., either an absolute maximum or an absolute minimum). Consequently, one of the extreme points must be located in the interior of the interval. Then we know (Proposition 15.8) that at that point, say x^*, the derivative of the AVC function vanishes, and so we have

(2.22) $x^* f'(x^*) - f(x^*) = 0.$

The Theorem of the Mean is now applied to the interval $[x^*, x]$ to yield

$$(x - x^*)f'(\xi_3) = f(x) - f(x^*),$$

where $x^* < \xi_3 < x$. Since f' is increasing at values of x exceeding x^*, we have

$$(x - x^*)f'(x) > (x - x^*)f'(\xi_3) = f(x) - f(x^*),$$

and hence

(2.23) $xf'(x) - f(x) > x^*f'(x) - f(x^*) > x^*f'(x^*) - f(x^*) = 0,$

where the equality follows from (2.22). Therefore, it is clear that AVC' is positive for all $x > x^*$, which means that at the extreme point x^*, the AVC function attains a minimum.

To complete the proof, we must show that the point x^* is unique. Suppose there exists another point, say x^{**}, at which the AVC function has a local minimum. Since we have already shown that the AVC function increases for all $x > x^*$, it follows that x^{**} must lie between x_0 and x^*. However, since at x^{**} the slope of the AVC function must vanish, we can use Eq. (2.22), and the reasoning following that equation, to obtain a result similar to that given in (2.23), and thus show that AVC' is positive for all $x > x^{**}$. That, however, contradicts the fact that at the point x^*, AVC' vanishes, hence the point x^{**} cannot exist. Consequently, the point x^* satisfies the conditions of the proposition which was to be proved.

2.1.4 The Case of n Products

If the firm produces more than one product, then the cost of producing a given amount of one product may depend on the amounts produced of the other products. If the firm produces n products ($n \geqslant 2$), the various cost functions depend in general on the n variables $x^1, x^2, ..., x^n$, where x^i is the amount produced of the ith product. Thus we can write

$$TC = f(x^1, x^2, ..., x^n) + c.$$

As in the one-product case, it is reasonable to assume that $f(0, 0, ..., 0) = 0$. For each of the n products we define marginal cost as $MC^i = f_i$. Subscripts attached to functional symbols denote partial derivatives; thus

$$f_i = \frac{\partial f(x)}{\partial x^i}, \qquad i = 1, 2, ..., n.$$

As a measure of economy, we shall sometimes use the notation x to denote the vector $(x^1, x^2, ..., x^n)$.

Average cost functions may be defined for each product as follows:

$$ATC^i = \frac{f(x) + c}{x^i}; \quad AVC^i = \frac{f(x)}{x^i}; \quad AFC^i = \frac{c}{x^i}; \quad x^i \neq 0, \quad i = 1, 2, ..., n.$$

The relationships between ATC and MC (and AVC and MC) which we derived in Section 2.1.2 hold for each product. Accordingly,

ATC^i *is decreasing if and only if* $MC^i < ATC^i$.

ATC^i *is increasing if and only if* $MC^i > ATC^i$.

ATC^i *is constant if and only if* $MC^i = ATC^i$.

Similar statements hold for AVC^i. Finally, if we impose conditions on the f_{ii} similar to those in (2.4), then it can be shown that the AVC^i and ATC^i functions are U-shaped.

2.2 THE LONG RUN

The reader will recall that the short run is defined by the existence of fixed factors of production, and hence fixed cost. For convenience, the fixed factors can be lumped together and referred to as the "size of plant." Short-run analysis is, therefore, concerned with the firm's operating conditions for a given size of plant.

In the long run, by definition, all factors and costs are variable. Thus, long-run cost functions reflect not only the effects on cost of changes in the level of output, but also the effects of variations in the size of the plant. In this section, we shall demonstrate the construction of long-run cost functions and indicate some of their properties.

If we let z denote the size of plant (x still denoting the level of output), we can write

(2.24a) $$\mathrm{SAC}_1 = f^*(x, z_1),$$

where SAC stands for *short-run average total cost*, and the subscript indicates the particular size of plant, that is, $z = z_1$. For any fixed level of z, the function f^* represents an ordinary U-shaped ATC function of the type discussed in Section 2.1. Thus, for z constant, say $z = z_1$, we have

$$f^*(x, z_1) = \frac{f(x) + c}{x},$$

where $f(x)$ and c are defined as in (2.1b). But now we are concerned with the effect on short-run cost as the size of plant is changed. We make the following assumptions:

For any two different sizes of plant z_1 and z_2, and $z_1 < z_2$, there exists a level of output x_0 (depending on both z_1 and z_2) such that

(2.25a) $f^*(x, z_1) < f^*(x, z_2)$ for $x < x_0,$

(2.25b) $f^*(x, z_1) > f^*(x, z_2)$ for $x > x_0,$

(2.25c) $f^*(x, z_1) = f^*(x, z_2)$ at $x = x_0.$

This assumption can be interpreted as stating that at levels of output which are small relative to the plants in question, the smaller of the two plants incurs a lower unit cost of production, but as output exceeds a certain level, the larger of the two plants is more efficient.

In Fig. 2.3 is shown a set of cost curves consistent with this assumption, the basis for which is quite reasonable: At relatively low levels of output, the larger plant is less efficient than the smaller plant because, compared to the smaller plant, it has more unused capacity, and it also has a higher fixed cost. (Fixed cost increases as the size of the plant increases.) At relatively high levels of output, on the other hand, the smaller plant uses a greater portion of its capacity, and hence is more "crowded" than the larger plant.

We make further assumptions concerning the relative positions of various SAC functions. These assumptions are stated as follows:

There exists a size of plant, say z_m, such that

(2.26) $\min f^*(x, z_m) < \min f^*(x, z_i)$ for all $i, i \neq m,$

(2.27a) $\min f^*(x, z_i) > \min f^*(x, z_j)$ for $i < j \leqslant m,$

(2.27b) $\min f^*(x, z_i) < \min f^*(x, z_j)$ for $m \leqslant i < j.$

In words, starting from some relatively small size of plant, the minimum of the SAC functions falls as the size of plant is increased, reaches its minimum when the size of plant is equal to z_m, and rises as the size of plant is increased beyond z_m, as shown in Fig. 2.3.

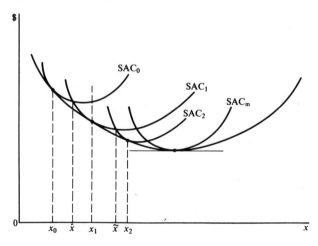

Figure 2.3

Finally, we assume that there exists a U-shaped function which constitutes an envelope curve to the family of SAC curves. That is, there exists a U-shaped curve such that at each of its points the curve is tangent to exactly one SAC curve, no two points of the curve being tangent to the same SAC curve.

We shall next show how the envelope curve can be derived, given the family of SAC curves. For convenience, let us denote the left-hand side (lhs) of (2.24a) by C (*cost*) and write. .

(2.24b) $C = f^*(x, z),$

where z is now permitted to vary. Since every point on the envelope curve is a point of tangency with one particular member of the family of U-shaped SAC curves which are generated by giving z different values, it is clear that each of these tangency points is associated with a unique value of z, and, conversely, each value of z is associated with a unique point on the envelope curve. Therefore, each of the two coordinates (C, x) of any point on the envelope curve is associated with a unique value of z. These relationships can be written as

(2.28a) $$C = \gamma(z),$$

(2.28b) $$x = \xi(z).$$

In other words, the relationship between C and x along the envelope curve can be represented in parametric form, z being the parameter. If we substitute for C and x in (2.24b) from (2.28), we get

(2.29) $$\gamma(z) = f^*[\xi(z), z],$$

which is an identity in z.

Now, the slope of any of the U-shaped curves given by (2.24b) is represented by

(2.30) $$\frac{dC}{dx} = f_x^*,$$

and the slope of the envelope curve is given by

(2.31) $$\frac{dC}{dx} = \frac{\gamma'}{\xi'} \qquad \text{by (2.28)}.$$

(Since the envelope curve is assumed to be U-shaped, it follows that $\xi' \neq 0$.) Since every point on the envelope curve is a tangency point, the slopes in (2.30) and (2.31) must be equal; hence

(2.32) $$f_x^* = \frac{\gamma'}{\xi'}.$$

Differentiating (2.29) with respect to z yields

(2.33) $$\gamma' = f_x^* \, \xi' + f_z^*,$$

and after substituting for f_x^* in (2.33) from (2.32), we obtain

(2.34) $$f_z^* = 0.$$

This means that the partial derivative of each U-shaped SAC function with respect to z vanishes *at the point at which the* SAC *function is tangent to the envelope curve.* But it does not vanish at other points on the SAC function. In fact, we shall now show that assumptions (2.25) imply that $f^*(x, z)$ is a U-shaped function with respect to z for any given value of x.

Let us assume that SAC_1 is tangent to the envelope curve at x_1, and SAC_0, which is the cost curve for a smaller plant, is tangent to the envelope curve at x_0. (See Fig. 2.3.) Then, by assumption (2.25c), there exists a level of x, say $\hat{x}$, such that $f^*(\hat{x}, z_0) = f^*(\hat{x}, z_1)$. It is clear that $\hat{x} < x_1$, therefore it follows from (2.25b) that $f^*(x_1, z_0) > f^*(x_1, z_1)$. This means that if x_1 is the desired level of output, cost can be reduced by switching from plant size z_0 to size z_1. A similar argument shows that switching from size z_1 to z_2 raises the cost of producing output x_1. Clearly, the cost of producing x_1 is minimized by using plant size z_1.

More formally, consider the problem of minimizing the cost of some given level of output x_1 with respect to the size of plant; that is, minimize $C = f^*(x_1, z)$. The necessary condition for this is $dC/dz = f_z^*(x_1, z) = 0$, which is exactly the same as condition (2.34). The second-order condition for this minimization problem is also satisfied, since we have shown that $f^*(x_1, z)$ is U-shaped. Therefore any particular point on the envelope curve can be interpreted as follows:

The plant whose SAC *curve is tangent to the envelope curve at some level of output, say* x_1, *is capable of producing output* x_1 *at less than the cost of producing* x_1 *with any other plant.*

For this reason, the envelope curve is the *long-run average total cost* (LAC) function, where it is understood that any chosen level of output is produced by using the plant whose SAC curve is tangent to the LAC function at the output in question.

The formal derivation of the LAC function can now be completed by considering Eqs. (2.24) and (2.34). Equation (2.34) may be solved explicitly for z, so that we can write

$$(2.35) \qquad\qquad\qquad z = \zeta(x).$$

We can now reduce Eqs. (2.24) and (2.35) to one equation by eliminating z. The resultant equation, which can be written as

$$(2.36) \qquad\qquad LAC = f^*[x, \zeta(x)] = F(x),$$

is the relationship which we were seeking. As was mentioned earlier, it is generally assumed that the LAC function is U-shaped. The downward-sloping segment of the LAC function describes the phenomenon of *economies of scale*, and the upward-sloping part shows *diseconomies of scale*.

Once the LAC function is given, we can immediately construct two more long-run cost functions: *long-run total cost* (LTC), and *long-run marginal cost* (LMC). Thus

$$(2.37) \qquad\qquad\qquad LTC = xF(x),$$

$$(2.38) \qquad\qquad LMC = LTC' = F(x) + xF'.$$

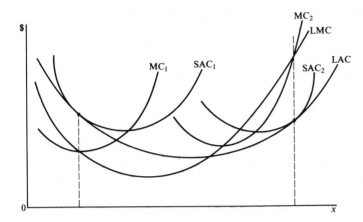

Figure 2.4

The relationship between LAC and LMC is of the same nature as that between ATC and MC as shown in Section 2.1.2.

Finally, there exists a particular relationship between LMC and the MC function of any particular SAC function. According to this relationship, LMC = MC at the level of output at which the respective SAC function is tangent to the LAC function as illustrated in Fig. 2.4. This can be proved as follows:

Multiplying (2.24) by x yields

$$(2.39) \qquad \text{TC } (\textit{short-run total cost}) = xf^*(x, z_1).$$

Suppose that SAC_1 is tangent to LAC at x_1. If we differentiate (2.39) with respect to x, and evaluate the derivative at the point of tangency, we get

$$(2.40) \qquad MC = f^*(x_1, z_1) + x_1 f_x^*(x_1, z_1).$$

But at the point of tangency, $SAC_1 = LAC$, hence

$$(2.41) \qquad f^*(x_1, z_1) = F(x_1).$$

Furthermore, the slopes of the two curves which are tangent to each other must also be equal at that point, and so

$$(2.42) \qquad f_x^*(x_1, z_1) = F'(x_1),$$

from which it follows, by combining (2.40), (2.41), and (2.42), that

$$F(x_1) + x_1 F'(x_1) = f^*(x_1, z_1) + x_1 f_x^*(x_1, z_1).$$

Example 2.2. Let us consider the following:

$$TC = ax^3 + (b - z)^2 x + cz^2, \qquad a, b, c > 0.$$

The above implies that $TFC = cz^2$, which increases with the size of plant.

Differentiating the TC function with respect to x yields

(2.43) $$MC = 3ax^2 + (b - z)^2$$

which is always positive. Dividing TC by x, we get

(2.44) $$C = ax^2 + (b - z)^2 + \frac{cz^2}{x} = f^*(x, z).$$

If we hold the size of the plant constant (that is, $z =$ constant), then $C =$ SAC. For the particular example chosen here, the SAC curve is U-shaped. This can be verified by differentiating (2.44) with respect to x. This gives

(2.45) $$SAC' = 2ax - \frac{cz^2}{x^2} = f_x^*(x, z).$$

It is clear that, for sufficiently small levels of output, the slope of the SAC function is negative, and for sufficiently large outputs it is positive. The slope is zero (that is, SAC has its minimum) at $x = (cz^2/2a)^{1/3}$.

If we now hold the level of output constant, and differentiate (2.44) with respect to z, we get

$$\frac{\partial C}{\partial z} = 2z \frac{(x + c)}{x} - 2b = f_z^*(x, z),$$

which indicates that C, as a function of z, is also U-shaped. The above derivative, as was shown in (2.34), must vanish at the point of tangency. Therefore,

(2.46) $$z = \frac{bx}{(x + c)} = \zeta(x).$$

Equation (2.46) determines the size of the plant which minimizes the cost of producing any given level of output. It is easy to see that $dz/dx > 0$, which means that as the level of output is increased, cost minimization requires the use of a larger size of plant.

Equations (2.44) and (2.46) define the LAC (envelope) curve. Substituting for z in (2.44) from (2.46), we get

(2.47) $$LAC = ax^2 + \frac{b^2 c}{(x + c)}.$$

Differentiating (2.47), we get

$$LAC' = 2ax - \frac{b^2 c}{(x + c)^2},$$

which indicates that the LAC curve is U-shaped. Multiplying both sides of

(2.47) by x, we obtain

$$(2.48) \qquad \mathrm{LTC} = ax^3 + \frac{b^2 cx}{(x + c)},$$

and by differentiating (2.48) we get

$$(2.49) \qquad \mathrm{LMC} = 3ax^2 + \frac{b^2 c^2}{(x + c)^2}.$$

Finally, if we substitute for z in (2.43) from (2.46), we get

$$\mathrm{MC} = 3ax^2 + \frac{b^2 c^2}{(x + c)^2},$$

and hence $\mathrm{MC} = \mathrm{LMC}$. This verifies the fact that, at the level of output at which a particular SAC curve is tangent to the LAC curve, the respective MC function intersects the LMC function.

BIBLIOGRAPHICAL NOTES

The literature on cost functions as a specialized topic is rather limited. However, treatises on production (some of which are listed at the end of Chapter 3) normally also include some discussion on cost. An item which is of some historical interest is Jacob Viner, "Cost Curves and Supply Curves," *Zeitschrift für Nationalökonomie*, **3**, 23–46 (1931). This has been reprinted in K. E. Boulding and G. J. Stigler (eds.), *Readings in Price Theory*, Chicago: Irwin, 1952, pp. 198–232, and also in D. R. Kamerschen (ed.), *Readings in Microeconomics*, Cleveland: World, 1967, pp. 197–228. The geometrically inclined may also consult L. W. McKenzie, "A Method for Drawing Marginal Curves," *Journal of Political Economy*, **58**, 434–435 (1950), and E. J. Mishan, "A Single Geometric Measure for Elasticity of Demand and Supply," *Review of Economic Studies*, **26**, 63–65 (1958).

CHAPTER 3

THEORY OF PRODUCTION

3.1 THE PRODUCTION FUNCTION

In Chapter 2 we made no direct reference to the technological conditions governing the production process, but it is clear that production cost depends, among other things, directly on the available technology. In this chapter we shall deal with certain technological principles underlying the type of production principles assumed in elementary economic theory, and their relationship to the firm's cost functions. Essentially, these principles refer to the quantitative relationships between the inputs used in the production process, and the output produced by that process. The basic relationship between the inputs and the output is referred to as a production function, and may be written as

$$(3.1) \qquad x = \phi(z^1, z^2, ..., z^n),$$

where x is the level of output and z^i represents the ith input, per period of time. All variables are measured in appropriate physical units of measurement. The function is defined for nonnegative values of the z^i, and takes only nonnegative values in the domain of definition. The function ϕ may be interpreted in either one of the following equivalent ways:

a) If the amounts of the n inputs are given, then x represents the maximum *level of output that can be produced with the given amounts of the inputs.*

b) If the amounts of all the inputs except, say, the kth are given, and the level of output is also specified, then the function gives the minimum *amount of the kth input necessary to produce the specified level of x.*

In general, some of the inputs may be variable, others fixed. As in the case of cost functions, we distinguish between the short run and the long run on the basis of the existence or absence of fixed inputs. Since those aspects of production theory which we wish to discuss in the present chapter are not affected in any substantive way by the fixed inputs, no serious loss of generality is incurred if we assume that all the arguments of the production function represent variable inputs.

We make certain basic assumptions about the production function. The first of these is

(3.2) $\phi_i > 0$ for all i and z,

where z denotes the vector of the z^i. Subscripts are again used to denote partial derivatives. For example, $\phi_i = \partial\phi/\partial z^i$, and $\phi_{ij} = \partial^2\phi/(\partial z^i\, \partial z^j)$. Condition (3.2) states that when the quantity of the ith input is increased, all other inputs being held constant, the level of ouptut increases as well. It is, of course, possible to think of physical situations in which the application of additional units of a certain input will *diminish* the level of output. But since such an operation makes no economic sense, it is excluded from the present analysis.

The function ϕ_i is referred to as the *marginal product* (MP) function of the ith input. Thus a verbal version of (3.2) would say that every input has a positive marginal product.

Furthermore, we make the following assumptions about certain second-order partial derivatives of the production function:

There exist input levels z_0^i such that

(3.3a) $\phi_{ii} > 0$ for $0 \leqslant z^i < z_0^i,$

(3.3b) $\phi_{ii} < 0$ for $z^i > z_0^i,$ $\Big\}$ for all i.

(3.3c) $\phi_{ii} = 0$ at $z^i = z_0^i,$

These conditions say, in effect, that if all inputs except the ith are held constant, and the amount of the ith input is between 0 and z_0, then a small increase in z^i will cause output to increase at an *increasing rate* (except when $z_0^i = 0$); but when the amount of z^i is increased beyond z_0^i, then output increases at a *decreasing rate*.

Another way of interpreting these conditions is to say that between 0 and z_0^i the MP function of the ith input increases, whereas at levels higher than z_0^i it decreases. It should be pointed out that, in general, the dividing point between these two ranges, that is, the point z_0^i, depends on the level at which the other inputs are held constant. Condition (3.3b) is also known as the *Law of Diminishing Returns*.

Frequently we will also be interested in the *average product* (AP) of the ith input; that is, the output per unit of the ith input used. Thus we define

(3.4) $$\mathrm{AP}^i = \frac{\phi(z)}{z^i}, \qquad z^i \neq 0.$$

From what has so far been said about the production function, it follows immediately that AP^i and MP^i are governed by the same type of relationships as are ATC and MC, as stated in Section 2.1.2. Furthermore, it can be shown (along the lines of the proof given in Section 2.1.3) that each AP^i function (as a function of z^i) has the shape of an inverted U.

Finally, we introduce the concept of an *isoquant*. An isoquant may be thought of as a collection of points in the input space at which the production function has the same value. Thus, for any specified level of output the production function defines an implicit function between the inputs. This implicit function may be obtained directly from (3.1) by fixing the level of x at some desired value. For example, for the output x_0 we have

$$(3.5) \qquad\qquad x_0 = \phi(z^1, z^2, ..., z^n).$$

To study the properties of isoquants in greater detail, we shall make matters somewhat easier by taking as an example a two-input production function. Then the isoquant for the output x_0 may be obtained from

$$(3.6) \qquad\qquad x_0 = \phi(z^1, z^2),$$

which is an implicit function in two variables. Since $\phi_1 \neq 0$ by assumption (3.2), we can solve (3.6) explicitly for z^1 as a function of z^2 and x_0. (See the section on Implicit Functions in Chapter 15.) In other words, we can say that there exists a function ψ such that

$$(3.7) \qquad\qquad z^1 = \psi(z^2; x_0).$$

The above is the isoquant for output level x_0. In fact, the function ψ defines a whole *family* of isoquants—one isoquant for each particular level of x. Thus, each isoquant depends on the parameter x, and the different members of the family can be generated from (3.7) by giving x different values.

First we shall investigate the slope of the isoquant. To that end we substitute for z^1 in (3.6) from (3.7) to obtain

$$(3.8) \qquad\qquad x_0 = \phi[\psi(z^2; x_0), z^2].$$

Differentiating (3.8) with respect to z^2, we get

$$(3.9) \qquad\qquad 0 = \phi_1\psi' + \phi_2,$$

where $\psi' = d\psi/dz^2$, and so

$$(3.10) \qquad\qquad \psi' = -\frac{\phi_2}{\phi_1} < 0 \qquad \text{by (3.2).}$$

Thus, the slope of the isoquant is negative. This makes sense; when one input is increased, and output is to remain constant, then, since every input has a positive marginal product, the other input must be decreased. In other

words, it is possible to produce a given level of output by substituting one
input for another. The absolute value of the slope of the isoquant, that is
ϕ_2/ϕ_1, indicates the rate at which the two inputs must be substituted so as
to keep output constant. For that reason, the ratio ϕ_2/ϕ_1 at any given point
(z^1, z^2) is called the *marginal rate of technical substitution* (MRTS).

In general, the MRTS will vary from one point on the isoquant to another.
To study the behavior of the MRTS along an isoquant we differentiate (3.10)
with respect to z^2, and get

$$(3.11) \quad \psi'' = \frac{d\left[\dfrac{-\phi_2(z^1, z^2)}{\phi_1(z^1, z^2)}\right]}{dz^2} = \frac{-(\phi_{21}\psi' + \phi_{22})}{\phi_1} + \frac{\phi_2(\phi_{11}\psi' + \phi_{12})}{\phi_1^2}$$

After substituting for ψ' from (3.10), and rearranging terms, we get

$$(3.12) \qquad \psi'' = -\frac{1}{\phi_1^3}(\phi_{11}\phi_2^2 - 2\phi_{12}\phi_1\phi_2 + \phi_{22}\phi_1^2),$$

where we have also used the fact that we can interchange the subscripts of
second-order cross-partial derivatives, that is, $\phi_{12} = \phi_{21}$. Now, only ϕ_1
and ϕ_2 are of known sign, whereas the signs of ϕ_{11} and ϕ_{22} depend on the
point at which they are evaluated. Furthermore, we have made no assumption
whatsoever about ϕ_{12}; that is, we have said nothing about what happens to
the marginal product of an input as the quantity of the other input is increased.
All this means that the sign of ψ'' is, in general, indeterminate; in other words,
the assumptions which we have made up to this point in no way place any
restriction on the curvature of the isoquant. However, we shall now *assume*
that $\psi'' > 0$. This means that as z^2 is increased, the slope of the isoquant
increases. However, since that slope is always negative, the condition $\psi'' > 0$

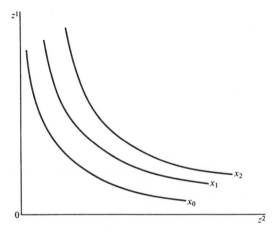

Figure 3.1

implies that the *absolute value* of the slope diminishes. Thus, if plotted in the $z^1 z^2$-plane, the isoquants are assumed to be strictly convex to the origin, as shown in Fig. 3.1. The above assumption is also known as the principle of *diminishing marginal rate of technical substitution*.

3.2 OUTPUT MAXIMIZATION

Let us look now at the following problem: Suppose that in each period of time, a firm has available a certain amount of money which it can use for the purchase of various factors of production (inputs). How much of each input should the firm purchase so as to maximize its output? Formally, this is a constrained maximization problem. Most problems in the theory of the firm are really set in the more general framework of profit maximization, but as we shall see, the conditions for output maximization are necessary conditions for profit maximization. For simplicity, we continue to use for our exposition the two-input production function. We shall work out the problem by two different methods.

The Substitution Method. The formal statement of the problem is as follows:

Maximize

$$(3.13) \qquad\qquad x = \phi(z^1, z^2),$$

subject to

$$(3.14a) \qquad\qquad p_0^1 z^1 + p_0^2 z^2 = C_0,$$

where p_0^1 and p_0^2 are the given (positive) market prices of the two inputs, respectively, and C_0 is the given spendable amount of money. The last three quantities are the parameters of the problem, while the zs are the decision variables. Equation (3.14a) is the cost, or budget, equation, which states that the amount spent on the two inputs must be equal to C_0 dollars.*

The first step of the present method consists of solving (3.14a) explicitly for one of the variables, say z^1. This yields

$$(3.14b) \qquad\qquad z^1 = \frac{C_0 - p_0^2 z^2}{p_0^1}.$$

---

* As a matter of fact, the budget restriction of this problem can be stated in a somewhat weaker form by replacing the strict equality in (3.14a) by the inequality $p_0^1 z^1 + p_0^2 z^2 \leqslant C_0$. However, it can be shown, and it should be intuitively obvious, that in order to maximize its output, the firm will always spend its entire budget.

Substituting for z^1 in (3.13) from (3.14b), the production function can be written as

$$(3.15) \qquad x = \phi\left(\frac{C_0 - p_0^2 z^2}{p_0^1}, z^2\right).$$

The problem can now be solved by maximizing (3.15) without any direct reference to the constraint. Of course, the constraint is bound to be satisfied because the substitution which we performed restricts the choice of z^1 to those values which, given any choice of z^2, satisfy condition (3.14).

If we assume that the function in (3.15) has an interior maximum (that is, a maximum at a point at which neither z^1 nor z^2 is zero), then the first derivative of the function must be zero. (See Section 15.1.3.) We therefore require

$$(3.16a) \qquad \frac{dx}{dz^2} = \phi_1 \frac{dz^1}{dz^2} + \phi_2 = 0.$$

Differentiating (3.14b) with respect to z^2, we obtain

$$(3.17) \qquad \frac{dz^1}{dz^2} = -\frac{p_0^2}{p_0^1},$$

and after substituting for dz^1/dz^2 in (3.16a) from (3.17), we get

$$(3.16b) \qquad \frac{dx}{dz^2} = -\phi_1 \frac{p_0^2}{p_0^1} + \phi_2 = 0,$$

or

$$(3.16c) \qquad \frac{\phi_1}{\phi_2} = \frac{p_0^1}{p_0^2}.$$

Condition (3.16c) states that, at the point at which output is maximized, the ratio of the MPs of the two inputs must be equal to the ratio of the input prices. Recall, also, that the ratio of the MPs is referred to as the MRTS, so that (3.16c) can also be interpreted as requiring the MRTS to be equal to the ratio of the respective input prices. The values of the zs at the extreme point—say $\bar{z}^1$ and $\bar{z}^2$—can be found by solving Eqs. (3.14) and (3.16) simultaneously. The existence of a solution to the above system of equations follows, of course, directly from our assumption about the existence of an interior maximum.

In order for the extreme point $(\bar{z}^1, \bar{z}^2)$ to furnish a regular maximum (rather than a minimum) the second derivative, evaluated at $(\bar{z}^1, \bar{z}^2)$, must be negative. To evaluate this derivative, we differentiate (3.16b) [that is, we differentiate (3.15) twice]. Constraining this derivative to be negative, we get

$$(3.18a) \qquad \frac{d^2x}{d(z^2)^2} = -\frac{p_0^2}{p_0^1}\left(\phi_{11}\frac{dz^1}{dz^2} + \phi_{12}\right) + \phi_{21}\frac{dz^1}{dz^2} + \phi_{22} < 0,$$

and after substituting for dz^1/dz^2 from (3.17), and rearranging terms, we get

(3.18b) $$\frac{d^2x}{d(z^2)^2} = \frac{1}{(p_0^1)^2}[\phi_{11}(p_0^2)^2 - 2\phi_{12}p_0^1 p_0^2 + \phi_{22}(p_0^1)^2] < 0.$$

Finally, substituting for p_0^2 from (3.16c), we have

(3.18c) $$\frac{d^2x}{d(z^2)^2} = \frac{1}{\phi_1^2}(\phi_{11}\phi_2^2 - 2\phi_{12}\phi_1\phi_2 + \phi_{22}\phi_1^2) < 0.$$

The reason for the above manipulations was to obtain a form of the second-order condition stated entirely in terms of the properties of the production function.

Comparing (3.12) and (3.18c), we can see that $d^2x/d(z^2)^2 = -\psi''\phi_1$, and hence our earlier assumption that $\psi'' > 0$ implies that condition (3.18) is satisfied. We can now see that the assumption about strictly convex isoquants has the advantage of enabling us to assume the existence of a unique interior maximum. If the convexity assumption is relaxed (for example, by allowing isoquants to be concave, or linear, in certain ranges), we can still obtain a maximum which, however, may not be unique, or which may be located at a "corner," that is, a point at which either $\bar{z}^1$ or $\bar{z}^2$ is zero. The last two cases are avoided in the present approach not necessarily on grounds of economic common sense (or lack of it), but merely as a means of simplifying the analysis.

The Lagrange Method. Let us combine the function to be maximized (the production function in this particular example) and the constraint function in the following manner:

(3.19) $$\phi(z^1, z^2) + \lambda(p_0^1 z^1 + p_0^2 z^2 - C_0),$$

where λ is an unknown, the value of which may be determined from the maximization process. The expression in (3.19) is called the *Lagrangian form* of the problem on hand, and λ is called a *Lagrange multiplier*, after the eighteenth-century French mathematician.

According to this method (see Section 15.1.5), if the objective function possesses an interior extreme point which satisfies the constraint, then such a point may be found by setting the first-order partial derivatives of the Lagrangian form with respect to the zs equal to zero. To the equations thus obtained, one adds the constraint, and the entire system is solved simultaneously. In our problem, this procedure yields

(3.20a) $$\phi_1 + \lambda p_0^1 = 0,$$

(3.20b) $$\phi_2 + \lambda p_0^2 = 0,$$

and the constraint

(3.14a) $$p_0^1 z^1 + p_0^2 z^2 = C_0.$$

Here we have three equations in three unknowns (z^1, z^2, λ), and if an interior extreme point exists, then the above system has a solution. To see the similarity between the two methods more clearly, we can reduce the above system to one of two equations. This may be done by combining (3.20a) and (3.20b) into one equation, and eliminating λ in the process. Then we obtain the system

(3.20c)
$$\frac{\phi_1}{\phi_2} = \frac{p_0^1}{p_0^2},$$

(3.14a)
$$p_0^1 z^1 + p_0^2 z^2 = C_0,$$

which is identical to the two equations (3.16c) and (3.14a), from which we found $\bar{z}^1$ and $\bar{z}^2$ by the substitution method.

We have still to examine the second-order condition in order to guarantee that the extreme point $(\bar{z}^1, \bar{z}^2)$ yields a maximum. In the present example, this condition requires that the relevant bordered Hessian determinant be positive; that is,

(3.21a)
$$\begin{vmatrix} \phi_{11} & \phi_{12} & p_0^1 \\ \phi_{21} & \phi_{22} & p_0^2 \\ p_0^1 & p_0^2 & 0 \end{vmatrix} > 0.$$

Using the rule for the expansion of a determinant (see Section 15.2.2), we obtain

(3.21b)
$$-[\phi_{11} (p_0^2)^2 - 2\phi_{12} p_0^1 p_0^2 + \phi_{22} (p_0^1)^2] > 0$$

which, after the substitution for p_0^2 from (3.20c) and multiplication of both sides of the inequality by -1, becomes

(3.21c)
$$(p_0^1/\phi_1)^2 (\phi_{11} \phi_2^2 - 2\phi_{12} \phi_1 \phi_2 + \phi_{22} \phi_1^2) < 0.$$

This condition is equivalent to condition (3.18c), since both conditions require that the expression in parentheses (the same expression in each case) be negative. This establishes the equivalence of the two methods.

Example 3.1. Production functions which exhibit both increasing and diminishing returns are likely to be somewhat complicated, and hence are not very suitable as illustrations for our problems. But in order to assure the reader that such functions actually exist, we shall suggest one particular function which may serve as a candidate for a legitimate production function.

Consider the example

$$x = a_1 \arctan (z^1 - b_1) + a_2 \arctan (z^2 - b_2) + c = \phi(z^1, z^2),$$
$$a_1, b_1, a_2, b_2 > 0.$$

The above happens to be a trigonometric function with a somewhat forbidding appearance. This fact, however, should not give cause to undue alarm, because the derivatives of this function turn out to be quite manageable. It should be pointed out that if $c = -a_1 \arctan(-b_1) - a_2 \arctan(-b_2)$, which is just a number, then the function has the property that when both variable inputs are zero, the level of output is also zero.

Taking partial derivatives, we get

$$\phi_i = \frac{a_i}{1 + (z^i - b_i)^2}, \qquad i = 1, 2,$$

which is positive for any value of z^i.

Differentiating again, we have

$$\phi_{ii} = \frac{-2a_i(z^i - b_i)}{[1 + (z^i - b_i)^2]^2},$$

from which we can see that

$$\phi_{ii} > 0 \quad \text{for} \quad 0 \leqslant z^i < b_i, \quad \text{and} \quad \phi_{ii} < 0 \quad \text{for} \quad z^i > b_i, \quad i = 1, 2.$$

In this particular example, the MP function of each input is independent of the other input, and the ith input exhibits diminishing returns at levels exceeding b_i.

Example 3.2. In order to illustrate the output maximization problem, we shall use a simpler production function—one that has diminishing returns for every input combination.

Let

$$x = a_1 \ln(z^1 + 1) + a_2 \ln(z^2 + 1) = \phi(z^1, z^2), \qquad a_1, a_2 > 0.$$

Note that $\phi(0, 0) = 0$. The first-order partial derivatives are

$$\phi_i = \frac{a_i}{z^1 + 1}, \qquad i = 1, 2,$$

so that condition (3.20c) takes the form

$$\frac{a_1(z^2 + 1)}{a_2(z^1 + 1)} = \frac{p_0^1}{p_0^2}.$$

The above can be solved simultaneously with (3.14a) to yield the extreme points

$$\bar{z}^1 = a_1 \frac{(C_0 + p_0^1 + p_0^2)}{p_0^1(a_1 + a_2)} - 1; \qquad \bar{z}^2 = a_2 \frac{(C_0 + p_0^1 + p_0^2)}{p_0^2(a_1 + a_2)} - 1.$$

Of course, the solution will be economically meaningful only if $\bar{z}^1 \geqslant 0$, and $\bar{z}^2 \geqslant 0$.

Taking second-order partial derivatives, we find

$$\phi_{ii} = \frac{-a_i}{(z^i + 1)^2}, \qquad i = 1, 2, \qquad \text{and} \qquad \phi_{ij} = 0, \qquad i \neq j,$$

so that the second-order condition is

$$\begin{vmatrix} \dfrac{-a_1}{(z^1 + 1)^2} & 0 & p_0^1 \\[2mm] 0 & \dfrac{-a_2}{(z^2 + 1)^2} & p_0^2 \\[2mm] p_0^1 & p_0^2 & 0 \end{vmatrix} > 0.$$

Expanding the above determinant, we find

$$\frac{a_1(p_0^2)^2}{(z^1 + 1)^2} + \frac{a_2(p_0^1)^2}{(z^2 + 1)^2} > 0 \quad \text{for all } z^1 \text{ and } z^2,$$

and therefore the point $(\bar{z}^1, \bar{z}^2)$ does indeed furnish a maximum. The value of the maximum output can be computed by substituting $\bar{z}^1$ and $\bar{z}^2$ for z^1 and z^2, respectively, in the production function.

3.3 COST MINIMIZATION

In this section we consider a problem which is related to the one discussed in Section 3.2; the nature of this relationship will become evident as soon as the problem is worked out. Instead of assuming that the firm has a fixed budget for its inputs, we assume that the firm wishes to produce some specified level of output, and the problem is to find an input combination which minimizes the cost of producing that level of output. This is, therefore, a constrained minimization problem, and is formally stated as follows:

Minimize

$$(3.22) \qquad\qquad C = p_0^1 z^1 + p_0^2 z^2,$$

subject to

$$(3.23) \qquad\qquad x_0 = \phi(z^1, z^2),$$

where C is the cost of the chosen input combination, and x_0 is the desired level of output. The Lagrangian form of this problem is

$$(3.24) \qquad\qquad p_0^1 z^1 + p_0^2 z^2 + \lambda [x_0 - \phi(z^1, z^2)],$$

and the necessary conditions (assuming the existence of a regular interior minimum) take the form

(3.25a) $$p_0^1 - \lambda\phi_1 = 0,$$

(3.25b) $$p_0^2 - \lambda\phi_2 = 0,$$

and the constraint

(3.23) $$x_0 = \phi(z^1, z^2).$$

The above system may be reduced by eliminating λ. This gives

(3.25c) $$\frac{p_0^1}{p_0^2} = \frac{\phi_1}{\phi_2},$$

(3.23) $$x_0 = \phi(z^1, z^2).$$

The second-order condition requires that the relevant bordered Hessian determinant be negative (since we are seeking a minimum), hence

(3.26a) $$\begin{vmatrix} -\lambda\phi_{11} & -\lambda\phi_{12} & -\phi_1 \\ -\lambda\phi_{21} & -\lambda\phi_{22} & -\phi_2 \\ -\phi_1 & -\phi_2 & 0 \end{vmatrix} < 0.$$

If we substitute for the ϕ_i from (3.25a and b), and perform a number of suitably chosen multiplications on the rows and columns of the determinant in (3.26a) (see Section 15.2.2), it is possible to show that condition (3.26a) is equivalent to

(3.26b) $$-\lambda \begin{vmatrix} \phi_{11} & \phi_{12} & p_0^1 \\ \phi_{21} & \phi_{22} & p_0^2 \\ p_0^1 & p_0^2 & 0 \end{vmatrix} < 0,$$

and since $\lambda > 0$ [by (3.25) and the fact that the ϕ_i and p_0^i are positive], the above is equivalent to

(3.26c) $$\begin{vmatrix} \phi_{11} & \phi_{12} & p_0^1 \\ \phi_{21} & \phi_{22} & p_0^2 \\ p_0^1 & p_0^2 & 0 \end{vmatrix} > 0.$$

This condition is the same as (3.21a).

Recalling for a moment the output maximization problem of the preceding section, let us suppose that x_0 is the greatest output that can be produced with C_0 dollars. Since the isoquants are assumed to be strictly convex, there exists only one point on the isoquant for x_0 at which the absolute value of the slope is equal to p_0^1/p_0^2. This means that the point $(\bar{z}^1, \bar{z}^2)$, which is the solution to the maximum problem posed in Section 3.2, is at the same time the solution to the present problem of minimizing the cost of producing the output x_0. Therefore, the minimum cost must be C_0 dollars.

Thus, each of these problems may be said to be the *dual* of the other. More specifically, if x_0 is the maximum output that can be produced with a budget of C_0 dollars, then C_0 is also the minimum cost of producing x_0 units of x; or, if C_0 is the minimum cost of producing x_0 units of x, then x_0 is the highest level of output that can be produced with C_0 dollars. In each case the extremum is attained at the same point, that is, by using the same combination of inputs. Of course, this duality holds only if the input prices are the same in each case.

3.4 FROM THE PRODUCTION FUNCTION TO COST FUNCTIONS

3.4.1 The Derivation of the TVC Function

The purpose of this section is to demonstrate the nature of the relationship between the present chapter and the preceding one. In what follows, we shall show to what extent the properties of the cost functions depend on the properties of the production function.

In order to discuss one of the cost functions, the TVC function, we need to consider three relationships. The first of these is the production function, from which we can determine the amounts of the various inputs necessary to produce any given level of output. And since we are interested only in the *minimum* cost of producing any given level of output, we must also consider the necessary conditions for efficient (i.e., least-cost) production. Finally, to obtain the actual cost of any chosen input combination, we must make use of the cost equation. These relationships have already been discussed in the preceding sections of this chapter, but we reproduce them here for convenience (still assuming a two-input production function).

(3.27a) $\qquad p_0^1 - \lambda \phi_1 = 0,$

(3.27b) $\qquad p_0^2 - \lambda \phi_2 = 0,$ $\qquad$ (efficiency conditions)

(3.27c) $\qquad \phi(z^1, z^2) - x = 0,$ $\qquad$ (production function)

(3.28) $\qquad\qquad C = p_0^1 z^1 + p_0^2 z^2.$ $\qquad$ (cost equation)

Now, the equations in (3.27) constitute a system of three implicit equations in the four variables z^1, z^2, λ, and x, and the two parameters p_0^1 and p_0^2. We may solve this system for the first three variables in terms of x, p_0^1, and p_0^2. (We are invoking here the Implicit Function Theorem, which is applicable by virtue of the second-order conditions for cost minimization. See Proposition 15.15.) In other words, there exist three functions, say h^1, h^2, and h^3, such that

(3.29a) $$\bar{z}^1 = h^1(x; \; p_0^1, p_0^2),$$

(3.29b) $$\bar{z}^2 = h^2(x; \; p_0^1, p_0^2),$$

(3.29c) $$\lambda = h^3(x; \; p_0^1, p_0^2).$$

The bars on top of the zs indicate that these are values of the inputs satisfying the efficiency conditions in (3.27); that is, for any given x and input prices, the functions h^1 and h^2 determine the least-cost input combination. If we now substitute for the zs in (3.28) from (3.29), then we obtain the function that we are seeking; that is,

(3.30a) $$\text{TVC} = p_0^1 h^1(x; \; p_0^1, p_0^2) + p_0^2 h^2(x; \; p_0^1, p_0^2).$$

We refer to the above as a TVC function, since it is a relation between the (minimum) variable cost, and the level of output (rather than the levels of inputs). In fact, if we suppress the prices in the above equation, then it becomes the same TVC function that we first introduced in (2.1) in Chapter 2; formally,

(3.30b) $$p_0^1 h^1(x; \; p_0^1, p_0^2) + p_0^2 h^2(x; \; p_0^1, p_0^2) = f(x).$$

We now wish to investigate the extent to which the properties of the production function determine the properties of the TVC function. Differentiating (3.30) with respect to x gives

(3.31) $$f' = \text{MC} = p_0^1 h_x^1 + p_0^2 h_x^2,$$

where $h_x^i = \partial h^i / \partial x$, and differentiating (3.27c) with respect to x, after substituting for the z^i from (3.29), yields

(3.32) $$\phi_1 h_x^1 + \phi_2 h_x^2 = 1.$$

If we now substitute for ϕ_1 and ϕ_2 in (3.32) from (3.27a) and (3.27b), and rearrange terms, we get

(3.33a) $$p_0^1 h_x^1 + p_0^2 h_x^2 = \lambda,$$

which, by virtue of (3.31), can also be written as

(3.33b) $$\text{MC} = \lambda.$$

We see, therefore, that the Lagrange multiplier of the cost minimization problem is equal to MC. We can also substitute for λ in (3.33b) from (3.27a) and (3.27b) and write

(3.34) $$\text{MC} = \frac{p_0^1}{\phi_1} = \frac{p_0^2}{\phi_2}.$$

These equations indicate that when production is carried out in an efficient manner, MC equals the price of any input (used in the production process) divided by the MP of that input. Here we have an explicit relationship between the derivatives of the production function and the slope of the TVC function.

To pursue this investigation a little further, we shall try to establish a relationship between the curvature of the TVC function and the derivatives of the production function. For this purpose we differentiate (3.33b) with respect to x, after substituting for λ from (3.29c). This gives

$$(3.35) \qquad MC' = h_x^3.$$

In order to evaluate h_x^3, it is necessary to differentiate each of the equations in (3.27). This yields the following system of equations:

$$(3.36a) \qquad -\lambda\phi_{11}h_x^1 - \lambda\phi_{12}h_x^2 - \phi_1 h_x^3 = 0,$$

$$(3.36b) \qquad -\lambda\phi_{21}h_x^1 - \lambda\phi_{22}h_x^2 - \phi_2 h_x^3 = 0,$$

$$(3.36c) \qquad \phi_1 h_x^1 + \phi_2 h_x^2 = 1.$$

The above may be viewed as a system of linear equations in the three unknowns h_x^1, h_x^2, and h_x^3; the solutions may be obtained by using Cramer's rule (see the section on Simultaneous Equations in Chapter 15). For the derivative in which we are interested, we get

$$(3.37) \qquad h_x^3 = \frac{\lambda^2(\phi_{11}\phi_{22} - \phi_{12}^2)}{D},$$

where

$$D = \begin{vmatrix} -\lambda\phi_{11} & -\lambda\phi_{12} & -\phi_1 \\ -\lambda\phi_{21} & -\lambda\phi_{22} & -\phi_2 \\ \phi_1 & \phi_2 & 0 \end{vmatrix}.$$

First, we may observe the relationship between the determinant D, and the determinant in condition (3.26a). If we denote the latter by D^*, then we see that

$$(3.38) \qquad D = -D^* > 0 \quad \text{(since we required } D^* < 0\text{)}.$$

Even though this establishes the sign of the denominator in (3.37), the sign of the term h_x^3 is still indeterminate, since the sign of the expression in parentheses is unknown. However, equation (3.37) clearly shows the close relationship between the MC function and the production function. For example, if the two inputs are technologically independent, that is, if $\phi_{12} = 0$, and both inputs are subject to diminishing returns, then the MC function is increasing. We may remark parenthetically that the expression in parentheses in (3.37) is the (unbordered) Hessian determinant of the production function.

3.4.2 The Effects of Price Changes

In the preceding analysis we considered input prices as fixed parameters. It is of interest to investigate how the TVC function is affected by changes in those prices; in other words, we wish to investigate how the cost of producing any given level of output changes when one of the input prices changes. To do so, we simply go back to (3.30), and consider prices as variables. However, since this makes TVC a function of three variables (x, p^1, p^2), we must use a different functional symbol. Accordingly, we write the generalized version of (3.30) as

$$(3.39) \qquad p^1 h^1(x;\; p^1, p^2) + p^2 h^2(x;\; p^1, p^2) = \hat{f}(x;\; p^1, p^2).$$

Equation (3.39) shows that, when input prices are allowed to vary, the variable cost is represented by a *family* of one-dimensional TVC functions, where each member of this family is associated with a particular set of input prices. What we wish to investigate now is the relationship between the different members of this family of TVC functions, and this requires us to determine the signs of the partial derivatives of the function $\hat{f}$ with respect to the input prices.

Differentiating (3.39) with respect to, say, p^1, holding x and p^2 constant, we get

$$(3.40a) \qquad \qquad \hat{f}_1 = \bar{z}^1 + p^1 h_1^1 + p^2 h_1^2,$$

where $\hat{f}_j = \partial \hat{f} / \partial p^j$, and $h_j^i = \partial h^i / \partial p^j$, while differentiation of (3.27c), after substituting for the z^i from (3.29), yields

$$(3.41) \qquad \qquad \phi_1 h_1^1 + \phi_2 h_1^2 = 0.$$

We can now substitute for p^1 and p^2 in (3.40a) from (3.27a) and (3.27b), and hence can write

$$(3.40b) \qquad \qquad \hat{f}_1 = \bar{z}^1 + \lambda(\phi_1 h_1^1 + \phi_2 h_1^2).$$

But the expression in parentheses is zero by (3.41), so that

$$(3.40c) \qquad \qquad \hat{f}_1 = \bar{z}^1 > 0.$$

By a similar process we can show that

$$(3.42) \qquad \qquad \hat{f}_2 = \bar{z}^2 > 0.$$

We see, therefore, that the cost of producing any (positive) level of output increases as one of the inputs becomes more expensive. Geometrically speaking, as the price of a variable input rises, the TVC function shifts upward.

We shall now reveal another property of the function $\hat{f}$. From (3.40) and (3.42) we see that

(3.43) $$\hat{f}_1 p^1 + \hat{f}_2 p^2 = \bar{z}^1 p^1 + \bar{z}^2 p^2.$$

But the rhs of (3.43) is the same as the rhs of (3.28); that is, it represents TVC as a function of the inputs and their prices. Therefore it is also equal to TVC as we have expressed it in (3.39), and so we can write

(3.44) $$\hat{f}_1 p^1 + \hat{f}_2 p^2 = \hat{f}(x;\ p^1,p^2) \quad \text{for all } x,\ p^1, \text{ and } p^2.$$

This shows that the function $\hat{f}$ is homogeneous of degree one in the two prices. Consequently, when *all* prices change by some percentage, then TVC changes by the same percentage.

This last result may also be deduced from the following argument. We see that the efficiency conditions (Eqs. 3.27a and 3.27b, or 3.25c) are invariant to a proportionate change in all prices, since such a change does not affect the *ratio* of the prices. This means that the input combination which is optimal before such a price change is also optimal following the price change. From this it follows that when all prices change by the same proportion, then the cost equation in (3.28) becomes a linear function in the ps, from which it follows that the cost (TVC) changes by the same proportion as the prices.

Example 3.3. Let us consider the production function

$$x = a_1\sqrt{z^1} + a_2\sqrt{z^2}, \qquad a_1, a_2 > 0.$$

For this function the efficiency condition is

$$\frac{a_1}{a_2}\sqrt{\frac{z^2}{z^1}} = \frac{p^1}{p^2}.$$

By eliminating from the above two equations one input at a time, we get the following:

$$\bar{z}^1 = \frac{x^2(a_1 p^2)^2}{(a_1^2 p^2 + a_2^2 p^1)^2} = h^1(x;\ p^1,p^2),$$

$$\bar{z}^2 = \frac{x^2(a_2 p^1)^2}{(a_1^2 p^2 + a_2^2 p^1)^2} = h^2(x;\ p^1,p^2).$$

These are the optimal levels of the two inputs for any chosen level of output, given some fixed input prices. Substituting for $\bar{z}^1$ and $\bar{z}^2$ in the cost equation (3.28), we obtain the following generalized TVC function:

$$\text{TVC} = \frac{x^2 p^1 p^2}{a_1^2 p^2 + a_2^2 p^1} = \hat{f}(x;\ p^1,p^2).$$

It can easily be verified that this function is homogeneous of degree one in both prices. If we think of the prices as being constant, then we can write

$$\text{TVC} = bx^2 = f(x) \quad \text{where} \quad b = \frac{p^1 p^2}{a_1^2 p^2 + a_2^2 p^1}.$$

We see that each member of the family of TVC functions in this example is a quadratic function in x, and hence the MC function f' and the AVC function are linear. However, the ATC function is U-shaped, its minimum occurring at $x = \sqrt{\text{TFC}/b}$.

3.5 MULTIPRODUCT PRODUCTION

A situation in which a firm produces a number of different products has been briefly discussed in Section 2.1.4 in connection with cost functions. In this section we wish to generalize the main results of the chapter so as to allow for multiproduct production. We shall assume that the firm produces m products, and makes use of n inputs. Under these circumstances, it is convenient to define the production function in implicit form, and so we write

$$(3.45) \qquad \phi(x^1, x^2, ..., x^m; \; z^{m+1}, z^{m+2}, ..., z^{m+n}) = 0.$$

The above function is defined for nonnegative values of its arguments, and, like the one-product production function, it can be given one of the following interpretations:

a) If the amounts of the n inputs and the amounts of all but the kth product are given, then the function gives the maximum *amount of the kth output that can be produced with the given inputs.*

b) If the amounts of the m products and the amounts of all but the kth input are given, then the function gives the minimum *amount of the kth input necessary to produce the given amounts of the outputs.*

As for the properties of the derivatives of ϕ, at this stage we shall point out only that the first-order partial derivatives of ϕ with respect to the inputs must all be of the same sign; essentially, because the general nature of the role of the inputs in the production process is the same for each input. [These derivatives need not be positive, however, because we can multiply both sides of (3.45) by -1 without materially affecting the specifications of the technology which are embodied in the function ϕ. If we carry out such a multiplication, then all the partial derivatives of ϕ will change sign.] For a similar reason, all the partial derivatives with respect to the outputs must be of the same sign. Further restrictions will be obtained later on in the context of specific problems.

Let us next derive one of the isoquants associated with the function given in (3.45). Before we do so, however, two remarks are in order. First, when we speak about a fixed level of output then, unless otherwise specified, we mean a fixed amount of *each* of the m products. In other words, by the expression a "fixed (or given) level of output" we mean a *vector*, each of whose m components is given. Second, if there are more than two inputs, that is, if $n > 2$, then the geometric representation of an isoquant is not a curve, but a surface.

If we fix the level of output, then (3.45) can be written as

$$(3.46) \qquad \phi(x_0; \; z^{m+1}, \; z^{m+2}, \; ..., z^{m+n}) = 0,$$

where $x_0 = (x_0^1, x_0^2, ..., x_0^m)$. The above equation defines an implicit relationship between the inputs, and this relationship is, of course, the isoquant surface. As in the two-input case, we may arbitrarily choose one of the inputs and express it explicitly in terms of the remaining $n - 1$ inputs. Thus, we may write

$$(3.47) \qquad z^{m+i} = \psi^{m+i}(z^{m+1}, z^{m+2}, ..., z^{m+i-1}, z^{m+i+1}, ..., z^{m+n}; \; x_0).$$

In order to evaluate the derivatives of ψ^{m+i}, we substitute for z^{m+i} in (3.46) from (3.47), and differentiate (3.46) with respect to z^{m+j}. This gives

$$(3.48) \qquad \psi_s^r = - \frac{\phi_s}{\phi_r} \quad \text{for} \quad r, s = m + 1, \; m + 2, ..., m + n, \; r \neq s,$$

where $\psi_s^r = \partial \psi^r / \partial z^s$, and $\phi_r = \partial \phi / \partial z^r$. Since ϕ_r and ϕ_s are of the same sign, it follows that the slope of the isoquant surface is negative along any coordinate.

We shall also assume again that the MRTS is diminishing, that is, $\psi_{jj}^i > 0$, for $i, j = m + 1, \; m + 2, ..., m + n, \; i \neq j$. If we differentiate (3.48) partially with respect to z^{m+j}, it can be shown that

$$(3.49) \qquad \psi_{jj}^i = - \frac{1}{\phi_i^3} (\phi_{ii} \phi_j^2 - 2\phi_{ij} \phi_i \phi_j + \phi_{jj} \phi_i^2) > 0,$$
$$i, j = m + 1, \; m + 2, ..., \; m + n, ..., \; i \neq j.$$

The reader may note the similarity between (3.49) and (3.12).

In the context of a multiproduct problem, it may be of interest to obtain a relationship between the amounts of the various products that can be produced under the assumption that the inputs are fixed at some given levels. If we fix the levels of the inputs, then (3.45) can be written as

$$(3.50) \qquad \phi(x^1, x^2, ..., x^m; \; z_0) = 0,$$

where $z_0 = (z_0^{m+1}, z_0^{m+2}, ..., z_0^{m+n})$. The relationship in (3.50) defines all possible product combinations that a firm can produce with the given fixed levels of inputs. In the two-product case, such a relationship is referred to as a *transformation curve*, but in the general case ($m \geqslant 2$) it may more properly be called a *transformation surface*.

We may solve (3.50) explicitly for one of the products, and write

(3.51) $x^i = \Psi^i(x^1, x^2, ..., x^{i-1}, x^{i+1}, ..., x^m; z_0)$.

Substituting for x^i in (3.50) from (3.51), and differentiating (3.50) with respect to x^j, we get

(3.52) $\Psi^i_j = -\dfrac{\phi_j}{\phi_i}$, $i, j = 1, 2, ..., m$, $i \neq j$,

where $\Psi^i_j = \partial\Psi^i/\partial x^j$, and $\phi_i = \partial\phi/\partial x^i$. Since ϕ_i and ϕ_j have the same sign, it follows that the slope of the transformation surface is negative along any coordinate. The slope of the transformation surface is referred to as the *marginal rate of product transformation* (MRPT).

Finally, if we let both the inputs and the outputs vary, then a substitution for x^i in (3.45) from (3.51) and differentiation with respect to z^j yields

(3.53) $\Psi^i_j = -\dfrac{\phi_j}{\phi_i}$, $i = 1, 2, ..., m$, $j = m + 1, m + 2, ..., m + n$,

where $\Psi^i_j = \partial\Psi^i/\partial z^j$. The expressions in (3.53) represent the marginal product of the jth input in the production of the ith output, all other inputs and outputs being held constant. Since we require that all marginal products be positive, the function ϕ must satisfy the condition $\phi_j/\phi_i < 0$ for $i = 1, 2, ..., m$, and $j = m + 1, m + 2, ..., m + n$.

The use of a multiproduct production function may be illustrated in the context of the following cost minimization problem.

Minimize

$$\sum_{i=m+1}^{m+n} p^i_0 z^i$$

subject to

(3.54) $\phi(x_0; z^{m+1}, z^{m+2}, ..., z^{m+n}) = 0$.

Using the Lagrangian method, we obtain the following necessary conditions (assuming the existence of a regular interior minimum):

(3.55a) $p^i_0 + \lambda\phi_i = 0$, $i = m + 1, m + 2, ..., m + n$.

By eliminating λ from (3.55a), these conditions can be stated as

(3.55b) $\dfrac{p^i_0}{p^j_0} = \dfrac{\phi_i}{\phi_j}$, $i, j = m + 1, m + 2, ..., m + n$,

which are the familiar conditions equating the MRTS between any two inputs with the ratio of their respective prices. Equations (3.54) and (3.55) may be used to determine the optimal levels of the inputs $\bar{z}^{m+1}, \bar{z}^{m+2}, ..., \bar{z}^{m+n}$.

The second-order condition involves the bordered Hessian determinant and its principal minors of order three and up. All of these must be negative. This condition may be expressed as follows:

(3.56a)

$$(-1)^k \begin{vmatrix} \lambda\phi_{m+1,\,m+1} & \lambda\phi_{m+1,\,m+2} & \cdots & \lambda\phi_{m+1,\,m+k} & \phi_{m+1} \\ \lambda\phi_{m+2,\,m+1} & \lambda\phi_{m+2,\,m+2} & \cdots & \lambda\phi_{m+2,\,m+k} & \phi_{m+2} \\ \vdots & & & \vdots & \\ \lambda\phi_{m+k,\,m+1} & \lambda\phi_{m+k,\,m+2} & \cdots & \lambda\phi_{m+k,\,m+k} & \phi_{m+k} \\ \phi_{m+1} & \phi_{m+2} & \cdots & \phi_{m+k} & 0 \end{vmatrix} < 0, \qquad k = 2, 3, \ldots, n.$$

By proper multiplications of the rows and the columns in the above determinants, this condition can be shown to be equivalent to

(3.56b)

$$(-1)^k \lambda^{k-1} \begin{vmatrix} \phi_{m+1,\,m+1} & \phi_{m+1,\,m+2} & \cdots & \phi_{m+1,\,m+k} & \phi_{m+1} \\ \phi_{m+2,\,m+1} & \phi_{m+2,\,m+2} & \cdots & \phi_{m+2,\,m+k} & \phi_{m+2} \\ \vdots & & & \vdots & \\ \phi_{m+k,\,m+1} & \phi_{m+k,\,m+2} & \cdots & \phi_{m+k,\,m+k} & \phi_{m+k} \\ \phi_{m+1} & \phi_{m+2} & \cdots & \phi_{m+k} & 0 \end{vmatrix} < 0, \qquad k = 2, 3, \ldots, n.$$

Finally, the derivation of the multiproduct TVC functions proceeds in a fashion similar to the one-product case. The basis for the derivation is the following system:

(3.57) $$\phi_i + \lambda p_0^i = 0, \qquad i = m + 1, m + 2, \ldots, m + n,$$

(3.58) $$\phi(x^1, x^2, \ldots, x^m; \ \bar{z}^{m+1}, \bar{z}^{m+2}, \ldots, \bar{z}^{m+n}) = 0,$$

(3.59) $$C = \sum_{i=m+1}^{m+n} p_0^i \bar{z}^i.$$

This system contains $n + 2$ equations, and by eliminating λ and the n $\bar{z}$'s, it can be reduced to one relationship between $C(\text{TVC})$, the m products, and the n input prices. It can be shown that when the relationship thus obtained is differentiated partially with respect to the products, one obtains the marginal cost of each product. These are given by

$$\text{MC}^k = -\frac{p_0^1}{\phi_{m+1}}\,\phi_k = -\frac{p_0^2}{\phi_{m+2}}\,\phi_k = \cdots = -\frac{p_0^n}{\phi_{m+n}}\,\phi_k, \quad k = 1, 2, \ldots, m,$$

where $\phi_k = \partial\phi/\partial x^k$. Since it was shown that $\phi_k/\phi_j < 0$ for $k = 1, 2, \ldots, m$, and $j = m + 1, m + 2, \ldots, m + n$, it follows (as is to be expected) that $\text{MC}^k > 0$ for all k.

BIBLIOGRAPHICAL NOTES

A fairly complete, yet relatively short, treatment of production may be found in a recently reissued monograph by S. Carlson, *A Study on the Pure Theory of Production*, New York: Kelley, 1965. Ragnar Frisch, in his *Theory of Production*, Chicago: Rand McNally, 1965, presents a highly specialized and comprehensive exposition of production theory, while C. E. Ferguson deals with a variety of topics related to production theory in his *The Neoclassical Theory of Production and Distribution*, Cambridge: Cambridge University Press, 1969. Among shorter pieces on this subject, Chapter 4, "A Comprehensive Restatement of the Theory of Cost and Production," in P. A. Samuelson's *Foundations of Economic Analysis*, Cambridge: Harvard University Press, 1947, is a rigorous summary of the important results in this area. Certain aspects of production functions that are not treated in standard texts are discussed by G. H. Borts and E. J. Mishan in "Exploring the 'Uneconomic Region' of the Production Function," *Review of Economic Studies*, **29**, 300–312 (1962).

PROFIT MAXIMIZATION
UNDER PURE COMPETITION:
THE SUPPLY OF OUTPUT

In this chapter we shall analyze a typical decision problem of a firm under the special conditions of pure competition. We think here of an industry in which a great number of firms produce an identical product. From the point of view of this analysis, the most important behavioral implication of pure competition is the fact that the typical firm in such a market considers all market prices as given. In other words, from the point of view of the individual firm, prices are parameters rather than decision variables. In Section 4.1 the decision problem is posed in the framework of a short-run situation, while Section 4.2 deals with the long run.

4.1 THE SHORT RUN

4.1.1 The Conditions for Profit Maximization

In this model, the firm is concerned with choosing an optimal level of output. Naturally, in order to produce the chosen level of output, the firm also makes a choice of inputs. In fact, as we have seen in Chapter 3, given the production function, and assuming that the efficiency conditions are satisfied, then a choice of output implies a particular input combination, and vice versa. Thus, the problem of profit maximization can be analyzed by using either one of the following approaches: (a) the choice of output, (b) the choice of inputs. This chapter is concerned exclusively with the former approach, while Chapter 5 deals with the latter.

The quantity which the firm wishes to maximize is defined as

$$(4.1a) \qquad \pi = TR - TC,$$

where π denotes profit, and TR denotes *total revenue*; TC has already been defined in Chapter 2. All quantities are measured over some given period of time (a week, a month, a year) which represents the planning period, and they are expressed in some suitable monetary unit.

TR may be defined directly in terms of price and output, namely

$$(4.2) \qquad TR = p_0 x,$$

45

where p denotes the market price of product x. The subscript on the p reflects the fact that in any particular period, the market price is considered to be a given parameter. If we make use of the functional notation of Chapter 2, that is, $TC = f(x) + c$, then the problem on hand can be stated as follows:

Maximize

(4.1b) $$\pi = p_0 x - f(x) - c.$$

This is a function of one variable, and if we assume that the function has an extremum at some positive level of x, then the necessary condition is

(4.3a) $$\frac{d\pi}{dx} = p_0 - f' = 0.$$

If we define *marginal revenue* (MR) = TR$'$, then, since in this case MR = p_0 (TR being a linear function of x), condition (4.3a) can also be stated as

(4.3b) $$MR = MC.$$

The second-order condition for this problem is

(4.4a) $$\frac{d^2\pi}{dx^2} = -f'' < 0,$$

which is equivalent to

(4.4b) $$f'' > 0.$$

Thus, at the optimal level of output the MC function must be increasing. The optimal level of output, $\bar{x}$, is found by solving equation (4.3a).

At this point, we must emphasize the fact that the assumption about the existence of a point satisfying conditions (4.3) and (4.4) does not really ensure that such a point furnishes the maximum level of profit. The question we are raising here has to do with the uniqueness of extreme points, as well as the distinction between *local* (relative) and *global* (absolute) extrema. Since these issues are discussed and illustrated in some detail in Section 15.1.3, we shall merely raise two points that are directly relevant to the problem on hand.

First, there may exist more than just one point satisfying conditions (4.3) and (4.4). In such an event, one must compute the profit level at each of these points in order to find the one that yields the highest profit.

Second, even if we were to assume (as we shall implicity do) that the point satisfying (4.3) and (4.4) is unique (i.e., that the profit function has only one "hump"), the optimality of this point would not necessarily be guaranteed. Since output can assume only nonnegative values, the profit function is defined only on the nonnegative half-line. In that case, the boundary of the domain of definition, that is, the point $x = 0$, is necessarily an extreme point (at least a local extreme point) even if conditions (4.3) and (4.4) are not satisfied at that point. Hence, it is always necessary to compare the profit at the interior extreme point, such as $\bar{x}$, with the profit at the origin. In fact, since we know that at the origin the profit is equal to $-$TFC dollars, it is clear that the firm will choose to produce a positive level of output only if its profit will exceed $-$TFC dollars. Two possible profit functions are illustrated in Figure 4.1, where in each of the two diagrams the point $\bar{x}$ satisfies conditions (4.3) and (4.4).

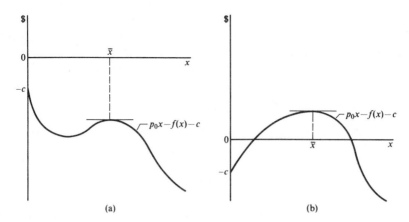

Fig. 4.1 (a) The optimal output is zero. (b) The optimal output is $\bar{x}$.

A condition for determining whether the interior extreme point is the optimal output can be derived as follows. The firm should shut down (i.e., produce zero output) if

(4.5a) $$\pi(\bar{x}) < -\text{TFC}.$$

Substituting for $\pi(\bar{x})$ in (4.5a) from (4.1a) (and adding bars to indicate that the respective functions are evaluated at the point $\bar{x}$), we get

(4.5b) $$\overline{\text{TR}} - \overline{\text{TC}} < -\text{TFC}.$$

Substituting for $\overline{\text{TC}}$ from (2.1a), we have

(4.5c) $$\overline{\text{TR}} - \overline{\text{TVC}} - \text{TFC} < -\text{TFC},$$

which may be written as

(4.5d) $$\overline{\text{TR}} < \overline{\text{TVC}}.$$

This condition states that the firm should shut down if its revenues are insufficient to cover the cost of the variable inputs. If we divide both sides of (4.5d) by $\bar{x}$ and make use of the definitions of TR and TVC, we get

(4.5e) $$p_0 < \overline{AVC},$$

which is an alternative version of condition (4.5d).

One of the quantities involved in (4.5e), namely p_0, is known to the firm in advance, but in order to evaluate $\overline{AVC}$, the firm must first find $\bar{x}$. It is, however, possible to change condition (4.5e) slightly so as to enable the firm to decide whether it should shut down or not without computing $\bar{x}$.

Let AVC_{min} denote the minimum value of the AVC function. Since $AVC_{min} \leqslant \overline{AVC}$, it is clear that, if $p_0 < AVC_{min}$, then also $p_0 < \overline{AVC}$. On the other hand, if $p_0 \geqslant AVC_{min}$, then, since at $\bar{x}$ we have $p_0 = MC$ by (4.3a), we have $p_0 \geqslant \overline{AVC}$ (because in the range in which the AVC function is rising, MC exceeds AVC, as was shown in Section 2.1.2). Thus, the condition for profit maximization can be summarized as follows:

(4.6a)   If $p_0 \geqslant AVC_{min}$, the firm should produce $\bar{x}$, $\bar{x}$ being the level of output satisfying conditions (4.3) and (4.4).

(4.6b)   If $p_0 < AVC_{min}$, the firm should shut down.

(If $p_0 = AVC_{min}$, it makes no difference, as far as the profit situation is concerned, whether the firm shuts down or not; in either case its profit is equal to $-$TFC.)

4.1.2 The Supply Function

From the foregoing discussion, it is clear that the market price of the product (together with the cost structure of the firm) determines whether the firm will produce a positive level of output, and if so, at what level. Thus, the optimal level of output is functionally related to the market price. This relationship can be obtained by solving (4.3) for $\bar{x}$ in terms of p for those values of p satisfying (4.6a). Thus,

(4.7) $$\bar{x} = g(p), \qquad p \geqslant AVC_{min}.$$

The subscript has been removed from the p because we now wish to study the effects of changes in the market price on the output of the firm. Since the function g indicates the level of output which the firm will produce at any given price, the function is called the firm's *supply function*.

Let us first indicate the relationship between the supply function, and the firm's cost functions. If we substitute for x in (4.3a) from (4.7), remove the subscript from the p, and differentiate (4.3a) with respect to p, we get

(4.8a) $$1 - f''g' = 0,$$

or

(4.8b) $$g' = \frac{1}{f''}.$$

Thus, we see that the slope of the supply function is equal to the reciprocal of the slope of the MC function [which is positive by (4.4)]. In fact, since from (4.3a) we have $p = f'(\bar{x})$, it is obvious that (4.7) is obtained by inverting the function f'. Thus if f'^{-1} denotes the inverse function of f' in the range in which $f' \geqslant \text{AVC}_{\min}$, then $g(p) = f'^{-1}(p)$.

Since the slope of a function is not invariant to a change in the units in which the variables are measured, economists use a different criterion by which relationships such as supply and demand functions can be characterized and compared with each other. This is the concept of *elasticity*, which may be defined as follows.

For discrete changes in price, the following definition is used:

$$\text{arc elasticity} = E = \frac{\dfrac{\Delta x}{x}}{\dfrac{\Delta p}{p}} = \frac{\Delta x}{\Delta p}\frac{p}{x},$$

where Δ denotes "change in." Thus, arc elasticity measures the percentage change in quantity (supplied or demanded, as the case may be) for a one-percent change in price.

As Δp approaches zero, the definition of arc elasticity becomes

$$\text{point elasticity} = e = \frac{dx}{dp}\frac{p}{x}.$$

Since most of the analysis in this text deals with infinitesimal changes, we shall primarily use the concept of point elasticity, and for simplicity refer to it as "elasticity."

Since price and output are nonnegative quantities, it follows that the sign of the elasticity is the same as the sign of the slope of the function in question. It is customary to distinguish between various ranges of elasticity on the basis of the absolute value of the elasticity. This classification is given below:

At·a point at which $|e| > 1$, the function is said to be elastic.

At a point at which $|e| < 1$, the function is said to be inelastic.

At a point at which $|e| = 1$, the function is said to be unit-elastic (or of unitary elasticity).

The individual supply function serves as the basis for constructing a market supply function. The latter indicates the total market supply (i.e., the supply of all the firms in the market) at any given price. Therefore, if the supply functions of all the firms in the market are given, the market supply function can be obtained by "summing" the individual supply functions. If $g^i(p)$ denotes the supply function of the ith firm, then we define

$$(4.9) \qquad g(p) = \sum_{i=1}^{m} g^i(p),$$

where $g(p)$ denotes the market supply function, and m is the number of firms in the market.

Differentiating (4.9), we get

$$(4.10) \qquad g' = \sum_{i=1}^{m} g^{i\prime}.$$

Since $g^{i\prime} > 0$ for all i, it follows that $g' > 0$. The elasticity of the market supply function is defined by

$$(4.11) \qquad e = g' \frac{p}{x},$$

where $x = \sum_{i=1}^{m} x^i$, and x^i is the output of the ith firm.

Multiplying both sides of (4.10) by p/x, we have

$$(4.12a) \qquad e = \sum_{i=1}^{m} \frac{p}{x} g^{i\prime}.$$

But since $pg^{i\prime} = x^i e^i$, where e^i denotes the elasticity of the ith firm's supply function, we get

$$(4.12b) \qquad e = \sum_{i=1}^{m} \frac{x^i e^i}{x}.$$

Thus, the elasticity of the market supply function is a *weighted average* of the elasticities of the individual supply functions, where a typical weight, that is, x^i/x, is the ith firm's share of the total market supply.

It is also clear that if every individual supply function is elastic (inelastic), then the market supply function is also elastic (inelastic). And a similar result holds if the word "elastic" in the preceding sentence is replaced by "unit-elastic."

Example 4.1. Let us take the TVC function from Example 2.1, and let c denote TFC. Then we form the profit function

$$\pi = px - (x - a)^3 - bx - a^3 - c.$$

Setting the first derivative equal to zero, we get the quadratic equation $p - 3(x - a)^2 - b = 0$. This equation has the solutions

$$\text{a)} \quad x = a + \frac{\sqrt{3(p - b)}}{3}, \qquad \text{b)} \quad x = a - \frac{\sqrt{3(p - b)}}{3}.$$

The second-order condition requires

$$-6(x - a) < 0, \quad \text{or} \quad x > a.$$

Therefore we have

$$\bar{x} = a + \frac{\sqrt{3(p - b)}}{3} = g(p), \qquad p \geqslant \text{AVC}_{\min}.$$

Since the AVC function has its minimum at $x = \frac{3}{2}a$, we find that $\text{AVC}_{\min} = \frac{3}{4}a^2 + b$. Thus, the firm will shut down whenever $p < \frac{3}{4}a^2 + b$.

4.1.3 Multiproduct Production

A firm may conceivably produce a number of different products all of which are sold in purely competitive markets. If the firm produces n different products, then its profit function takes the form

$$(4.13) \qquad \pi = \sum_{i=1}^{n} p_0^i x^i - f(x) - c,$$

where x^i is the output of the ith product, $f(x)$ is a multiproduct TVC function of the type discussed in Section 2.1.4, and $x = (x^1, x^2, ..., x^n)$. If an interior extremum exists, then the necessary conditions are

$$(4.14a) \qquad p_0^i - f_i = 0, \qquad i = 1, 2, ..., n,$$

where $f_i = \partial f / \partial x^i$. The above condition may also be stated as

$$(4.14b) \qquad \text{MR}^i = \text{MC}^i, \qquad i = 1, 2, ..., n,$$

which says that the MR of each product must be equal to its MC.

The second-order condition takes the form

$$(4.15)$$

$$-f_{11} < 0, \quad \begin{vmatrix} -f_{11} & -f_{12} \\ -f_{21} & -f_{22} \end{vmatrix} > 0, \quad ..., \quad (-1)^n \begin{vmatrix} -f_{11} & -f_{12} & \cdots & -f_{1n} \\ -f_{21} & -f_{22} & \cdots & -f_{2n} \\ \vdots & & & \vdots \\ -f_{n1} & -f_{n2} & \cdots & -f_{nn} \end{vmatrix} > 0.$$

The question of whether the firm should produce the amounts given by the interior extreme point, or shut down, is not quite as simple as in the one-product case. The reason for this is that as an alternative to producing the positive amounts given by the interior extreme point, the firm may either shut down *completely* (that is, produce zero of every product), or shut down *partially* (that is, produce positive amounts of some products, zero of the others). We shall illustrate this problem for the two-product case.

First, let us denote the solution to conditions (4.14), for $n = 2$, by $\bar{x}^1$, $\bar{x}^2$, where it is assumed that this point also satisfies the second-order condition (4.15). Now, a second alternative available to the firm is not to produce Product 2 at all, and to maximize profit by producing only Product 1. This problem calls for maximizing the profit function $p_0^1 x^1 - f(x^1, 0) - c$, and if this function has an interior maximum, then the solution is found by solving the first-order condition

$$p_0^1 - f_1(x^1, 0) = 0.$$

The optimal amount of x^1 is denoted by $\hat{x}^1$, and it may be pointed out that, in general, $\hat{x}^1 \neq \bar{x}^1$. Similarly, the firm may consider producing only Product 2, and the solution to this problem is found by maximizing $p_0^2 x^2 - f(0, x^2) - c$. The first-order condition now takes the form

$$p_0^2 - f_2(0, x^2) = 0,$$

and the solution to this equation is denoted by $\hat{x}^2$ (in general, different from $\bar{x}^2$). Finally, the last alternative the firm may consider is to shut down completely, in which case

$$x^1 = x^2 = 0.$$

We see, therefore, that in the present example the firm must consider four alternative production plans, and, of course, it will choose the plan that produces the highest level of profit. It is also clear that the firm will shut down (that is, choose the last alternative) if, and only if, none of the other three alternatives generates enough revenues to cover the respective variable cost. Thus, the firm shuts down if the following three inequalities hold:

(4.16) $p_0^1 \bar{x}^1 + p_0^2 \bar{x}^2 < f(\bar{x}^1, \bar{x}^2), \qquad p_0^1 \hat{x}^1 < f(\hat{x}^1, 0), \qquad p_0^2 \hat{x}^2 < f(0, \hat{x}^2).$

In general, if the firm may potentially produce n different products, it must consider 2^n different production plans.

If the absolute maximum is in the interior, the solution to (4.14) gives the firm's supply functions for its n products, and these can be written as

(4.17) $\bar{x}^i = g^i(p), \qquad i = 1, 2, ..., n,$

where $p = (p^1, p^2, ..., p^n)$. The partial derivatives of the g^i can be found by implicit differentiation of (4.14a), considering the p^j as variables. [Such a differentiation has already been performed in (3.36)]. Using Cramer's rule to solve for the various derivatives, we obtain

$$(4.18) \qquad\qquad g_j^i = -\frac{D_{ji}}{D},$$

where $g_j^i = \partial g^i/\partial p^j$, D is the $n \times n$ determinant given in (4.15), and D_{ji} is the cofactor of the element in row j and column i of D. (Cofactors are defined in Section 15.2.2.) Now, D_{ii} is an $(n-1) \times (n-1)$ determinant which, according to (4.15), has a sign opposite to that of D. Therefore $D_{ii}/D < 0$, and hence $g_i^i > 0$ for all i. This means that, as in the one-product case, the firm will always increase the production (and hence the supply) of a product when the price of that product rises. However, condition (4.15) places no restrictions on the off-diagonal cofactors D_{ji} so that in general it is impossible to determine the effect of a change in the price of product j on the supply of product i.

4.2   THE LONG RUN

4.2.1   Equilibrium of the Firm

The problem of profit maximization in the long run is very similar to that of short-run profit maximization. Long-run profit is defined as

$$(4.19) \qquad\qquad \pi = p_0 x - xF(x),$$

where p_0 may be interpreted as the price which is expected to prevail in the long run, and F is the LAC function, which we first introduced in (2.36). Note the absence of fixed cost.

If there exists a maximum for a positive value of x, the conditions for profit maximization are

$$(4.20a) \qquad\qquad p_0 - F(x) - xF' = 0,$$

or

$$(4.20b) \qquad\qquad p_0 = \text{LMC},$$

$$(4.21a) \qquad\qquad -2F' - \bar{x}F'' < 0,$$

or

$$(4.21b) \qquad\qquad 2F' + \bar{x}F'' > 0,$$

where $\bar{x}$ is the solution to (4.20). Condition (4.21) states that LMC must be increasing at the optimal level of output.

The long-run counterpart to condition (4.5) of Section 4.1.1 requires that the long-run market price be not less than LAC. While the firm cannot avoid the fixed cost in the short run, it can avoid long-run losses by leaving the market altogether. Thus, if the long-run market price is less than LAC, the firm shuts down, that is, leaves the market.

The conditions for long-run profit maximization can be summarized as follows:

(4.22a)   *If $p \geqslant \text{LAC}_{\min}$, the firm should produce $\bar{x}$, $\bar{x}$ being the level of output which satisfies conditions (4.20) and (4.21).*

(4.22b)   *If $p < \text{LAC}_{\min}$, the firm should leave the market.*

It must be understood, of course, that $\bar{x}$ is to be produced with the plant whose SAC curve is tangent to LAC at $\bar{x}$. (The justification for this and the computation of the optimal size of plant have already been explained in Section 2.2.)

The firm's long-run supply function can be obtained by solving (4.20) for $\bar{x}$ in terms of p. This solution can be written as

(4.23) $\bar{x} = G(p), \qquad p \geqslant \text{LAC}_{\min}.$

The function G is the inverse of the LMC function in the range of x for which LAC is increasing, and, like that of the LMC function, the slope of the function G is positive.

It is also possible to derive a direct relationship between the market price and the optimal size of plant. This is done by substituting for x in (2.35) from (4.23). Thus

(4.24) $z = \zeta[G(p)] = Z(p),$

which is an increasing function. This relationship may be interpreted as the firm's demand function for input z (that is, plant).

Example 4.2. This is a somewhat lengthy example since it demonstrates how short-run and long-run profit maximization can be integrated into a unified problem. In this example, we derive the short-run and the long-run supply functions, the long-run cost functions, and the optimal size of plant. We assume the following short-run cost functions:

$$\text{TVC} = ax^3 + (b - cz)x; \qquad \text{TC} = ax^3 + (b - cz)x + dz^2; \qquad a, b, c, d > 0.$$

Before we begin with the analysis itself, we impose certain restrictions on the parameters and the variables of the model in order to ensure that the implications of the model make economic (and technological) sense. These restrictions are:

(4.25) $x > \sqrt{(cz - b)/a}, \qquad \text{if } (cz - b) > 0,$

(4.26) $b > c^4/16ad^2.$

Condition (4.25) places a lower bound on the output level produced in a plant whose size exceeds b/c; it may be interpreted as saying that in plants which are larger than b/c, output levels below the minimum bound are technically unfeasible. In those plants, condition (4.25) also replaces the condition $p \geqslant \text{AVC}_{\min}$, since the AVC function associated with the above TVC function has no minimum (remembering that AVC is not defined for $x = 0$). Formally, condition (4.25) prevents TVC from becoming negative. [Since $\text{TVC} \geqslant 0$ for $x \geqslant 0$ whenever $(cz - b) \leqslant 0$, the restriction becomes effective only if $(cz - b) > 0$.]

Condition (4.26) is a restriction on the relative magnitudes of the parameters of the model, the reason for which will become apparent as we proceed with the analysis of the example.

Differentiating TC with respect to x yields

$$MC = 3ax^2 + (b - cz),$$

which, in view of (4.25), is always positive.

Dividing TC by x, we get

(4.27) $$SAC = ax^2 + (b - cz) + dz^2/x,$$

which, for any given value of z, is a U-shaped function with a minimum at

$$x = (dz^2/2a)^{1/3}.$$

Applying the conditions for short-run profit maximization (4.3) and (4.4), we obtain the firm's short-run supply function

$$\bar{x} = \sqrt{(cz - b + p)/3a} = g(p), \qquad \text{subject to (4.25).}$$

In order to generate the LAC function, we first minimize SAC with respect to z, holding x constant. This yields

$$-c + 2dz/x = 0,$$

or

(4.28) $$z = cx/2d,$$

which determines the optimal size of plant for any chosen level of output. The LAC function can now be obtained by substituting for z in (4.27) from (4.28), which gives

$$LAC = ax^2 - c^2x/4d + b.$$

This is a U-shaped function with a minimum at $x = c^2/8ad$. The value of LAC at that point is equal to $b - c^4/64ad^2$, which is positive by (4.26).

To derive the other long-run cost functions we multiply LAC by x, and get

$$LTC = ax^3 - c^2x^2/4d + bx,$$

and differentiating LTC gives

$$LMC = 3ax^2 - c^2x/2d + b.$$

The LMC function is also U-shaped, and has a minimum at $x = c^2/12ad$. At that point we have LMC $= b - c^4/48ad^2 > 0$ by (4.26).

To find the optimal long-run level of output, we apply condition (4.20) which takes the form

$$p - 3ax^2 + c^2x/2d - b = 0,$$

and has the solutions

$$x = \frac{c^2 \pm \sqrt{c^4 + 48ad^2(p - b)}}{12ad}.$$

But the second-order condition (4.21) requires that

$$- 6ax + c^2/2d < 0,$$

or

$$x > c^2/12ad,$$

hence we get the long-run supply function

(4.29) $$\bar{x} = \frac{c^2 + \sqrt{c^4 + 48ad^2(p - b)}}{12ad} = G(p), \quad p \geqslant b - \frac{c^4}{64ad^2}.$$

It remains to test the model for internal consistency; i.e., to test whether the long-run output satisfies condition (4.25). This test is necessary because once the long-run output is chosen, and the optimal size of plant is built, the firm is thereby placing itself in a short-run position which is characterized by the appropriate set of short-run cost curves. We must, therefore, verify that the chosen level of output does not give rise to negative costs.

Substituting for z in (4.25) from (4.28), we have

$$x > \sqrt{c^2x/2ad - b/a}, \quad \text{assuming } (cz - b) > 0,$$

and squaring both sides, we get

$$x^2 > c^2x/2ad - b/a, \quad \text{or} \quad x^2 - c^2x/2ad + b/a > 0.$$

This last inequality holds if the equation $x^2 - c^2x/2ad + b/a = 0$ has no real solution. This, in turn, will be the case if its discriminant is negative; that is, if

$$c^4/4a^2d^2 - 4b/a < 0,$$

which is identical to (4.26). This proves that the long-run output satisfies condition (4.25), provided that the size of plant is chosen so as to minimize the cost of producing that output, as it is determined by (4.28).

4.2.2 Adjustment to Price Changes

For the discussion of the firm's reaction to price changes, it will be useful to introduce the concept of *equilibrium*. Broadly speaking, equilibrium means a state of affairs in which certain variables remain constant over time. With respect to the firm, we distinguish between short-run equilibrium and long-run equilibrium. We say that the firm is in *short-run equilibrium* whenever, given the market prices, it produces the optimal level of output, that is, the output which maximizes short-run profit. We refer to this situation as an equilibrium because the firm has no reason, so long as prices and other parameters stay constant, to change its level of output. Thus, the output which yields maximum profit in the short run may also be referred to as the firm's short-run equilibrium output.

Similarly, we say that the firm is in *long-run equilibrium* whenever its production plan is consistent with long-run profit maximization. This means that the firm produces the profit-maximizing level of output, and uses the optimal plant for that output. In the next section, we shall also apply the concept of equilibrium to an entire market.

It is obvious that if the firm is in long-run equilibrium, it is also in short-run equilibrium, but the converse is not necessarily true. In long-run equilibrium we have $p = $ LMC. But the SAC function of the optimal size of plant is tangent to the LAC function at the long-run level of output; therefore, at that level of output we also have LMC $=$ SMC, and so $p = $ SMC, which is the first-order condition for short-run profit maximization. Since, in long-run equilibrium, the firm always operates in the nondecreasing range of the LAC function, it follows that under these conditions it also operates in the nondecreasing range of the SAC function of the optimal plant (since LAC and SAC are tangent at the equilibrium output). This implies that, at the long-run equilibrium level of output, the SMC function is increasing, so that the second-order condition for short-run profit maximization is also satisfied.

If the firm is in long-run equilibrium and the market price changes, then the equilibrium, is disrupted and the firm will find it necessary to adjust its production plan. For example, if the market price rises, long-run profit maximization calls for an increase in the level of output, and an increase in the size of plant. However, changing the size of plant normally requires a fairly long period of time; certainly, it requires more time than merely changing the level of output. It is, therefore, reasonable to assume that the adjustment to the new long-run equilibrium is made in two phases. In the first phase, the firm moves to a new short-run equilibrium by making an appropriate change in output, using the initial size of plant. In the second phase the firm moves to the new plant, and also adjusts its output to the long-run equilibrium level. Formally, this adjustment can be summarized as follows.

Let the initial market price and SAC function of the optimal plant be p_0 and SAC_0, respectively, and let p_1 and SAC_1 denote the new price and SAC function of the optimal plant for the new long-run equilibrium, respectively. Then as the price changes from p_0 to p_1, the firm immediately chooses a new level of output which satisfies the condition $p_1 = SMC_0$. Doing so places the firm in a new short-run equilibrium, but it is still not in long-run equilibrium. In the second phase the firm moves into the plant with cost function SAC_1, and produces the output satisfying $p_1 = \text{LMC} = \text{SMC}_1$. On the completion of phase two, the firm is again in long-run equilibrium, as well as in new short-run equilibrium.

4.2.3 Market Equilibrium

So much for the two types of equilibrium of a single firm. The short-run equilibrium of the market, on the other hand, is defined in terms of *excess demand*, that is, quantity demanded minus quantity supplied. If $h(p)$ and $g(p)$ denote the short-run market demand and supply functions, respectively, then excess demand is defined as $h(p) - g(p)$.* When excess demand is zero, the market is said to be in short-run equilibrium. When excess demand is zero, the market clears, and hence there will be no tendency for the market price to change, thus maintaining the current level of output and purchases.

For the market to be in long-run equilibrium, however, we require not only that excess demand be zero, but also that each firm in the market earn zero profit. Underlying this condition is the assumption that if some firms in the market earn excess profit (that is, more than zero profit), then, in the long run, firms from other markets will enter into the more lucrative market, and thereby upset the equilibrium. Similarly, firms which earn a negative profit will leave the market in the long run. Essentially, therefore, long-run equilibrium is attained when the number of firms in the market remains constant, and hence the condition requiring that the profit of every firm be zero.

The process by which the market attains a long-run equilibrium has not been fully developed; in fact, this problem has not even been satisfactorily solved for a single firm. One of the difficulties is that the adjustment of an entire market usually involves a movement of firms between different markets, and this adds an entirely new dimension to the problem. Essentially, the problem is of a nature which makes it necessary to take into account the interdependence between different markets. For example, if the long-run adjustment involves substantial changes in output, then input prices are likely to change, and this will be reflected in a shift of the entire (short-run and long-run) cost structure of each firm, thus further complicating the analysis.

The main reason for this brief excursion into these problems is to point out that adjustments in output and plant made by individual firms may be explained in terms of a prevailing state of disequilibrium, either short-run or long-run. And even if we still have no satisfactory formulation of the adjustment process to equilibrium, the specification of the different kinds of equilibria helps us to distinguish between the different forces that are at work during the adjustment process, and it provides us with a set of conditions that characterize the positions to which a firm or a market may be moving.

---

*The derivation of the market demand function is discussed in Chapter 10.

BIBLIOGRAPHICAL NOTES

Mathematical expositions of the competitive firm may be found in most texts in mathematical economics; for instance, J. M. Henderson and R. E. Quandt, *Microeconomic Theory*, New York: McGraw-Hill, 1958. Since throughout the present text it is assumed that firms wish to maximize profit, the reader may be well advised to acquaint himself with some of the criticism of that assumption, as well as alternative assumptions that have appeared in the literature. To this end, the following references may be offered: J. Margolis, "The Analysis of the Firm: Rationalism, Conventionalism, and Behaviorism," *Journal of Business*, **31**, 187–199 (1958); A. B. Cohan, "The Theory of the Firm: A View on Methodology," *Journal of Business*, **36**, 316–324 (1963); H. T. Koplin, "The Profit Maximization Assumption," *Oxford Economic Papers*, **15**, 130–139 (1963); and J. Encarnación, "Constraints and the Firm's Utility Function," *Review of Economic Studies*, **31**, 113–120 (1964).

PROFIT MAXIMIZATION
UNDER PURE COMPETITION:
THE DEMAND FOR INPUTS

In this chapter, we re-examine the problem discussed in Chapter 4, but from a different point of view. In the preceding chapter, the technological conditions entered into the problem only through their effect on the shape of the cost functions, and we made no direct reference to the amounts of the various inputs which were required to produce the desired level of output. In the present approach, the emphasis is changed by introducing the production function explicitly into the model. From a formal point of view, the difference between the two approaches may be stated as follows: in Chapter 4, the level of output played the role of the decision variable, and the optimization process led to the derivation of the firm's supply function; in this chapter, the levels of inputs are the decision variables, and the optimization process yields the firm's demand functions. Or, to put it differently, Chapter 4 examined the behavior of the firm as a seller of output, while this chapter considers the behavior of the firm as a buyer of inputs.

5.1 THE CONDITIONS FOR PROFIT MAXIMIZATION

Profit, which is still defined as the difference between revenues and cost, depends now directly on the levels of the inputs, and the profit function takes the form

$$(5.1) \qquad \pi = p_0^x \phi(z^1, z^2, ..., z^n) - \sum_{i=1}^{n} p_0^i z^i - c,$$

where p_0^x is the price of product x, p_0^i is the price of the ith input, ϕ is the production function whose arguments are the n variable inputs z^i, and c is the fixed cost associated with the firm's fixed size of plant. The assumption of pure competition is reflected in the fact that all prices are assumed to be parameters that are not under the control of the producer.

Assuming that the profit function possesses an interior maximum, we have the necessary conditions

$$(5.2a) \qquad p_0^x \phi_i - p_0^i = 0, \qquad i = 1, 2, ..., n.$$

The first term on the lhs of (5.2a) represents the MP of the ith input multiplied by the price of the product, and therefore it represents the contribution to the firm's revenues of an infinitesimal increase in the ith input. This quantity is referred to as the *marginal revenue product* (MRP) of the ith input. (The reader should be careful not to confuse MRP and MR; MRP is a function of inputs, MR is a function of output.) And since p_0^i represents the increase in the firm's cost resulting from an infinitesimal increase in the ith input, p_0^i is referred to as the *marginal input cost* (MIC) (which is different from MC).

Thus, condition (5.2a) may be stated as

$$(5.2b) \qquad \text{MRP}^i = \text{MIC}^i, \qquad i = 1, 2, ..., n.$$

If we take any two equations from (5.2a) and eliminate p_0^x, we get

$$(5.3) \qquad \frac{\phi_i}{\phi_j} = \frac{p_0^i}{p_0^j}, \qquad i, j = 1, 2, ..., n,$$

which is identical with the necessary conditions for cost minimization as given in (3.25c) of Chapter 3. Hence the conclusion that cost minimization is a necessary condition for profit maximization.

Another version of the necessary conditions may be obtained by dividing both sides of (5.2a) by ϕ_i. Then we can write

$$(5.2c) \qquad p_0^x = \frac{p_0^i}{\phi_i}, \qquad i = 1, 2, ..., n.$$

Now, in (3.34) it was shown that $p_0^i/\phi_i = \text{MC}$, so that (5.2c) becomes

$$(5.2d) \qquad p_0^x = \text{MC},$$

which is the necessary condition for profit maximization as given in (4.3). Thus, the equivalence between conditions (4.3) and (5.2) shows that the approach to the problem of profit maximization which we are following in this chapter leads to the same solution as that which we analyzed in Chapter 4.

The second-order conditions for this problem take the form

$$(5.4) \qquad p_0^x \phi_{11} < 0, \qquad \begin{vmatrix} p_0^x \phi_{11} & p_0^x \phi_{12} \\ p_0^x \phi_{21} & p_0^x \phi_{22} \end{vmatrix} > 0, ...,$$

$$(-1)^n \begin{vmatrix} p_0^x \phi_{11} & p_0^x \phi_{12} & \cdots & p_0^x \phi_{1n} \\ p_0^x \phi_{21} & p_0^x \phi_{22} & \cdots & p_0^x \phi_{2n} \\ \vdots & & & \vdots \\ p_0^x \phi_{n1} & p_0^x \phi_{n2} & \cdots & p_0^x \phi_{nn} \end{vmatrix} > 0.$$

Since prices are assumed to be positive, it is clear the condition (5.4) implies $\phi_{ii} < 0$ for all i. In words, if the profit-maximizing production program requires a positive amount of each input, then the firm operates in a range of the production function in which each input is subject to diminishing returns.

The shut-down condition is essentially the same as condition (4.5), except that we shall use slightly different terminology and notation. This is necessary since, in this chapter, revenue and cost are functions of inputs rather than output (as was the case in Chapter 4). Thus, the receipts from sales are referred to as *total revenue product* (TRP), and the cost of the variable inputs is called *total input cost* (TIC); that is,

$$\text{TRP} = p_0^x \phi(z^1, z^2, ..., z^n) \text{ and TIC} = \sum_{i=1}^{n} p_0^i z^i.$$

(Note that MRP^i is the partial derivative of TRP with respect to z^i, and MIC^i is the partial derivative of TIC with respect to z^i.) The shut-down condition can now be stated as

(5.5) $$\overline{\text{TRP}} < \overline{\text{TIC}}.$$

At this point, we should point out that a complete analysis of the present problem should also include an investigation of boundary solutions (that is, partial shut-downs) of the type discussed in Section 4.1.3. In the present context, a boundary solution means that the highest level of profit is realized from an input combination in which some inputs are zero. Of course, this can happen only if it is technologically feasible to produce some amount of the output without using all of the n inputs. In any event, in order to avoid repetition, we exclude the possibility of boundary maxima, and assume that the maximum occurs either in the interior of the input space, or at the origin.

In view of the exclusion of boundary maxima, we can state the profit maximization conditions as follows:

(5.6a)   *If* $\overline{\text{TRP}} \geq \overline{\text{TIC}}$, *the firm should purchase and use the amounts given by* $\bar{z}$, *where* $\bar{z}$ *is the vector of the* z^i *satisfying conditions* (5.2) *and* (5.4).

(5.6b)   *If* $\overline{\text{TRP}} < \overline{\text{TIC}}$, *the firm should shut down.*

5.2 THE INPUT DEMAND FUNCTIONS

The assumption about the existence of an interior maximum allows us to solve (5.2a) for the optimal levels of the inputs in terms of the prices. These solutions are the firm's *input demand functions*, and they may be written as

(5.7)
$$\bar{z}^i = h^i(p^x; p^1, p^2, ..., p^n), \quad i = 1, 2, ..., n, \text{ for all } p \text{ such that } \overline{\text{TRP}} \geq \overline{\text{TIC}}.$$

Let us first investigate the effect of a change in the price of the firm's product on the firm's purchases of inputs; in other words, we wish to investigate the sign of $h_x^i = \partial h^i / \partial p^x$, regarding prices now as independent variables.

Differentiating (5.2a) implicity with respect to p^x yields the following system of equations:

$$(5.8) \qquad p^x \sum_{i=1}^{n} \phi_{ji} h_x^i = -\phi_j, \qquad j = 1, 2, ..., n.$$

Solving for h_x^i by means of Cramer's rule, we get

$$(5.9) \qquad h_x^i = -\sum_{j=1}^{n} \phi_j \frac{D_{ji}}{D}, \qquad i = 1, 2, ..., n,$$

where D is the determinant of the $n \times n$ matrix $[p^x \phi_{ij}]$, and D_{ji} is the cofactor of the element in row j and column i of the latter matrix. Since we know only the signs of the diagonal cofactors D_{ii} (from the second-order conditions), it follows that the sign of h_x^i is indeterminate.

Now, this result may at first glance appear somewhat unusual. We saw in Section 4.1.2 that when the price of the output rises, the competitive firm will increase its supply of output; and this suggests that the firm will require larger amounts of the inputs in order to produce the higher level of output. Hence, we would expect that $h_x^i > 0$. However, in order to increase its production, the firm need not necessarily use more of *all* inputs, so that the amounts of some inputs may in fact be reduced, or kept unchanged, as output expands. Consequently, $h_x^i \leq 0$ is indeed possible. We shall discuss this matter further in Section 5.3.

We now turn to the effects of changes in the input prices. Differentiating (5.2a) with respect to p^j, and using Cramer's rule, we find

$$(5.10) \qquad h_j^i = \frac{D_{ji}}{D}, \qquad i, j = 1, 2, ..., n,$$

where $h_j^i = \partial h^i / \partial p^j$. Here we see that for $i \neq j$, the sign of h_j^i is indeterminate, but for $i = j$, we have $h_i^i < 0$ by virtue of (5.4). Thus, we have obtained a *law of demand* for the competitive firm which says that when the price of input i rises (falls), the firm reduces (increases) its purchase (and use) of that input. But the law is not applicable to the effects of such a price increase on the other inputs. However, because of the symmetry of the matrix $[p^x \phi_{ij}]$, it is clear that $D_{ji} = D_{ij}$, and hence we have $h_j^i = h_i^j$ for all i and j.

Another property that input demand functions possess is homogeneity. This may be demonstrated by forming the following expressions:

$$(5.11a) \qquad h_x^i p^x = -\sum_{j=1}^{n} p^x \phi_j \frac{D_{ji}}{D} \qquad \text{by (5.9),}$$

$$(5.12) \qquad \sum_{j=1}^{n} h_j^i p^j = \sum_{j=1}^{n} p^j \frac{D_{ji}}{D} \qquad \text{by (5.10),}$$

$$\left. \right\} \ i = 1, 2, ..., n.$$

Substituting for the $p^x \phi_j$ in (5.11a) from (5.2a), we get

$$(5.11\text{b}) \qquad h^i_x p^x = - \sum_{j=1}^{n} p^j \frac{D_{ji}}{D}, \qquad i = 1, 2, \ldots, n,$$

from which follows

$$(5.13) \qquad h^i_x p^x + \sum_{j=1}^{n} h^i_j p^j = - \sum_{j=1}^{n} p^j \frac{D_{ji}}{D} + \sum_{j=1}^{n} p^j \frac{D_{ji}}{D} = 0, \qquad i = 1, 2, \ldots, n.$$

Then it follows, from Euler's theorem, that the input demand functions are homogeneous of degree zero in all prices. Thus, a proportionate change in all input prices and the price of the output has no effect on the firm's optimal choice of inputs.

The input demand functions of the individual firms may be summed to obtain market demand functions. If $h^{ik}(p)$ denotes the kth firm's demand function for input i, and $p = (p^x;\ p^1, p^2, \ldots, p^n)$, then we have

$$(5.14) \qquad h^i(p) = \sum_{k=1}^{mi} h^{ik}(p),$$

where $h^i(p)$ denotes the market demand function for the ith input, and m^i is the number of firms using input i. Like individual demand functions, the market demand function is homogeneous of degree zero in all prices, and it satisfies the law of demand.

5.3 THE INDIRECT PRODUCTION FUNCTION

Since the optimal levels of inputs depend on the prices, and since the level of output depends on the amounts of the inputs used, the market prices indirectly determine the firm's profit-maximizing level of output. We can, therefore, derive a functional relationship between the prices and the output, and we may refer to it as an *indirect* production function (because it expresses output indirectly as a function of prices). This relationship is obtained by replacing the input variables in the production function by their respective demand functions, and it can be written as

$$(5.15) \qquad \bar{x} = \phi[h^1(p), h^2(p), \ldots, h^n(p)] = \Phi(p^x;\ p^1, p^2, \ldots, p^n).$$

It should be pointed out that, since (5.15) expresses output as a function of prices, it can be interpreted as a supply function, and we may refer to it as such. Moreover, since it depends on *all* prices (unlike the supply function derived in Section 4.1.2), it is a *generalized* supply function. If we hold the input prices constant, allowing only p^x to vary, then the generalized supply function in (5.15) reduces to the one-dimensional supply function given in (4.7); thus

$$(5.16) \qquad \Phi(p^x;\ p^1_0, p^2_0, \ldots, p^n_0) = g(p^x) \quad \text{for all } p^x \text{ such that } \overline{\text{TRP}} \geqslant \overline{\text{TIC}}.$$

This result has an important methodological implication. We see that the present model makes it possible to derive both the demand functions and the supply function of the firm, whereas the profit-maximization model analyzed in Chapter 4 yields only the firm's supply function. The present approach is, therefore, more general. The reason for this is that in the present model we are making use of a specification (the production function) that is more basic than the specification (the cost function) which served as the main building block for the model presented in Chapter 4. (As we have shown in Section 3.4, the cost function may itself be derived from the production function, hence its secondary status.) Consequently, the present model is capable of generating all the behavioral, or technological, relationships and hypotheses that can be derived from the model in Chapter 4, and others as well. This does not mean, however, that the model in Chapter 4 is entirely superfluous; it may be more convenient to work with when interest is focused only on the behavior of the firm as a seller.

We now examine the properties of the generalized supply function. Differentiating (5.15) with respect to p^x, we get

$$(5.17) \qquad \Phi_x = \sum_{i=1}^{n} \phi_i h_x^i = - \sum_{i=1}^{n} \sum_{j=1}^{n} \phi_i \phi_j \frac{D_{ji}}{D},$$

where the second equation follows from (5.9).

The double summation in the above equation may be recognized as a quadratic form in the variables ϕ_i and ϕ_j. The matrix of coefficients associated with this form is the matrix $[D_{ji}/D]$, which turns out to be the inverse of the matrix whose determinant is the Hessian determinant D. (The definition of the inverse matrix in terms of cofactors is given in Section 15.2.2). But it is known that if a matrix is negative definite (i.e., if the associated quadratic form is negative definite), then its inverse is also negative definite. Since the matrix $[D_{ji}/D]$ is the inverse of the matrix $[p^x \phi_{ij}]$, and since the latter matrix was assumed to be negative definite by condition (5.4), it follows that $[D_{ji}/D]$ is negative definite, and hence it is clear that $\Phi_x > 0$. This is, of course, exactly what we would expect, since we already know from Chapter 4 that an increase in the price of the output causes the firm to increase its output.

Differentiating (5.15) with respect to p^j, we get

$$(5.18) \qquad \Phi_j = \sum_{i=1}^{n} \phi_i h_j^i = \sum_{i=1}^{n} \phi_i \frac{D_{ji}}{D}, \qquad j = 1, 2, ..., n,$$

where the second equation follows from (5.10).

The sign of Φ_j is indeterminate, but suppose it is positive. This would mean that as the price of input j rises, the firm increases its output. But from the law of demand for inputs [condition (5.10) for $i = j$], we know that a rise in the input price always brings about a decrease in the use of that input, so that $\Phi_j > 0$ implies that the *expansion* in output is accompanied by a *reduction* in the amount of input j. In that case, input j is said to be an *inferior* input.

Opposite changes in output and an inferior input may also occur when input prices are fixed; it may happen, for instance, when output is changed in response to a change in the price of output. We see from (5.9) and (5.18) that $\Phi_j = -h_x^j$, so that $\Phi_j > 0$ is equivalent to $h_x^j < 0$. The latter inequality says that when the price of output increases (which, in turn, will cause output to increase), the demand for input j falls. Here, again, an increase in the level of production requires a reduction in the use of input j.

Naturally, it is not possible for all inputs to be inferior at the same time (i.e., for any given set of prices), since, in order to increase output, it is necessary to use more of some inputs. This may be demonstrated as follows. A comparison of (5.17) and (5.18) shows that

$$(5.19) \qquad \sum_{j=1}^{n} \phi_j \Phi_j = -\Phi_x = \sum_{i=1}^{n} \sum_{j=1}^{n} \phi_i \phi_j \frac{D_{ji}}{D}.$$

But the quadratic form in (5.19) was shown to be negative definite, hence it is not possible for all the Φ_j to be positive (or zero).

Finally, since the input demand functions were shown to be homogeneous of degree zero in all prices, it follows from an inspection of (5.15) that the function Φ is also homogeneous of degree zero in all prices; that is, when all prices change by the same percentage, the firm will not change its level of output.

5.4 THE INDIRECT PROFIT FUNCTION

It may also be of interest to examine the effects of price changes on the firm's profit. This may be done by constructing an indirect profit function; that is, a relation expressing profit as a function of prices.

If we replace the z^i in (5.1) by their respective demand functions, then profit becomes a function of the market prices, taking the form

$$(5.20) \qquad \pi = p^x \Phi(p) - \sum_{i=1}^{n} p^i h^i(p) - c = \rho(p).$$

The desired effects can now be investigated by differentiating $\rho(p)$. Differentiating (5.20) with respect to p^x yields

$$(5.21a) \qquad \rho_x = \bar{x} + p^x \Phi_x - \sum_{i=1}^{n} p^i h_x^i,$$

where $\rho_x = \partial\rho/\partial p^x$. Making use of (5.17) to eliminate Φ_x, we can write

$$(5.21b) \qquad \rho_x = \bar{x} + \sum_{i=1}^{n} h_x^i (p^x \phi_i - p^i).$$

But since the expression in parentheses in (5.21b) is zero for all i by (5.2a), we have

$$(5.21c) \qquad \rho_x = \bar{x}.$$

This shows that an increase in the price of the product increases the firm's level of profit, the rate of increase being equal to the optimal level of output. It can also be shown that the percentage increase in profit is always greater than the percentage increase in price; in other words, the output-price elasticity of the function ρ, that is, $\rho_x p^x / \rho(p)$, is greater than unity. Multiplying both sides of (5.21c) by $p^x/\rho(p)$, assuming $\rho(p) > 0$, we get

$$(5.22) \qquad \rho_x \frac{p^x}{\rho(p)} = \frac{p^x \bar{x}}{\rho(p)}.$$

But total revenue is always greater than profit, hence $p^x \bar{x}/\rho(p) > 1$.

Differentiating (5.20) with respect to p^j yields

$$(5.23a) \qquad \rho_j = p^x \Phi_j - \sum_{i=1}^{n} p^i h_j^i - \bar{z}^j, \qquad j = 1, 2, ..., n,$$

where $\rho_j = \partial\rho/\partial p^j$. Substituting for Φ_j from (5.18) we get

$$(5.23b) \qquad \rho_j = \sum_{i=1}^{n} h_j^i (p^x \phi_i - p^i) - \bar{z}^j = -\bar{z}^j \qquad \text{for all } j \text{ by (5.2a).}$$

Profit, therefore, falls when the price of an input rises, the rate of decrease being equal to the optimal amount of the respective input.

Example 5.1. To illustrate the model examined in the preceding sections we shall use the n-input version of the production function given in Example 3.2. The firm's profit function can then be written as

$$\pi = p_0^x \sum_{i=1}^{n} a_i \ln(z^i + 1) - \sum_{i=1}^{n} p_0^i z^i - c, \qquad a_i, c > 0 \qquad \text{for all } i,$$

and the first-order conditions are

$$\frac{p_0^x a_i}{z^i + 1} - p_0^i = 0, \qquad i = 1, 2, ..., n.$$

The second-order conditions are

$$\frac{-p_0^x a_1}{(z^1 + 1)^2} < 0, \quad \begin{vmatrix} \dfrac{-p_0^x a_1}{(z^1 + 1)^2} & 0 \\ 0 & \dfrac{-p_0^x a_2}{(z^2 + 1)^2} \end{vmatrix} > 0, \ \ldots,$$

$$(-1)^n \begin{vmatrix} \dfrac{-p_0^x a_1}{(z^1 + 1)^2} & 0 & \cdots & 0 \\ 0 & \dfrac{-p_0^x a_2}{(z^2 + 1)^2} & \cdots & 0 \\ \vdots & & & \vdots \\ 0 & 0 & \cdots & \dfrac{-p_0^x a_n}{(z^n + 1)^2} \end{vmatrix} > 0,$$

which are obviously satisfied in this particular example.

The optimal amounts of the inputs can be obtained by solving the first-order conditions for the z^i, and these solutions take the form

$$\bar{z}^i = \frac{p^x a_i}{p^i} - 1 = h^i(p), \quad i = 1, 2, \ldots, n \quad \text{for all } p \text{ such that } \overline{\text{TRP}} \geqslant \overline{\text{TIC}}.$$

(The reader may observe that this model will yield an interior maximum only if $p^x a_i > p_i$ for all i.)   It is easy to see that $h_x^i = a_i/p_i > 0$, $h_i^i = -p^x a_i/(p^i)^2 < 0$, and $h_j^i = 0$, $i \neq j$.   Since the optimal amounts of the inputs depend only on price *ratios*, proportionate changes in all prices have no effect on the optimal levels of the inputs.

To construct the indirect production function we replace the z^i in the production function by their demand functions, and thus get

$$\bar{x} = \sum_{i=1}^{n} a_i \ln \left(\frac{p^x a_i}{p^i} \right) = \Phi(p).$$

If the p^i are held constant, then the indirect production function becomes the firm's supply function. Thus

$$\bar{x} = \sum_{i=1}^{n} a_i \ln \left(\frac{p^x a_i}{p_0^i} \right) = g(p^x) \quad \text{for all } p \text{ such that } \overline{\text{TRP}} \geqslant \overline{\text{TIC}},$$

and

$$g' = \Phi_x = \sum_{i=1}^{n} \frac{a_i}{p^x} > 0.$$

If input prices are also allowed to vary, then we have

$$\Phi_j = -\frac{a_j}{p^j} < 0,$$

which also verifies the fact that $\Phi_j = -h_x^j$. Therefore, in the example chosen here, an expansion of output always requires more of each input, and hence a rise in the price of an input will result in a contraction of output. Hence, none of the inputs is inferior.

Profit can now be expressed as a function of prices. This gives

$$\pi = p^x \sum_{i=1}^{n} a_i \ln\left(\frac{p^x a_i}{p^i}\right) - \sum_{i=1}^{n} (p^x a_i - p^i) - c = \rho(p).$$

Differentiating with respect to p^x, we get

$$\rho_x = \bar{x} + \sum_{i=1}^{n} a_i - \sum_{i=1}^{n} a_i = \bar{x},$$

and differentiating with respect to p^j, we have

$$\rho_j = -\frac{p^x a_j}{p^j} + 1 = -\bar{z}^j.$$

5.5 HOMOGENEOUS PRODUCTION FUNCTIONS

In many economic problems, especially those of the macro variety, it is customary to assume that the production function is homogeneous of degree one in all inputs. In this section we shall briefly examine the implications of the homogeneity assumption with respect to the model presented in this chapter.

If the production function is homogeneous of degree one, then equiproportionate changes in all inputs will cause a change in output by the same proportion. For example, if each input is increased by, say, k percent, then output will also increase by k percent. In that case, both revenue (TRP) and cost (TIC) will increase by k percent, and so will *gross* profit (profit exclusive of fixed cost). Therefore, under these circumstances, gross profit is also homogeneous of degree one.

Suppose now that prices are such that, for some input vector z, gross profit is positive, then it is possible to increase profit indefinitely by increasing all inputs by the same proportion. Therefore, the profit function has no maximum (provided, of course, there are no restrictions on the availability of the inputs). In order to demonstrate this more formally, let us write the profit function as

$$(5.24) \qquad \pi = p_0^x \phi(k z_0^1, k z_0^2, \ldots, k z_0^n) - \sum_{i=1}^{n} p_0^i k z_0^i - c,$$

which may be regarded as a function of the single variable k. The reason for writing the profit function in this way is that a change in k results in equi-proportionate changes in all inputs. Differentiating the profit function with respect to k gives

$$(5.25\text{a}) \qquad \frac{d\pi}{dk} = p_0^x \sum_{i=1}^{n} \phi_i z_0^i - \sum_{i=1}^{n} p_0^i z_0^i,$$

which, by virtue of the homogeneity assumption, can also be written as

$$(5.25\text{b}) \qquad \frac{d\pi}{dk} = p_0^x x_0 - \sum_{i=1}^{n} p_0^i z_0^i.$$

Thus, $d\pi/dk$ is equal to gross profit. Hence, if gross profit is positive for some positive value of k (and some vector z_0), profit can always be increased further by increasing k (since $d\pi/dk > 0$), and so we see that the profit function cannot attain a maximum for any finite value of k.

On the other hand, if gross profit is zero for some positive value of k, then it will be zero for all values of k. In that special case, of course, the profit function attains a maximum for any value of k, the maximum level of profit being equal to zero. (In this special case, gross profit, when plotted against k, is a constant function.)

We may investigate the reasons for these results in a still different way. Let us reproduce the first-order conditions for profit maximization as given in (5.2a); that is,

$$(5.26) \qquad p_0^x \phi_i(z^1, z^2, ..., z^n) - p_0^i = 0, \qquad i = 1, 2, ..., n.$$

Now, if the function ϕ is homogeneous of degree one in all the z^i, then the functions ϕ_i are homogeneous of degree zero in the z^i; that is, equipro-portionate changes in the z^i will not change the value of the functions ϕ_i. We may, therefore, multiply each z^i in (5.26) by the factor $1/z^n$, and write the conditions in (5.26) in the equivalent form

$$(5.27\text{a}) \qquad p_0^x \phi_i\left(\frac{z^1}{z^n}, \frac{z^2}{z^n}, ..., \frac{z^{n-1}}{z^n}, 1\right) - p_0^i = 0 \qquad \left.\begin{array}{c} \\ \\ \\ \end{array}\right\} \quad i = 1, 2, ..., n,$$

or

$$(5.27\text{b}) \qquad p_0^x \phi_i(\zeta^1, \zeta^2, ..., \zeta^{n-1}, 1) - p_0^i = 0$$

where $\zeta^i = z^i/z^n$.

We see from (5.27b) that the first-order conditions in this problem consist of n equations in $n-1$ independent variables. In general, however, such a system of equations may be inconsistent; in other words, it may not be possible to find values for the $n-1$ variables satisfying all n equations simul-taneously. If this is the case, the first-order conditions are not satisfied, and hence the profit function cannot have an interior maximum. This situation will occur, as we have already pointed out, when prices are such as to yield a positive gross profit for some vector z, in which case the profit function cannot attain a maximum.

The only case in which the first-order conditions can be satisfied is when gross profit is zero. Suppose that prices are such as to make (5.27b) a consistent system of equations, and let the $\bar{z}^i$ denote the values satisfying these equations. Multiplying both sides of the ith equation by $\bar{z}^i$, we get

$$(5.28) \qquad p_0^x \phi_i \bar{z}^i - p_0^i \bar{z}^i = 0, \qquad i = 1, 2, \ldots, n,$$

and, summing these equations, we have

$$(5.29) \qquad p_0^x \sum_{i=1}^{n} \phi_i \bar{z}^i - \sum_{i=1}^{n} p_0^i \bar{z}^i = 0.$$

The expression in (5.29) is the same as that in (5.25), and the latter was seen to be equal to gross profit. Thus, according to (5.29), if the first-order conditions are fulfilled, then gross profit is zero. We may point out, though, that the optimal levels $\bar{z}^i$ are not unique, since a proportionate change in each $\bar{z}^i$ will leave the equations in (5.27) unaffected.

Finally, by virtue of Euler's theorem on homogeneous functions, we have

$$(5.30) \qquad \sum_{i=1}^{n} \phi_i z^i = \phi(z).$$

Differentiating (5.30) with respect to z^j, we have

$$(5.31) \qquad \sum_{i=1}^{n} \phi_{ij} z^i + \phi_j = \phi_j,$$

and so we have

$$(5.32) \qquad \sum_{i=1}^{n} \phi_{ij} z^i = 0, \qquad j = 1, 2, \ldots, n.$$

The equations in (5.32) imply that the rows (columns) of the $n \times n$ matrix, whose determinant is given in (5.4), are linearly dependent. (See Section 15.2.3.) Hence the Hessian determinant in condition (5.4) vanishes, and it follows, therefore, that the profit function cannot have a regular interior maximum. Of course, the Hessian vanishes even in the special case in which the maximum gross profit is zero. This poses no contradiction, however, since the nonvanishing of the Hessian is necessary only if the maximum is a regular maximum. In the present case, the maximum is not a regular maximum because the first-order conditions are invariant to equiproportionate changes in the $\bar{z}^i$.

What the above results have shown is that under competitive conditions the maximization process breaks down if the production function is homogeneous of degree one since, in general, the profit function will not possess a maximum. Only one special case may yield a solution, and in that case gross profit is zero.

5.6 MULTIPRODUCT PRODUCTION

For the case of a multiproduct production process we shall make use of a multiproduct production function of the kind introduced in Section 3.5. The firm's profit function takes the form

$$(5.33) \qquad \pi = \sum_{i=1}^{m} p_0^i x^i - \sum_{j=m+1}^{m+n} q_0^j z^j - c,$$

where p_0^i denotes the price of the ith product, q_0^j denotes the price of the jth input, and the m products x^i are related to the n inputs z^i by the implicit production function $\phi(x^1, x^2, ..., x^m; z^{m+1}, z^{m+2}, ..., z^{m+n}) = 0$. We shall adopt the same notational conventions as in Chapter 3; that is,

$$\phi_i = \frac{\partial \phi}{\partial x^i} \quad \text{for} \quad i = 1, 2, ..., m,$$

$$\phi_j = \frac{\partial \phi}{\partial z^j} \quad \text{for} \quad j = m + 1, m + 2, ..., m + n.$$

It will be convenient to use the Lagrangian method, and so we set up the Lagrangian form

$$(5.34) \qquad \sum_{i=1}^{m} p_0^i x^i - \sum_{j=m+1}^{m+n} q_0^j z^j - c + \lambda \phi(x; z),$$

where $x = (x^1, x^2, ..., x^m)$ and $z = (z^{m+1}, z^{m+2}, ..., z^{m+n})$.

If the profit function has an interior maximum, then we obtain the first-order conditions

$$(5.35a) \qquad p_0^i + \lambda \phi_i = 0, \qquad i = 1, 2, ..., m,$$

$$(5.36a) \qquad -q_0^j + \lambda \phi_j = 0, \qquad j = m + 1, m + 2, ..., m + n,$$

$$(5.37) \qquad \phi(x; z) = 0.$$

By eliminating λ from (5.36a) we get

$$(5.36b) \qquad \frac{q_0^j}{q_0^k} = \frac{\phi_j}{\phi_k}, \qquad j, k = m + 1, m + 2, ..., m + n.$$

Now, in (3.48) it was shown that the rhs of (5.36b) is the slope (in absolute value) of the isoquant surface, that is, the MRTS between inputs j and k. Therefore, condition (5.36b) is the same as condition (5.3) in the one-product case.

If we eliminate λ from (5.35a), we get

(5.35b) $$\frac{p_0^i}{p_0^k} = \frac{\phi_i}{\phi_k}, \qquad i, k = 1, 2, \ldots, m,$$

which equates the MRPT between any two products with the ratio of the respective product prices.

Finally, by combining pairs of equations, one equation from (5.35a) and (5.36a) each, we get

(5.38a) $$- p_0^i \frac{\phi_j}{\phi_i} - q_0^j = 0, \quad i = 1, 2, \ldots, m, \quad j = m+1, m+2, \ldots, m+n.$$

The ratio $-\phi_j/\phi_i$ is the MP of the jth input in the production of product i [see (3.53)], and is assumed to be positive. Hence we can write (5.38a) as

(5.38b) $$p_0^i \left| \frac{\phi_j}{\phi_i} \right| - q_0^j = 0, \quad i = 1, 2, \ldots, m, \quad j = m+1, m+2, \ldots, m+n,$$

which is the analog of condition (5.2a) in the one-product case.

The second-order conditions can be stated as follows:

(5.39a)
$$(-1)^k \begin{vmatrix} \lambda\phi_{11} & \lambda\phi_{12} & \cdots & \lambda\phi_{1k} & \phi_1 \\ \lambda\phi_{21} & \lambda\phi_{22} & \cdots & \lambda\phi_{2k} & \phi_2 \\ \vdots & & & \vdots & \vdots \\ \lambda\phi_{k1} & \lambda\phi_{k2} & \cdots & \lambda\phi_{kk} & \phi_k \\ \phi_1 & \phi_2 & \cdots & \phi_k & 0 \end{vmatrix} > 0, \qquad k = 2, 3, \ldots, m+n,$$

and this is equivalent to

(5.39b)
$$(-1)^k \lambda^{k-1} \begin{vmatrix} \phi_{11} & \phi_{12} & \cdots & \phi_{1k} & \phi_1 \\ \phi_{21} & \phi_{22} & \cdots & \phi_{2k} & \phi_2 \\ \vdots & & & \vdots & \vdots \\ \phi_{k1} & \phi_{k2} & \cdots & \phi_{kk} & \phi_k \\ \phi_1 & \phi_2 & \cdots & \phi_k & 0 \end{vmatrix} > 0, \qquad k = 2, 3, \ldots, m+n.$$

The firm's supply and demand functions can be obtained from Eqs. (5.35) through (5.37), and can be written as

(5.40a) $$\bar{x}^i = g^i(p; q), \qquad i = 1, 2, \ldots, m,$$

(5.40b) $$\bar{z}^j = h^j(p; q), \qquad j = m+1, m+2, \ldots, m+n,$$

where $p = (p^1, p^2, \ldots, p^m)$ and $q = (q^{m+1}, q^{m+2}, \ldots, q^{m+n})$.

Partial differentiation of Eqs. (5.40) with respect to the various prices yields the following:

$$(5.41) \qquad \frac{\partial g^i}{\partial p^j} = g^i_j = -\frac{D_{ji}}{D}, \qquad i, j = 1, 2, \ldots, m,$$

$$(5.42) \qquad \frac{\partial g^i}{\partial q^j} = g^i_j = \frac{D_{ji}}{D}, \qquad i = 1, 2, \ldots, m, \quad j = m+1, m+2, \ldots, m+n,$$

$$(5.43) \qquad \frac{\partial h^j}{\partial p^i} = h^j_i = -\frac{D_{ij}}{D}, \qquad i = 1, 2, \ldots, m, \quad j = m+1, m+2, \ldots, m+n,$$

$$(5.44) \qquad \frac{\partial h^j}{\partial q^i} = h^j_i = \frac{D_{ij}}{D}, \qquad i, j = m+1, m+2, \ldots, m+n,$$

where D is the $(m + n + 1) \times (m + n + 1)$ determinant given in (5.39a), and D_{ji} is a typical cofactor.

The properties of the above derivatives, deduced from the second-order conditions given in (5.39), are consistent with our findings in the more special cases discussed earlier in the chapter. The following derivatives have determinate signs:

$$(5.45) \qquad g^i_i > 0, \qquad i = 1, 2, \ldots, m.$$

[g^i_i corresponds to g^i_i as defined in (4.18), and to Φ_x in (5.17).]

$$(5.46) \qquad h^j_j < 0, \qquad j = m + 1, m + 2, \ldots, m + n.$$

[h^j_j corresponds to h^j_j given in (5.10).]

All other derivatives are of indeterminate signs. However, due to the symmetry of D, we also have the following:

$$(5.47) \qquad g^i_j = g^j_i, \qquad i, j = 1, 2, \ldots, m,$$

$$(5.48) \qquad h^i_j = h^j_i, \qquad i, j = m + 1, m + 2, \ldots, m + n,$$

$$(5.49) \qquad g^i_j = -h^j_i, \qquad i = 1, 2, \ldots, m, \qquad j = m + 1, m + 2, \ldots, m + n.$$

It is easy to show that the functions in (5.40) are homogeneous of degree zero in all prices. For example,

$$(5.50a) \qquad \sum_{j=1}^{m} g^i_j p^j + \sum_{j=m+1}^{m+n} g^i_j q_j = -\sum_{j=1}^{m} p^j \frac{D_{ji}}{D} + \sum_{j=m+1}^{m+n} q^j \frac{D_{ji}}{D}, \quad i = 1, 2, \ldots, m.$$

Substituting for the p^j and q^j in (5.50a) from (5.35a) and (5.36a), respectively, we have

$$(5.50b) \qquad \sum_{j=1}^{m} g^i_j p^j + \sum_{j=m+1}^{m+n} g^i_j q^j = \lambda \sum_{j=1}^{m+n} \phi_j \frac{D_{ji}}{D} = 0, \qquad i = 1, 2, \ldots, m,$$

where the second equality follows from the theorem about the expansion of determinants by alien cofactors. (See Section 15.2.2.) The same proof can be used to demonstrate the homogeneity of the input demand functions.

Finally, we can write the profit function as

$$(5.51) \qquad \pi = \sum_{i=1}^{m} p^i g^i(p; \ q) - \sum_{j=m+1}^{m+n} q^j h^j(p; \ q) - c = \rho(p; \ q).$$

Then, by invoking once more the above theorem about determinant expansion, it can be shown that

$$(5.52) \qquad \frac{\partial \pi}{\partial p^i} = \rho_i = \bar{x}^i, \qquad i = 1, 2, ..., m,$$

and

$$(5.53) \qquad \frac{\partial \pi}{\partial q^j} = \rho_j = - \bar{z}^j, \qquad j = m + 1, m + 2, ..., m + n,$$

which are the generalizations of the results obtained in (5.21c) and (5.23b).

BIBLIOGRAPHICAL NOTES

The derivation of input demand functions, and the analysis of their properties, is carried out in P. A. Samuelson, *Foundations of Economic Analysis*, Cambridge: Harvard University Press, 1947, Chapter 4, and in J. M. Henderson and R. E. Quandt, *Microeconomic Theory*, New York: McGraw-Hill, 1958, Chapter 3. Recently, several writers have paid special attention to the case of inferior inputs, and have examined the implications of this case; for example, D. V. T. Bear, "Inferior Inputs and the Theory of the Firm," *Journal of Political Economy*, **73**, 287–289 (1965); T. Rader, "Normally, Factor Inputs are Never Gross Substitutes," *Journal of Political Economy*, **76**, 38–43 (1968); and C. E. Ferguson, " 'Inferior Factors' and the Theories of Production and Input Demand," *Economica*, **35**, 140–150 (1968). The effects on input demand functions resulting from a relaxation of the profit-maximization assumption are discussed in R. D. Portes, "Input Demand Functions for the Profit-Constrained Sales-Maximizer: Income Effects in the Theory of the Firm," *Economica*, **35**, 233–248 (1968). The relationship between the approach presented in Chapter 4 and this chapter is illustrated graphically in J. Hirshleifer, "An Exposition of the Equilibrium of the Firm: Symmetry Between Product and Factor Analyses," *Economica*, **29**, 263–268 (1962); it is reprinted in D. R. Kamerschen (ed.), *Readings in Microeconomics*, Cleveland: World Publishing Company, 407–413 (1967).

CHAPTER 6

PROFIT MAXIMIZATION
UNDER PURE MONOPOLY:
THE SUPPLY OF OUTPUT

We turn now to a discussion of the market behavior of a firm which is the only seller in the market. Unlike the pure competitor, the pure monopolist does not view the market price as a given parameter, but rather as a decision variable. Since the monopolist is the only seller in the market, the quantities that he will be able to sell depend directly on the price at which he will offer his product for sale. This relationship between price and quantity demanded is given by the market demand function. The derivation of the market demand function is discussed in Chapter 10, and for the purpose of the present analysis we shall merely assume that quantity demanded decreases with price.

6.1 THE CONDITIONS FOR PROFIT MAXIMIZATION

The monopolist's profit function takes the form

(6.1) $$\pi = xh(x) - f(x) - c,$$

where $p = h(x)$ represents the market demand function, and $f(x)$ the TVC function. (It is perhaps more appropriate to refer to $h(x)$ as the *inverse* demand function since, from the buyer's point of view, the output x is the dependent, rather than the independent, variable. We choose to use the inverse demand function in this formulation, but will, for simplicity, continue to refer to it as the "demand function.") The inclusion of fixed cost in the profit function implies, of course, that we are dealing here with a short-run decision problem.

If the profit function possesses a regular interior maximum, then the first-order condition is

(6.2a) $$h(x) + xh' - f' = 0.$$

Since the first two terms in (6.2a) represent the first derivative of TR with respect to x, condition (6.2a) can be rewritten as

(6.2b) $$MR = MC,$$

which is identical with condition (4.3b).

The second-order condition requires

(6.3a) $$2h' + \bar{x}h'' - f'' < 0,$$

where $\bar{x}$ is the value of x satisfying (6.2). The above condition can also be stated as

(6.3b) $$MR' < MC'.$$

It may be observed that condition (6.3) is less specific than the corresponding condition (4.4) for the competitive firm inasmuch as (4.4) is a special case of (6.3). Thus, while under competitive conditions the MC function must be increasing at the optimal level of output, the monopolist's MC function may be falling at the optimal output, provided it falls less rapidly than the MR function.

The shut-down condition is essentially the same as that for the competitive firm, except that the price is not predetermined. Thus, the analog of condition (4.5e) is

(6.4) $$\bar{p} < \overline{AVC},$$

where $\bar{p} = h(\bar{x})$, and $\bar{x}$ is the level of x satisfying conditions (6.2) and (6.3). We may summarize these conditions as follows:

(6.5a)   *If $\bar{p} \geqslant \overline{AVC}$, the monopolist should produce $\bar{x}$, $\bar{x}$ being the level of output satisfying conditions (6.2) and (6.3).*

(6.5b)   *If $\bar{p} < \overline{AVC}$, the monopolist should shut down.*

The optimal output level $\bar{x}$ can be found by solving (6.2) for x. But since Eq. (6.2) contains no explicit parameters, the solution is just a number (rather than a function). This means that technology, demand, and the input prices together determine a unique level of output.

If we remove the fixed cost from the profit function, and replace the TVC function by the monopolist's LTC function, then the above analysis gives us the conditions for long-run profit maximization. Of course, in that case one also has to interpret $h(x)$ as the firm's *expected* long-run market demand function. We shall not repeat the analysis itself, but merely state the conclusions:

(6.6a)   *If $\bar{p} \geqslant \overline{AVC}$, the monopolist should produce $\bar{x}$, $\bar{x}$ being the level of output satisfying conditions (6.2) and (6.3) after replacing $f(x)$ by the LTC function.*

(6.6b)   *If $\bar{p} < \overline{AVC}$, the monopolist should leave the market.*

It may be pointed out that, since LMC need not be increasing at the optimal level of output, the monopolist, unlike the pure competitor, may attain a long-run equilibrium position on the *downward* sloping segment of his LAC function.

Example 6.1. For the present example, we shall use the TVC function from Example 2.1. The market demand function will be assumed to be a linear function of the form

$$p = r - sx = h(x) \qquad r, s > 0,$$

so that we have the following profit function:

$$\pi = rx - sx^2 - (x - a)^3 - bx - a^3 - c.$$

Setting the first derivative equal to zero, we get

$$r - 2sx - 3(x - a)^2 - b = 0,$$

which has the solutions

$$x = \frac{(3a - s)}{3} \pm \frac{\sqrt{(3a - s)^2 - 3(3a^2 + b - r)}}{3}.$$

To ensure a maximum, the second derivative of the profit function is required to be negative, hence

$$-2s - 6(x - a) < 0, \qquad \text{or} \qquad x > \frac{3a - s}{3},$$

so that

$$\bar{x} = \frac{(3a - s)}{3} + \frac{\sqrt{(3a - s)^2 - 3(3a^2 + b - r)}}{3}.$$

It may, of course, be necessary to make some assumptions about the parameters of the model (a, b, c, r, s) in order to exclude nonsensical results. First, we want to make sure that $\bar{x}$ is real. For this purpose, we must assume

(6.7) $$(3a - s)^2 - 3(3a^2 + b - r) \geqslant 0.$$

Second, we require $\bar{x} \geqslant 0$. It is easy to verify that if $(3a - s) \geqslant 0$, then $\bar{x} \geqslant 0$. This condition is stronger than necessary, but we shall make this assumption just the same because of its simple form.

Having made appropriate assumptions about the parameters, we must test whether the output $\bar{x}$ generates sufficient revenues to defray the variable cost; that is, whether $\bar{p} \geqslant \overline{\text{AVC}}$, or equivalently, whether $\overline{\text{AVC}} - \bar{p} \leqslant 0$. Applying the latter inequality to the present example, we get

(6.8) $$\bar{x}^2 - (3a - s)\bar{x} + 3a^2 + b - r \leqslant 0.$$

We shall go about testing this inequality in an indirect manner. Let us assume first that $3a - s = 0$. This implies, by (6.7), that $3a^2 + b - r \leqslant 0$, in which case we have

$$\bar{x} = \frac{\sqrt{-3(3a^2 + b - r)}}{3}.$$

Making use of this equation, we can show that condition (6.8) is satisfied, so that the monopolist will not shut down.

Suppose now that we decrease s slightly, holding all other parameters constant. This is a legitimate procedure, since it will not violate condition (6.7). Given the profit level for the initial level of s (that is, $s = 3a$), we can see from the profit function that a slight decrease in s will increase profit, assuming the level of output is held constant. Of course, a change in the value of a parameter will in general require an adjustment in the optimal level of output, so that if we allow output to be adjusted following the decrease in s, profit will increase still more. From this argument we can conclude that when $(3a - s) \geqslant 0$, and given also (6.7), then $\bar{x}$ is indeed the monopolist's optimal level of output.

6.2 PRICE DISCRIMINATION

When a monopolist charges different prices for an identical product in the same period of time, he is said to practice *price discrimination*. Such a practice becomes feasible when the total market for the monopolist's product consists of a number of effectively separated submarkets each of which may be represented by its own demand function. For the purpose of price discrimination, the separation between the submarkets must be such as to discourage the buyers in any submarket from reselling the monopolist's product in any other submarket; if such transactions did take place on a large scale, the monopolist would not be able to maintain price differentials in the different markets. Thus, price discrimination may conceivably take place when markets are separated geographically, when the monopolist's product is highly perishable, when the existence of price differentials can be kept secret, or under any other set of conditions that make intermarket transactions either technically unfeasible, or too costly. Naturally, the reason for engaging in price discrimination, whenever it is feasible, is the desire to earn a higher level of profit.

6.2.1 The Conditions for Profit Maximization

When a monopolist is confronted with a number of effectively separated markets for his product x, his profit function takes the form

(6.9) $$\pi = \sum_{i=1}^{m} x^i h^i(x^i) - f\left(\sum_{i=1}^{m} x^i\right) - c,$$

where x^i is the quantity of x sold in the ith market, $p^i = h^i(x^i)$ represents the demand function of the ith market, and m is the number of markets. If the profit function has a regular interior maximum, then we have the first-order conditions

(6.10a) $$h^i(x^i) + x^i h^{i\prime} - f' = 0, \qquad i = 1, 2, ..., m.$$

Since $x^i h^i(x^i)$ represents total revenue from the ith market, condition (6.10a) may also be stated as

(6.10b) $$\mathrm{MR}^i = \mathrm{MC}, \qquad i = 1, 2, ..., m,$$

where MR^i denotes the marginal revenue in the ith market. The necessary conditions for profit maximization equate the MR in each market with MC of the total output. These conditions imply, of course, that at the optimal distribution of sales, the MRs must be equal in all markets.

The second-order conditions may be stated in the following fashion:

(6.11) $$\mathrm{MR}^{1\prime} - \mathrm{MC}' < 0,$$

$$\begin{vmatrix} \mathrm{MR}^{1\prime} - \mathrm{MC}' & -\mathrm{MC}' \\ -\mathrm{MC}' & \mathrm{MR}^{2\prime} - \mathrm{MC}' \end{vmatrix} > 0, ...,$$

$$(-1)^m \begin{vmatrix} \mathrm{MR}^{1\prime} - \mathrm{MC}' & -\mathrm{MC}' & \cdots & -\mathrm{MC}' \\ -\mathrm{MC}' & \mathrm{MR}^{2\prime} - \mathrm{MC}' & \cdots & -\mathrm{MC}' \\ \vdots & & & \vdots \\ -\mathrm{MC}' & -\mathrm{MC}' & \cdots & \mathrm{MR}^{m\prime} - \mathrm{MC}' \end{vmatrix} > 0.$$

These conditions require, among other things, that the change in MC exceed the exchange in MR in each market. The optimal levels of sales in the different markets, $\bar{x}^i$, are found by solving the system (6.10), and the optimal prices can be determined from the equations $\bar{p}^i = h^i(\bar{x}^i)$, $i = 1, 2, ... m$.

As for the shut-down situation, the discriminating monopolist is in a position similar to that of the multiproduct firm. This issue was discussed in Section 4.1.3, and given the conclusion which we reached in that discussion, we can say that if the monopolist faces m different submarkets, then he must, when choosing his optimal strategy, select from among 2^m different sales plans. Here we simplify the analysis by excluding partial shut-downs, i.e., we exclude plans which call for selling positive quantities in some submarkets, and zero in others; instead, we assume that the maximum is attained either at an interior point, or at the origin. Under these assumptions the shut-down condition is given by

(6.12a) $$\sum_{i=1}^{m} \bar{p}^i \bar{x}^i < f(\bar{x}),$$

where $\bar{x} = \sum_{i=1}^{m} \bar{x}^i$. If we replace $f(\bar{x})$ by $\bar{x}\,\overline{\mathrm{AVC}}$, and divide both sides of (6.12a) by $\bar{x}$, we get

(6.12b) $$\sum_{i=1}^{m} \frac{\bar{p}^i \bar{x}^i}{\bar{x}} < \overline{\mathrm{AVC}}.$$

This inequality bears some resemblance to condition (6.4), except that whereas the latter condition involves only one price, condition (6.12) involves the m prices charged by the monopolist in the different markets. In fact, the lhs of (6.12) may be interpreted as a *price index*, i.e., a weighted average of m prices. In this particular case, the weights that appear in the index are the shares of total output sold in the respective markets.

6.2.2 The Relative Price and Output Levels

When the monopolist exercises price discrimination, the relative levels of the prices in the m submarkets depend on the elasticities of the demand functions. In order to demonstrate this relationship, we first derive a useful formula relating marginal revenue, price, and elasticity. If we differentiate the equation $TR = xh(x)$, we get

$$(6.13a) \qquad\qquad MR = p + xh'.$$

The expression on the rhs can be rearranged to yield

$$(6.13b) \qquad\qquad MR = p\left(1 + \frac{x}{p}h'\right).$$

But $(x/p)h' = 1/e$, where e is the elasticity of the demand function $x = h^{-1}(p)$, and since $e < 0$, we can write

$$(6.13c) \qquad\qquad MR = p\left(1 - \frac{1}{|e|}\right).$$

Since, in general, $MR > 0$ at the optimal output, we shall assume $|e| > 1$.

Now, since under conditions of price discrimination all the MR^i have to be equal, by (6.10b), we get from (6.13c)

$$(6.14) \qquad p^1\left(1 - \frac{1}{|e^1|}\right) = p^2\left(1 - \frac{1}{|e^2|}\right) = \ldots = p^m\left(1 - \frac{1}{|e^m|}\right).$$

Then, for any two markets, it is clear that the price will be higher in the market in which the absolute value of the elasticity at the optimal level of output is lower; that is, if $|e^i| < |e^j|$, then $p^i > p^j$ for all i and j. It is also clear from (6.14) that, if $e^i = e^j$ for all i and j, then $p^i = p^j$ for all i and j. In that case no discrimination takes place even though the monopolist chooses his prices in accordance with condition (6.10). It is, therefore, clear that if the m submarkets have identical demand functions, then the monopolist will not find it profitable to charge different prices. This, however, is not the only case in which price discrimination is not an optimal strategy. Another case is that in which all the demand functions are linear, and intersect the price axis at the same point; that is, if the $h^i(x^i)$ are linear, and if $h^i(0) = h^j(0)$ for all i and j.

A qualitative comparison of the different levels of output is also possible, but additional assumptions are necessary to obtain conclusive results. For this purpose, we first rewrite the profit function given in (6.9) in terms of the inverses of the functions h^i. We write

$$(6.15) \qquad \pi = \sum_{i=1}^{m} p^i \hat{h}^i(p^i) - f\left[\sum_{i=1}^{m} \hat{h}^i(p^i)\right] - c,$$

where $x^i = \hat{h}^i(p^i)$. This formulation yields the first-order conditions

$$(6.16a) \qquad \hat{h}^i(p^i) + p^i \hat{h}^{i\prime} - f' \hat{h}^{i\prime} = 0, \qquad i = 1, 2, ..., m,$$

which may also be stated as

$$(6.16b) \qquad mr^i = mc^i, \qquad i = 1, 2, ..., m.$$

Here we are using a different notation for the expressions in (6.16b) since, unlike those given in (6.10b), they are functions of the p^i (rather than the x^i). Thus, mr^i is the change in TR as p^i is increased by a small amount, and mc^i is the change in TC resulting from a small increase in p^i. It also follows from (6.16) that

$$(6.17) \qquad \frac{mr^i}{\hat{h}^{i\prime}} = \frac{mr^j}{\hat{h}^{j\prime}} \qquad \text{for all } i \text{ and } j.$$

By rearranging the expression for mr^i, it can be shown that

$$(6.18) \qquad mr^i = x^i(1 - |e^i|),$$

and hence, in view of (6.17), we obtain the analog of conditions (6.14), namely

$$(6.19) \qquad \frac{x^1(1 - |e^1|)}{\hat{h}^{1\prime}} = \frac{x^2(1 - |e^2|)}{\hat{h}^{2\prime}} = \cdots = \frac{x^m(1 - |e^m|)}{\hat{h}^{m\prime}}.$$

(The bars which we sometimes place on top of variables to denote optimal values have been removed here as a measure of economy.)

Conditions (6.19) involve both the elasticities and the slopes of the demand functions, and therefore one cannot make a qualitative comparison of the levels of output on the basis of the elasticities alone. In the special case in which all demand functions have the same slope at the optimal distribution of sales, we have the following: If $|e^i| > |e^j|$, then $x^i < x^j$, for all i and j. If $|e^i| = |e^j|$ for all i and j, in which case there is no discrimination, then if $\hat{h}^{i\prime} > \hat{h}^{j\prime}$, then $x^i < x^j$. But since all demand functions are assumed to be downward sloping, we can say that in the absence of discrimination, given any two markets, output will be greater in the market which has the steeper demand function (output being expressed as a function of price).

6.2.3 Average Revenue under Discrimination

As we have seen, when the monopolist's total market is separated into several submarkets, profit is maximized when prices are set so as to equate the MRs in the different markets. This is, of course, also true if the level of total output is predetermined; in other words, in order to maximize the total revenue from a given level of output, prices should be set according to the conditions for price discrimination. Thus, if we rule out the special case in which the equalization of the MRs results in a uniform price, then for any given x we have

$$\text{(6.20)} \qquad \sum_{i=1}^{m} p^{*i} x^i > px,$$

where $p = h(x)$, $h(x)$ is the total market demand function, $p^{*i} = h^i(x^i)$, and the x^i satisfy the conditions for price discrimination as well as the condition $\sum_{i=1}^{m} x^i = x$. If we divide both sides of (6.20) by x, we get

$$\text{(6.21a)} \qquad \sum_{i=1}^{m} \frac{p^{*i} x^i}{x} > p,$$

or

$$\text{(6.21b)} \qquad AR^* > AR,$$

where AR denotes *average revenue* (that is, revenue per unit of output).

Condition (6.21) simply says that when the monopolist practices price discrimination, then the revenue that he receives per unit of output (that is, AR*) exceeds the average revenue (that is, $AR = p$) that he receives when he charges a uniform price for his product. (This difference is, of course, the source of the extra profit that price discrimination produces.) Both of these revenue concepts can be expressed as functions of the total output x. We already have the relationship $AR = p = h(x)$, and that between AR* and x can be written as $AR^* = h^*(x)$. Given these two functional relationships, we can write (6.21b) as

$$\text{(6.22)} \qquad h^*(x) > h(x),$$

which says that the function h^* lies above the market demand function h. The function h^* is a useful analytical concept, but before we illustrate some of the applications to which it may be put, we show how this function can be derived, and examine its slope.

First, we restate the conditions for price discrimination

(6.23) $h^i(x^i) + x^i h^{i\prime} = h^j(x^j) + x^j h^{j\prime}$,   for all i and j,

and the condition

(6.24) $\sum_{i=1}^{m} x^i = x.$

The above conditions contain m independent equations in $m + 1$ variables. By virtue of the Implicit Function Theorem it is, in general, possible to solve this system for the x^i in terms of x. These solutions can be stated as

(6.25) $x^i = \eta^i(x),$ $i = 1, 2, \ldots, m,$

and it follows from (6.24) and (6.25) that

(6.26) $\sum_{i=1}^{m} \eta^{i\prime} = 1.$

Since $\text{AR*} = \sum_{i=1}^{m} \dfrac{h^i(x^i)x^i}{x}$, we can substitute for the x^i in the latter expression from (6.25), and this gives us the desired relationship

(6.27) $h^*(x) = \sum_{i=1}^{m} \dfrac{h^i[\eta^i(x)]\eta^i(x)}{x}.$

To show that the slope of $h^*(x)$ is negative, we differentiate (6.27). This gives

(6.28a) $h^{*\prime} = \sum_{i=1}^{m} \dfrac{[h^i(x^i)\eta^{i\prime} + x^i h^{i\prime}\eta^{i\prime}]}{x} - \dfrac{h^*(x)}{x},$

which can also be stated as

(6.28b) $h^{*\prime} = \sum_{i=1}^{m} \dfrac{\eta^{i\prime}\text{MR}^i}{x} - \dfrac{\text{AR*}}{x}.$

But since all the MR^i are equal by (6.23), we can write

(6.28c) $h^{*\prime} = \dfrac{\text{MR}}{x} \sum_{i=1}^{m} \eta^{i\prime} - \dfrac{\text{AR*}}{x} = \dfrac{\text{MR} - \text{AR*}}{x},$

where MR is the common value of the MR^i, and the second equation follows by virtue of (6.26). Since we are assuming that all demand functions are downward sloping, it follows that $\text{MR}(=\text{MR}^i) < p^i$ for all i. However, AR* is a weighted average of the p^i in which the weights add up to one [see (6.21a)], from which it is obvious that $\text{MR} < \text{AR*}$, and hence $h^{*\prime} < 0$. The function $h^*(x)$ is illustrated in Fig. 6.1, in which the total market is assumed to consist of two submarkets each of which has a linear demand function.

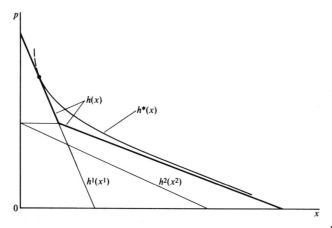

Figure 6.1

When price discrimination is in effect, the function $h^*(x)$ plays a role in the analysis similar to that of the ordinary demand function $h(x)$ in the absence of discrimination. For example, we can make use of $h^*(x)$ in the statement of the shut-down condition, and write the latter as $h^*(\bar{x}) < \overline{AVC}$, and it is clear from the similarity between the two inequalities that by means of the function $h^*(x)$ we are able to reduce the formal difference between the two models to a minimum. The similarity between the shut-down conditions also enables us to draw an interesting conclusion about a possible economic effect of price discrimination. Suppose that $h(x) < AVC$, from which it follows that if the monopolist were to adopt a nondiscriminatory pricing policy, he would not be able to cover his variable cost, and hence would be forced to shut down. On the other hand, since $h^*(x) > h(x)$, there may exist some range of x such that $h^*(x) > AVC$. This shows that the introduction of price discrimination may make it possible for the monopolist to operate in a market in which he could not survive if he were not able to implement price discrimination.

To carry the formal similarity between the two models a step further, we can specify the discriminating monopolist's environment *as if* it consisted (like that of a nondiscriminating monopolist) of only one market whose demand function is given by $h^*(x)$. The monopolist's choice of total output is then found by maximizing the profit function

$$(6.29) \qquad \pi = xh^*(x) - f(x) - c.$$

To prove this, we derive the necessary condition for the maximization of the function given in (6.29). This condition is

$$(6.30a) \qquad h^*(x) + xh^{*\prime} - f' = 0.$$

Substituting for $h^{*'}$ in (6.30a) from (6.28), we have

(6.30b) $h^*(x) + MR - h^*(x) - f' = MR - f' = 0.$

However, MR is the common value of the MR^i, hence conditions (6.30b) and (6.10) are equivalent. Of course, in order to compute the outputs and prices in the different submarkets, we must make use of the equations in (6.25), as well as the individual demand functions $p^i = h^i(x^i)$.

As a concluding remark, we may point out that in spite of the similarity in the formal structure of the profit functions given in (6.1) and (6.29), the profit-maximizing level of total output may, in general, be different in each case. The result depends on the relative curvatures of the demand functions of the submarkets. A special case occurs when the demand functions $h^i(x^i)$ are linear: in this case, total output in the absence of discrimination will be equal to that produced under a discriminatory policy.

Example 6.2. Let us suppose that the monopolist's market can be separated into two submarkets with the following demand functions:

$$\text{Submarket 1} \quad x^1 = \frac{a_1}{p^1} - b_1 = \hat{h}^1(p^1), \qquad a_1, b_1 > 0.$$

$$\text{Submarket 2} \quad x^2 = \frac{a_2}{p^2} - b_2 = \hat{h}^2(p^2), \qquad a_2, b_2 > 0.$$

We can then construct the total market demand function by summing the above functions, that is,

$$x = \frac{a_1}{p} - b_1 + \frac{a_2}{p} - b_2 = \frac{a}{p} - b = \hat{h}(p),$$

where $a = a_1 + a_2$, and $b = b_1 + b_2$.

We shall first determine the monopolist's optimal output under a non-discriminatory policy. For simplicity, we assume that the TVC function is linear. If we invert the total market demand function we get $p = a/(b + x) = h(x)$, and consequently the profit function takes the form

$$\pi = \frac{ax}{b + x} - dx - c, \qquad c, d > 0.$$

Since the p-intercept of the market demand function is equal to a/b, the optimal output will be positive if MC is smaller than that intercept. Therefore we assume $d < a/b$.

Setting the first derivative of the profit function equal to zero, we get

$$\frac{ab}{(b + x)^2} - d = 0,$$

from which we obtain the solution

$$\bar{x} = -b + \sqrt{\frac{ab}{d}} .$$

Substituting this value of $\bar{x}$ into the market demand function $h(x)$, we find

$$\bar{p} = \sqrt{\frac{ad}{b}} ,$$

and by substituting for x in the profit function we obtain the monopolist's maximum profit

$$\pi = a - 2\sqrt{abd} + db - c.$$

The quantities sold in each submarket can be found by replacing p^1 and p^2 by $\bar{p}$ in the respective demand functions. This yields

$$x^1 = a_1 \sqrt{\frac{b}{ad}} - b_1, \qquad x^2 = a_2 \sqrt{\frac{b}{ad}} - b_2.$$

To determine whether the monopolist could increase his profit by practicing price discrimination, we compute the MRs in the two markets. Inverting the two demand functions, we get $p^i = a_i/(b_i + x^i)$, $i = 1, 2$, and by differentiating the products $TR^i = a_i x^i/(b_i + x^i)$, we obtain $MR^i = a_i b_i/(b_i + x^i)^2$, $i = 1, 2$. After substituting in the latter equations, respectively, the values of the x^i computed above, we get

$$MR^1 = \frac{b_1 \, ad}{a_1 \, b}, \qquad MR^2 = \frac{b_2 \, ad}{a_2 \, b}.$$

Since we have placed no restrictions (other than positivity) on the parameters of the demand functions, we can in general expect that $MR^1 \neq MR^2$, in which case a redistribution of the total output between the two markets will result in a higher profit.

Assuming now that the monopolist wishes to practice discrimination, we make use of the inverted demand functions of the two submarkets, and write the profit function as

$$\pi = \frac{a_1 x^1}{b_1 + x^1} + \frac{a_2 x^2}{b_2 + x^2} - d(x^1 + x^2) - c.$$

This formulation yields the first-order conditions

$$\frac{a_i b_i}{(b_i + x^i)^2} - d = 0, \qquad i = 1, 2,$$

which have the solutions

$$\bar{x}^i = \sqrt{\frac{a_i b_i}{d}} - b_i, \qquad i = 1, 2.$$

The optimal prices in the two markets are found by replacing x^i by $\bar{x}^i$ in the inverse demand functions $p^i = a_i/(b_i + x^i)$. This gives

$$\bar{p}^i = \sqrt{\frac{a_i d}{b_i}}, \qquad i = 1, 2.$$

As is to be expected, if the two demand functions are identical, then there will be no discrimination. That is, if $a_1 = a_2$ and $b_1 = b_2$, then $\bar{p}^1 = \bar{p}^2$. But this is not the only case which rules out discrimination in the present example. We see also that if $a_1/b_1 = a_2/b_2$, then $\bar{p}^1 = \bar{p}^2$. Now, a_i/b_i is the p-intercept of the demand function of the ith submarket. This means that if the demand functions in our example have the same p-intercept, the monopolist will not find it profitable to charge different prices, even though each demand function may have a different slope. On the other hand, if the intercepts are different, discrimination will take place, and the market with the higher intercept will be charged the higher of the two prices.

The completion of this example, i.e., the comparison of the total output and profit levels under a uniform and a discriminatory pricing policy, respectively, is left to the reader as an exercise.

6.3 PRICE CONTROL

A monopolist may be restricted in his choice of an optimal production plan by price control. This could take the form of a price ceiling which prohibits the monopolist from charging a price in excess of the specified ceiling. In which case, the monopolist maximizes his profit function subject to the constraint $p \leqslant p_0$, where p_0 is the price ceiling.

An optimization problem in which some (or all) variables are constrained by inequalities is usually referred to as a *programming* problem, linear or nonlinear, as the case may be. Strictly speaking, the problems we have considered so far (as well as others we shall consider in the succeeding chapters) are programming problems, because they involve variables that are subject to the nonnegativity restriction. But since, for the most part, we have assumed that the maximum (minimum) occurs at an interior point, we have in fact made the nonnegativity restriction redundant, and thus obviated the necessity of dealing with some of the typical issues of programming problems. Consequently, except for our occasional analysis of the shut-down condition, we were able to use the traditional mathematical methods for finding and characterizing the solutions to optimization problems. The nature of the present problem, however, is such that, short of assuming the entire problem away, boundary solutions have to be considered explicitly. Therefore, we will have to introduce some elementary concepts and techniques of nonlinear programming in order to analyze the problem satisfactorily. As will be seen in the analysis that follows, the "trick" is to set up the problem in a way which permits us to invoke the results of the traditional methods and, in particular, the necessary conditions for interior extreme points.

We assume that in the absence of the ceiling the monopolist charges a price which is higher than the ceiling. That is, it is assumed that $\hat{p} > p_0$, where $\hat{p}$ is the solution to maximizing

$$(6.31) \qquad \pi = ph(p) - f[h(p)] - c,$$

where $x = h(p)$ is the market demand function, and $f(x)$ again denotes the TVC function. Since the first-order condition to this problem is

$$(6.32) \qquad h(p) + ph' - f'h' = 0,$$

it is also correct to say that $\hat{p}$ is the root of Eq. (6.32).

In the formulation of the present problem, we shall relax the assumption that the quantity of output chosen by the monopolist at some price equals the quantity demanded by the market at that price; instead, we allow the former quantity to be smaller than the latter. Put differently, we permit the market to be in a state of excess demand. Under these conditions the monopolist is confronted with the following problem:

Maximize

$$(6.33) \qquad \pi = px - f(x) - c,$$

subject to

$$(6.34a) \qquad x \leqslant h(p),$$

$$(6.35a) \qquad p \leqslant p_0.$$

In order to analyze this problem, we first change the form of the constraints through the introduction of two dummy variables, v_1 and v_2. The modified (but equivalent) version of the problem now states: Maximize (6.33) subject to

$$(6.34b) \qquad x + v_1 = h(p),$$

$$(6.35b) \qquad p + v_2 = p_0,$$

$$(6.36) \qquad v_1 \geqslant 0,$$

$$(6.37) \qquad v_2 \geqslant 0.$$

The purpose of this reformulation is to change the inequalities in (6.34a) and (6.35a) into strict equalities. Of course, at the same time it is necessary to restrict the dummy variables to nonnegative values in order to ensure that the original inequalities (6.34a) and (6.35a) hold. Even though the dummy variables play only an auxiliary role in this problem, they may be given an economic interpretation: v_1 represents excess demand in the market at any given price, and v_2 represents *excess ceiling*, that is, the amount by which the ceiling exceeds the price chosen by the monopolist.

The problem now involves four unknowns (p, x, v_1, and v_2) and is subject to four constraints. If we assume that the optimal price and output (that is, $\bar{p}$ and $\bar{x}$) are positive, then the solution to the problem must fall into one of the following four exhaustive cases:

$$1. \qquad \bar{v}_1, \bar{v}_2 > 0,$$

$$2. \qquad \bar{v}_1 = 0, \quad \bar{v}_2 > 0,$$

$$3. \qquad \bar{v}_1 > 0, \quad \bar{v}_2 = 0,$$

$$4. \qquad \bar{v}_1 = \bar{v}_2 = 0,$$

where bars denote optimal values. We shall now investigate each of the above possibilities.

Case 1. Under the specification of this case, the solution is entirely in the interior (i.e., all the four optimal values are positive), and hence the Lagrangian method is applicable. If we set up the Lagrangian form

$$(6.38) \qquad px - f(x) - c + \lambda_1[x + v_1 - h(p)] + \lambda_2(p + v_2 - p_0),$$

where λ_1 and λ_2 are Lagrange multipliers, and set the appropriate first-order partial derivatives equal to zero, we obtain

$$(6.39) \qquad x - \lambda_1 h' + \lambda_2 = 0 \quad \text{(differentiating with respect to } p),$$

$$(6.40) \qquad p - f' + \lambda_1 = 0 \quad \text{(differentiating with respect to } x),$$

$$(6.41) \qquad \lambda_1 = 0 \quad \text{(differentiating with respect to } v_1),$$

$$(6.42) \qquad \lambda_2 = 0 \quad \text{(differentiating with respect to } v_2).$$

Thus, under the assumption that there exists an interior maximum, the solution must satisfy conditions (6.39) through (6.42). But the above conditions imply that $\bar{x} = 0$ (since $\lambda_1 = \lambda_2 = 0$), which contradicts our assumption that $\bar{x} > 0$. Therefore, the problem cannot have an interior solution, i.e., not all four variables can be positive at the maximum.

Case 2. This case assumes that excess demand is zero (i.e., the monopolist chooses a price-output combination which is represented by a point *on* the market demand function). This permits us to eliminate condition (6.34b) and the variable x by substituting $h(p)$ for x in the profit function. However, since the remaining variables (p and v_2) are assumed to be positive, we have again an interior solution (but to a problem which is of a slightly different form from Case 1). The Lagrangian form can now be written as

$$(6.43) \qquad ph(p) - f[h(p)] - c + \lambda(p + v_2 - p_0).$$

and the first-order conditions are

$$(6.44) \qquad\qquad h(p) + ph' - f'h' + \lambda = 0,$$

$$(6.45) \qquad\qquad\qquad\qquad \lambda = 0.$$

Now, if the demand and cost functions are sufficiently "well behaved," so that in the absence of a price ceiling the profit function possesses a unique maximum (that is, at $\hat{p}$), then, since $\lambda = 0$ by (6.45), Eqs. (6.44) and (6.32) have the same solution—namely, $\hat{p}$. But $\hat{p} > p_0$ (by assumption), which implies $v_2 < 0$ by (6.35b). This is a contradiction of our assumption that $v_2 > 0$, and therefore the profit function cannot have a maximum under the conditions of Case 2.

Case 3. In this case, we eliminate condition (6.35b) and the variable p, so that the problem is reduced to one with the two unknowns x and v_1, both of which are assumed to be positive at the maximum. This yields the following Lagrangian form and first-order conditions, respectively:

$$(6.46) \qquad\qquad p_0 x - f(x) - c + \lambda[x + v_1 - h(p_0)],$$

$$(6.47) \qquad\qquad\qquad p_0 - f' + \lambda = 0,$$

$$(6.48) \qquad\qquad\qquad\qquad \lambda = 0.$$

The first-order conditions imply that the monopolist chooses the output which equates the price with MC, and hence the solution is qualitatively the same as that of a purely competitive firm.

Case 4. This case is the simplest of all four cases, since by setting $v_1 = 0$ in (6.34b), and $v_2 = 0$ in (6.35b), one immediately obtains the solutions $\bar{p} = p_0$ and $\bar{x} = h(p_0)$.

So, the solutions obtained under Cases 3 and 4 are the only possible results of the imposition of a price ceiling when the latter is less than the monopolist's optimal price in the absence of any control. In general, of course, one cannot tell in advance which of these two cases applies. It should, however, be pointed out that if Case 3 prevails, then the existing excess demand is likely to force the price up, since some buyers may be willing to pay more than the legal ceiling in order to guarantee for themselves an adequate supply of the commodity. To prevent this from happening, the imposition of the price ceiling may, in such a case, have to be accompanied by some form of rationing. It should also be pointed out that the imposition of the price ceiling has the effect of reducing the monopolist's profit. This is so because if at the ceiling price p_0 his profit were greater than at $\hat{p}$, the monopolist would have chosen to charge p_0 (rather than $\hat{p}$) in the first place.

Some possible outcomes are illustrated in Figs. 6.2(a), (b). In the absence of a ceiling, the monopolist chooses $\hat{p}$ and $\hat{x}$. Under the conditions of Fig. 6.2(a), price ceilings set at the levels p_1 and p_2 bring about outputs x_1 and x_2, respectively. Both of these events fall into Case 4. If the ceiling is set at p_3, the monopolist produces x_3, and there exists excess demand equal to $x_4 - x_3$ units. This, therefore, is an example of Case 3.

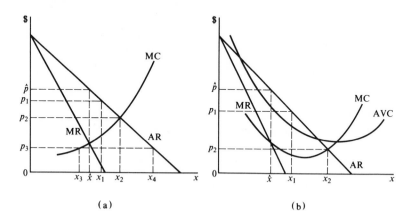

Figure 6.2

Under the conditions illustrated in Fig. 6.2(b), all solutions fall into Case 4, as, for example, when the ceiling is set at p_1. Now, in our discussion of price control, we have made no mention of the shut-down condition, since we have assumed (for simplicity) that the optimal output is always positive. But it can easily be seen that if the ceiling were set at p_2, then a monopolist who faced the conditions depicted in Fig. 6.2(b) would shut down, since at the price p_2 no output which is equal to, or less than, x_2 can generate enough revenues to cover TVC (AVC being higher than p_2). Thus, whenever the ceiling is sufficiently high to enable the monopolist to produce a positive level of output, the solution is of the type described by Case 4.

6.4 TAXATION

The introduction of taxes, like the imposition of a price ceiling, may force the monopolist to choose a new optimal combination of price and output. Taxes may be thought of as either fixed or variable. A fixed tax—also known as a lump-sum tax—is independent of the level of output, and therefore its effect is the same as, say, a change in fixed cost. Since the first-order condition, as well as the shut-down condition, is independent of the level of TFC, the monopolist's optimal choice remains unchanged in this case; the sole effect of the tax is to reduce the monopolist's profit by the amount of the tax.

Variable taxes may be of various forms, some of which will be examined below.

6.4.1 Profit Tax

This tax requires the monopolist to surrender a certain portion of his profit (but not of his loss). If we let π^* denote profit exclusive of the tax, then

(6.49) $\pi = (1 - t)\,\pi^*$ if $\pi^* > 0$,

                          $\pi = \pi^*$ if $\pi^* \leqslant 0$,

where $t \cdot 100$ is the percentage of profit which has to be paid as tax, and $0 < t < 1$. If gross profit is positive, then the profit function takes the form

(6.50) $\pi = (1 - t)\,[xh(x) - f(x) - c]$,

which leads to the first-order condition

(6.51) $(1 - t)\,[h(x) + xh' - f'] = 0$.

Since $1 - t \neq 0$, it follows that condition (6.51) is equivalent to condition (6.2) which (in the case of an interior maximum) must hold in the absence of a tax.

If $\pi^* \leqslant 0$, then the monopolist will produce a positive level of output so long as revenues are sufficient to pay for the variable cost. Thus, the profit tax has no effect on the monopolist's choice of price and output, but in those situations in which he earns a positive profit, the monopolist loses an amount of profit equal to his tax payment. Needless to say, if the profit tax is graduated, so that t itself is a function of π^*, then the imposition of (or changes in) the tax rate will normally call for an adjustment in price and output.

6.4.2 Specific Tax

A specific tax is a fixed payment per unit of output. We thus have

(6.52) $\pi = \pi^* - tx$,

where t is the specific tax, and π^* is as defined in Section 6.4.1. In this case, the monopolist maximizes

(6.53) $\pi = xh(x) - f(x) - c - tx$,

and the first-order condition is

(6.54a) $h(x) + xh' - f' - t = 0$,

which can also be stated as

(6.54b) $MR - MC - t = 0$.

The tax can be thought of either as a part of variable cost, or as a deduction from revenues. In the former case, we can write (6.54b) as

(6.54c) $MR = MC + t,$

and in the latter, as

(6.54d) $MR - t = MC.$

The second-order condition (6.3) is not affected by the tax, since t vanishes upon differentiation. However, since the total tax payment varies with the level of output, the shut-down condition does depend on t. We may state it as either

(6.55a) $\bar{p} < \overline{AVC} + t,$

or

(6.55b) $\bar{p} - t < \overline{AVC},$

where $\bar{p} = h(\bar{x})$, $\overline{AVC} = f(\bar{x})/\bar{x}$, and $\bar{x}$ is the level of x satisfying (6.54). Since $\bar{x}$ depends on the parameter t, we can write

(6.56) $\bar{x} = g(t),$

which is the solution of (6.54), and can be thought of as the monopolist's supply of x as a function of the tax rate, subject to (6.55). If this function is evaluated at the origin, that is, at $t = 0$, it yields the same level of x as the solution to (6.2).

The function $g(t)$ may be used for studying the effects of the tax on the monopolist's level of output, price, and profit. Substituting for x in (6.54a) from (6.56), and differentiating, yields

(6.57a) $2h'g' + \bar{x}h''g' - f''g' - 1 = 0,$

which can also be written as

(6.57b) $g' = \dfrac{1}{2h' + \bar{x}h'' - f''} < 0,$

where the inequality follows from the fact that the denominator of the middle term is negative by the second-order condition. Therefore, an increase in the tax leads to a decrease in output.

If we differentiate the inverse demand function $\bar{p} = h[g(t)]$ we get

(6.58) $\dfrac{d\bar{p}}{dt} = h'g' > 0,$

where the inequality follows from the assumption that the demand function is downward sloping. According to (6.58), the monopolist's response to an increase in the tax is to raise his price. Furthermore, if both p and t are measured in the same unit of measurement (say, the dollar), then if $d\bar{p}/dt > 1$, the increase in the price exceeds the increase in the tax, and the opposite occurs if $d\bar{p}/dt < 1$. For example, $d\bar{p}/dt > 1$ holds if, and only if, $h' + \bar{x}h'' - f'' > 0$. The latter inequality will hold if either the MC function is falling rapidly ($f'' < 0$) in the relevant range, or the demand function is sufficiently convex to the origin ($h'' > 0$), or both.

The effect of the tax on the monopolist's profit can be determined by differentiating the profit function after substituting for x from (6.56). This yields

$$(6.59) \qquad \frac{d\pi}{dt} = g'[h(\bar{x}) + \bar{x}h' - f' - t] - \bar{x} = -\bar{x} < 0,$$

where the second equality follows by virtue of (6.54a). The fact that profit diminishes as a result of the tax is, of course, to be expected; if it weren't so, the monopolist could always profit from voluntarily levying a tax on his own product (and pocketing the tax himself, to boot!).

For any given tax rate, we can easily compare the magnitude of the monopolist's loss of profit with the amount of tax collected from him. If $\hat{\pi}$ denotes the maximum profit when the tax is zero, and $\bar{\pi}$ the maximum profit when the tax is equal to t, we can compare the monopolist's loss $\hat{\pi} - \bar{\pi}$ with the total tax payment $t\bar{x}$. Making use of the definition in (6.52) we can write

$$(6.60a) \qquad\qquad \bar{\pi} = \pi^* - t\bar{x},$$

or

$$(6.60b) \qquad\qquad \pi^* = \bar{\pi} + t\bar{x}.$$

Now, π^* is also equal to the amount of profit which the monopolist would earn if he chose to produce $\bar{x}$ units of x in the absence of any tax. But when $t = 0$, his optimal output is not $\bar{x}$, but, say $\hat{x}$, which yields the profit $\hat{\pi}$. Therefore we have

$$(6.61a) \qquad\qquad \hat{\pi} > \pi^*,$$

which, in view of (6.60), may be written as

$$(6.61b) \qquad\qquad \hat{\pi} > \bar{\pi} + t\bar{x},$$

and hence

$$(6.61c) \qquad\qquad \hat{\pi} - \bar{\pi} > t\bar{x}.$$

In words, the amount of profit which the monopolist loses as a result of the imposition of the tax is greater than the tax payment collected from him.

(*Question*: What happens to the difference?) Note that this result does not depend on the amount by which the monopolist raises his price following the increase in the tax.

6.4.3 Sales Tax

A sales tax is an *ad valorem* (as opposed to a specific) tax which is expressed as a certain percentage of the *value* (i.e., price) of one unit of the output. The effects of a sales tax are similar to those of a specific tax. To avoid repetition, we shall only formulate the problem, and state the main results. The monopolist maximizes the profit function

$$(6.62) \qquad \pi = (1 - t)xh(x) - f(x) - c,$$

where $t \cdot 100$ is the percentage of the price levied in the form of a sales tax. This problem has the first-order condition

$$(6.63) \qquad (1 - t)\,\mathrm{MR} = \mathrm{MC},$$

and the second-order condition

$$(6.64) \qquad (1 - t)\,\mathrm{MR}' < \mathrm{MC}',$$

while the shut-down condition states

$$(6.65) \qquad (1 - t)\,\bar{p} < \overline{\mathrm{AVC}}.$$

If $\bar{x} = g(t)$ denotes the solution to (6.63), then we again have

$$(6.66) \qquad g' < 0,$$

$$(6.67) \qquad \frac{d\bar{p}}{dt} = h'g' > 0,$$

and

$$(6.68) \qquad \frac{d\pi}{dt} = -\bar{p}\bar{x} < 0.$$

And it is easily shown that when the tax is increased from zero to t, the monopolist's loss in profit exceeds the quantity $t\bar{p}\bar{x}$.

Example 6.3. Let the monopolist's demand function be given by $x = (a/p) - b$, $a, b > 0$,   so that the inverse demand function is $p = a/(b + x)$. Assuming a linear cost function, the monopolist's profit function can be written as

$$\pi = \frac{ax}{b + x} - dx - c - tx, \qquad d, c > 0,$$

where $t \geqslant 0$ is a specific tax. The first-order condition is

$$\frac{ab}{(b+x)^2} - (d+t) = 0,$$

and the second-order condition is

$$\frac{-2ab}{(b+x)^3} < 0,$$

which is satisfied for all nonnegative values of x. Since marginal cost (inclusive of the tax) is fixed at $d + t$, the optimal level of output will be positive if the p-intercept of the demand function (a/b) is above that of marginal cost. Hence we assume $a/b > d + t$. (See Fig. 6.3.)

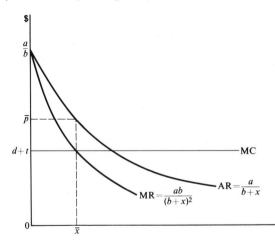

Figure 6.3

Solving for x from the first-order condition, we get

$$\bar{x} = \sqrt{\frac{ab}{d+t}} - b = g(t).$$

The optimal price can be obtained by inserting the value of $\bar{x}$ in the inverse demand function. This yields

$$\bar{p} = \sqrt{\frac{a}{b}(d+t)}.$$

The monopolist will produce a positive level of output so long as

$$\bar{p} \geqslant \overline{AVC} + t,$$

which, in this example, requires

$$\sqrt{\frac{a}{b}(d+t)} \geqslant d + t.$$

Since both sides of this inequality are positive, we can square them to get

$$\frac{a}{b}(d + t) \geqslant (d + t)^2, \qquad \text{or} \qquad \frac{a}{b} \geqslant d + t,$$

which is satisfied in view of our earlier assumption (Fig. 6.3).

The effect of changes in the tax on the optimal level of output can be studied by differentiating the function g. This gives

$$g' = -\frac{\sqrt{ab}}{2(d + t)^{3/2}} < 0,$$

which shows that an increase in the tax rate will induce the monopolist to contract his output. The accompanying change in price is given by

$$\frac{d\bar{p}}{dt} = \left[\frac{a}{4b(d + t)}\right]^{1/2} > 0.$$

However, the magnitude of the change in price is indeterminate. For example, if

$$\frac{a}{b} < 4(d + t),$$

then the increase in price is less than the increase in the tax, and if the inequality is reversed, the change in price will exceed the change in tax. The actual outcome depends, therefore, on the relative magnitudes of the parameters of the cost and demand functions, and on the level of the tax.

BIBLIOGRAPHICAL NOTES

One of the earliest, if not the first, mathematical treatment of monopoly (as well as that of other types of markets) is to be found in Augustin Cournot's *Researches into the Mathematical Principles of the Theory of Wealth*. This was first published, in the original French version, in 1838. Two chapters of this book have recently been reprinted (in English) under the title "Of Monopoly and of the Influence of Taxation on Commodities Produced under a Monopoly," in R. A. Musgrave and C. S. Shoup (eds.), *Readings in the Economics of Taxation*, Homewood, Illinois: Irwin, 1959, pp. 240–255. A more recent work is J. Robinson, *The Economics of Imperfect Competition*, London: Macmillan, 1933; while not mathematical, the scope of this work is comprehensive and it makes extensive use of diagrammatical analysis. A particular aspect of price discrimination is analyzed in E. O. Edwards, "The Analysis of Output under Discrimination," *Econometrica*, **18**, 163–172 (1950). Analyses of the effects of taxation are usually found in texts on taxation and public finance. An example is R. A. Musgrave, *The Theory of Public Finance*, New York: McGraw-Hill, 1959, Chapter 13. A brief comparison of the effects of taxation under different market structures may be found in J. Hadar, "Tax-Shifting and Profit-Protection—A Clarification," *Finanzarchiv*, **25**, 52–59 (1966).

CHAPTER 7

PROFIT MAXIMIZATION UNDER PURE MONOPOLY AND PURE MONOPSONY: THE DEMAND FOR INPUTS

The monopolist's demand for inputs can be analyzed in a fashion similar to that carried out in Chapter 5. This, it will be recalled, is done by reformulating the profit maximization problem so as to introduce the production function and the input prices explicitly. In the first section, we examine the model of a monopolist who purchases his inputs under competitive conditions, while in the second section, we consider the purchase of inputs under conditions other than competitive. The discussion in Section 7.1 will be quite brief because of the similarity of the analysis with material that has already been discussed in the preceding chapters.

7.1 PURE MONOPOLY

15504

We shall let $p^x = H(x)$ denote the (inverse) market demand function, $x = \phi(z^1, z^2, ..., z^n)$ the production function, and p^i the market price of the ith input.

The monopolist's profit function takes the form

(7.1)
$$\pi = \phi(z)H[\phi(z)] - \sum_{i=1}^{n} p_0^i z^i - c,$$

where $z = (z^1, z^2, ..., z^n)$. The monopolist now maximizes his profit function with respect to the n inputs z^i. If the function possesses a regular interior maximum, then the first-order conditions are

(7.2a) $\phi_i H[\phi(z)] + \phi(z) H' \phi_i - p_0^i = 0, \qquad i = 1, 2, ..., n.$

In order to clarify the meaning of the necessary conditions (7.2a), we rewrite them as

(7.2b) $\phi_i(p^x + xH') = p_0^i,$ ⎫

and hence   ⎬ $i = 1, 2, ..., n.$

(7.2c) $\mathrm{MP}^i \cdot \mathrm{MR} = p_0^i,$ ⎭

The lhs of (7.2c) represents the increment in output due to a small change in the ith input (MP^i) multiplied by the contribution to total revenue of the incremental output (MR); it, therefore, represents what has been defined in Section 5.1 as the MRP (marginal revenue product) of the ith input. The quantity p_0^i is, of course, the marginal increase in cost resulting from a small increase in z^i. Thus we can write

(7.2d) $$MRP^i = MIC^i, \qquad i = 1, 2, \ldots, n,$$

which is equivalent to conditions (5.2b) for the competitive case. Of course, the two models are not identical, since the MRP^i in the present model are more complicated functions than those in the competitive case. The comparison between conditions (5.2b) and (7.2d), however, is designed to point out the similarity in the formal structures of the two models.

Eliminating MR from any two equations in (7.2b), we get

(7.3) $$\frac{\phi_i}{\phi_j} = \frac{p_0^i}{p_0^j}, \qquad i, j = 1, 2, \ldots, n,$$

which, like (5.3), are the necessary conditions for cost minimization.

Finally, if we manipulate conditions (7.2) once more, we can write

(7.2e) $$MR = \frac{p_0^i}{MP^i}, \qquad i = 1, 2, \ldots, n,$$

and since the ratios p_0^i/MP^i have been shown to be equal to MC [Eq. (3.34)], we have

(7.2f) $$MR = MC.$$

This establishes the equivalence of the present approach to that of Chapter 6.

The second-order conditions, as in any multivariable problem, involve a series of Hessian determinants. The elements of these determinants are the second-order partial derivatives of the profit function. A typical element can be obtained by differentiating the lhs of (7.2a); this yields

$$\frac{\partial^2 \pi}{\partial z^i \, \partial z^j} = \phi_{ij}\{H[\phi(z)] + \phi(z)H'\} + \phi_i \phi_j (2H' + xH'').$$

A more compact form of this expression is $\phi_{ij} MR + \phi_i \phi_j MR'$. Thus the second-order conditions can be stated as

(7.4)
$$\phi_{11}MR + (\phi_1)^2 MR' < 0, \begin{vmatrix} \phi_{11}MR + (\phi_1)^2 MR' & \phi_{12}MR + \phi_1\phi_2 MR' \\ \phi_{21}MR + \phi_2\phi_1 MR' & \phi_{22}MR + (\phi_2)^2 MR' \end{vmatrix} > 0, \ldots$$

$$(-1)^n \begin{vmatrix} \phi_{11}MR + (\phi_1)^2 MR' & \phi_{12}MR + \phi_1\phi_2 MR' & \ldots & \phi_{1n}MR + \phi_1\phi_n MR' \\ \phi_{21}MR + \phi_2\phi_1 MR' & \phi_{22}MR + (\phi_2)^2 MR' & \ldots & \phi_{2n}MR + \phi_2\phi_n MR' \\ \vdots & & & \vdots \\ \phi_{n1}MR + \phi_n\phi_1 MR' & \phi_{n2}MR + \phi_n\phi_2 MR' & \ldots & \phi_{nn}MR + (\phi_n)^2 MR' \end{vmatrix} > 0.$$

The first inequality in these conditions states that the MRP of input 1 (and hence of each input) must be diminishing as the amount of that input is increased slightly. However, unlike in the competitive case (Chapter 5), the second-order conditions do not require diminishing returns to inputs. Thus we may have $\phi_{ii}MR + (\phi_i)^2 MR' < 0$, even though $\phi_{ii} \geqslant 0$. If the change in MR (which under pure competition is zero) is less than zero, and of sufficient magnitude, then the second-order conditions may be satisfied with increasing returns to inputs.

The shut-down condition is the same as that for the competitive case. We can summarize the conditions for profit maximization (ruling out partial shut-downs) in the following statements:

(7.5a) *If* $\overline{TRP} \geqslant \overline{TIC}$, *then the monopolist should purchase and use the amounts* $\bar{z}$, *where* $\bar{z}$ *is the vector of the* z^i *satisfying conditions* (7.2) *and* (7.4).

(7.5b) *If* $\overline{TRP} < \overline{TIC}$, *then the monopolist should shut down.*

The monopolist's input demand functions can be obtained by solving (7.2a) for the z^i in terms of the input prices. These functions can be written as

(7.6) $\bar{z}^i = h^i(p^1, p^2, \ldots, p^n)$, $i = 1, 2, \ldots, n$,   for all p such that $\overline{TRP} \geqslant \overline{TIC}$.

Note that the price of the monopolist's output is not an argument of these demand functions. [Compare with (5.7).]

The properties of the input demand functions can be studied by differentiation of the first-order conditions with respect to the prices. Differentiating the system (7.2a) with respect to p^j [after substituting for the z^i from (7.6), and using Cramer's rule], we get

(7.7) $h^i_j = \dfrac{D_{ji}}{D}$, $i, j = 1, 2, \ldots, n$,

where D is the determinant of the $n \times n$ matrix appearing in condition (7.4), and D_{ji} is a cofactor of the latter matrix. Since the signs of the off-diagonal cofactors are indeterminate, we cannot say anything about the sign of h^i_j. But since the above matrix is symmetric, we have $D_{ji} = D_{ij}$, and so $h^i_j = h^j_i$. For $j = i$ we have $D_{ii}/D < 0$ by (7.4), and hence $h^i_i < 0$. We thus see that the law of demand for inputs applies to the monopolist as well as to the pure competitor; that is, like a competitive firm, the monopolist reduces the purchase of an input when the price of that input rises. Unlike the demand functions of the competitive firm, those of the monopolist are not homogeneous of degree zero in all prices.

Next, we construct the monopolist's indirect production function by substituting the input demand functions into the production function. This gives

$$(7.8) \qquad \bar{x} = \phi[h^1(p), h^2(p), ..., h^n(p)] = \Phi(p),$$

where p denotes the vector of the n input prices. The function Φ may also be interpreted as the monopolist's supply of output as a function of the input prices. Upon differentiation of Φ with respect to p^j, we get

$$(7.9) \qquad \Phi_j = \sum_{i=1}^{n} \phi_i h^i_j = \sum_{i=1}^{n} \phi_i \frac{D_{ji}}{D} \qquad \text{by (7.7),} \qquad j = 1, 2, ..., n.$$

These expressions are, of course, of indeterminate signs. If $\Phi_j > 0$, then the jth input is an inferior input. (We have already defined and discussed inferior inputs in Section 5.3.) Here we merely add the observation that, since the sign of Φ_j is indeterminate, we see that the phenomenon of inferior inputs is not an exclusive characteristic of competitive environments.

Finally, replacing the z^i in the profit function, we get

$$(7.10) \qquad \pi = \phi[h(p)] H\{\phi[h(p)]\} - \sum_{i=1}^{n} p^i h^i(p) - c = \rho(p),$$

where $h(p) = [h^1(p), h^2(p), ..., h^n(p)]$. Differentiating $\rho(p)$ with respect to p^j, yields

$$(7.11) \qquad \rho_j = \sum_{i=1}^{n} h^i_j[\phi \cdot (p^x + \bar{x}H') - p^i] - \bar{z}^j = -\bar{z}^j \qquad \text{by (7.2b),}$$
$$j = 1, 2, ..., n.$$

This result is the same as that obtained in (5.23) for the competitive firm.

7.2 PURE MONOPSONY

When a producer is the only buyer in an input market, he is said to be a *pure monopsonist*. Under these conditions, the producer can no longer take the input prices as given parameters. Since the monopsonist purchases the entire amount of input which is being exchanged, he must expect a change in the price per unit of input whenever the quantity to be exchanged varies. In general, the price which the monopsonist must pay depends on the conditions under which the input is produced. If the sellers of the input are pure competitors, the market supply function of the input will be an increasing function. In the present analysis we shall assume, for simplicity, that the producer sells his output under competitive conditions.

7.2.1 The Conditions for Profit Maximization

The producer's profit function under these circumstances is of the form

$$(7.12) \qquad \pi = p_0^x \phi(z) - \sum_{i=1}^{n} g^i(z^i) z^i - c,$$

where $\phi(z)$ again denotes the production function, $p^i = g^i(z^i)$ is the (inverse) market supply function of the ith input, and it is assumed that $dg^i/dz^i = g^{i\prime} > 0$ for all i. Assuming the existence of a regular interior maximum, we get the first-order conditions

$$(7.13a) \qquad p_0^x \phi_i - [g^i(z^i) + z^i g^{i\prime}] = 0, \qquad i = 1, 2, ..., n.$$

The first term on the lhs of (7.13a) has already been identified as the MRP of the ith input (Section 5.1). The bracketed term represents the MIC of the ith input. Thus, (7.13a) can be written as

$$(7.13b) \qquad MRP^i = MIC^i, \qquad i = 1, 2, ..., n.$$

In Chapter 5, we saw that under conditions of pure competition, MIC^i equals the price of the ith input [see (5.2a)], but since under conditions of monopsonistic buying the price of the input rises with quantity purchased, we have $MIC^i = p^i + z^i g^{i\prime} > p^i$. From this it follows that $MRP^i > p^i$. That is, the price paid by the monopsonist per unit of input is less than the MRP of the input, a feature which distinguishes this model from the competitive model of Section 5.1.

If we eliminate p_0^x from the equations in (7.13a), we can also write

$$(7.14) \qquad \frac{\phi_i}{\phi_j} = \frac{MIC^i}{MIC^j}, \qquad i, j = 1, 2, ..., n,$$

which says that at the maximum, the MRTS (marginal rate of technical substitution) between any two inputs must equal the ratio of their MICs.

Differentiating the lhs of (7.13a), first with respect to z^i and then with respect to z^j, we get the expressions $p_0^x \phi_{ii} - (2g^{i\prime} + z^i g^{i\prime\prime})$ and $p_0^x \phi_{ij}$, respectively. Writing $2g^{i\prime} + z^i g^{i\prime\prime}$ as $MIC^{i\prime}$, we get the second-order conditions

$$(7.15) \quad p_0^x \phi_{11} - MIC^{1\prime} < 0, \quad \begin{vmatrix} p_0^x \phi_{11} - MIC^{1\prime} & p_0^x \phi_{12} \\ p_0^x \phi_{21} & p_0^x \phi_{22} - MIC^{2\prime} \end{vmatrix} > 0,$$

$$\ldots (-1)^n \begin{vmatrix} p_0^x \phi_{11} - MIC^{1\prime} & p_0^x \phi_{12} & \cdots & p_0^x \phi_{1n} \\ p_0^x \phi_{21} & p_0^x \phi_{22} - MIC^{2\prime} & \cdots & p_0^x \phi_{2n} \\ \vdots & & & \vdots \\ p_0^x \phi_{n1} & p_0^x \phi_{n2} & \cdots & p_0^x \phi_{nn} - MIC^{n\prime} \end{vmatrix} > 0.$$

Just as in the preceding model [see (7.4)], but for slightly different reasons, diminishing returns need not prevail at the maximum.

Since the shut-down condition is the same as under conditions of competitive buying, we can summarize it without further discussion:

(7.16a) *If* $\overline{TRP} \geqslant \overline{TIC}$, *then the monopsonist should purchase and use the amounts* $\bar{z}$, *where* $\bar{z}$ *is the vector of the* z^i *satisfying conditions (7.13) and (7.15).*

(7.16b) *If* $\overline{TRP} < \overline{TIC}$, *then the monopsonist should shut down.*

The optimal levels of the inputs can be found by solving (7.13) for the zs. These solutions can be written as

$$(7.17) \quad \bar{z}^i = h^i(p^x), \quad i = 1, 2, \ldots, n, \quad \text{for } p^x \text{ such that } \overline{TRP} \geqslant \overline{TIC}.$$

These are the monopsonist's demand functions for inputs. Unlike the functions in (7.6), those in (7.17) depend on the price of the monopsonist's product. This is so because, in the monopsony model, the input prices are not parameters, but variables whose values depend directly on the monopsonist's choice of inputs. The actual prices paid by the monopsonist can be computed by substituting the $\bar{z}^i$ into the functions $g^i(z^i)$.

If the price of product x increases, then the monopsonist, being a competitive seller (by assumption), will increase his output. But when a producer expands his output, he may use more of some inputs, and perhaps less of others; in general, therefore, as in the preceding models, the derivative of the function h^i is indeterminate. To verify this fact, we substitute for the z^i in (7.13a) from (7.17), differentiate, and use Cramer's rule to solve for the $dh^i/dp^x = h_x^i$.* This yields

$$(7.18) \quad h_x^i = -\sum_{j=1}^n \phi_j \frac{D_{ji}}{D}, \quad i = 1, 2, \ldots, n,$$

where D is the determinant of the $n \times n$ matrix in (7.15), and D_{ji} is a cofactor

---

* Here we are using the notation for a partial derivative even though the function $h^i(p^x)$ has only one argument. This is done in order to facilitate comparison with similar results in other models; for example, Eq. (5.9).

of the latter matrix. The indeterminancy of the signs of the h_x^i follows from the fact that the D_{ji} are of indeterminate signs.

The monopsonist's indirect production function can be constructed by substituting the $h^i(p^x)$ into the production function. Then we can write

$$(7.19) \qquad \bar{x} = \phi[h^1(p^x), h^2(p^x), ..., h^n(p^x)] = \Phi(p^x),$$

which may also be interpreted as the monopsonist's supply function of product x. Here, upon differentiation, we get

$$(7.20) \qquad \Phi_x = \sum_{i=1}^{n} \phi_i h_x^i = -\sum_{i=1}^{n} \sum_{j=1}^{n} \phi_i \phi_j \frac{D_{ji}}{D} > 0,$$

where the second equation follows from (7.18), and the inequality follows from the fact that the expression on the lhs of the inequality is a negative-definite quadratic form. [See (5.17), and the following discussion.]

Finally, we insert the $h^i(p^x)$ into the profit function and write

$$(7.21) \qquad \pi = p^x \phi[h(p^x)] - \sum_{i=1}^{n} g^i[h^i(p^x)] \, h^i(p^x) - c = \rho(p^x),$$

where $h(p^x) = [h^1(p^x), h^2(p^x), ..., h^n(p^x)]$. Differentiating $\rho(p^x)$ with respect to p^x, we get

$$(7.22) \qquad \rho_x = \sum_{i=1}^{n} h_x^i [p^x \phi_i - g^i(\bar{z}^i) - \bar{z}^i g^{i\prime}] + \bar{x} = \bar{x} \qquad \text{by (7.13a).}$$

As is to be expected, an increase in the price of his product increases the monopsonist's profit. This result is the analog of the result in (5.21c) for a competitive firm.

7.2.2 Taxation

The effect of taxation on a producer's output has been discussed in Chapter 6; there it was shown that, with some exceptions, taxation tends to raise the price of the product, and to lower the level of production. In this section, we shall examine the effects of taxation on the monopsonist's purchasing behavior. Specifically, we shall impose a specific tax on one of the inputs purchased by the monopsonist.

If the tax is collected from the seller of the input, it is first necessary to modify the supply function of the taxed input. If we think of the tax as an addition to cost, then the MC of the taxed producer increases by t (the specific tax), and since we know that the supply function of a competitive seller coincides with (a certain portion of) his MC function (see Section 4.1.2), we have

$$(7.23) \qquad p^j = g^j(z^j) + t,$$

where j denotes the taxed input. The supply function in (7.23) indicates that, if the monopsonist purchased some fixed quantity of the jth input, then after the imposition of the tax, the price per unit of z^j would increase by t. In order to determine whether the monopsonist will, in fact, leave his purchases unchanged following the imposition of the tax, we must derive his demand functions for inputs.

The monopsonist's profit function now takes the form

$$(7.24) \qquad \pi = p_0^x \, \phi(z) - \sum_{\substack{i=1 \\ i \neq j}}^{n} g^i(z^i) z^i - [g^j(z^j) + t] z^j - c,$$

which yields the first-order conditions

$$(7.25a) \quad p_0^x \phi_i - [g^i(z^i) + z^i g^{i\prime}] = 0, \qquad i = 1, 2, ..., n, \quad i \neq j,$$

$$(7.25b) \quad p_0^x \phi_j - [g^j(z^j) + z^j g^{j\prime} + t] = 0.$$

The second-order conditions are the same as those in (7.15), and the shut-down condition is also the same as in the preceding model.

The demand functions now depend on both p^x and t, and hence we write

$$(7.26) \qquad \bar{z}^i = h^i(p^x, t), \qquad i = 1, 2, ..., n.$$

Evaluating the derivative of h^i with respect to t, h^i_t, by the method used to evaluate the h^i_x in (7.18), we find

$$(7.27) \qquad h^i_t = \frac{D_{ji}}{D}, \qquad i = 1, 2, ..., n.$$

From previous investigations, we know that the signs of the cofactors D_{ji} are indeterminate, but $(D_{jj}/D) < 0$ by the second-order conditions. Therefore, the effect of the tax is to reduce the purchase of the taxed input, but the model yields no determinate conclusions about the changes in the purchases of the nontaxed inputs. It can also be shown that the effect on the monopsonist's output is indeterminate, while his profit will fall, the rate of decrease being equal to $\bar{z}^j$.

7.2.3 Price Discrimination

The phenomenon of price discrimination in a product market served by a monopolist (Section 6.2) has its counterpart in an input market in which a monopsonist is able to separate the suppliers of an input into a number of groups. In that case, each group is represented by its own market supply function, and even though each of these groups is assumed to produce an identical input, differences in their production conditions may account for differences in their supply functions.

In the present example we shall assume, in order to illustrate the model, that discrimination is feasible with respect to one input, say z^j, while all other inputs are assumed to be purchased by the monopsonist in fixed quantities, and at given prices. As in the preceding section, we assume that the monopsonist sells his output in a competitive market.

We write the monopsonist's profit function as

$$(7.28) \qquad \pi = p_0^x \phi\left(\sum_{i=1}^{m} z^i, z_0^{-j} \right) - \sum_{i=1}^{n} g^i(z^i)\, z^i - c.$$

Here, the superscript i denotes the market in which the jth input is purchased; thus, $p^i = g^i(z^i)$ represents the supply function of the ith market for input j, and z^i the amount of input j purchased in market i. (The superscript j, which should be affixed to the p^i and z^i, is omitted in order to simplify the notation.) The expression $\sum_{i=1}^{m} z^i$ represents the total quantity of input j purchased (and used) by the monopsonist, and z_0^{-j} denotes the vector of the fixed amounts of the remaining inputs. There are m markets for input j. The constant c may now be interpreted as representing the usual fixed cost, as well as the cost of the inputs which are held constant in this example.

If a regular interior maximum exists, then the first-order conditions are

$$(7.29a) \qquad p_0^x \phi_j - [g^i(z^i) + z^i g^{i\prime}] = 0, \qquad i = 1, 2, \ldots, m.$$

The first term on the lhs of (7.29a) is the MRP of the jth input. (The notation ϕ_j denotes the partial derivative of ϕ with respect to the jth input.) The second term represents the MIC of input j in the ith market. These conditions may, therefore, be stated as

$$(7.29b) \qquad \text{MRP}^j = \text{MIC}^i, \qquad i = 1, 2, \ldots, m,$$

and for any two markets we have

$$(7.30) \qquad \text{MIC}^i = \text{MIC}^k, \qquad i, k = 1, 2, \ldots, m,$$

which says that at the optimal distribution of purchases, the MICs must be equal in all markets.

Differentiating the lhs of (7.29a) with respect to z^i, we get

$$p_0^x \phi_{jj} - (2g^{i\prime} + z^i g^{i\prime\prime}), \text{ or } \text{MRP}^{j\prime} - \text{MIC}^{i\prime},$$

and differentiating with respect to z^k, we get $p_0^x \phi_{jj} = \text{MRP}^{j\prime}$. Therefore, we write the second-order conditions as

$$(7.31) \quad \text{MRP}^{j\prime} - \text{MIC}^{1\prime} < 0, \quad \begin{vmatrix} \text{MRP}^{j\prime} - \text{MIC}^{1\prime} & \text{MRP}^{j\prime} \\ \text{MRP}^{j\prime} & \text{MRP}^{j\prime} - \text{MIC}^{2\prime} \end{vmatrix} > 0,$$

$$\ldots (-1)^n \begin{vmatrix} \text{MRP}^{j\prime} - \text{MIC}^{1\prime} & \text{MRP}^{j\prime} & \ldots & \text{MRP}^{j\prime} \\ \text{MRP}^{j\prime} & \text{MRP}^{j\prime} - \text{MIC}^{2\prime} & \ldots & \text{MRP}^{j\prime} \\ \vdots & & & \vdots \\ \text{MRP}^{j\prime} & \text{MRP}^{j\prime} & \ldots & \text{MRP}^{j\prime} - \text{MIC}^{m\prime} \end{vmatrix} > 0.$$

Among other things, these conditions require that the change in MIC in each market exceed the change in MRP^j.

The shut-down condition, given the exclusion of partial shut-downs, is of the general form $\overline{TRP} < \overline{TIC}$, so that we can summarize:

(7.32a) *If* $\overline{TRP} \geqslant \overline{TIC}$, *then the discriminating monopsonist should purchase the quantities* $\bar{z}$ *of the jth input, where* $\bar{z}$ *is the vector of the* z^i *satisfying conditions (7.29) and (7.31).*

(7.32b) *If* $\overline{TRP} < \overline{TIC}$, *then the monopsonist should shut down.*

The relative levels of the prices paid for the jth input in the different markets depend on the elasticities of the market supply functions. It will be recalled that $MIC^i = p^i + z^i g^{i\prime}$. Since the elasticity of supply is defined as $\dfrac{dz^i}{dp^i}\dfrac{p^i}{z^i}$, and since the latter can also be written as $\dfrac{1}{g^{i\prime}}\dfrac{p^i}{z^i}$, we can write

$$(7.33) \qquad MIC^i = p^i\left(1 + \frac{1}{e^i}\right), \qquad i = 1, 2, \ldots, m,$$

where e^i denotes the elasticity of supply in the ith market. (It is unnecessary here to distinguish between the absolute value and the algebraic value of the elasticity because the latter, in the case of an upward-sloping supply function, is positive.) Since at the optimal distribution of purchases the MICs in the different markets must be equal [by (7.30)], we have

$$(7.34) \qquad p^1\left(1 + \frac{1}{e^1}\right) = p^2\left(1 + \frac{1}{e^2}\right) = \ldots = p^m\left(1 + \frac{1}{e^m}\right).$$

We can see from the above equations that if, at the optimal distribution, the elasticities are equal, then the monopsonist will pay the same price in each market, and no discrimination takes place. However, if discrimination does take place, then for any two markets it is obvious that in the more elastic market the sellers will be paid a higher price; that is, $e^i > e^k$ implies $p^i > p^k$ for all i and k. It is interesting to compare this result with the conditions for discrimination on the part of a seller; according to those conditions (Section 6.2), it is the *less* (rather than the *more*) elastic market that is charged more.

7.3 BILATERAL MONOPOLY

A unique situation arises when a market consists of only two traders—one seller and one buyer. Such a situation is referred to as *bilateral monopoly*. Because both traders occupy a monopolistic position, the normal market mechanism fails to operate, and consequently the terms of trade are settled by bilateral bargaining. The situation will be illustrated by a few simple cases.

The seller in this market produces product x, and operates under cost conditions given by TVC $= f(x)$. The buyer, on the other hand, uses product x as an input, and the revenues that he can obtain from various amounts of this input are given by the function TRP $= g(x)$. We begin the illustration with two cases which are somewhat unrealistic in the context of bilateral monopoly, but they may help in illuminating the peculiarities of this type of market.

Case 1. Let us assume that the monopsonist chooses to behave like a competitor, in the sense that he will offer to purchase various quantities of x at prices specified by the monopolist. In other words, the monopsonist will confront the monopolist with his demand function, which, assuming that the monopsonist is a profit maximizer, is the same as his MRP function. [See the necessary conditions for profit maximization (5.2b).] The MRP function, under the notation used in this chapter, is given by $g'(x)$. Under these conditions, the monopolist's profit function is given by

$$(7.35) \qquad\qquad \pi = g'x - f(x) - c,$$

and the first-order condition by

$$(7.36) \qquad\qquad g' + xg'' = f'.$$

This is the familiar condition equating the seller's MR and MC. (Second-order conditions are assumed to hold in all cases, and no trader is forced to shut down.) The quantity of x exchanged, $\bar{x}_1$, is the solution to Eq. (7.36), and the price per unit of x can be computed by evaluating the function g' at the point $\bar{x}_1$. See Fig. 7.1, which shows the relevant functions as viewed by the monopolist.

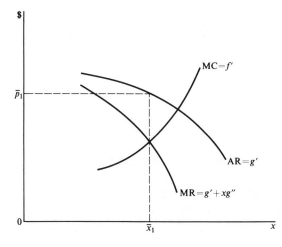

Figure 7.1

Case 2. We now reverse the roles of the two traders, and assume that the seller chooses to act like a competitor. The monopsonist is now confronted with the monopolist's supply curve, which is, of course, the monopolist's MC function. The monopsonist thus maximizes

$$(7.37) \qquad \pi = g(x) - xf' - c,$$

which requires

$$(7.38) \qquad g' = f' + xf''.$$

The monopsonist equates his MRP with his MIC, and the level of x satisfying (7.38) is the quantity exchanged. See Fig. 7.2. It is clear that the two problems will have the same solution if the two first-order conditions are identical. Combining (7.36) and (7.38), we see that this will be the case if at the extreme point we have $- g'' = f''$. In words, if, at the extreme point, the absolute value of the slope of the buyer's MRP function is equal to the slope of the seller's MC function, then the level of x traded will be the same, regardless of which of the two traders acts like a competitor.

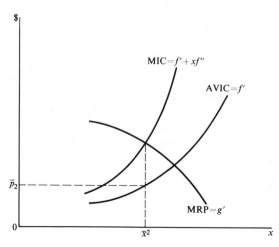

Figure 7.2

The price, on the other hand, will be different in each case so long as all the relevant functions have nonzero slopes. Nor is it difficult to see that the price will be higher in the case in which the monopsonist chooses to behave like a competitor, that is, Case 1.

Case 3. Under the conditions of bilateral monopoly, it is more reasonable to assume that both traders will try to exercise their monopoly power. We may, for example, suppose that each trader assumes his opponent to act like a competitor, while he himself will offer terms of trade in accordance with his monopolistic position. This will result in the trade offers determined in Cases 1 and

2, respectively. Hence agreement is likely to be reached at most with respect
to the amount of x to be traded. The price remains undetermined, except that
if the traders finally do settle on acceptable terms, the price will lie between $\bar{p}_1$
and $\bar{p}_2$—the two price levels established in Cases 1 and 2.

We shall now consider another approach to bilateral monopoly, in which
each trader not only insists on taking full advantage of his monopoly, but also
attempts to drive the hardest bargain possible short of forcing his opponent
out of business. For simplicity, we shall first consider the cases in which such
behavior is attributed to only one trader at a time, and then consider the case
of similar behavior on the part of both traders simultaneously.

Case 4. It is assumed that the monopolist has information about the form of
the monopsonist's ARP function. The monopolist attempts to sell his product
on terms at which the monopsonist will derive no profit from the transaction,
and consequently he will offer to sell any quantity of x at a price which equals
the ARP of x at that point. Put differently, the monopolist will attempt to
force the monopsonist to act as if his ARP function were his demand function
for x. In that case, the monopolist's profit function is given by

$$(7.39) \qquad\qquad \pi = g(x) - f(x) - c,$$

which leads to the first-order condition

$$(7.40) \qquad\qquad g' = f'.$$

Since the monopolist considers the ARP function to be the monopsonist's AR
(demand) function, condition (7.40) simply requires the monopolist to equate
his MR with his MC. If $\bar{x}$ is the level of x satisfying (7.40), then the monopo-

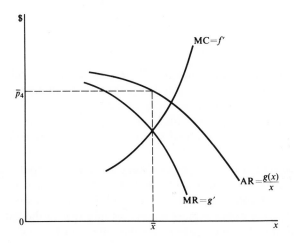

Figure 7.3

list will offer to sell $\bar{x}$ units of x at $g(\bar{x})/\bar{x}$ dollars per unit of x. The determination of the monopolist's offer is illustrated in Fig. 7.3.

Case 5. Reversing the roles of the traders, we assume that the monopsonist wishes to force the monopolist to sell him his output x at cost. In other words, the monopsonist attempts to compel the monopolist to behave as if his AVC function were his supply function of x. Then the monopsonist maximizes

$$(7.41) \qquad\qquad \pi = g(x) - f(x) - c,$$

which has its maximum at the point which satisfies

$$(7.42) \qquad\qquad g' = f'.$$

This latter equation is satisfied at the same point as that which satisfies (7.40), but the price offered by the monopsonist is equal to $f(\bar{x})/x$. The solutions to Cases 4 and 5 are shown in Fig. 7.4.

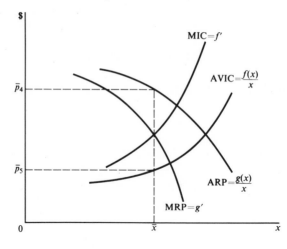

Figure 7.4

Case 6. If both traders attempt simultaneously to pursue their objectives as described in Cases 4 and 5, respectively, then they will agree to exchange $\bar{x}$ units of x, but the price remains undetermined; the monopolist asks $\bar{p}_4$, while the monopsonist offers $\bar{p}_5$. The final outcome depends on the relative bargaining skill of the two traders, about which, however, our model has nothing to say.

In conclusion, it may be observed that the level of output resulting under the conditions of Cases 4, 5, and 6 is larger than either of the two output levels in Cases 1 and 2; that is, $\bar{x} > \bar{x}_1$, and $\bar{x} > \bar{x}_2$. This is so because, in Cases 1 and 2, the relevant marginal curves intersect to the left of the intersection of g' and f' which determines the output in Cases 4, 5, and 6. We thus have a somewhat unusual example in which competitive behavior on the part of some traders results in a smaller level of output than is the case when they act like monopolists.

BIBLIOGRAPHICAL NOTES

A general discussion of monopsony and related issues is contained in J. Robinson, *The Economics of Imperfect Competition,* London: Macmillan, 1933, especially Books 6 and 9. A departure from the standard treatment of bilateral monopoly was undertaken by L. Foldes in "A Determinate Model of Bilateral Monopoly," *Economica,* **31,** 117–131 (1964). Certain aspects of price discrimination, with references to monopsony and bilateral monopoly, can be found in C. G. F. Simkin, "Some Aspects and Generalizations of the Theory of Discrimination," *Review of Economic Studies,* **15,** 1–13 (1947).

CHAPTER 8

MONOPOLISTIC COMPETITION

Markets that are neither purely competitive nor pure monopolies belong in the broad category called *monopolistic competition*. Firms in this category—called *monopolistic competitors*—differ from purely competitive firms inasmuch as they need not produce a homogeneous product; that is, one feature that we may observe in a monopolistically competitive market (but not necessarily in all such markets) is the phenomenon of product differentiation. On the other hand, compared to pure monopoly, the number of firms in monopolistically competitive markets is greater than one: if there are two firms, the market is called *duopoly*; if there are a few firms, it is called *oligopoly*; in all other cases it is simply referred to as monopolistic competition.

Since the conditions of monopolistic competition are distinctly different from those of either pure competition or pure monopoly, it is necessary to make different assumptions concerning the decision-making process of firms operating under conditions of monopolistic competition. As the range between the two opposite market structures (competition and monopoly) encompasses an extremely large variety of possible market conditions, there exists an equally large number of environmental and behavioral specifications that may be used in setting up suitable theoretical constructs for the analysis of various aspects of monopolistic competition. It is because of this diversity that there exists no general theory of monopolistic competition; instead, we have a collection of different models (theories), each designed to deal with a particular subset of monopolistically competitive markets. We do not intend, in this chapter, to examine the entire list of such models, but to present a selected sample to bring out the most typical features of monopolistic competition. As the chosen examples will show, the most common elements of these markets are: (a) the interdependence between the firms in the market, and (b) the uncertainty about the actions of one's competitors.

We begin by examining several fairly simple models. These models are not, perhaps, the most typical representatives of monopolistic competition, but placing them at the beginning of the chapter makes pedagogical sense. Later on in this chapter, we shall deal with the problem of advertising, and examine models in which the interdependence among the firms plays a crucial role.

8.1 MARKET LEADERSHIP

In this section, we consider markets in which, owing to the size distribution (and hence the distribution of power) among the firms, some firms are in a position to exercise leadership over the market. For simplicity, we assume that there exists one dominant firm (the "leader") and a number of small firms, which will be referred to as the "competitive fringe." As the latter term implies, the small firms elect to behave, essentially, like pure competitors, and this, in some sense, makes the leader a pure monopolist. The leadership provided by the dominant firm may manifest itself through the establishment of either a price policy, or an output policy, for the entire market. Each of these possibilities will be considered separately.

8.1.1 Price Leadership

We assume that the firms in the market produce a homogeneous product; or, to be more specific, we assume that the product under consideration is sufficiently homogeneous to make it possible to represent total market demand by a single demand function. Since the firms in the competitive fringe act like pure competitors, they choose their levels of output on the basis of the price set by the leader. The market behavior of the competitive fringe can, therefore, be described by its supply function, which is simply the sum of the supply functions of all the small firms. [See Eq. (4.9).] Now, if the leader sets a particular price, the market will demand a certain quantity, of which the competitive fringe will sell the amount given by its supply function at the quoted price. The remaining quantity, i.e., the difference between the quantity demanded by the market and the quantity supplied by the competitive fringe, makes up the leader's share of the market. Thus if $h(p)$ denotes the market demand function, and $g(p)$ the supply function of the competitive fringe, then the leader's demand function is given by $h(p) - g(p)$.

    The problem can now be viewed as that of a profit-maximizing monopolist. The leader's profit function can be written as

(8.1) $$\pi = p[h(p) - g(p)] - f[h(p) - g(p)] - c,$$

where $f(x)$ is the leader's TVC function. If the profit function has a regular interior maximum, then the following conditions hold:

(8.2) $$h(p) - g(p) + (p-f')(h' - g') = 0,$$

(8.3) $$2(h' - g') + (p - f')(h'' - g'') - f''(h' - g')^2 < 0.$$

The solution of Eq. (8.2) is the price chosen by the leader, and by evaluating the functions h and g at that point, one can find the total quantity produced, as well as the shares sold by the competitive fringe and the leader, respectively.

Example 8.1. Suppose the relevant relationships are of the following form:

Market demand function $\qquad x = \dfrac{a}{p} - b = h(p) \qquad a, b > 0,$

Supply function of the competitive fringe $\qquad x = d - \dfrac{e}{p} = g(p) \qquad d, e > 0,$

TVC function of the leader $\qquad \text{TVC} = sx = f(x) \qquad s > 0.$

In order to ensure an interior maximum, it is assumed that

$$\frac{a}{b} > \frac{e}{d}, \quad \text{and} \quad s < \frac{a + e}{b + d}.$$

The leader's profit function is given by

$$\pi = a + e - (b + d)p - s\left[\frac{(a + e)}{p} - (b + d)\right] - c.$$

For profit maximization we must have

$$-(b + d) + \frac{s(a + e)}{p^2} = 0,$$

and $\qquad\qquad\qquad -\dfrac{2s(a + e)}{p^3} < 0,$

the latter of which is certainly satisfied, since all the parameters are positive.

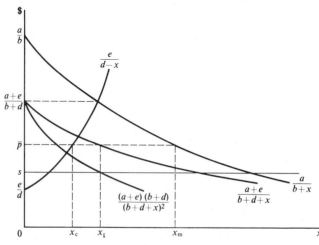

Figure 8.1

Solving the first-order condition, we get

$$\bar{p} = \sqrt{\frac{s(a + e)}{(b + d)}},$$

which can be used to evaluate the levels of output. The equilibrium quantities of output are shown graphically in Fig. 8.1 in which x_c, x_l, and x_m denote competitive output, leader's output, and market output, respectively.

8.1.2 Market Sharing

The relationship between leader and followers may take the form of an agreement to share the market in some prespecified proportions. For example, the leader may take a certain percentage of the market for himself, and assign the remainder to the competitive fringe. Once the shares are determined, the leader takes it upon himself to set the price at which the industry's output will be sold (if the product is homogeneous). This particular arrangement may, therefore, involve market sharing as well as price leadership. We shall examine the decision process under this type of arrangement for both homogeneous and differentiated products.

Homogeneous products. The leader's decision making proceeds as follows: If $h(p)$ is the market demand function, then $kh(p)$, $0 < k < 1$, represents the demand function facing the leader, k being the leader's share of the market. The leader's profit function takes the form

(8.4) $\pi = pkh(p) - f[kh(p)] - c,$

which, at an interior maximum, must satisfy

(8.5a) $k[h(p) + (p - f')h'] = 0,$

or, equivalently,

(8.5b) $[h(p) + (p - f')h'] = 0.$

The second-order condition is

(8.6a) $k[2h' + (p - f')h'' - kf''(h')^2] < 0,$

or

(8.6b) $[2h' + (p + f')h'' - kf''(h')^2] < 0.$

The solution to (8.5) is the market price. If we substitute this value into the function $h(p)$, we obtain the total market output, and given the value of k, we can also compute the amounts supplied by the leader and the competitive fringe, respectively. (The allocation of the fringe's share among its members is not considered here.)

It is easy to prove (and intuitively obvious) that the leader's profit is an increasing function of k; he would, therefore, be better off the larger the value of k. In general, however, the leader may not be able to set the value of k at its maximum value $k = 1$ (except by acquiring the competitive firms); nor, for that matter, would it always be in his best interest to do so (in view of other than profit considerations). In any event, the determination of k is subject to agreement between the leader and the competitive fringe, but the process by which such an agreement might be reached will not be discussed here.

It is of some interest to examine what impact the market-sharing agreement has on the buyers in this market. If we write the solution to (8.5) as

$$(8.7) \qquad\qquad\qquad \bar{p} = \theta(k),$$

and then differentiate (8.5) with respect to k, after substituting for p from (8.7), we get

$$(8.8) \qquad\qquad\qquad \theta' = \frac{h(p)\, h'\, f''}{D},$$

where $D = 2h' + (p - f')\, h'' - kf''(h')^2$. Since $h' < 0$ by assumption, and $D < 0$ by (8.6), it is clear that the sign of θ' is the same as that of f''. The most likely case is $f'' > 0$. This indicates that the higher the value of k, the higher the market price. In this case, then, it would be correct to say that an increase in the monopoly power of the leader (monopoly power being measured by k) brings about a higher price, and consequently a smaller level of output. In the special case in which the leader's cost function is linear, and hence $f'' = 0$, the buying public would be indifferent as to the agreement reached by the leader and the competitive fringe, since the market price is independent of k.

Example 8.2. Using the same demand and TVC functions as in Example 8.1, and assuming $s < a/b$, we get the leader's profit function

$$\pi = k(a - bp) - sk\left(\frac{a}{p} - b\right) - c.$$

Profit maximization yields the conditions

$$-kb + \frac{ska}{p^2} = 0,$$

and

$$-\frac{2ska}{p^3} < 0.$$

From the first-order condition, we get

$$\bar{p} = \sqrt{\frac{sa}{b}}, \qquad \text{and hence } x_m \text{ (market output)} = \sqrt{\frac{ab}{s}} - b.$$

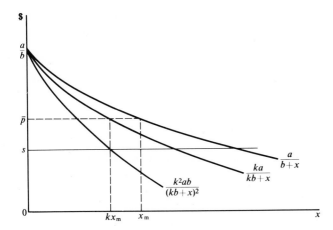

Figure 8.2

The leader's output is kx_m, and that of the competitive fringe is $(1 - k)\,x_m$. The example is illustrated in Fig. 8.2.

Differentiated products. Sometimes it makes sense to talk about the total market, or shares of the total market, of an industry in which firms produce differentiated products which are sold under different brand names. (For instance, it is meaningful to talk about the total annual output of electric office typewriters, and the percentages of that total produced by each firm in that market.) One may, therefore, imagine a market-sharing agreement under which each firm in the competitive fringe agrees to produce a certain percentage of the total industry output, or, equivalently, a certain percentage of the leader's output. This arrangement differs from that which applies to homogeneous products, however, in that each firm may charge a different price for its product.

In the case of differentiated products, the quantity that any one firm can sell depends not only on the price of the firm's own product, but also on the prices, or quantities sold, of all other products in the same market. The (inverse) demand function of a typical firm is, therefore, a relationship between its price and the quantities of all the products in the market. If the percentages assigned to each firm are known to everyone, then, given the leader's planned level of output, each firm in the competitive fringe is in a position (assuming it knows the nature of its demand function) to set the price of its product at a level which will bring about the agreed-upon share of market.

Thus, if there are n firms in the market, then the demand function of a typical firm can be written as $p = h(x^1, x^2, ..., x^n)$. If, for simplicity, Firm 1 is the leader, the remaining firms being in the competitive fringe, and k^i denotes the ith firm's share of the leader's output, that is, $x^i = k^i x^1$, $i = 2, 3, ..., n$, then the demand function of the ith firm in the competitive fringe can be written as

$p^i = h^i(x^1, k^2x^1, k^3x^1, ..., k^nx^1)$. Hence, given the leader's chosen level of output, each firm can compute the price for its product that will yield the assigned level of output k^ix^1.

The leader will, of course, choose a level of output for his own product which maximizes his profit. Given the shares of the firms in the competitive fringe, the leader's profit function takes the form

$$(8.9) \qquad \pi = h^1(x^1, k^2x^1, k^3x^1, ..., k^nx^1)\, x^1 - f(x^1) - c.$$

If the function has a regular interior maximum, then we have

$$(8.10) \qquad h^1(x^1, k^2x^1, k^3x^1, ..., k^nx^1) + x^1 \sum_{i=1}^{n} h_i^1 k^i - f' = 0,$$

where $k^1 = 1$, and $h_i^1 = \partial h^1/\partial x^i$. The second-order condition is

$$(8.11) \qquad 2 \sum_{i=1}^{n} h_i^1 k^i + x^1 \sum_{i=1}^{n} \sum_{j=1}^{n} h_{ij}^1 k^i k^j - f'' < 0,$$

where $h_{ij}^1 = \partial h_i^1/\partial x^j$.

The leader's optimal level of output is found by solving (8.10), which depends only on x^1.

Given this value of x^1, say, $\bar{x}^1$, each firm in the competitive fringe computes its price by substituting $\bar{x}^1$ into the demand function h^i.

8.2 CARTELS

When the conditions that are conducive to the emergence of some form of market leadership are absent, and firms are of more or less equal size, the rivalry among the firms may put them under considerable pressures. These pressures stem from the fact that each firm must be constantly on guard, to guarantee for itself as large a share of the market as possible. In economic terms, this means that the firm may have to incur considerable expenses for such purposes as advertising and market research. One way in which the firms may escape these extra costs (as well as other unpleasant burdens) is to give up their freedom of independent decision making, and to control certain aspects of their operations by means of joint decision making. Such an arrangement is usually referred to as a *cartel*. In fact, the formation of a cartel may be justified (i.e., explained) under less restrictive conditions: even in the absence of any additional costs for such purposes as advertising or market research, joint profit maximization always results in higher profits than independent profit maximization. From a formal point of view, the formation of a cartel has the effect of transforming the monopolistically competitive market into a pure monopoly. In our analysis, we shall again distinguish between industries that produce homogeneous products and those that produce differentiated products.

8.2.1 Homogeneous Products

The price and output decisions of a cartel are explained in terms of the desire to maximize profit for the cartel as a whole. We shall let $h(x)$ denote the (inverse) market demand function, and $f^i(x^i)$ the TVC function of the ith firm. Cartel profit is given by

(8.12) $$\pi = xh(x) - \sum_{i=1}^{n} [f^i(x^i) + c^i],$$

where $x = \sum_{i=1}^{n} x^i$, and n is the number of firms in the cartel. If the profit function possesses a regular interior maximum, the following conditions hold:

(8.13a) $$h(x) + xh' - f^{i\prime} = 0, \qquad i = 1, 2, ..., n,$$

$$2h' + xh'' - f^{1\prime\prime} < 0,$$

$$\begin{vmatrix} 2h' + xh'' - f^{1\prime\prime} & 2h' + xh'' \\ 2h' + xh'' & 2h' + xh'' - f^{2\prime\prime} \end{vmatrix} > 0, \ ...$$

(8.14)

$$(-1)^n \begin{vmatrix} 2h' + xh'' - f^{1\prime\prime} & 2h' + xh'' & ... & 2h' + xh'' \\ 2h' + xh'' & 2h' + xh'' - f^{2\prime\prime} & ... & 2h' + xh'' \\ \vdots & & & \vdots \\ 2h' + xh'' & 2h' + xh'' & ... & 2h' + xh'' - f^{n\prime\prime} \end{vmatrix} > 0.$$

The first-order conditions may also be stated as

(8.13b) $$MR = MC^i, \qquad i = 1, 2, ..., n,$$

which says that, at the optimal distribution of outputs, the MC of each member firm must be equal to the MR of the total cartel output; from which it follows, of course, that at that point the MCs of all the firms in the cartel must be equal. It may also be pointed out parenthetically that conditions (8.13) and (8.14) are precisely the same as those which apply to a monopolist who operates a number of different plants in which he produces an identical product. This equivalence justifies the formal conceptualization of the cartel as a monopoly.

At this point, we should once again draw the reader's attention to the possibility of boundary solutions. If in the present problem the maximum does not occur in the interior of the output space, then the cartel maximizes its profit at a distribution of outputs which assigns a zero output to one or more members of the cartel. (Naturally, any firm that is asked to shut down receives a share of the cartel profit that is at least as large as the profit it earned prior to joining the cartel.) This may conceivably happen if there exist marked differences in the cost conditions of the member firms, in which case output is shifted from high-cost firms to low-cost firms. Essentially, the formation of a cartel creates an opportunity for bringing about a more efficient allocation of resources than that which prevails when firms operate independently. This increased efficiency is, of course, the source of the higher profit that the cartel is able to earn.

8.2.2 Differentiated Products

Under the assumption of differentiated products, total market demand can no longer be represented by a single functional relationship; instead, it must be represented by a set of interrelated functions. These may be written as

$$(8.15) \qquad x^i = \hat{h}^i(p^1, p^2, ..., p^n), \qquad i = 1, 2, ..., n.$$

We shall continue to assume that demand functions are downward sloping; that is, an increase (decrease) in the price of a product causes a decrease (increase) in the quantity demanded of that product. As for the cross-relationships, since we are concerned here with different brands of a certain type of product, the products (i.e., brands) produced by the firms are substitutes. Thus, if one firm raises its price, all other prices remaining fixed, buyers will shift from the product that has become relatively more expensive to the other products. This assumption may be stated in terms of the partial derivatives of the functions $\hat{h}^i$:

$$(8.16a) \qquad \hat{h}^i_i < 0 \text{ for all } i,$$

$$(8.16b) \qquad \hat{h}^i_j \geqslant 0 \text{ for all } i \text{ and } j, \qquad i \neq j.$$

Often it is more convenient to work with the inverse demand functions given by

$$(8.17) \qquad p^i = h^i(x^1, x^2, ..., x^n), \qquad i = 1, 2, ..., n.$$

If the inverse relationship between the price of a product and quantity demanded of that product is to be preserved, and if the products are substitutes as defined by (8.16b), then the derivatives of the functions h^i must satisfy

$$(8.18a) \qquad h^i_i < 0 \text{ for all } i,$$

$$(8.18b) \qquad h^i_j \leqslant 0 \text{ for all } i \text{ and } j, \qquad i \neq j.$$

In the present model we make use of the functions given in (8.17). The cartel's profit function can be stated as

$$(8.19) \qquad \pi = \sum_{i=1}^{n} [x^i h^i(x) - f^i(x^i) - c^i],$$

where $x = (x^1, x^2, ..., x^n)$. Assuming a regular interior maximum, we have the first-order conditions

$$(8.20a) \qquad h^i(x) + x^i h_i^i + \sum_{\substack{j=1 \\ j \neq i}}^{n} x^j h_i^j - f^{i\prime} = 0, \qquad i = 1, 2, ..., n.$$

Now, the term $h^i(x) + x^i h_i^i$ is the change in total revenue from product i due to an infinitesimal change in x^i, hence we denote it by TR_i^i. The term $x^j h_i^j$, on the other hand, represents the change in total revenue from product j due to an infinitesimal change in x^i, hence we denote it by TR_i^j. (Note that superscripts identify the firm, or product, and subscripts denote partial derivatives.) Using this shorthand notation, we can write conditions (8.20a) as

$$(8.20b) \qquad \sum_{j=1}^{n} TR_i^j = MC^i, \qquad i = 1, 2, ..., n.$$

Thus, at the maximum, the MC of the ith product must equal the sum of the changes in the revenues from *all* the n products as product i is changed by a small amount.

We now define the partial derivatives of the TR_i^j as follows:

$$(8.21) \qquad TR_{ik}^j = \begin{cases} 2h_i^i + x^i h_{ii}^i & \text{for } i = j = k, \\ h_k^j + x^j h_{jk}^j & \text{for } i = j, \ k \neq j, \\ h_i^j + x^j h_{ij}^j & \text{for } i \neq j, \ k = j, \\ x^j h_{ik}^j & \text{for } i \neq j, \ k \neq j, \end{cases}$$

where $h_{ik}^j = \partial h_i^j / \partial x^k$. We shall also denote $f^{i\prime\prime}$ by MC_i^i. Then we can state the second-order conditions as

$$\sum_{j=1}^{n} TR_{11}^j - MC_1^1 < 0, \qquad \begin{vmatrix} \sum_{j=1}^{n} TR_{11}^j - MC_1^1 & \sum_{j=1}^{n} TR_{12}^j \\ \sum_{j=1}^{n} TR_{21}^j & \sum_{j=1}^{n} TR_{22}^j - MC_2^2 \end{vmatrix} > 0,$$

$$(8.22)$$

$$...(-1)^n \begin{vmatrix} \sum_{j=1}^{n} TR_{11}^j - MC_1^1 & \sum_{j=1}^{n} TR_{12}^j & \cdots & \sum_{j=1}^{n} TR_{1n}^j \\ \sum_{j=1}^{n} TR_{21}^j & \sum_{j=1}^{n} TR_{22}^j - MC_2^2 & \cdots & \sum_{j=1}^{n} TR_{2n}^j \\ \vdots & & & \vdots \\ \sum_{j=1}^{n} TR_{n1}^j & \sum_{j=1}^{n} TR_{n2}^j & \cdots & \sum_{j=1}^{n} TR_{nn}^j - MC_n^n \end{vmatrix} > 0.$$

Let us take another look at the first-order conditions (8.20). From condition (8.18b) and the definition of TR_i^j, we can see that

$$\sum_{\substack{j=1 \\ j \neq i}}^{n} \mathrm{TR}_i^j < 0.$$

(Strictly speaking, according to (8.18b), the latter summation may also be zero. However, if there is any interdependence at all between the different brands in the market, then some of the h_j^i will be strictly negative, hence the negativity of the above summation.) However, this implies $\mathrm{TR}_i^i > \mathrm{MC}^i$. Of course, TR_i^i is nothing but the marginal revenue of firm i (with respect to a change in its own product). Hence the equality between MR and MC which characterizes the optimal output of a firm operating independently is not satisfied. Moreover, since in this case we have MR > MC, the present situation may suggest to the typical firm that it could increase its profit by increasing its output (by lowering its price) to the point where MR = MC. This strategy, however, may not work. If one of the firms increases its output beyond the level assigned to it by the cartel, i.e., as given by (8.20), the amounts sold (or prices received) by the other firms are bound to change as well, and in such a way as to lower the profits of these firms. The latter may then attempt to recover, or reduce, their losses by making appropriate adjustments in their prices and outputs. This, in turn, will reduce, or eliminate, any additional gains realized by the firm which was the first to deviate from the cartel solution.

The point of all this is that the cartel will maximize its profit only if each member firm abides by the solution as it is dictated by the first-order conditions. True, by increasing its own output so as to equate its own MR and MC, a firm may possibly increase its own profit if the other firms make no corrective changes in *their* prices and outputs, and if no change is made in the distribution of the cartel profit among its members. However, it is unlikely that countermeasures on the part of firms whose profits decline will be delayed for long, so that any additional gains that a firm might make by "cheating" will be only temporary. Clearly, repeated deviations from the optimal solution are likely to result in the disintegration of the cartel.

8.3 COMPETITION WITH ADVERTISING

In a market in which firms produce differentiated products, each firm faces its own demand function. Such a function depends, in general, on the prices (or outputs) of all the firms in the market. [See the demand functions in (8.15) and (8.17).] Given the prices (or outputs) of all other firms in the market (and ruling out such special arrangements as market leadership or cartels), each firm sets its own price at a level that maximizes its profit. The ability to formulate an independent price policy is, of course, one of the behavioral characteristics that distinguishes a monopolistic competitor from a pure competitor;

unlike the pure competitor, the monopolistic competitor who produces a differentiated product need not lose all his sales if he raises his price above that of his competitors, nor will he necessarily drive his rivals out of business by setting his price below that of the other firms in the market.

Competition in a monopolistically competitive market, however, may assume forms other than price competition. For example, firms may exert considerable efforts designed to increase the rate of their sales at some given price. This may be done by engaging in advertising, or other types of promotional activities. Now, if the price of the product is fixed, the demand for the product can increase only as a result of a *shift* in the demand function. Hence, from a formal point of view, we may think of promotional activities as attempts to shift the demand function in a direction away from the origin.

In this section, we consider the general nature of the effects of promotional activities, and examine the properties of models in which such activities are explicitly incorporated. For simplicity, all promotional activities will be referred to as "advertising."

8.3.1 The Single Firm—A General Model

Since in this section we wish to concentrate on the effects of advertising, we shall ignore the cross-relationships between the firms in the market; consequently, we will be concerned only with the price, output, and advertising of a single firm. (A more general model is presented in Section 8.4.3.)

The firm's demand function. The (inverse) demand function of the firm may be written as

$$(8.23) \qquad p^x = h(x, y^1, y^2, ..., y^n),$$

where, as before, x and p^x denote output and its price, respectively, while y^i denotes the level of the ith advertising medium. The y^i are measured in appropriate physical (rather than monetary) units, such as minutes of television time, inches of newspaper column, square feet of billboard, etc.

It should be obvious that under the assumption that there exist n different advertising media, the firm, in trying to maximize its profit, must choose not only a total level of advertising expenditure, but also a distribution of that total among the different media. To simplify the present exposition, it will be convenient to restrict the problem to the choice of the optimal advertising expenditure, and therefore we shall deal only with the single variable y. This approach is consistent with either one of two assumptions: (a) the firm makes use of only one advertising medium; or (b) the prices of the different advertising media always change by the same proportion, in which case the variable y can be interpreted as a composite good.

Under the present approach, we write the firm's demand function as

$$(8.24) \qquad p^x = h(x, y).$$

We assume, as usual, that price and output are inversely related; that is,

$$(8.25) \qquad\qquad h_x < 0,$$

where $h_x = \partial h/\partial x$. As for the effect of advertising, we assume that an increase in advertising increases the quantity demanded at any fixed price; or, equivalently, it increases the price that buyers are willing to pay for a unit of the product, given some fixed total level of output. In other words, the effect of an increase in advertising is to shift the demand function away from the origin; hence

$$(8.26) \qquad\qquad h_y > 0,$$

where $h_y = \partial h/\partial y$.

The conditions for profit maximization. The firm's profit function can now be stated as

$$(8.27) \qquad\qquad \pi = xh(x, y) - f(x) - p^y y - c,$$

where $f(x)$ again denotes the TVC function, and p^y is the price of advertising. If the profit function possesses a regular interior maximum, then the first-order conditions are

$$(8.28\text{a}) \qquad\qquad h(x, y) + xh_x - f' = 0,$$

$$(8.29\text{a}) \qquad\qquad xh_y - p^y = 0.$$

The first of these conditions is the familiar equality between marginal revenue and marginal cost. The expression xh_y in (8.29a) represents the change in total revenue due to an infinitesimal increase in y, and may appropriately be called the *marginal revenue product* (MRP) of advertising. (It makes sense to think of advertising as an input—one that creates demand, and hence revenue, rather than a physical output. It is, therefore, proper to apply to advertising the terminology usually applied to a factor of production.) On the other hand, p^y represents the marginal cost of y. We may, therefore, rewrite the above conditions as

$$(8.28\text{b}) \qquad\qquad \text{MR} = \text{MC},$$

$$(8.29\text{b}) \qquad\qquad \text{MRP} = \text{MIC}.$$

The second-order conditions take the form

$$(8.30\text{a}) \qquad\qquad 2h_x + xh_{xx} - f'' < 0,$$

$$(8.30\text{b}) \qquad\qquad xh_{yy} < 0,$$

$$(8.30\text{c}) \qquad\qquad \begin{vmatrix} 2h_x + xh_{xx} - f'' & h_y + xh_{xy} \\ h_y + xh_{yx} & xh_{yy} \end{vmatrix} > 0,$$

where $h_{xx} = \partial h_x/\partial x$, $h_{yy} = \partial h_y/\partial y$, and $h_{xy} = h_{yx} = \partial h_x/\partial y = \partial h_y/\partial x$.

One of the implications of these conditions is $h_{yy} < 0$; this may be defined as diminishing returns of the advertising input.

In this model, it is of interest to take a closer look at the shut-down condition, and especially at the possibility of a boundary solution. Theoretically, there are two partial shut-downs to consider:

$$\text{Solution (1)} \qquad x = \bar{x} > 0, \qquad y = 0,$$
$$\text{Solution (2)} \qquad x = 0, \qquad y = \bar{y} > 0.$$

The second solution can be dismissed without any analysis: profit can never be maximized by spending money on advertising without producing any output, since a complete shut-down will always yield a higher profit (smaller loss). However, to market a product without engaging in advertising may turn out to be an optimal strategy. To see what factors determine the optimal solution, let us derive a condition that must hold if the interior solution (i.e., a positive output *and* a positive level of advertising) is to yield the highest level of profit.

Let $(\bar{x}, \bar{y})$ denote the interior solution, i.e., the solution to maximizing the profit function given in (8.27), and let $(\hat{x}, 0)$ be the solution to maximizing the profit function $\pi = xh(x, 0) - f(x) - c$. The latter profit function applies to a situation in which the firm makes an *a priori* decision to refrain from advertising. The interior solution (marketing with advertising) is optimal if it yields a higher profit than the boundary solution (marketing without advertising); that is, if

$$(8.31) \qquad \bar{x}h(\bar{x}, \bar{y}) - f(\bar{x}) - p^y\bar{y} - c > \hat{x}h(\hat{x}, 0) - f(\hat{x}) - c.$$

Since $\hat{x}$ is the profit-maximizing level of output for the no-advertising policy, is follows that

$$(8.32) \qquad \hat{x}h(\hat{x}, 0) - f(\hat{x}) - c \geqslant \bar{x}h(\bar{x}, 0) - f(\bar{x}) - c,$$

(since $\bar{x}$ is not optimal for this policy). Combining (8.31) and (8.32), we have

$$(8.33) \qquad \bar{x}h(\bar{x}, \bar{y}) - f(\bar{x}) - p^y\bar{y} - c > \bar{x}h(\bar{x}, 0) - f(\bar{x}) - c,$$

which, upon rearrangement, gives

$$(8.34) \qquad h(\bar{x}, \bar{y}) - h(\bar{x}, 0) > \frac{p^y\bar{y}}{\bar{x}}.$$

Now, $h(\bar{x}, \bar{y})$ is the price the firm charges in order to sell $\bar{x}$ units of x, given that its advertising level is $\bar{y}$. If, on the other hand, the firm wishes to sell $\bar{x}$ units of x without any advertising, it must lower its price from $h(\bar{x}, \bar{y})$ to $h(\bar{x}, 0)$. (The price must be *lowered* upon the reduction in advertising because we have assumed that $h_y > 0$.) Since $h(\bar{x}, \bar{y}) - h(\bar{x}, 0)$ is the cut in price which is necessary to offset the elimination of $p^y\bar{y}/\bar{x}$ dollars of advertising per unit of output, we refer to this difference as the *discount-equivalence* of the average advertising expenditure $p^y\bar{y}/\bar{x}$.

According to (8.34), the discount-equivalence must exceed its average advertising expenditure; that is, in order to maintain the level of demand $\bar{x}$ after reducing advertising to zero, the firm must lower its price by more than $p^y \bar{y}/\bar{x}$ dollars. This means that one dollar's worth of advertising per unit of output must in some sense be more effective than a discount of one dollar. We thus see that for a firm to engage in advertising, not only must advertising be *effective* (in the sense of causing a shift in the demand curve), it must also be *profitable*; i.e., it must be capable of bringing about a *sufficiently large* shift in the demand function. To see this point more clearly, let us apply the Theorem of the Mean to the function $h(x, y)$ over the interval $(\bar{x}, \bar{y}) - (\bar{x}, 0)$. We get

$$(8.35) \qquad\qquad h(\bar{x}, \bar{y}) - h(\bar{x}, 0) = h_y \bar{y},$$

where h_y is evaluated at a suitable point in the interior of the line segment $(\bar{x}, \bar{y}) - (\bar{x}, 0)$, and combining (8.34) and (8.35), we obtain

$$(8.36) \qquad\qquad h_y > \frac{p^y}{\bar{x}}.$$

This condition clearly shows that the assumption $h_y > 0$ is not sufficiently strong to guarantee the profitability of advertising; the shift in the demand function resulting from an increase in advertising from zero to $\bar{y}$ must be sufficiently large to satisfy the inequality in (8.36).

It should be remembered, however, that the conditions that we have derived, i.e., (8.34) and (8.36), are only *necessary* conditions for the profitability of advertising; in other words, these conditions hold if the interior solution $(\bar{x}, \bar{y})$ yields a higher profit level than the boundary solution $(\hat{x}, 0)$. But it may turn out that neither of these solutions is optimal because the revenue generated by the respective levels of output may fall short of variable cost. We must, therefore, also compare the interior solution with the complete shut-down solution. For the interior solution to be optimal, the following condition must hold:

$$(8.37) \qquad\qquad h(\bar{x}, \bar{y}) \geqslant \overline{\text{AVC}} + \frac{p^y \bar{y}}{\bar{x}}.$$

Thus, conditions (8.34) and (8.37) taken together constitute a set of necessary and sufficient conditions for the profitability of advertising. Condition (8.37) is the counterpart of the standard shut-down condition that we have used in previous models. As can be seen, in the present model the firm will produce a positive output and engage in advertising only if it is able to pay all its variable cost, including the cost of advertising.

Comparative statics. The solutions to the first-order conditions (8.28) and (8.29) can be written as functions of the price of advertising (which is a parameter of the model) as follows:

(8.38a) $$\bar{x} = g^x(p^y),$$

(8.38b) $$\bar{y} = g^y(p^y).$$

These are the firm's supply function of output and the demand function for advertising, respectively. In the present formulation of the model, changes in output and advertising are caused by changes in the price of advertising. In order to investigate the effects of these changes, we must determine the first derivative of the functions g^x and g^y, respectively. To do so, we differentiate (8.28a) and (8.29a) with respect to p^y, after substituting for x and y from (8.38), and using Cramer's rule for solving for the unknown derivatives. This yields

(8.39a) $$g^{x\prime} = \frac{-(h_y + xh_{xy})}{D},$$

(8.39b) $$g^{y\prime} = \frac{2h_x + xh_{xx} - f''}{D},$$

where D is the determinant given in condition (8.30c). It is clear that $g^{x\prime}$ is of indeterminate sign, but $g^{y\prime} < 0$. The latter inequality is simply a reconfirmation of the law of demand for inputs [Eq. (5.10)]. In fact, we may apply the definition of an inferior input (Section 5.3) to the present model, and say that if $g^{x\prime} > 0$, then advertising is an inferior input. Because of the indeterminacy of the sign of $g^{x\prime}$, it is clear that the effect on the price of the firm's product is likewise indeterminate.

Compared with other models considered so far in this text, the present model produces just about as many (or as few) behavioral hypotheses; of the two behavioral relations derived from the model, the slope of only one has a determinate sign. To some extent, of course, this stems directly from the fact that the model has only one parameter. But if we were to introduce other parameters into the model, the general nature of the results would not be changed substantially; for example, if a specific tax is introduced, it can be shown that an increase in the tax will decrease output, but the effects on price and advertising are indeterminate.

Given this state of affairs, one might indeed wonder whether the introduction of the advertising variable was a useful thing to do in the first place. On the other hand, if models of the firm with advertising are not to be discarded altogether, the question arises as to whether such models can be made to yield more hypotheses than the general model examined above. It is the purpose of the next section to suggest one way of modifying the general model so as to increase its predictive content.

8.3.2 The Single Firm—A More Specific Model

In studying the optimization models presented in this and preceding chapters, the reader may have observed that the determinancy of the comparative static properties (i.e., the effects of changes in a parameter on the optimal solution) depends on two sets of conditions: (a) the specifications of the decision maker's environment (i.e., the properties of such relations as production, cost, and demand functions), and (b) the conditions for optimization, especially the second-order conditions. The latter conditions are determined by the underlying mathematical theory, and there is little we can do to change them. Consequently, the only way of making a model yield more hypotheses is to make stronger assumptions about the environment. Technically speaking, this may not be a very difficult thing to do, but if the assumptions that are found to be capable of doing the trick turn out to be highly restrictive, then the model will be of only limited applicability; and this may be just as unsatisfactory as a general model that yields no, or only very few, hypotheses. We are, therefore, confronted with an inherent conflict between generality on the one hand, and predictive content on the other. Since both of these are desirable properties of a model, the best strategy is to steer a middle course, and to attempt to satisfy both criteria simultaneously. This, indeed, is the art of model building: to find a set of conditions that are capable of yielding meaningful hypotheses, yet which at the same time are sufficiently weak as to make the model applicable to a wide class of phenomena.

The model to be presented here differs from the general model examined in the preceding section in the restrictions that are placed on the firm's demand function. In addition to the usual assumptions about the first-order partial derivatives of the demand function (that is, $h_x < 0$, $h_y > 0$), we shall add certain conditions specifying the nature of the effect of advertising. These specifications have to do with the concept of discount-equivalence, which we have defined and discussed in the preceding section. This concept, it will be recalled, represents the price cut that is necessary in order to maintain the level of demand following the elimination of advertising. It is reasonable to assume that this cut in price is larger the higher the amount of advertising per unit of output. Formally, this implies the following two assumptions: (a) the discount-equivalence is a function of the average level of advertising, and (b) the latter function is an increasing one. If we let $z = y/x$, and $H(x) = h(x, 0)$, then the first assumption can be stated as

$$(8.40) \qquad h(x, y) = H(x) + \theta(z),$$

where θ is the discount-equivalence function. The function $H(x)$ represents the "ordinary" demand function, i.e., the demand function of a firm that never advertises, and we make the usual assumption that $H' < 0$.

The assumption in (8.40), which is a specification about the demand function $h(x, y)$, may be given the following interpretation: The (maximum) price which the firm can charge in order to sell x units of its product while advertising at a rate of y per period of time is the sum of the following two quantities: (a) the (maximum) price which the firm can charge in order to sell the output level x without any advertising, and (b) the discount-equivalence of y/x.

Our second assumption says that θ is an increasing function; formally,

$$(8.41) \qquad\qquad \theta' > 0 \quad \text{for all} \quad z.$$

Finally, it is also not unreasonable to suppose that beyond some point the effectiveness of advertising diminishes; that is, beyond a certain level of z the discount-equivalence increases at a decreasing rate. Hence, we assume that there exists a nonnegative number z_0 such that

$$(8.42) \qquad\qquad \theta'' < 0 \quad \text{for} \quad z > z_0.$$

Since the properties of the demand function play a crucial role in the model, we start out by obtaining the derivatives of the function h in terms of those of the functions H and θ. For this purpose, we differentiate (8.40) with respect to x and y, respectively. This yields

$$(8.43) \qquad\qquad h_x = H' - \frac{z}{x}\,\theta' < 0,$$

$$(8.44) \qquad\qquad h_y = \frac{\theta'}{x} > 0,$$

$$(8.45) \qquad\qquad h_{xy} = -\frac{1}{x^2}(\theta' + z\theta'') \gtrless 0,$$

$$(8.46) \qquad\qquad h_{yy} = \frac{\theta''}{x^2} < 0 \quad \text{for} \quad z > z_0.$$

In the determination of the signs of three of the above derivatives, we made use of conditions (8.41) and (8.42), and the assumption that $H' < 0$. It should be observed that the assumptions about the signs of h_x and h_y are identical to those which we made in the general model in the preceding section.

We are now ready to formulate the firm's profit function, and derive the firm's supply and demand functions. The profit function is essentially the same as that in (8.27), except that since we are primarily interested in the comparative static properties of the model, we shall also assume that the product of the firm is subject to a specific tax. Hence, we write

$$(8.47) \qquad \pi = xh(x, y) - f(x) - p^y y - tx - c = \rho(x, y),$$

where t denotes the specific tax. Assuming the existence of a regular interior maximum, we have the following first-order and second-order conditions:

$$(8.48) \qquad \rho_x = h(x, y) + xh_x - f' - t = 0,$$

$$(8.49) \qquad \rho_y = xh_y - p^y = 0,$$

$$(8.50) \qquad \rho_{xx} = 2h_x + xh_{xx} - f'' < 0,$$

$$(8.51) \qquad \rho_{yy} = xh_{yy} < 0,$$

$$(8.52) \qquad \begin{vmatrix} \rho_{xx} & \rho_{xy} \\ \rho_{yx} & \rho_{yy} \end{vmatrix} > 0.$$

The solutions to the first-order conditions can be written as

$$(8.53a) \qquad \bar{x} = g^x(p^y, t),$$

$$(8.53b) \qquad \bar{y} = g^y(p^y, t).$$

First, we investigate the effect of a change in the price of advertising. Differentiating (8.48) and (8.49) with respect to p^y, after substituting for x and y from (8.53), and using Cramer's rule, we get

$$(8.54a) \qquad g^x_p = \frac{D_{21}}{D},$$

$$(8.54b) \qquad g^y_p = \frac{D_{22}}{D},$$

where D is the determinant given in (8.52), and the D_{ij}, $i, j = 1, 2$, are co-factors. The derivatives in (8.54) are the counterparts of those given in (8.39). As in the general model, $g^y_p < 0$ by virtue of the second-order conditions. However, whereas in the general model the sign of g^x_p was found to be indeterminate, in the present model this indeterminancy disappears. We see that $D_{21} = -\rho_{xy} = -(h_y + xh_{xy})$. If we now make use of (8.44) and (8.45), we get $D_{21} = (z/x)\theta'' < 0$, where the inequality follows from (8.51) and (8.46). Hence, $g^x_p < 0$. Thus, when the price of advertising rises, the firm reduces both output and advertising. But the effect of a change in p^y on the price of the firm's product is indeterminate even in this model.*

---

* To simplify the notation, we have omitted the bars that indicate optimal values. It should be clear that in the present analysis (and in comparative static analysis in general) we consider only those values of x and y (and hence z) that satisfy the first-order conditions for a maximum (or minimum, as the case may be).

Turning now to the effects of changes in the tax rate, we differentiate the first-order conditions with respect to t. This gives

$$
(8.55a) \qquad g_t^x = \frac{D_{11}}{D},
$$

$$
(8.55b) \qquad g_t^y = \frac{D_{12}}{D}.
$$

Here we have $g_t^x < 0$ by the second-order conditions, and $g_t^y < 0$, since $D_{12}(= D_{21})$ was already shown to be negative. (In fact, we see that $g_t^y = g_p^x$.) Thus, like an increase in the price of advertising, an increase in the tax causes a reduction in both output and advertising.

We can obtain an additional result which is of interest. We see that $D_{11} = P_{yy} = \theta''/x$, while $D_{12} = (z/x)\theta''$; hence $D_{12} = zD_{11}$, and consequently, $g_t^y = zg_t^x$, or

$$
(8.56) \qquad \frac{g_t^y}{y} = \frac{g_t^x}{x}.
$$

According to (8.56), when the tax rate changes, output and advertising change by the *same percentage*, so that the ratio y/x remains constant. In other words, advertising per unit of output is invariant to changes in the tax rate; formally, $\partial z/\partial t = 0$. By virtue of this invariance, we can also determine the effect on the price of output. Differentiating (8.40) with respect to t, we have

$$
(8.57) \qquad \frac{\partial p^x}{\partial t} = H'g_t^x + \theta' \frac{\partial z}{\partial t} = H'g_t^x > 0,
$$

since both H' and g_t^x are negative.

To summarize briefly, the main purpose of the analysis in this section was to demonstrate how the predictive content of a model can be increased by strengthening the specifications of the environment. In this particular example, the strengthening consisted of making a more specific assumption about the nature of the advertising effect. However, this assumption does not appear to be unduly restrictive, since we did not force the demand functions to assume a particular form, nor did we assume that cross-effects, such as h_{xy}, were zero. In return for the stronger assumptions, we were able to determine the signs of certain comparative static properties which in the general model turn out to be ambiguous. Moreover, in our model, the advertising ratio y/x exhibits a certain invariance property which is in itself a testable hypothesis.

8.4 GROUP ADJUSTMENT AND EQUILIBRIUM

In this section we shall focus primarily on the interdependence among firms operating in a monopolistically competitive market. In so doing, we examine aspects of this interdependence affecting the behavior of a single firm, as well as the working of an entire market. To simplify matters, we at first exclude advertising, but generalize the results to a model with advertising in the last section of the chapter. Product differentiation is assumed throughout.

8.4.1 A Market Model

The market environment of each firm is described by an inverse demand function $p^i = h^i(x)$, where $x = (x^1, x^2, ..., x^n)$. This demand function is the same as that which we introduced in (8.17), in Section 8.2.2; it relates the price of firm (product) i to the amounts of all the products in the same market. The profit function of firm i can then be stated as

$$(8.58) \qquad \pi^i = x^i h^i(x) - f^i(x^i) - c^i, \qquad i = 1, 2, ..., n.$$

Now, each of the above profit functions depends on the n variables $x^1, x^2, ..., x^n$, but from the point of view of firm i, only x^i is a decision variable, whereas the output levels of competing firms must be regarded as unknowns. Clearly, unless these unknowns are given numerical values, the firm will not be able to maximize its profit; or, to put it differently, in order to maximize its profit function, the firm must first replace the *actual* output levels of its competitors by *expected* (or anticipated) outputs. If we let carets ($\hat{}$) denote expected quantities, then the profit function can be written as

$$(8.59) \qquad \hat{\pi}_t^i = x_t^i h^i(\hat{x}_t^1, \hat{x}_t^2, ..., \hat{x}_t^{i-1}, x_t^i, \hat{x}_t^{i+1}, ..., \hat{x}_t^n) - f^i(x_t^i) - c^i,$$
$$i = 1, 2, ..., n.$$

It is important to note that what each firm is really maximizing in this model is not actual profit, but expected profit. Since time enters explicitly into this model, we have affixed time subscripts to the variables to indicate the time period in question.

There remains one crucial step in the construction of the model: the specification of a rule by which each firm forms its expectations about its competitors' outputs. This problem can be treated in several different ways, some of which are quite sophisticated, but in this introductory analysis we shall use a very simple rule. According to this rule, *each firm expects that its competitors will produce in the current period the same level of output as in the preceding period.* Formally,

$$(8.60) \qquad\qquad\qquad \hat{x}_t^j = x_{t-1}^j.$$

In view of (8.60), we can now replace the $\hat{x}_t^j$ in (8.59) by x_{t-1}^j, and write

$$(8.61) \qquad \hat{\pi}_t^i = x_t^i h^i(x_{t-1}^1, x_{t-1}^2, ..., x_{t-1}^{i-1}, x_t^i, x_{t-1}^{i+1}, ..., x_{t-1}^n) - f^i(x_t^i) - c^i,$$
$$i = 1, 2, ..., n.$$

Each profit function is now a function of only one variable, x_t^i, the remaining symbols being known numbers.

Before turning to the formal analysis, we should comment on another aspect of the model. Suppose that firm i chooses to produce x_t^i units of its product in period t, then, given the expected outputs of the competing firms, the demand function of firm i determines the price

$$p_t^i = h^i(x_{t-1}^1, x_{t-1}^2, ..., x_{t-1}^{i-1}, x_t^i, x_{t-1}^{i+1}, ..., x_{t-1}^n).$$

This means that if the firm charges p_t^i for its product, it will be able to sell exactly x_t^i units in period t *if* the jth firm, $j \neq i$, sells in period t the expected quantity x_{t-1}^j. In general, however, the expectations of firm i will not be fully realized, which means that p_t^i will not be the "correct" price; that is, there will exist in the market either excess demand or excess supply. Since in the present model we do not wish to concern ourselves with the possible implications of such a state of affairs (for example, inventories and unfilled orders), we may assume that firm i chooses p_t^i to be its initial price at the beginning of period t, and that it varies the price, if necessary, during the period so as to bring about a clearing of the market. Under this assumption, the average revenue that firm i receives for its product will be different from p_t^i. This is precisely the reason why, in the present model, each firm is said to be maximizing *expected* profit.

Assuming the existence of a regular interior maximum for all x_{t-1}^j, we have the following first-order and second-order conditions:

(8.62)
$$h^i(x_{t-1}^1, x_{t-1}^2, ..., x_{t-1}^{i-1}, x_t^i, x_{t-1}^{i+1}, ..., x_{t-1}^n) + x_t^i h_i^i - f^{i\prime} = 0, \quad i = 1, 2, ..., n,$$

(8.63)
$$2h_i^i + x_t^i h_{ii}^i - f^{i\prime\prime} < 0, \qquad i = 1, 2, ..., n,$$

where $h_i^i = \partial h^i / \partial x_t^i$ and $h_{ii}^i = \partial h_i^i / \partial x_t^i$. The optimal output of firm i in period t can be found by solving the ith equation in (8.62). This solution depends on the expected outputs of all the remaining firms, and hence we can write the solutions (omitting the customary bars) as

(8.64)
$$x_t^i = g^i(x_{t-1}^{-i}), \qquad i = 1, 2, ..., n,$$

where x_{t-1}^{-i} is the vector of the $n - 1$ terms $x_{t-1}^j, j \neq i$. Since the functions g^i determine how a typical firm reacts to changes in the outputs of its competitors, they are called *reaction functions*. In fact, since the reaction functions show how the outputs change from one period to the next, it is clear that the equations in (8.64) constitute a dynamical system that traces out the movement of the variables x_t^i over time. The nature of these movements is an important aspect of this model, and one which we shall examine in some detail; but before doing so we shall say a few words about the equilibrium, or stationary state, of the model.

The market is said to be in equilibrium if the output of each firm remains constant over time; in symbols, if $x_t^i = x_{t+1}^i = x_{t+2}^i ...$ for all i. However, in the present model, the outputs in any period of time are completely determined by the outputs in the preceding period, hence if $x_{t-1}^i = x_t^i$ for all i, then the market is in equilibrium. Formally, we can define an equilibrium of the market as a vector of outputs, say $x = (x^1, x^2, ..., x^n)$, such that

(8.65) $x^i = g^i(x^{-i}),$ $i = 1, 2, ..., n.$

Mathematically speaking, the equilibrium vector is the solution to the system of simultaneous equations given in (8.65). It should, however, be pointed out that even though (8.65) consists of n equations in n unknowns, it need not necessarily possess a solution. Consequently, the dynamical market model defined by (8.64) may not have an equilibrium. We shall not study the question of the existence of a market equilibrium separately, but only in conjunction with the examination of the dynamical characteristics of the adjustment process. This is done in the next section.

8.4.2 Dynamic Properties

We begin by pointing out a general feature of the dynamic system in (8.64), namely, the fact that it is a *self-contained system*. This means that, given a set of initial conditions (outputs), the system determines the levels of output in any future period of time. For example, given the outputs x_{t-1}^i, the functions g^i determine the outputs x_t^i; replacing now the arguments x_{t-1}^i by the x_t^i, the functions g^i determine the values of the x_{t+1}^i; and so on. It is important to note that in order to generate the outputs in successive periods of time, we merely replace the arguments of the functions g^i, while the form of these functions remains unchanged. In other words, the time path of the process can be constructed by making use of the formulas in (8.64) recursively, and hence a system such as this is called a *recursive system*.

To study the general nature of the adjustment process, we must compute the derivatives of the reaction functions. We shall use the following notation:

$MR_i^i = 2h_i^i + x_t^i h_{ii}^i$
(rate of change in MR^i with respect to a small change in x_t^i),

$MR_j^i = h_j^i + x_t^i h_{ij}^i$
(rate of change in MR^i with respect to a small change in x_{t-1}^j),

$MC_i^i = f^{i\prime\prime}$
(rate of change in MC^i with respect to a small change in x_t^i).

The typical derivative $g_j^i (= \partial g^i / \partial x_{t-1}^j)$ is obtained by differentiating the ith equation in (8.62) with respect to x_{t-1}^j, after substituting for x_t^i from (8.64). This yields

(8.66) $g_j^i = - \dfrac{MR_j^i}{MR_i^i - MC_i^i},$ $i, j = 1, 2, ..., n,$ $i \neq j.$

Now, the denominator in (8.66) is negative by the second-order condition (8.63), but the numerator is indeterminate; since the products are substitutes, we know that $h_j^i \leqslant 0$ [by (8.18b)], but h_{ij}^i is of unknown sign. Let us assume (which, upon reflection, seems to be quite reasonable) that $h_{ij}^i < 0$, and hence $g_j^i < 0$.

To see the implications of this assumption, let us apply the Theorem of the Mean (Proposition 15.14), and write

$$g^i(x_t^{-i}) - g^i(x_{t-1}^{-i}) = \sum_{\substack{j=1 \\ j \neq i}}^{n} g_j^i (x_t^j - x_{t-1}^j),$$

or, by virtue of (8.64),

$$x_{t+1}^i - x_t^i = \sum_{\substack{j=1 \\ j \neq i}}^{n} g_j^i (x_t^j - x_{t-1}^j).$$

Suppose that initially all firms increase their outputs (that is, $x_t^j - x_{t-1}^j > 0$ for all j), then in the second period they will all lower their outputs, in the third period they will increase output again, and so on. Hence we see that if the initial adjustments are all in the same direction, then the dynamic pattern of the process is one of oscillations in output, all outputs moving in the same direction in each period. Admittedly, this is a special case since, in general, firms will not necessarily be making adjustments in the same direction; in that case, the fact that all the g_j^i are negative (or positive) is not enough to determine whether the output of a particular firm will oscillate, or move monotonically over time. The nature of this dynamic process depends, therefore, on the derivatives of the reaction functions, as well as on the initial conditions.

In order to establish the stability properties of the model, what we need to examine is not the signs of the g_j^i, but rather their magnitudes. Since each x_t^i can be thought of as an infinite sequence, the variable t assuming the values 1, 2, 3, ..., we can make use of appropriate theorems concerning the convergence of infinite sequences. First, if each function g^i satisfies a Lipschitz condition with a constant less than one at every point of its domain, then each sequence x_t^i converges to some finite limit. (See Section 15.1.6.) Second, each function g^i will satisfy such a condition if the sum of the absolute values of its first-order partial derivatives is bounded by a number less than one (Proposition 15.13). Hence, the system given by (8.64) will converge to a finite limit if there exists a positive number $k < 1$ such that

$$(8.67) \qquad \sum_{\substack{j=1 \\ j \neq i}}^{n} |g_j^i| \leqslant k \qquad \text{for all } x_{t-1}^{-i}, \qquad i = 1, 2, ..., n.$$

The limit to which the system converges under condition (8.67) is the market equilibrium, that is, a vector x such as that defined by (8.65). Let us denote the limit of x_t^i by x^i, $i = 1, 2, ..., n$, or in vector notation, $\lim_{t \to \infty} x_t = x$. Since the g^i are continuous functions, we have

$$\lim_{t \to \infty} g^i(x_{t-1}^{-i}) = g^i \left[\lim_{t \to \infty} x_{t-1}^{-i} \right] = g^i(x^{-i}).$$

Hence, in view of (8.64), we get

$$(8.68) \qquad \lim_{t \to \infty} x_t^i = \lim_{t \to \infty} g^i(x_{t-1}^{-i}), \qquad \text{or} \qquad x^i = g^i(x^{-i}), \qquad i = 1, 2, ..., n.$$

It is obvious that the vector x constitutes a market equilibrium; that is, if the system starts at the point x, then it will remain there.

We thus see that condition (8.67) accomplishes two objectives: (a) it guarantees the existence of a market equilibrium, i.e., a solution to the system of simultaneous equations in (8.65); and (b) it guarantees that the system will converge to the equilibrium point, regardless of its initial position. When a dynamic system has the property of converging to some finite limit, then it is said to be *stable*; otherwise it is said to be *unstable*.* If it converges to some point regardless of its initial position, it is said to be *globally stable*; if it converges to a finite limit only if it starts from a point in some proper subset of the domain of definition, it is said to be *locally stable*. Thus, under condition (8.67), the present model is globally stable.

One other property of the equilibrium point has to be mentioned: the uniqueness of the equilibrium. As it turns out, condition (8.67) guarantees not only the existence of an equilibrium, but also its uniqueness. This means that the system will always converge to a particular vector x, regardless of where it starts. This can be proved by contradiction. Suppose there exists another equilibrium vector denoted by $\hat{x}$, then by virtue of (8.68) we have $x^i = g^i(x^{-i})$ and $\hat{x}^i = g^i(\hat{x}^{-i})$ for all i. But the Lipschitz condition implies, in conjunction with these equations, that

$$|x^i - \hat{x}^i| \leqslant k|x^i - \hat{x}^i| < |x^i - \hat{x}^i| \quad \text{for all } i,$$

which is a contradiction (since a number cannot be smaller than itself), from which we conclude that the equilibrium is unique.

It remains to discuss what properties the demand and cost functions should possess in order that condition (8.67) be fulfilled. These properties have to do with the relative magnitudes of the derivatives of the MR^i and

---

* This classification of dynamic systems is, perhaps, somewhat oversimplified. Sometimes, a system is said to be stable even if it does not converge to a limit, provided there exists a value of t, say, t_0, such that the values of the variables remain inside a prespecified neighbourhood for all $t > t_0$.

MC^i. A sufficient condition for (8.67) is the following: There exists a number $k' > 1$ such that

$$(8.69) \quad (MC_i^i - MR_i^i) - k' \sum_{\substack{j=1 \\ j \neq i}}^{n} |MR_j^i| \geqslant 0 \quad \text{for all } x_t, \qquad i = 1, 2, ..., n.$$

Since the expression in parentheses is positive by condition (8.63), condition (8.69) will hold if the magnitudes of the MR_j^i are sufficiently small. But MR_j^i represents the change in MR^i due to a small change in the output of firm j, so that the MR_j^i can in some sense be regarded as measures of the interrelationships between the products in the market. Broadly speaking, therefore, the adjustment process will be stable if the interrelationships between the different products are sufficiently weak. In the limiting case (i.e., if the products are completely unrelated, in which case all the MR_j^i are zero), the stability of the adjustment process is automatically guaranteed; in fact, in that case, market equilibrium is attained instantaneously, i.e., in one period of time. Of course, this limiting case no longer represents a monopolistically competitive market, but rather n independent pure monopolies.

To prove that (8.69) implies (8.67), we write (8.69) as

$$- k' \sum_{\substack{j=1 \\ j \neq i}}^{n} |MR_j^i| \geqslant (MR_i^i - MC_i^i).$$

If we now divide both sides of this inequality by the expression in parentheses (which is negative), we get

$$- k' \sum_{\substack{j=1 \\ j \neq i}}^{n} \frac{|MR_j^i|}{(MR_i^i - MC_i^i)} \leqslant 1,$$

and dividing by k', we get

$$(8.70) \qquad - \sum_{\substack{j=1 \\ j \neq i}}^{n} \frac{|MR_j^i|}{(MR_i^i - MC_i^i)} \leqslant \frac{1}{k'} < 1 \qquad (\text{since } k' > 1).$$

Thus, in view of (8.70) and (8.66), it is clear that (8.67) is satisfied with $k = 1/k'$.

Example 8.3. The purpose of this example is twofold: to work out a simple model of monopolistic competition by using fully specified functions, and at the same time to suggest an alternative formulation to that presented in Section 8.4.1. In the latter model, it will be recalled, the emphasis was on the choice of the firms' outputs, and the adjustments in these outputs; changes in prices were not analyzed explicitly. In the present example, on the other hand, the model is formulated to yield a price adjustment mechanism.

For this illustration, we take the case of *duopoly*, that is, a market with two sellers. A typical demand function is given by

$$x^i = a^i - \frac{b^i p^i}{p^j} = h^i(p^1, p^2) \qquad a^i, b^i > 0, \qquad i, j = 1, 2, \quad i \neq j.$$

Since the two products are substitutes, the demand functions satisfy the conditions $h_j^i = \partial h^i / \partial p^j > 0$, $i \neq j$. The TVC functions are assumed to be linear, that is,

$$s^i x^i = f^i(x^i) \qquad s^i > 0, \qquad i = 1, 2.$$

As in the model discussed in Section 8.4.1, so in the present model each firm must form some expectations about the actions of its competitors in the current period. Since the present model is formulated in terms of prices, we must make an assumption about the formation of price expectations. For this purpose, we follow an approach similar to that in Section 8.4.1, and hence we adopt the rule that each firm assumes its competitors to charge in period t the same price as in period $t - 1$. Affixing time subscripts to the variables, we get the expected profit functions

$$\pi_t^i = a^i p_t^i - \frac{b^i (p_t^i)^2}{p_{t-1}^j} - s^i \left(a^i - \frac{b^i p_t^i}{p_{t-1}^j} \right) - c^i, \qquad i, j = 1, 2, \quad i \neq j.$$

In this model, actual profit may be different from expected profit since the price expectations may turn out to be false; consequently, actual sales may be different from expected sales. This, in turn, may result in either unsold stock, or unfulfilled orders. Ideally, these factors should also be incorporated into the model, since they are likely to affect the firm's choice of output and price. However, in order not to complicate this illustration, we shall confine ourselves to an analysis of the price adjustment process. (A model in which the consequences of excess demand and excess supply are considered explicitly is presented in Section 12.5.)

First- and second-order conditions are given by

$$a^i + \frac{b^i(s^i - 2p_t^i)}{p_{t-1}^j} = 0, \qquad -\frac{2b^i}{p_{t-1}^j} < 0, \qquad i, j = 1, 2, \quad i \neq j.$$

Solving the first-order conditions, we get the price reaction functions

$$p_t^i = \frac{s^i}{2} + \frac{a^i p_{t-1}^j}{2b^i} = g^i(p_{t-1}^j), \qquad i, j = 1, 2, \quad i \neq j.$$

It may be noted that the derivatives of the reaction functions are positive [unlike those in (8.66), which are negative]. The implication of this is that firms match (in direction) the price changes of their competitors, but the response is always delayed by one period. For example, if Firm 1 raises its price in period t, Firm 2 will raise *its* price (but not necessarily by the same amount) in period $t + 1$. And the same general pattern applies to price cuts.

As for the existence and stability of the market equilibrium, we may apply conditions (8.67), which in the present example require that the first derivative of each reaction function be bounded away from unity; that is, there must exist a number $k < 1$ such that $a^i/2b^i \leqslant k$, $i = 1, 2$.* The two reaction functions are plotted in Fig. 8.3. Since their slopes are less than one, the two functions are bound to intersect the 45° line, and hence intersect each other. (Note that the abscissa of the function g^2 is the vertical axis p^1.) The intersection of the reaction functions indicates the equilibrium price vector; in other words, $\bar{p}^1$ and $\bar{p}^2$ are the solutions to the system of equations given by the first-order conditions of this model. It is also obvious (from an inspection of Fig. 8.3) that if the reaction functions are linear, then it is not necessary that the slope of each function be less than one; the two functions will still intersect each other even if one function is very steep, provided the other is sufficiently flat.

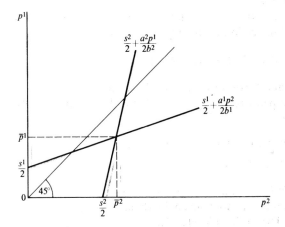

Figure 8.3

8.4.3   Group Adjustment with Advertising

In the preceding sections we examined output (and price) adjustments in the absence of advertising. In this last section we extend the analysis to a market in which firms also engage in advertising, and for this purpose we shall use the special model of a firm presented in Section 8.3.2. Since most of the relevant analysis has already been carried out in the preceding sections, we shall merely

---

* As a matter of fact, if the reaction functions are linear, it is sufficient if their derivatives be merely less than (rather than bounded away from) one; that is, each derivative can be arbitrarily close to (but less than) one. Existence and stability conditions for linear systems are, in general, less stringent than those required for nonlinear systems.

outline the model, and refer, whenever necessary, to results obtained in earlier sections.

In order to construct the model, we generalize Eq. (8.40) as follows:

$$(8.71) \qquad h^i(x, y^i) = H^i(x) + \theta^i(z^i), \qquad i = 1, 2, ..., n,$$

where $x = (x^1, x^2, ..., x^n)$, y^i is the level of advertising of the ith firm, θ^i is the discount-equivalence function of the ith firm, and $z^i = y^i/x^i$. The reader may note that the advertising levels of competing firms are not introduced directly into the demand function of the typical firm. This is not necessary in the present formulation, because the effects of the advertising efforts of one's rivals show up through the variations in their outputs. For example, assume that the jth firm increases its advertising in order to increase its demand at any fixed price. Then the resulting increase in the output of firm j causes an increase in the jth argument of the function H^i, so that if firm i intends to keep its demand unchanged, it will have to reduce its price, or increase its own advertising, or both.

We shall make the same assumption about the formation of expectations as in the preceding sections, hence the expected profit functions can be written as

$$(8.72) \quad \hat{\pi}^i_t = x^i_t h^i(x^i_t, y^i_t, x^{-i}_{t-1}) - f^i(x^i_t) - p^y y^i_t - c^i, \qquad i = 1, 2, ..., n,$$

where x^{-i}_{t-1} again denotes the vector of outputs produced in period $t - 1$ by the $n - 1$ competitors of firm i. First-order conditions for an interior maximum are:

$$(8.73a) \qquad h^i(x^i_t, y^i_t, x^{-i}_{t-1}) + x^i_t h^i_i - f^{i\prime} = 0,$$

$$(8.73b) \qquad x^i_t h^i_y - p^y = 0,$$

$$\left. \right\} \qquad i = 1, 2, ..., n,$$

where $h^i_i = \partial h^i/\partial x^i_t$, and $h^i_y = \partial h^i/\partial y^i_t$. The second-order conditions are virtually the same as those given in (8.50) through (8.52), and hence are omitted here. The optimal levels of output and advertising of each firm now depend on the expected output of its competitors, as well as on the price of advertising. The solutions (omitting bars) are written as

$$(8.74a) \qquad x^i_t = g^{xi}(x^{-i}_{t-1}; p^y),$$

$$(8.74b) \qquad y^i_t = g^{yi}(x^{-i}_{t-1}; p^y),$$

$$\left. \right\} \qquad i = 1, 2, ..., n.$$

Directing our attention first to the signs of the derivatives of the reaction functions, we proceed as in Section 8.4.2, and obtain

$$(8.75a) \qquad g^{xi}_j = - \frac{\mathrm{MR}^i_j \theta^{i\prime\prime}}{x^i_t D^i},$$

$$(8.75b) \qquad g^{yi}_j = - \frac{\mathrm{MR}^i_j z^i_t \theta^{i\prime\prime}}{x^i_t D^i},$$

$$\left. \right\} \qquad i = 1, 2, ..., n,$$

where $g_j^{xi} = \partial g^{xi}/\partial x_{t-1}^j$, $g_j^{yi} = \partial g^{yi}/\partial x_{t-1}^j$, MR_j^i as defined in (8.66), $z_t^i = y_t^i/x_t^i$, and D^i is the determinant given in (8.52) as it applies to the ith firm. If we assume, as in section 8.42, that $\mathrm{MR}_j^i < 0$, then we have $g_j^{xi} < 0$, and $g_j^{yi} < 0$. Thus, as in the model without advertising considered in the preceding sections, output adjustments are made in an opposite direction to those of one's competitors, while advertising changes in the same direction as output. Moreover, we see immediately from (8.75) that

$$(8.76) \qquad\qquad \frac{g_j^{xi}}{x_t^i} = \frac{g_j^{yi}}{y_t^i},$$

according to which output and advertising are always adjusted by the same percentage.

This invariance was already shown to hold in the model presented in Section 8.3.2 dealing with an isolated firm; here we see that this invariance also holds when firms are allowed to interact with one another. In the present model, this invariance means that the advertising-output ratio of each firm remains constant during the adjustment process, at least so long as the price of advertising remains constant, and provided no shifts occur in the discount-equivalence functions.

We see that Eqs. (8.74a), which are the counterparts of (8.64) of the no-advertising model, constitute a self-contained dynamic system; that is, given the initial output levels, and the price of advertising, the time path of each output is fully determined. The levels of advertising, which are determined by (8.74b), merely ride along, so to speak, and make no contributions whatsoever to the determination of the levels of outputs in the different periods of time. Because of the formal equivalence of systems (8.64) and (8.74a), the stability of the latter may be guaranteed by condition (8.67).

BIBLIOGRAPHICAL NOTES

General

One of the first mathematical expositions of monopolistically competitive markets is that of A. Cournot in his *Researches into the Mathematical Principles of the Theory of Wealth*, Homewood: Irwin, 1963, Chapter 7. The first comprehensive modern treatment of monopolistic competition, including such aspects as selling cost and product variations, is E. H. Chamberlin's work *The Theory of Monopolistic Competition*, Cambridge: Harvard University Press, first published in 1933. A critical examination of certain aspects of Chamberlin's theory is contained in H. Demsetz, "The Nature of Equilibrium in Monopolistic Competition," *Journal of Political Economy*, **67**, 21–30 (1959).

Comparative Statics and Stability

Chamberlin's theory has been criticized for, among other things, the indeterminancy of its comparative static properties. A detailed statement and analysis of this criticism may be found in two articles by G. C. Archibald: "Chamberlin versus

Chicago," *Review of Economic Studies*, **29**, 2–28 (1961), and "Profit-Maximising and Non-Price Competition," *Economica*, **31**, 13–22 (1964). A model which yields a larger number of determinate comparative static properties than does the general model is given by J. Hadar in "On the Predictive Content of Models of Monopolistic Competition," *Southern Economic Journal*, **36**, 67–73 (1969).

Stability aspects of markets with interdependent firms have interested economists for some time, and there is a fairly long list of articles on this topic. Most of the important results are included in the following selection (listed in chronological order): R. D. Theocharis, "On the Stability of the Cournot Solution on the Oligopoly Problem," *Review of Economic Studies, 27*, 133–134 (1960); F. M. Fisher, "The Stability of the Cournot Oligopoly Solution: The Effects of Speeds of Adjustment and Increasing Marginal Costs," *Review of Economic Studies, 28*, 125–135 (1961); F. H. Hahn, "The Stability of the Cournot Oligopoly Solution," *Review of Economic Studies*, **29**, 329–331 (1962); K. Okuguchi, "The Stability of the Cournot Oligopoly Solution: A Further Generalization," *Review of Economic Studies, 31*, 143–146 (1964); J. Hadar, "Stability of Oligopoly with Product Differentiation," *Review of Economic Studies, 33*, 57–60 (1966); and R. E. Quandt, "On the Stability of Price Adjusting Oligopoly," *Southern Economic Journal*, **33**, 332–336 (1967).

Expectations and Learning

The formation of expectations, and the possibility of linking expectations to a learning process, are two critical issues involved in modeling the decision making of interacting firms (and other decision makers as well). The following references examine different aspects of these issues, some in frameworks other than monopolistically competitive markets: K. J. Arrow and M. Nerlove, "A Note on Expectations and Stability," *Econometrica*, **26**, 297–305 (1958); C. E. Ferguson and R. W. Pfouts, "Learning and Expectations in Dynamic Duopoly Behavior," *Behavioral Science, 7*, 223–237 (1962); J. Hadar, "On Expectations and Stability," *Behavioral Science*, **13**, 445–454 (1968); and J. F. Muth, "Rational Expectations and the Theory of Price Movements," *Econometrica*, **29**, 315–335 (1961).

Advertising

A mathematical analysis of optimal advertising policy may be found in R. Dorfman and P. O. Steiner, "Optimal Advertising and Optimal Quality," *American Economic Review*, **44**, 826–836 (1954), and K. J. Arrow and M. Nerlove, "Optimal Advertising Policy under Dynamic Conditions," *Economica*, **29**, 129–142 (1962). A discussion of the effects of advertising with special references to empirical considerations is given in L. G. Telser, "Advertising and Competition," *Journal of Political Economy*, **72**, 537–562 (1964).

CHAPTER 9

PROFIT MAXIMIZATION
WITH LINEAR PROCESSES

In all of the forgoing discussion on the profit-maximizing firm it was assumed that the firm's technological environment was of a type which may, primarily for historical reasons, be referred to as "neoclassical" or "traditional." That is, it was assumed that the technology available to the firm was representable by a production function in which any given level of output could be produced by one of many (infinite) combinations of inputs. This property, it will be recalled, is reflected in the nature of the isoquants, each of which can be thought of as a continuous hypersurface in the input space. Under these conditions the firm is able to move freely (technologically speaking) over the isoquant surface, and choose to produce any given level of output by using any one of many different combinations of the various inputs included in the production function.

The assumption of perfect substitutability between inputs which characterizes the "traditional" production function is in some sense an idealization, inasmuch as in many concrete situations the firm may in fact have only limited freedom of substitution; indeed, in many cases the technology does not admit of any substitution at all, and requires that inputs be combined in fixed proportions for all levels of output. For example, if the production process uses only two inputs, say z^1 and z^2, then the technology of such a process may, in part, be characterized by the condition $z^1/z^2 = k$, where k is some positive constant. Changing the amounts of the inputs used in this process means, therefore, either using more of both inputs, or using less of both inputs; using more of one input while using less of the other is technologically not feasible. This means (since using more of both inputs implies more output) that any particular level of output can be produced with only one specific combination of inputs.

Another typical feature of such production processes is the fact that the level of output is always proportional to the levels of the inputs. In a two-input example, this implies the existence of two positive constants, say c_1 and c_2, such that $x = c_1 z^1$, and $x = c_2 z^2$, where x denotes the level of output. Naturally, the two constants are not independent; since $z^1/z^2 = k$, we have

$c^2/c^1 = k$. Thus, the nature of a linear process can be summarized by the following two statements:

i) *Whenever the levels of the inputs are to be changed, each input must be changed by the same percentage.*

ii) *Whenever the inputs are changed by some percentage, the level of output changes by the same percentage.*

In this chapter, we shall concern ourselves with decision problems (essentially profit maximization) which are subject to a technological environment of the type described above. As we shall see, methods which we have applied to problems with a traditional production function fail to work when the technology consists of linear processes.

9.1 THE NATURE OF LINEAR MODELS

In our examples, we shall assume that each process uses m different inputs. Then there exist $m - 1$ constants defining the fixed proportions between the m inputs; that is,

$$(9.1) \qquad \frac{z^i}{z^m} = k^i, \qquad i = 1, 2, ..., m - 1, \quad k^i > 0.$$

The above equations imply, among other things, that once the level of one of the inputs is given (or chosen), the levels of the remaining $m - 1$ inputs are determined. The proportionality between the inputs and the output is given by the equations

$$(9.2a) \qquad x = c_i z^i, \qquad i = 1, 2, ..., m, \quad c_i > 0.$$

As was pointed out in the introductory discussion, the c_i are not independent of the k^i, and it is easy to see that (9.1) and (9.2a) imply

$$(9.3) \qquad \frac{c_j}{c_i} = \frac{k^i}{k^j}, \qquad i, j, = 1, 2, ..., m,$$

where $k^m = 1$.

Even so, one cannot express all the properties of this production process in one single functional relationship similar to a traditional production function. It is, however, possible to represent a linear process in a form which is more compact than the above equations. We can, for instance, rewrite (9.2a) as

$$(9.2b) \qquad \frac{z^i}{x} = \frac{1}{c_i} = a_i, \qquad i = 1, 2, ..., m,$$

and it should be clear that a_i, as defined by (9.2b), represents the amount of input i necessary to produce one unit of output x. Therefore, the vector of the a_i, that is, $(a_1, a_2, ..., a_m)$, contains *all* the information about this particular process which the firm needs to know in order to make an optimal choice. As soon as the level of output is chosen, the vector of the technological co-efficients determines the necessary levels of the m inputs (through multiplication of each a_i by x). Furthermore, the a_i also indicate (indirectly) the proportions between the various inputs, since from (9.3) and (9.2b) we immediately have

$$(9.4) \qquad \frac{a_i}{a_j} = \frac{k^i}{k^j}, \qquad i, j = 1, 2, ..., m, \quad k^m = 1.$$

From what has been said so far about linear processes, it is already possible to draw a general distinction between the decision problems arising in the traditional models, and those which characterize the present set-up. When the technology is given by an ordinary production function, a production plan requires two separate decisions: one about the level of output to be produced, and another concerning the input combination for the selected output level. In the present model, on the other hand (and assuming there exists only one process), the choice of a desired level of output implies a *unique* input combination, so that the entire production program is completely specified by one single decision.

While the properties of linear processes simplify, in some respects at least, the decision making of the firm, difficulties are likely to arise if the firm happens to be in a position in which it can operate more than one process at a time. The latter situation may occur (a) if a given product is capable of being produced by two technologically different processes, or (b) when the firm produces different products each of which requires for its production a different process. For the purpose of our exposition, it is irrelevant which of the above two cases prevails; the only thing that really matters is the number of different processes available to the firm, and the levels at which they are operated. To maintain a sufficiently high level of generality, and to indicate the relationship between the particular problems to be discussed in this chapter and the more general class of problems involving linear processes, we shall adopt the terminology normally used in such problems and refer to a particular process as an "activity." Thus, in the context of the theory of the firm, given a linear technology, the operation of two different activities may mean either producing a single product by two different processes, or producing two different products with different processes.

More formally, an activity is defined by a vector of technological coefficients such as $(a_{1j}, a_{2j}, ..., a_{mj})$ for activity j. In general, a_{ij} denotes the (minimum) amount of input i required to operate activity j at the unit level. This last phrase is just a slightly disguised, but conventional, way of saying "to produce one unit of output j." Of course, output j need not necessarily be a concrete product, but could perhaps represent some sort of intangible service. In any case, the relationships between products, inputs, and technological coefficients are of the same general nature as those given in Eqs. (9.1) through (9.4). It is also important to note that the different activities (processes) are assumed to be independent of each other; that is, the input requirements of a particular activity are independent of the levels at which other activities are operated.

It is convenient to begin the formulation of a typical decision problem with the specification of the profit function. As for the revenue side, we associate a market price with each activity. If activities i and j involve the production of an identical product, then, of course, $p^i = p^j$. As usual, under conditions of pure competition, the market prices are given (positive) constants. Thus, total revenue is given by

$$\sum_{j=1}^{n} p^j x^j,$$

where it is assumed that the firm can operate n different activities, the levels of which being denoted by x^j.

Similarly, each of the m inputs has a market price denoted by q^i. Therefore, the cost of input i incurred by operating activity j at the level x^j equals $x^j q^i a_{ij}$, and the total variable input cost of the jth activity is given by

$$x^j \sum_{i=1}^{m} q^i a_{ij}.$$

Consequently, total variable input cost is equal to

$$\sum_{j=1}^{n} x^j \sum_{i=1}^{m} q^i a_{ij},$$

and so we can write

(9.5a)
$$\pi = \sum_{j=1}^{n} x^j \left(p^j - \sum_{i=1}^{m} q^i a_{ij} \right) - c.$$

Since the prices and the technological coefficients are constant, (9.5a) can conveniently be written as

(9.5b)
$$\pi = \sum_{j=1}^{n} x^j r^j - c,$$

where

$$r^j = p^j - \sum_{i=1}^{m} q^i a_{ij}.$$

The latter may be defined as the net revenue for one unit of activity j.

The reason for introducing version (9.5b) is to make sure the reader realizes that (9.5) is a linear function in the variables x^j. This fact has the following implications: If $r^j < 0$, then the firm maximizes profit by setting x^j equal to zero (since an activity cannot be operated at a negative level). If $r^j < 0$ for all j, then the firm shuts down. If, on the other hand, $r^j > 0$ for some j, then the profit function has no maximum, since profit can be made as large as one may wish by setting activity j at a sufficiently high level. Thus, one of two things may happen: the firm either shuts down (in which case we have nothing more to say about the problem), or else the problem has no solution (which is equally unfortunate).

In reality, however, firms which stay in the market do manage to find solutions to their production problems. The discrepancy between the implications of our model and observed behavior lies in the fact that our model is not yet sufficiently specified. While it is certainly true that a linear function (which is not a constant function) possesses no maximum, it is not true that firms can increase their profit indefinitely. The reason for their inability to do so is that firms have only limited resources at their disposal. In the short run, these limitations may take the form of a fixed size of plant and related facilities, and in the long run, firms may be faced with budgetary restrictions; in many situations both factors may be responsible for preventing firms from attaining infinitely high levels of profit. We shall, therefore, modify our model by adding to the profit function a set of restrictions which require the firm to use no more of each input than some given amount (without, however, specifying the source of each particular limitation). Since the amount of input i used for operating activity j is given by $a_{ij} x^j$, the total amount of input i used by the firm is given by

$$\sum_{j=1}^{n} a_{ij} x^j.$$

If we let $b_i (> 0)$ denote the maximum available amount of input i, then the modified formulation of our problem can be stated as:

Maximize (9.5) subject to

$$(9.6) \qquad \sum_{j=1}^{n} a_{ij} x^j \leqslant b_i, \qquad i = 1, 2, \ldots, m,$$

$$(9.7) \qquad x^j \geqslant 0, \qquad j = 1, 2, \ldots, n.$$

The problem is now in the standard form of a *linear programming* problem—so called because it involves the maximization of a linear function subject to a set of linear constraints. The constraints may, in general, be in the form of either equations or inequalities, or both. Because of the special nature (linearity and constraints in the form of inequalities) of problems such as the above, they cannot be solved with the traditional tools of the differential calculus. One procedure which has been developed for solving linear programming problems is called the *simplex* method, and in what follows we shall apply this method to the problem on hand.

9.2 THE SIMPLEX METHOD

The first step to be taken consists of transforming the inequalities in (9.6) into equalities. This is done by defining a set of artificial variables—called *slack variables*—which represent the difference between the amount of each input used and the amount available of the respective input. If x^{n+i} denotes the slack variable of the ith input, then we transform (9.6) into

$$(9.8) \qquad \sum_{j=1}^{n} a_{ij} x^j + x^{n+i} = b_i, \qquad i = 1, 2, ..., m.$$

Since by definition

$$x^{n+i} = b_i - \sum_{j=1}^{n} a_{ij} x^j,$$

then clearly, if we impose the additional restrictions $x^{n+i} \geqslant 0, i = 1, 2, ..., m$, the equations in (9.8) are equivalent to the inequalities in (9.6); that is, any set of nonnegative xs satisfying (9.8) will automatically satisfy (9.6). Therefore, the problem can now be viewed as maximizing (9.5), subject to (9.8), and the nonnegativity restrictions on all the variables. Note that the slack variables are not included in the profit function, since the firm is generally neither rewarded nor penalized for not making use of the maximum amounts of the available inputs. If in some particular problem it is meaningful and proper to attach a price (or cost) to the surplus amounts of the inputs, then the input restrictions will appear as equations (rather than inequalities) in the original problem, and there will be no need for artificial slack variables.

Once the restrictions are converted into equalities, the simplex method proceeds as follows: First, one attempts to find a subsystem of (9.8) consisting of m variables (activities) and m equations for which a solution exists. Given the values of the variables in this solution, the profit level is computed. One then tries to increase the profit level by replacing one of the m activities in the first solution by one of the activities not included in that solution. This gives rise to a new solution, and the new profit level is computed. This process is repeated, replacing one activity at a time, until the replacement of further activities no longer increases the profit level. The rationale of the simplex method lies in the fact that, if a linear programming problem possesses an optimal solution, then one can find that solution in a finite number of iterations. Of course, if the number of activities is large, then the actual computations are bound to be quite lengthy and complicated, but such problems can now be solved with the aid of electronic computers without much difficulty.

From the above brief description, it should be evident that the simplex method relies heavily on existence theorems for solutions of simultaneous equations. Like those given in (9.8), these equations are linear, and underlying such a system of equations is a matrix of coefficients which, in our problem, can be represented by the $m \times (n + m)$ matrix

$$
(9.9) \quad
\begin{bmatrix}
a_{11} & a_{12} & \cdots & a_{1n} & 1 & 0 & \cdots & 0 \\
a_{21} & a_{22} & \cdots & a_{2n} & 0 & 1 & \cdots & 0 \\
\vdots & & & & & & & \vdots \\
a_{m1} & a_{m2} & \cdots & a_{mn} & 0 & 0 & \cdots & 1
\end{bmatrix},
$$

and will be denoted by A. Associated with the matrix A is the *augmented* matrix of system (9.8), which is formed by adding to matrix A the column of the coefficients on the rhs of (9.8) If the augmented matrix is denoted by $\tilde{A}$, then we have

$$
(9.10) \quad \tilde{A} =
\begin{bmatrix}
a_{11} & a_{12} & \cdots & a_{1n} & 1 & 0 & \cdots & 0 & b_1 \\
a_{21} & a_{22} & \cdots & a_{2n} & 0 & 1 & \cdots & 0 & b_2 \\
\vdots & & & & & & & & \vdots \\
a_{m1} & a_{m2} & \cdots & a_{mn} & 0 & 0 & \cdots & 1 & b_m
\end{bmatrix}.
$$

These matrices are introduced here because the required existence theorems involve the ranks of these matrices. The rank of a matrix, it will be recalled, is equal to the maximum number of linearly independent columns in the matrix. (See Section 15.2.3.) Thus, if the rank of some matrix M is equal to r, then there exists a nonsingular $r \times r$ submatrix of M, and every $(r + 1) \times (r + 1)$ submatrix of M is singular. (A *singular* matrix is one whose determinant is zero.) Now, since A is in some sense a subset of $\tilde{A}$, in that every column of A is also a column of $\tilde{A}$, then it certainly follows that the rank of A cannot exceed that of $\tilde{A}$ (because any set of linearly independent columns in A also constitutes a set of linearly independent columns in $\tilde{A}$). Therefore, one of the following may be the case: (a) $R(A) < R(\tilde{A})$, or (b) $R(A) = R(\tilde{A})$, where $R(A)$ denotes the rank of matrix A.

If $R(A) < R(\tilde{A})$, then the system has no real solution, and is said to be *inconsistent*. The reason for this, briefly, is as follows: Since $\tilde{A}$ is the same as A except for the column of the bs, the latter column must be included in the set of linearly independent columns in $\tilde{A}$ [otherwise $R(\tilde{A})$ cannot exceed $R(A)$]. Therefore, the column vector $b = (b_1, b_2, \ldots, b_m)$ (shown here as a row vector for typographical convenience) is linearly independent of the columns of A, which means that the vector b cannot be written as a linear combination of the columns in A. Symbolically, there exist no real-valued xs such that

$$
\sum_{j=1}^{n} a_{ij} x^j + x^{n+i} = b_i, \qquad i = 1, 2, \ldots, m,
$$

which means, of course, that the system (9.8) has no solution.

If $R(A) = R(\tilde{A})$, then (9.8) has at least one real solution. It must be remembered, however, that, in our problem, to find just *any* solution won't do; we also require that the solution be nonnegative. If a solution to (9.8) involves only nonnegative values, then we refer to it as a *feasible* solution. Ultimately, of course, we want to find an *optimal* solution, that is, an element in the set of all feasible solutions which maximizes the profit function. The simplex method is nothing but a computational method which, through a process of elimination, finds an optimal solution (provided one exists).

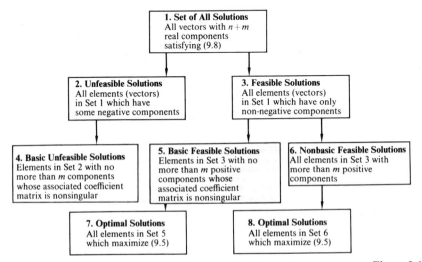

Figure 9.1

To be more precise, the simplex method examines not the entire set of feasible solutions, but only a certain subset of it—a subset whose elements are solutions which contain no more positive activities than the number of restrictions. In our example, this subset includes feasible solutions which require no more (possibly less) than m activities operated at positive levels, the remaining n activities being set equal to zero. A solution which is a member of this subset is called a *basic* feasible solution. Basic solutions must also be unique; in other words, a solution involving no more than m positive activities is a basic solution only if there exists exactly one set of values for these m activities which satisfies the system of equations under consideration.* The reason why the search for an optimal solution can be limited to the set of basic feasible solutions is the existence of a theorem according to which an optimal solution to a linear programming problem need not require more activities than the number

---

*To put it differently, a set of m activities constitutes a basic solution only if the associated matrix of coefficients is nonsingular.

of restrictions. Thus, even though the set of *all* optimal solutions (in the event
that this set has more than one element) may include solutions which require
more than m positive activities, one can always be sure to find in this set at
least one solution which uses no more than m activities; and from the point of
view of profit maximization, such a solution is just as good as one requiring
more than m activities. The relationship between the various types of solution
is shown schematically in Fig. 9.1.

Before proceeding with our problem, let us dwell briefly on those cases in
which a basic feasible solution has less than m positive activities. Such a solution is referred to as *degenerate*, and it arises when the vector b is linearly
dependent on a set of $m - 1$ columns of matrix A. Suppose, for example, that
the first m columns of A are linearly independent, so that the $m \times m$ submatrix of A consisting of these columns is nonsinglar. For simplification,
suppose further that the vector b is linearly dependent on the first $m - 1$ of
the above m column vectors. This last assumption implies (by definition) the
existence of a set of numbers, say y^j, not all zero, such that

$$(9.11) \qquad \sum_{j=1}^{m-1} a_{ij} y^j = b_i, \qquad i = 1, 2, \ldots, m.$$

However, the fact that the above m columns of matrix A are assumed to be
linearly independent implies, at the same time, that the system of equations
obtained from (9.8), by letting $x^j = 0$, $j = m + 1, m + 2, \ldots, m + n$, has a
unique solution. There exists, therefore, m unique values x^j such that

$$(9.12) \qquad \sum_{j=1}^{m} a_{ij} x^j = b_i, \qquad i = 1, 2, \ldots, m.$$

Subtracting (9.11) from (9.12), we get

$$(9.13) \qquad \sum_{j=1}^{m-1} a_{ij}(x^j - y^j) + a_{im} x^m = 0, \qquad i = 1, 2, \ldots, m.$$

The above is a system of homogeneous linear equations. Since it has the same
coefficients as system (9.12), it has a unique solution—namely, the so-called
trivial solution, with all variables being equal to zero. In this example, therefore, we have a case of degeneracy, since activity m is operated at the zero level.
Thus, degeneracy occurs when the vector representing the maximum available
amounts of the inputs happens to be a linear combination of $m - 1$ of the
technological vectors which characterize the different activities. Degeneracy,
therefore, is not inherent in either the technology or the economic environment
of the firm, but results from a particular combination of the two.

Returning now to our particular problem, we find that Set 5 in Fig. 9.1
has at least one element; in other words, one can always find at least one vector

with no more than m positive components satisfying (9.8). (Therefore, matrices A and $\tilde{A}$ above have the same rank.) This vector can be written as $(0, 0, ..., 0, b_1, b_2, ..., b_m)$, and, according to this solution, all the n real activities are set equal to zero, while each slack variable is set equal to the maximum amount of the respective input. Less formally, the firm's choice of producing nothing constitutes a basic feasible solution to the problem. Admittedly, this may appear to be a trivial result, but it is a convenient basis from which to start the iterative process. Note, too, that the basic feasible solution involving only the m slack variables is a unique solution, because the system of equations which obtains when all the first n variables in (9.8) are set equal to zero (which is what our first solution requires) has a nonsingular matrix—the identity matrix. (The latter is the submatrix of A formed from the last m columns of A.)

Having found an initial solution, how do we find a better one? What needs to be done now is to find another solution which yields a higher level of profit than does the first solution. (It requires no extensive computations to realize that the profit associated with the first solution is equal to $-c$.) Actually, at this stage of the process, our next move should be quite obvious: replace one of the slack variables by one of the real activities. But care must be exercised in order to ensure that the new solution has all the properties of a basic feasible solution.

First, we may want to verify that the new solution is a basic solution; that is, the matrix which obtains after the replacement of one vector in the initial (the identity) matrix should also be nonsingular. Here we make use of the fact that any set of linearly independent m-dimensional vectors (which, therefore, form a basis for an m-dimensional linear space) can be written as a linear combination of any other nonzero vector with m components. In terms of our problem, the vectors that make up the identity matrix can be written as a linear combination of any of the n vectors representing the n real activities. If we use the notation $e_k = (e_{1k}, e_{2k}, ..., e_{mk})$, $k = 1, 2, ..., m$, to represent the m unit vectors of the basic solution, and remembering that $a_j = (a_{1j}, a_{2j}, ..., a_{mj})$ is the technological vector of activity j, then the preceding statement says that there exist m numbers, say α_k, $k = 1, 2, ..., m$, not all zero, such that

$$(9.14) \qquad \sum_{k=1}^{m} \alpha_k e_{ik} = a_{ij}, \qquad i = 1, 2, ..., m.$$

Of course, since in this particular example e_k is a unit vector, that is, $e_{ik} = 1$ for $i = k$, and $e_{ik} = 0$ otherwise, it turns out that $\alpha_i = a_{ij}$, $i = 1, 2, ..., m$. We should also add (since the simplified notation fails to make this clear) that the αs depend on the js; that is, the "weights" in (9.14) depend on the vector a_j, which is to be expressed as a linear combination of the basic vectors.

Another theorem of linear algebra says that if in system (9.14) one of the αs, say α_r, is different from zero, then the matrix which is obtained by replacing e_r in the initial matrix by the vector a_j is nonsingular. In other words, replacing the rth slack variable in the initial basic solution by the jth activity yields another basic solution. But what is the meaning of the condition $\alpha_r \neq 0$? It was pointed out that $\alpha_r = a_{rj}$, where the latter indicates the amount of input r necessary to operate activity j at the unit level. If $\alpha_r = a_{rj} = 0$, then activity j makes no use of input r. However, if we remove the rth slack variable from the initial solution, we impose on the new solution the condition that all the available amount of input r (that is, b_r) be used up, and that is possible only if the activity (j) to be introduced into the solution requires some positive amount of input r. If $a_{rj} = 0$ for all j, then none of the activities makes use of input r, in which case the rth equation of (9.8) can be dropped, thereby reducing the system to one of $m - 1$ dimensions. Mathematically speaking, the introduction of an activity for which the respective "weight" (α) is zero creates linear dependence among the vectors of the new solution.

Assuming that we have found an eligible activity for our second basic solution, we still have the feasibility requirements to worry about; that is, we have to introduce the new activity in such a way that no variable in the new solution appears at a negative level. Since the activity to be introduced will require certain amounts of the limited inputs, it is conceivable that some of the variables carried over from the initial solution will have to be operated at reduced levels, and unless one is careful about it, such reductions may force some of these variables into negative levels. In the present problem, the second solution will require a reduction in some of the slack variables, but like the real activities, they too are restricted to nonnegative levels. (If a slack variable appears in a solution at a negative level, then the total input requirements of the real activities will be in excess of the available amount of the corresponding input.)

Fortunately, we can express the second solution in terms of the initial one, and this relationship provides us with a means for guaranteeing feasibility. Let us first rewrite system (9.8), inserting into it our initial basic feasible solution. This gives

$$(9.15) \qquad \sum_{k=1}^{m} e_{ik}\, \hat{x}^{n+k} = b_i, \qquad i = 1, 2, \ldots, m,$$

where carets ($\hat{}$) indicate the values of the variables in the initial basic feasible solution. Assuming that activity j is a candidate for the second basic solution, we can solve system (9.14) for the components of any vector e_k for which the corresponding α is not zero. Suppose $\alpha_r \neq 0$, then we have

$$(9.16) \qquad e_{ir} = \frac{a_{ij}}{\alpha_r} - \sum_{\substack{k=1 \\ k \neq r}}^{m} \frac{\alpha_k}{\alpha_r} e_{ik}, \qquad i = 1, 2, \ldots, m.$$

Substituting for e_{i_r} in (9.15) from (9.16), and rearranging terms we have

$$(9.17) \quad \sum_{\substack{k=1 \\ k \neq r}}^{m} e_{ik}\left(\hat{x}^{n+k} - \frac{\alpha_k}{\alpha_r}\hat{x}^{n+r}\right) + a_{ij}\frac{\hat{x}^{n+r}}{\alpha_r} = b_i, \quad i = 1, 2, ..., m.$$

What we have done here is this. We assumed that activity j is an eligible vector for the second basic solution; that is, that the vector a_j is a linear combination of the vectors in the initial basic solution. Since this assumption implies the existence of at least one $\alpha \neq 0$, we then solved (9.14) for e_{i_r}, assuming $\alpha_r \neq 0$, and substituted for e_{i_r} in the initial basic solution, obtaining (9.17). This means that if we replace the rth slack variable in the initial solution by activity j, then the resulting system of equations will have the form given in (9.17), with the new solution given by the expression in parentheses (for the $m - 1$ remaining slack variables), and the term multiplied by a_{ij} (for activity j). More formally,

$$(9.18a) \quad \hat{\hat{x}}^{n+k} = \hat{x}^{n+k} - \frac{\alpha_k}{\alpha_r}\hat{x}^{n+r}, \quad k = 1, 2, ..., m, \quad k \neq r,$$

$$(9.18b) \quad \hat{\hat{x}}^j = \frac{\hat{x}^{n+r}}{\alpha_r},$$

where two carets indicate the values of the variables in the second basic solution. Of course, in general, we can expect more than one of the αs in (9.14) to be different from zero, in which case we have a choice of several variables in the initial basic solution that can be replaced by activity j. By choosing the "correct" variable from among all the replaceable ones, we are in a position to ensure the feasibility of the second basic solution.

Ruling out degeneracy, we find from (9.18b) that the positivity of x^j requires $\alpha_r > 0$. We therefore consider for replacement only those vectors e_k for which $\alpha_k > 0$. Now, if the α_k, $k \neq r$, are all nonpositive, and e_r ($\alpha_r > 0$) is replaced by activity j, then it is clear from (9.18a) that the remaining $m - 1$ slack variables will assume nonnegative values in the new solution. In that case, the new solution is feasible. Now suppose that there are several αs (not just α_r) which are positive. If we adopt a labeling system such that the positive αs are numbered from 1 to s, then the nonnegativity requirements for the variables carried over from the initial solution can be stated as

$$(9.19) \quad \frac{\hat{x}^{n+r}}{\alpha_r} \leqslant \frac{\hat{x}^{n+k}}{\alpha_k}, \quad k = 1, 2, ..., s.$$

We are now faced with this question: How do we select the variable to be replaced without violating (9.19)? The answer to this is quite simple: we select for replacement the variable x^{n+r} by the rule

$$(9.20) \qquad \frac{\hat{x}^{n+r}}{\alpha_r} = \min \left(\frac{\hat{x}^{n+1}}{\alpha_1}, \frac{\hat{x}^{n+2}}{\alpha_2}, \ldots, \frac{\hat{x}^{n+s}}{\alpha_s} \right).$$

Suppose that $\hat{x}^{n+i}/\alpha_i$ is the smallest of the terms appearing in the parentheses in (9.20), then, according to the rule, the $(n + i)$th slack variable is removed from the initial basic solution and is replaced by activity j. Since from (9.20) we then have $\hat{x}^{n+r}/\alpha_r = \hat{x}^{n+i}/\alpha_i$, the values of the variables in the second basic feasible solution can be determined directly from (9.18). Substituting for $\hat{x}^{n+r}/\alpha_r$ in (9.18) from (9.20), we get

$$\hat{\hat{x}}^{n+i} = 0 \quad \text{(the replaced slack variable),}$$

$$\hat{\hat{x}}^{n+k} = \hat{x}^{n+k} - \frac{\alpha_k}{\alpha_i} \hat{x}^{n+i} > 0, \qquad k = 1, 2, \ldots, m, \quad k \neq i,$$

$$\hat{\hat{x}}^{j} = \frac{\hat{x}^{n+i}}{\alpha_i} > 0,$$

all of which satisfy the nonnegativity conditions.

Let us summarize briefly the whole procedure for finding a new solution. (Since we have used general notation for the vectors in the first basic solution, the procedure outlined above can, in general, be applied for moving from *any* basic feasible solution to the next one, and not only for the purpose of going from the first solution to the second.) Since any basic solution consists of m linearly independent vectors, any one of the vectors (activities) in matrix A not included in the basic solution can be written as a linear combination [such as (9.14)] of the vectors in the basic solution. Vectors in the original basic solution whose weights (αs) in this linear combination are positive are eligible to be replaced by an excluded activity. If activity r in the original basic solution is eligible for replacement (that is, $\alpha_r > 0$), and $\alpha_k \leqslant 0$ for all k, $k \neq r$, then the replacement of activity r by an excluded activity yields a new basic feasible solution. The levels (values) of the activities in the new solution are given by (9.18). If, when considering activity r for possible replacement, it is found that $\alpha_k > 0$ for several $k \neq r$, then the activity in the initial basic solution to be replaced by an excluded activity is determined by condition (9.20). This will again yield a new basic feasible solution whose values, as in the first case, are given by (9.18).

It will be helpful, at this point, to indicate the meaning of condition (9.20). To do so, however, we must first find an interpretation of the αs. Earlier, it was shown that, when the first solution consists exclusively of slack variables, then for any excluded activity j it is true that $\alpha_i = a_{ij}, i = 1, 2, \ldots, m$. It then follows from the definition of a_{ij}, that α_i can be interpreted as the amount by which the ith slack variable will have to be reduced in order to make room for one unit of the new activity j. For greater clarity, we shall now affix a superscript j to the α_i to indicate their dependence on the activity to be introduced, and demonstrate that α_i^j can, in general, be interpreted as the amount by which the ith activity in the basic feasible solution has to be changed (not necessarily reduced) for every unit of the excluded activity j brought into the solution.

If we solve system (9.15) for the values of the variables in the initial basic feasible solution, using Cramer's rule, we get

$$(9.21) \qquad \hat{x}^{n+k} = \sum_{i=1}^{m} b_i \frac{D_{ik}}{D}, \qquad k = 1, 2, ..., m,$$

where D is the determinant of the matrix of the coefficients e_{ik}, and D_{ik} is a cofactor of D. (Again, if the first solution is made up entirely of slack variables, then $D_{ik} = 0$ for $i \neq k$, $D_{ii} = 1$ for all i, $D = 1$, and $\hat{x}^{n+k} = b_k$ for all k. We are using general notation here because the proof holds for any basic feasible solution.) Now, if the excluded activity j is to be operated at the unit level, the amounts of the m inputs required for this activity must be subtracted from the amounts available for the activities already in the solution, that is, the rhs of (9.15). Thus, the adjusted levels of the activities in the initial solution are found by solving the system

$$(9.22) \qquad \sum_{k=1}^{m} e_{ik} x^{n+k} = b_i - a_{ij}, \qquad i = 1, 2, ..., m,$$

and if we denote the adjusted values of the variables by $\overset{*}{x}^{n+k}$, then we can write

$$(9.23) \qquad \overset{*}{x}^{n+k} = \sum_{i=1}^{m} (b_i - a_{ij}) \frac{D_{ik}}{D}, \qquad k = 1, 2, ..., m.$$

[Note that (9.23) is the same as (9.21) except for the coefficients in parentheses.] The amount by which activity $n + k$ has to be changed following the introduction of one unit of activity j may be denoted by Δx^{n+k}_j, and is defined to be equal to $\hat{x}^{n+k} - \overset{*}{x}^{n+k}$. (For convenience, we have defined the above change in such a way that $\Delta x^{n+k}_j > 0$ implies a *reduction* in x^{n+k}.) From (9.21) and (9.23), we have

$$(9.24) \qquad \Delta x^{n+k}_j = \sum_{i=1}^{m} a_{ij} \frac{D_{ik}}{D}, \qquad k = 1, 2, ..., m.$$

Now, let us go back to (9.14), which we can view as a system of equations in the m unknowns $\alpha_k^j, k = 1, 2, ..., m$. We see immediately that systems (9.14) and (9.15) share the same matrix of coefficients, although the constants on the rhs of the equations are different in the two cases. Solving (9.14), we have

$$(9.25) \qquad \alpha_k^j = \sum_{i=1}^{m} a_{ij} \frac{D_{ik}}{D}, \qquad k = 1, 2, ..., m,$$

and hence, in view of (9.24) and (9.25), we obtain the desired result $\Delta x^{n+k} = \alpha_k^j$ for all j and $k, j \neq k$.

If α_k^j is equal to the necessary change in activity $n + k$ (which is the case when considering the first basic solution), and if the introduction of activity j forces a *reduction* in x^{n+k} [as it does if $\alpha_k^j > 0$, see (9.18)], then x^{n+k}/α_k^j represents the number of units of activity j which, upon the introduction of activity j into the solution, will reduce the level of activity $n + k$ to zero. Thus, to pick the smallest of the terms x^{n+k}/α_k^j simply means to identify the variable in the basic solution which will be the first (or among the first) to reach zero as successive increments of activity j are introduced into the solution. Hence, if activity i satisfies condition (9.20), but instead one were to replace activity k, where $x^{n+k}/\alpha_k^j > x^{n+i}/\alpha_i^j$, then activity i would assume a negative level in the new solution. Note also that condition (9.20) not only indicates the variable in the initial solution which is to be replaced, but also determines, by (9.18), the level at which the new activity j enters the new solution.

Two further comments are now in order. It may happen, when applying (9.20), that two or more of the terms in parentheses are found to have the lowest value. Then, since only one activity is to be replaced, it follows from (9.18a) that one or more of the variables in the new solution will be zero. To put it differently, if the minimum in (9.20) is not unique, then the new solution is degenerate. In the above exposition, degeneracy was excluded by assumption. A second complication may arise if none of the αs in (9.14) is positive. If this occurs, then the profit function has no maximum—a contingency which we also find convenient to assume away.

It remains to perform one additional, indeed, very crucial, step: to compute the profit level associated with the new solution; or, to be more precise, to compare the latter with the profit from the preceding solution. First, we insert into the profit function (9.5b) the values of the variables in the initial basic feasible solution, obtaining thereby the profit level associated with the original solution. This can be written as

$$(9.26) \qquad \hat{\pi} = \sum_{k=1}^{m} \hat{x}^{n+k} r^{n+k} - c,$$

where r^j is defined as in (9.5b). Of course, since our *first* basic feasible solution has only slack variables, it follows that $r^{n+k} = 0$ for all k, and hence $\hat{\pi} = -c$. However, we shall continue to use general notation as in (9.26), because the comparison to be made applies to any two successive solutions of the simplex method. For the new solution we have, making use of (9.18),

$$(9.27) \qquad \hat{\hat{\pi}} = \sum_{k=1}^{m} \left(\hat{x}^{n+k} - \frac{\alpha_k^j}{\alpha_i^j} \hat{x}^{n+i} \right) r^{n+k} + \frac{\hat{x}^{n+i}}{\alpha_i^j} r^j - c.$$

It is assumed here that the second solution is obtained by replacing activity i in the first solution by activity j. Note also that the summation in (9.27) includes the term for which $k = i$, which is obviously equal to zero. Subtracting (9.26) from (9.27), we get

$$(9.28a) \qquad \hat{\hat{\pi}} - \hat{\pi} = \frac{\hat{x}^{n+i}}{\alpha_i^j} r^j - \frac{\hat{x}^{n+i}}{\alpha_i^j} \sum_{k=1}^{m} \alpha_k^j r^{n+k},$$

which can be rearranged and written as

$$(9.28b) \qquad \hat{\hat{\pi}} = \hat{\pi} + \hat{x}^j \left(r^j - \sum_{k=1}^{m} \alpha_k^j r^{n+k} \right).$$

According to this equation, the new level of profit is equal to the previous one, plus a certain quantity (of generally indeterminate sign) which is multiplied by the level of the new (jth) activity in the new solution. Clearly, whether the new solution constitutes an improvement compared to the previous one depends directly on the sign of the expression in parentheses in (9.28b).

In the latter expression, we easily recognize r^j as the marginal net revenue of activity j. The r^j must certainly be positive since any activity whose marginal net revenue is nonpositive will not be included in any production program. Since α_k^j represents the necessary change in the level of activity k upon the introduction of activity j, the term $\alpha_k^j r^{n+k}$ is the change in the net revenue from activity k, and $\sum_{k=1}^{m} \alpha_k^j r^{n+k}$ represents the change in total net revenue brought about by the inclusion of activity j in the new solution. It is, therefore, proper to call the expression in parentheses in (9.28b) the *marginal profitability* of activity j. We can now conclude that if the marginal profitability of an excluded activity is positive, then by including it in the new basis one obtains an improved basic feasible solution. If, on the other hand, the marginal profitability of an excluded activity is negative, then it should not be included in the new solution, and the attempt to improve the initial solution must be repeated by considering a different activity. If at any stage of this iterative process no excluded activity has a positive marginal profitability, then the last basic feasible solution is an optimal solution. As we pointed out earlier, if an optimal solution exists, the above procedure will find it in a finite number of iterations.

As a final comment to this discussion we should point out that, in general, a given linear programming problem need not necessarily be of the form in which we have cast our example. First of all, it is conceivable that a certain problem may require that the objective function be *minimized*. This calls for certain changes at some stages of the simplex method as described above. Fortunately, there is a simple way of avoiding these changes, and that is to convert the problem into a maximization problem. Since minimizing a function is equivalent to maximizing its negative (and conversely), the conversion procedure requires no more than a multiplication by -1 of the coefficients of the objective function. For example, minimizing

$$\sum_{j=1}^{n} c_j x^j$$

is the same as maximizing

$$\sum_{j=1}^{n} (-c_j) x^j.$$

Therefore, no loss of generality is incurred by studying only the method for solving maximization problems.

Our exposition may also appear to have been somewhat one-sided with respect to the form of the constraints, all of which involved conditions such as $\leqslant b_i$. Again, in certain contexts, the restrictions of the problem on hand, or at least some of them, may impose conditions of the form $\geqslant b_i$. In that case, one of the following can be done. If the ith constraint involves the condition $\geqslant b_i$, then multiplication by -1 of both sides of the inequality will reverse the direction of the inequality without, of course, changing the meaning of the constraint itself. By doing so, one can always modify any original problem in a manner such that all the constraints appear in the same form as in our example above. If, for some reason, such multiplication is not desired, and if the ith constraint involves the condition $\geqslant b_i$, then the column vector of the coefficients of the slack variable for the ith constraint must have the coefficient -1 (rather than 1) in its ith row. Then the resulting system of equations will be equivalent to the original set of inequality constraints, assuming that all variables, including the slack variables, are restricted to nonnegative values.

Example 9.1. Let us consider a hypothetical firm which produces three different products x^1, x^2, and x^3, the production of each of which requires the two inputs z^1 and z^2. The technological specifications are given by the three vectors

$$
\begin{array}{rclcll}
 & & z^1 & & z^2 & \\
a_1 & = & (1 & , & 1 &), \\
a_2 & = & (6/5 & , & 4/5), \\
a_3 & = & (3 & , & 1 &),
\end{array}
$$

where subscripts on the *a*s denote the corresponding product. Market prices are as follows:

Product prices   Input prices

$p^1 = \$6,$ $q^1 = \$3,$

$p^2 = \$6,$ $q^2 = \$2.$

$p^3 = \$13.$

In addition, there are restrictions on the amounts of the two inputs that the firm can use in each period of time. These are

$$z^1 \leqslant 18 = b_1,$$
$$z^2 \leqslant 14 = b_2.$$

Formally, the problem on hand can be stated as:

Maximize $\pi = x^1(6 - 3 \cdot 1 - 2 \cdot 1) + x^2(6 - 3 \cdot 6/5 - 2 \cdot 4/5)$
$\qquad\qquad + x^3(13 - 3 \cdot 3 - 2 \cdot 1) - c$

subject to $\qquad x^1 + 6/5x^2 + 3x^3 \leqslant 18,$

$\qquad\qquad\quad x^1 + 4/5x^2 + \ x^3 \leqslant 14,$

$\qquad\quad x^1, x^2, x^3 \geqslant 0.$

The first thing that we may want to do is to compute the net revenue per unit of each product in order to verify that they are all positive. This yields

$$r^1 = \ 6 - 3 - 2 = 1,$$
$$r^2 = \ 6 - 18/5 - 8/5 = 4/5,$$
$$r^3 = 13 - 9 - 2 = 2,$$

hence we have no reason, at this point, to exclude any activity from the production program even though we know that if the problem has an optimal solution, it will require no more than two activities.

We denote the two slack variables by x^4 and x^5, and are now ready for the first basic feasible solution which is given below.

Basis 1

$$1 \cdot x^4 + 0 \cdot x^5 = 18, \qquad \text{[the equivalent of (9.15)].}$$
$$0 \cdot x^4 + 1 \cdot x^5 = 14,$$

The solution to this system is $x^4 = 18$, $x^5 = 14$, and $\pi = -c$.

Let us now consider x^1 as a candidate for the next solution, and therefore express a_1 as a linear combination of the vectors in the first basis; that is,

$$1 \cdot \alpha_4^1 + 0 \cdot \alpha_5^1 = 1, \qquad \text{[the equivalent of (9.14)],}$$
$$0 \cdot \alpha_4^1 + 1 \cdot \alpha_5^1 = 1,$$

and hence $\alpha_4^1 = 1$, and $\alpha_5^1 = 1$. Since both αs are positive, either one of the slack variables may be replaced. However, before computing the level at which activity 1 is to be operated, we want to make sure that the introduction of this activity will increase the value of the profit function. We do this by evaluating the marginal profitability [the expression in parentheses in (9.28b)] for the activity in question. For this we have

$$\Delta\pi_1 = 1 - 1 \cdot 0 - 1 \cdot 0 = 1 > 0 \qquad (\text{since } r^4 = r^5 = 0),$$

where the notation $\Delta\pi_j$ refers to the change in profit due to the introduction of one unit of activity j, all other activities in the solution being adjusted so as to satisfy the feasibility requirements.

Now that the admissibility of x^1 has been established, we determine the variable to be replaced by using condition (9.20). We have

$$x^4/\alpha_4^1 \qquad x^5/\alpha_5^1$$
$$\min (\ 18/1\ , \quad 14/1\ ) \quad = \quad 14/1,$$

and therefore we remove x^5 from the first solution.

Basis 2

$$x^4 + x^1 = 18,$$
$$x^1 = 14.$$

The above yields $x^1 = 14$, $x^4 = 4$, and $\pi = 14 - c$. As we expected (since $\Delta\pi_1 > 0$), the second solution is an improvement compared with the first one.

Considering now activity 2 for inclusion in the next solution, we form the linear combination

$$\alpha_4^2 + \alpha_1^2 = 6/5,$$
$$\alpha_1^2 = 4/5,$$

from which we get $\alpha_1^2 = 4/5$, and $\alpha_4^2 = 2/5$. The feasibility of the next solution will, therefore, not be jeopardized if we remove either x^1 or x^4. Computing the marginal profitability of activity 2, we find.

$$\Delta\pi_2 = 4/5 - 4/5 = 0.$$

The above equation tells us that the introduction of x^2 into the solution will not increase the value of the profit function, and we are, therefore, just as well off leaving x^2 outside. Let us, then, try x^3. The relevant linear combination is given by

$$\alpha_4^3 + \alpha_1^3 = 3,$$
$$\alpha_1^3 = 1,$$

so that $\alpha_1^3 = 1$, and $\alpha_4^3 = 2$. The marginal profitability of activity 3 is given by

$$\underset{3}{\Delta\pi} = 2 - 1 = 1 > 0,$$

indicating that the substitution of x^3 for either x^1 or x^4 will increase the level of profit. In order to select the activity to be replaced, we apply the rule

$$x^4/\alpha_4^3 \qquad x^1/\alpha_1^3$$
$$\min (\ 4/2 \ , \quad 14/1 \ ) = 4/2,$$

and consequently we remove x^4.

Basis 3

$$3x^3 + x^1 = 18,$$
$$x^3 + x^1 = 14.$$

The solution to the third basis is $x^1 = 12$, $x^3 = 2$, and it yields a profit of $12 + 2\cdot2 - c = 16 - c$.

If we now pause for a moment and examine the preceding iterations, we find that we have either considered, or actually selected, for inclusion in one of the solutions each of the five variables at least once; nevertheless, we must continue to seek improved solutions, since it is possible that an activity which is removed from the basis at some stage of the iterative process will wind up in the optimal solution. With this possibility in mind, we now compute the marginal profitabilities of the three excluded activities, respectively, starting with activity 2.

Solving first for the αs, we have

$$3\alpha_3^2 + \alpha_1^2 = 6/5,$$
$$\alpha_3^2 + \alpha_1^2 = 4/5,$$

yielding $\alpha_1^2 = 3/5$, and $\alpha_3^2 = 1/5$, and consequently

$$\underset{2}{\Delta\pi} = 4/5 - 3/5 - 2/5 = - 1/5 < 0.$$

For activity 4, we get

$$3\alpha_3^4 + \alpha_1^4 = 1,$$
$$\alpha_3^4 + \alpha_1^4 = 0,$$

so that $\alpha_1^4 = - 1/2$, and $\alpha_3^4 = 1/2$, from which it follows that

$$\underset{4}{\Delta\pi} = 0 + 1/2 - 1 = - 1/2 < 0,$$

and for activity 5,

$$3\alpha_3^5 + \alpha_1^5 = 0,$$
$$\alpha_3^5 + \alpha_1^5 = 1,$$

hence $\alpha_1^5 = 3/2$, $\alpha_3^5 = -1/2$, and so

$$\Delta\pi_5 = 0 - 3/2 + 1 = -1/2 < 0.$$

Since all the excluded activities have negative marginal profitabilities, we are entitled to conclude that the solution of the third basis is the optimal solution, and hence $\bar{x}^1 = 12$, $\bar{x}^3 = 2$, and the maximum profit is $16 - c$ dollars. In this example, the optimal solution has no slack variables, which means that the included activities use up the entire amounts of the two limited inputs.

9.3 IMPUTED VALUES

In problems in which the firm is faced with restrictions on the available amounts of the inputs, it is often of interest to compute the "cost" of these restrictions. We are not referring here to any direct expenses incurred by the firm, but to the profit which the firm must forgo as a result of the input limitations. More specifically, we may ask the following question: "What would be the change in the firm's profit if the available amount of input k were increased by one unit?" This potential change in profit is referred to as the *imputed value* of one unit of input k, and it may also be thought of as the highest price that the firm would be willing to pay for an additional unit of that input. It is important to note that the imputed value is not the same as the market price of the input, or any other type of cost that the firm may assign to a limited input when computing the net revenue associated with the various activities. Since the imputed value of an input cannot be observed in the same way, for instance, as a market price, it is sometimes also called a *shadow price*.

The total imputed value of input k is obtained by multiplying the imputed value of one unit of the input by the total amount used of that input. Thus, if v^k denotes the imputed value of one unit of input k, and V^k the *total* imputed value of that input, then we define

$$(9.29a) \qquad V^k = v^k \sum_{j=1}^{m} a_{kj}\bar{x}^j, \qquad k = 1, 2, \ldots, m,$$

where bars denote the levels of the activities in the optimal solution, and the activities in the optimal solution are numbered from 1 to m. One of the properties of an optimal solution to a linear programming problem is the fact that the sum of all the total imputed values of the inputs is equal to gross profit, i.e., profit exclusive of fixed cost. Formally,

$$(9.30) \qquad \sum_{k=1}^{m} V^k = \pi + c,$$

the proof of which is as follows.

We may assume, without loss of generality, that the firm uses the entire amount available of each input, so that we can restate (9.29a) as

(9.29b) $$V^k = v^k b_k, \qquad k = 1, 2, ..., m.$$

The equivalence of the two definitions given in (9.29) stems from the fact (to be proved later) that if the firm is not using all the available amount of some input, that is, if $\sum_{j=1}^{m} a_{kj} \bar{x}^j < b_k$ for some k, then $v^k = 0$, in which case it makes no difference (as far as the definition of V^k is concerned) what number is being multiplied by v^k.

Strictly speaking, if the available amount of input k is increased by one unit, then it may happen that the new optimal solution will require a different set of activities. Since condition (9.30) is to be proved for the solution which is optimal with respect to the original input restrictions, we shall define v^k as the rate of change in the profit level due to an infinitesimal increase in b_k; that is,

(9.31) $$v^k = \frac{d\pi}{db_k}.$$

Since the optimal solution depends on the available amounts of the inputs, we can think of the $\bar{x}^j$ as functions of the b_k. If we then differentiate the profit function (9.5b) after inserting into it the optimal solution, we get

(9.32) $$\frac{d\pi}{db_k} = \sum_{j=1}^{m} r^j \frac{d\bar{x}^j}{db_k}, \qquad k = 1, 2, ..., m.$$

The optimal solution does, of course, satisfy the input restrictions, so that we also have

(9.33) $$\sum_{j=1}^{m} a_{ij} \bar{x}^j = b_i, \qquad i = 1, 2, ..., m.$$

[Eqs. (9.33) are obtained from (9.8) after the insertion of the optimal values of the activities.] Differentiating (9.33), we get

(9.34) $$\sum_{j=1}^{m} a_{ij} \frac{d\bar{x}^j}{db_k} = \xi_i, \qquad i, k, = 1, 2, ..., m,$$

where $\xi_i = 1$ for $i = k$, and $\xi_i = 0$ otherwise. Solving for the derivatives in (9.34) by Cramer's rule, we get

(9.35) $$\frac{d\bar{x}^j}{db_k} = \frac{D_{kj}}{D}, \qquad j, k = 1, 2, ..., m,$$

where D is the determinant of the matrix of the coefficients a_{ij}, and D_{kj} is a cofactor. Therefore, from (9.35), (9.32), and (9.31), we have

$$(9.36) \qquad v^k = \sum_{j=1}^{m} r^j \frac{D_{kj}}{D}, \qquad k = 1, 2, ..., m,$$

so that

$$(9.37) \qquad v^k b_k = b_k \sum_{j=1}^{m} r^j \frac{D_{kj}}{D}, \qquad k = 1, 2, ..., m,$$

and

$$(9.38) \qquad \sum_{k=1}^{m} V^k = \sum_{k=1}^{m} v^k b_k = \sum_{k=1}^{m} b_k \sum_{j=1}^{m} r^j \frac{D_{kj}}{D}.$$

Solving now for the optimal values of the activities from (9.33), we can write

$$(9.39) \qquad \bar{x}^j = \sum_{k=1}^{m} b_k \frac{D_{kj}}{D}, \qquad j = 1, 2, ... m,$$

which, in turn, implies

$$(9.40) \qquad \bar{x}^j r^j = r^j \sum_{k=1}^{m} b_k \frac{D_{kj}}{D}, \qquad j = 1, 2, ..., m,$$

and summing over all j gives

$$(9.41) \qquad \sum_{j=1}^{m} \bar{x}^j r^j = \sum_{j=1}^{m} r^j \sum_{k=1}^{m} b_k \frac{D_{kj}}{D}.$$

Since the rhs's of (9.38) and (9.41) are equal, we see that, in view of (9.5b), condition (9.30) is satisfied.

Finally, we show that when the optimal solution requires less than the maximum amount available of some input, then the imputed value of that input is zero. For simplicity, let us assume that the optimal solution uses less than b_1 units of input 1. In that case, one of the activities in the optimal solution is a slack variable, and we shall denote it by x^m. The column vector of the technological coefficients of the slack variable x^m has the coefficient one in the first row (because we assumed an "excess supply" of input 1), and zeros elsewhere. From this it follows that $D_{1j} = 0$, $j = 1, 2, ..., m - 1$ (since each of these cofactors has one column all of whose components are zero). And since the net revenue of the slack variable (r^m) is also zero, we get, using (9.36)

$$v^1 = \sum_{j=1}^{m} r^j \frac{D_{1j}}{D} = 0.$$

9.4 DUALITY

Given any linear programming problem, there exists another which bears a unique relationship to it. The original problem is usually referred to as the *primal*, and the associated problem as the *dual*. (Whether a particular problem is a primal or a dual depends, of course, entirely on the interest of the re-searcher; which is to say, there is nothing inherent in the formal structure of a linear programming problem which makes it either a primal or a dual.) It will be recalled that in the primal problem discussed in the preceding sections, we were trying to find numbers x^j which make the expression

$$\sum_{j=1}^{n} x^j r^j - c$$

as *large* as possible, but which at the same time satisfy the restrictions

$$\sum_{j=1}^{n} a_{ij} x^j \leqslant b_i, \qquad i = 1, 2, ..., m,$$

$$x^j \geqslant 0, \qquad j = 1, 2, ..., n.$$

In the above problem, the coefficients r^j, c, a_{ij}, and b_i are known. In the dual problem associated with the above primal, we seek a set of numbers v^i which make the expression

(9.42) $$\sum_{i=1}^{m} v^i b_i$$

as *small* as possible, subject to the restrictions

(9.43) $$\sum_{i=1}^{m} a_{ij} v^i \geqslant r^j, \qquad j = 1, 2, ..., n,$$

(9.44) $$v^i \geqslant 0, \qquad i = 1, 2, ..., m.$$

One aspect of the intimate relationship between the primal and the dual is the fact that both problems involve the same set of known coefficients, but at the same time it should be observed that they play a different role in each problem. Specifically, the coefficients of the objective function of the primal appear as the limiting values of the constraints of the dual, whereas the limiting values of the constraints of the primal constitute the coefficients of the objective function of the dual; the coefficients multiplying the variables in the constraints (a_{ij}) are the same in both problems.

Now, the fact that we have denoted the unknowns of the dual problem by the symbols v^i is not accidental; we did so because, like the v^i in Section 9.3, they represent the imputed values of the inputs appearing in the primal problem. This can easily be demonstrated by making use of an important property of linear programming problems according to which the existence of an optimal solution to the primal problem implies the existence of an optimal solution to the dual. It is, furthermore, known that if activity x^k (which is not a slack variable) is included in the optimal solution to the primal, then the kth constraint in the dual holds as an equality. Thus, if we assume that there are no slack variables in the optimal solution to the primal, and the variables included in that solution are numbered from 1 to m, then the constraints to the dual can be written as

$$(9.45a) \qquad \sum_{i=1}^{m} a_{ij} v^i = r^j, \qquad j = 1, 2, ..., m,$$

$$(9.45b) \qquad \sum_{i=1}^{m} a_{ij} v^i \geqslant r^j, \qquad j = m + 1, m + 2, ..., n.$$

Solving for the v^k from (9.45a), we get

$$(9.46) \qquad v^k = \sum_{j=1}^{m} r^j \frac{D_{jk}}{D}, \qquad k = 1, 2, ..., m.$$

Note that the matrix of coefficients underlying the system of Eqs. (9.45a) is the transpose of the matrix underlying system (9.33) (because, in the former system, the summation is over the index i, and in the latter, over j), therefore, $D_{jk} = D_{kj}$, and hence (9.46) is identical to (9.36).

In the event of one of the activities in the optimal solution to the primal, say x^m, being a slack variable, then the mth constraint in (9.45) is of the form

$$\sum_{i=1}^{m} a_{im} v^i \geqslant 0 \qquad \text{(since } r^m = 0\text{)},$$

which, however, is automatically satisfied since all the a_{ij} and v^i are already required to be nonnegative; consequently, this constraint can be dropped from the system, and doing so places no fewer effective restrictions on the v^i than would otherwise be the case. But if x^m is a slack variable, then $v^m = 0$, so that in this case (9.45a) is reduced to an $(m - 1)$-dimensional system, and the identity between (9.46) and (9.36) still holds.

It is now obvious that the objective function of the dual problem represents the total value of the limited inputs appearing in the primal problem. Since that latter quantity has already been shown [in (9.30)] to be equal to the maximum level of gross profit, we have further evidence of the interesting relationship between the two problems: the values of the two objective functions are the same when evaluated at their respective optimal solutions. (Strictly speaking, this is true only if we ignore the fixed cost c. We should, however, be quite willing to do so since the addition of a constant to a function has no effect whatsoever on the values of the variables at which the function attains a maximum or a minimum.)

With these results in mind, the dual problem may be interpreted as an attempt to find a set of numbers (imputed values) which will make the total imputed values of all the limited inputs as small as possible. But what is the reason for desiring such numbers? One way of answering this question is to suggest that what the firm is trying to do is to allocate its (gross) profit (as a matter of accounting) among the inputs it is using. After all, it is the use of these inputs in the various activities that creates whatever profit the firm is earning, and it therefore makes sense that the firm should want to determine what share of the profit it ought to assign to each input. However, this distribution of profit is meant not simply to allocate total profit among the inputs, but rather to allocate the profit *from each activity* to the *inputs used in that activity*. In other words, the values imputed to the various inputs must be such that the cost of each activity, evaluated in terms of the imputed values of the inputs used in that activity, should exhaust the profit from that activity.

This last condition explains the reason for the constraints of the dual. To see this, recall that a_{ij} is the amount of input i necessary to operate activity j at the unit level. Then the cost of input i (in terms of its imputed value) required for one unit of activity j is $a_{ij}v^i$, and the cost incurred by $\bar{x}^j$ units (the optimal level) of activity j is equal to $a_{ij}v^i \bar{x}^j$. Summing over all inputs we get $\sum_{i=1}^{m} a_{ij}v^i \bar{x}^j$, which represents the total imputed input cost of activity j operated at the optimal level. The profit from activity j, on the other hand, is simply $\bar{x}^j r^j$. Hence, the condition requiring the total imputed input cost of each activity to account for the total profit from that activity can be stated as

$$\sum_{i=1}^{m} a_{ij} v^i \bar{x}^j \geq \bar{x}^j r^j, \qquad j = 1, 2, ..., n.$$

Dividing both sides of these inequalities by $\bar{x}^j$, we get conditions (9.43). The reason for stating this condition in terms of inequalities (rather than equalities) is essentially mathematical, and has to do with the fact that the number of activities may in general be different from the number of inputs. However, as was pointed out earlier, if there are no slack variables in the solution to the primal, then the first m constraints in (9.43) hold as equations, so that for each activity, the imputed input cost is exactly equal to the profit. (In fact, this last result is true even if there are slack variables in the optimal solution to the primal.)

Aside from their purely economic significance, the duality properties have certain practical implications which may turn out to be of considerable help from the computational point of view. For example, if the primal problem has relatively few activities, but a large number of constraints, then the basic solutions will also involve a large number of variables (though many of them will be slack variables), since the dimensionality of the basic solution is the same as the number of constraints. The dual of that primal, however, will in general be easier to solve, since it will have only as many constraints as the number of real activities in the primal.

Solving the dual instead of the primal may in many situations provide all the desired information. The solution to the dual indicates not only the maximum value of the objective function of the primal, but it also tells us which of the activities are included in the optimal solution to the primal, and which, if any, of the inputs are not fully used up. In many problems, of course, the optimal values of the activities themselves are part of the desired information, but once the activities that are included in the optimal solution to the primal are identified (by inspection of the solution to the dual), one can set up a system of equations such as (9.33), and solve it for the $\bar{x}^j$. As a matter of fact, if the computational algorithm for the dual problem is set up properly, the values of the $\bar{x}^j$ are obtained as one of the outputs of the process by which the optimal values of the v^i are computed.

Example 9.2. It may be instructive to consider here the dual to the primal problem presented in Example 9.1. This dual takes the following form:

Minimize
$$V = 18v^1 + 14v^2,$$

subject to

$$v^1 + \quad v^2 \geqslant 1,$$
$$6/5v^1 + 4/5v^2 \geqslant 4/5,$$
$$3v^1 + \quad v^2 \geqslant 2,$$
$$v^1, \quad v^2, \geqslant 0.$$

This problem is, of course, computationally more difficult to solve than the primal, because it has three (rather than two) constraints, and so the basic solutions involve three simultaneous equations. We shall spare ourselves these efforts, and rather than apply the simplex method directly to this dual (which is, of course, a legitimate approach, since the dual is just another linear programming problem), we shall obtain the solution by making use of the solution to the primal.

We note that the optimal solution to the primal problem includes activities 1 and 3, therefore the contraints of the dual can be written as

$$v^1 + \quad v^2 = 1,$$
$$6/5v^1 + 4/5v^2 \geqslant 4/5,$$
$$3v^1 + \quad v^2 = 2.$$

The two equations in the above system can now be used to solve for v^1 and v^2. This gives $\bar{v}^1 = 1/2$, and $\bar{v}^2 = 1/2$, and so $V = 9 + 7 = 16$, which is equal to the maximum level of gross profit. We also observe that the optimal values of v^1 and v^2 satisfy the inequality constraint in the above system (which was not used for finding the solution).

BIBLIOGRAPHICAL NOTES

The formulation of the general linear programming problem, and the development of the simplex method, is due to G. B. Dantzig. The results of Dantzig's work were first published in his short paper "Maximization of A Linear Function of Variables Subject to Linear Inequalities," in T. C. Koopmans (ed.), *Activity Analysis of Production and Allocation* (Cowles Foundation Monograph No. 13), New York: Wiley, 1951, pp. 339-347. Since then, the general theory of linear models has undergone further developments and refinements, and these are found in most texts on the subject. Two examples are: D. Gale, *The Theory of Linear Economic Models,* New York: McGraw-Hill, 1960, and G. Hadley, *Linear Programming,* Reading: Addison-Wesley, 1962. The application of linear models to economic problems has been especially emphasized in R. Dorfman, P.A. Samuelson and R. M. Solow, *Linear Programming and Economic Analysis,* New York: McGraw-Hill, 1958, and K. E. Boulding and W. A. Spivey, *Linear Programming and the Theory of the Firm,* New York: Macmillan, 1960.

CHAPTER 10

THE BASIC THEORY
OF CONSUMER BEHAVIOR

The theory of the consumer and the theory of the firm have a great deal in common. Perhaps the most important aspect of this similarity is the fact that both theories are based on the fundamental assumption that the decision maker's actions are motivated by his desire to attain a certain objective. In the case of the firm, it was assumed that the objective is the maximization of profit over a typical planning period. Thus, it was assumed that, of any two feasible levels of output, a firm always prefers, and chooses, that level of output which yields the higher profit. The profit-maximization assumption, therefore, provides us with an explanation of the actual choice of output made by the firm under different sets of circumstances. Likewise, the purpose of the theory of consumer behavior is to find an explanation of the consumer's choice of action under a variety of environmental conditions.

Most basic models of consumer behavior deal with the consumer's role as a buyer of goods, where the term "goods" may also include services. Consequently, our task here is to construct a model which will explain, for instance, why the consumer chooses one particular bundle of goods, and not some other bundle. As it turns out, in the construction of such a model one encounters certain difficulties which do not arise (or only to a lesser degree) in the context of the theory of the firm. These difficulties derive from (a) the fact that the object of choice is not a single quantity (like the level of output of a single-product firm), but a multidimensional bundle of goods, and (b) the subjective nature of some of the factors which play a central part in the consumer's decision-making process. We find it, therefore, appropriate to begin this chapter with a brief discussion of some of the central concepts in the theory of the consumer.

10.1 THE NATURE OF PREFERENCES

As was mentioned above, the object of the consumer's choice (in the basic consumer model) is a bundle of goods. By the term "bundle of goods" is meant a collection of different goods, the quantity of each good in the collection being given. As for notation, if there are n goods denoted by x^1, x^2,

..., x^n, then a bundle is formally represented by the vector $x = (x^1, x^2, ..., x^n)$. When it is necessary to distinguish one bundle from others, a particular bundle may be identified by subscripts (or other auxiliary notation) such as $x_0 = (x_0^1, x_0^2, ..., x_0^n)$. By the nature of the problem, bundles in our model will contain only nonnegative quantities. At times we shall also use equality and inequality notation to compare bundles (vectors). These symbols (when applied to vectors) will have the following meaning:

Vectors		Numbers		
$x_0 = x_1$	means	$x_0^i = x_1^i$	for all	i.
$x_0 \geqq x_1$	means	$x_0^i \geqslant x_1^i$	for all	i.
$x_0 \geqslant x_1$	means	$x_0^i \geqslant x_1^i$	for all	i, and
		$x_0^i > x_1^i$	for at least one	i.
$x_0 > x_1$	means	$x_0^i > x_1^i$	for all	i.

The goods which the consumer purchases in the market are ordinarily meant to satisfy the consumer's (or his dependants') consumption needs rather than to serve as a means from which he derives a monetary gain (as in the case of the inputs purchased by a producer). Thus, in considering any two different bundles of goods, the consumer chooses that bundle which, in his own eyes and according to his own personal preferences, will best fulfill his needs. In general, a person other than the consumer in question, by merely comparing the contents of any two bundles, will not be able to tell which of the two bundles the consumer prefers; the determination of the preferred bundle must necessarily be made by the consumer himself, since it is entirely a matter of subjective choice. While we do not intend to embark here on an extensive study of the psychological factors determining the consumer's structure of preferences, a few basic assumptions about this matter need to be made to facilitate the construction of the model, and to be able to derive hypotheses from it.

The first assumption (by no means a trivial one, despite its innocuous appearance) is designed to rule out the possibility of indecision on the part of the consumer. By which we mean that if the consumer is shown any two bundles of goods, say bundles x_0 and x_1, and is asked to state his preference, he will never answer (given ample time for contemplation): "I don't know." What we expect him to say is one of the following:

a) "I prefer bundle x_0 to bundle x_1."

b) "I prefer bundle x_1 to bundle x_0."

c) "I am indifferent between the two bundles."

Note that the case of indifference (c) is not the same as indecision, which we have ruled out by assuming that the consumer will always be able to give one of the above three answers. Now, it is possible (and perhaps formally more elegant) to reduce the above set of alternative answers from three to two. Thus, if either (a) or (c) is the case, the consumer will describe his preference correctly by saying that, from his point of view, "bundle x_0 is at least as good (or desirable) as bundle x_1," and if either (b) or (c) holds, the consumer can express his preference by saying "bundle x_1 is at least as good as bundle x_0."

It will be convenient to denote the phrase "is at least as good as" by the symbol $\succsim$, so that if the consumer either prefers the bundle x_0 to the bundle x_1, or is indifferent between them, we write "$x_0 \succsim x_1$." If the consumer actually prefers x_0 to x_1, then his preference is described correctly by the statement: "$x_0 \succsim x_1$ and not $x_1 \succsim x_0$," which may also be stated in the shorter form "$x_0 \succ x_1$"; if the consumer is indifferent between x_0 and x_1, we write "$x_0 \succsim x_1$ and $x_1 \succsim x_0$," or simply, "$x_0 \sim x_1$."

The first assumption about the consumer's preferences can now be stated formally as follows:

A.10.1   Completeness. *Given any set of bundles, then for every two bundles x_0 and x_1 in that set, either $x_0 \succsim x_1$, or $x_1 \succsim x_0$.*

The second—the *transitivity* assumption—states that if bundle x_0 is at least as good as bundle x_1, and bundle x_1 is at least as good as bundle x_2, then bundle x_0 is at least as good as bundle x_2. In some sense, the transitivity assumption imposes a certain consistency restriction on the consumer's preferences. Formally, we state:

A.10.2   Transitivity. *For any three bundles x_0, x_1, and x_2, if $x_0 \succsim x_1$, and $x_1 \succsim x_2$, then $x_0 \succsim x_2$.*

Broadly speaking, Assumptions A.10.1 and A.10.2 impose a ranking on the bundles which makes it possible to order them in accordance with the consumer's preferences. In fact, any set (not just bundles of goods) whose elements satisfy assumptions such as A.10.1 and A.10.2 is said to be *completely preordered*. More precisely, in the present example the set of all bundles is completely preordered by the relation $\succsim$; or, stated differently, the relation $\succsim$ constitutes a *complete preordering* on the set of all bundles.* Thus, the two assumptions made so far amount to postulating the existence of a complete preordering on the set of all bundles.

We must now add another assumption to the above two which may, if you will, be regarded as a concession to human nature; it is the formal recognition of the fact that human beings are basically greedy. In the context of the theory of consumer behavior, this property is represented by the assumption

---

* The preordering is said to be "complete" because the relation $\succsim$ (or its negation) holds between *any two* bundles in the set. Sometimes, a preordering such as the above is also referred so as "weak," because of the inclusion of indifference.

that of any pair of bundles, the consumer always strictly prefers the "larger" of the two. By the term "larger" we mean that the bundle has more of at least one good, and no less of any good, than the other (i.e., "smaller") bundle. Using the inequality notation for vectors introduced earlier, we say that x_0 is "larger" than x_1 (or x_1 is "smaller" than x_0) if, and only if, $x_0 \geqq x_1$. The third assumption about the consumer's preferences can, therefore, be stated as:

A.10.3 Greediness. *For any two bundles x_1 and x_1, if $x_0 \geqq x_1$, then $x_0 \} x_1$.*

It may be noted here that, in general, the converse of A.10.3 need not hold; that is, a consumer may prefer a bundle to another even if the preferred bundle is not "larger" than the other. Of course, the preferred bundle cannot be "smaller" than the other bundle, since that would violate the greediness assumption. What this means, then, is that a bundle x_0 may be preferred to bundle x_1 when neither $x_0 \geqq x_1$ nor $x_1 \geqq x_0$. In such a case, we say that (as far as "size" is concerned), x_0 and x_1 are *noncomparabie* (but, as far as preference is concerned, any two bundles are always comparable by virtue of A.10.1).*

These are the substantive assumptions we make about the consumer's structure of preferences. They are really quite general, and do not place unduly restrictive conditions on the psychological factors which are involved in these considerations. Essentially, we have assumed that the consumer knows his preferences, that, in some sense, preferences are consistent, and that the consumer always prefers to have "more" rather than "less."

There remains one more-or-less formal aspect of consumer preferences that needs to be examined. We pointed out earlier that Assumptions A.10.1 and A.10.2 make it possible to order all bundles in a way which reflects the consumer's preferences. It is, therefore, natural to ask whether it is also possible to attach numbers to all possible bundles in such a way that for any two bundles it would be true that the consumer always prefers the bundle with the larger number. In general (i.e., if there are infinitely many bundles), Assumptions A.10.1 and A.10.2 do not guarantee this possibility. The reason for our being interested in this question is, of course, that if such numbering were possible, the consumer's decision rule could be conveniently described by saying that, of any given set of bundles, the consumer always chooses that bundle whose number is larger than (or at least as large as) that of any other bundle in the set. Since the analysis of consumer behavior is greatly simplified if a numbering scheme of the above kind can be carried out, we shall make the

---

* The above example of two noncomparable vectors shows that the set of all (two-dimensional or higher) vectors cannot be completely preordered by the relation $\geqq$ ("is greater than"). Hence, the latter relation is only a *partial* ordering on the set of all vectors.

additional assumption that the consumer's system of preferences is indeed of a type which makes that possible.

The existence of a numbering scheme really means the existence of a rule of correspondence, or functional relationship, whose domain is the set of all possible bundles (which, in general, is some region in an n-dimensional space) and whose range is the set of real numbers. If such a function exists, then we say that the system of preferences is *representable*, and the function itself is referred to as a *utility function*. Hence our last basic assumption:

A.10.4 Representability. *The consumer's system of preferences is representable.**

Since the utility function embodies all the properties of the preference system that are relevant to the analysis of consumer behavior, it is not necessary to include in the formal model both the preference structure itself (such as Assumptions A.10.1 and A.10.2) and the utility function; since the utility function, by its very nature, reflects all the properties of the preference structure, it is quite capable of fully representing the consumer's preferences in the model. (Indeed, discussions about consumer behavior quite often begin with the specification of a utility function without making any reference to the underlying structure of preferences.) At the same time, we cannot take just any function and call it a utility function; in order to qualify as an admissible utility function, a function must possess certain basic properties. These will be discussed in the following section.

10.2 THE UTILITY FUNCTION

A function can be a utility function only if it is an *order-preserving* function. In the present context, the utility function must preserve the ranking of all bundles in accordance with the consumer's preferences. This condition requires (as we have already mentioned earlier) that, given any two bundles, the function should assign a higher value to the preferred bundle; if the consumer is indifferent between the two bundles, then the function must assign the same value to each bundle. If we write the utility function as

$$(10.1) \qquad u = \phi(x^1, x^2, ..., x^n),$$

where u is referred to as the *utility index*, then for any two bundles x_0 and x_1, we require

$$(10.2a) \qquad \phi(x_0) > \phi(x_1) \qquad \text{if and only if} \qquad x_0 \} x_1,$$

$$(10.2b) \qquad \phi(x_0) = \phi(x_1) \qquad \text{if and only if} \qquad x_0 \sim x_1.$$

---

* The additional restriction which has to be imposed on the preferences in order to guarantee the existence of a utility function is a certain continuity condition.

Taken together, the above two conditions imply

(10.3) $\phi(x_0) \geqslant \phi(x_1)$ if and only if $x_0 \genfrac{}{}{0pt}{}{\}{\succeq} x_1.$

It may be remarked parenthetically that the relation $\geqslant$ constitutes a complete ordering of the set of real numbers; that is, it satisfies assumptions such as A.10.1 and A.10.2. This can easily be verified. If a and b are any two real numbers, then it is obviously true that either $a \geqslant b$, or $b \geqslant a$; and for any three real numbers a, b, and c it is true that $a \geqslant b$ and $b \geqslant c$ imply $a \geqslant c$. The relevance of this observation to the present discussion is that if the real number system did not possess this property (of being completely ordered by the relation $\geqslant$), then we would not be able to use real-valued functions as utility functions.

In the absence of further information about the consumer's preferences we cannot say much more about the properties of the utility function. We did, however, make one assumption about the general nature of preferences which places another restriction on the function ϕ. According to Assumption A.10.3 the consumer always prefers a "larger" bundle to a "smaller" one, and therefore the utility function must assign a higher value to the "larger" of any two bundles. To put it differently, Assumption A.10.3 and the order-preserving property in (10.2) together imply the following condition:
For any two bundles x_0 and x_1,

(10.4)   if $x_0 \geqslant x_1$, then $\phi(x_0) > \phi(x_1)$.

[Note that in the first part of the statement in (10.4) the inequality notation applies to *vectors*, while in the second part it compares *numbers*.] Assuming (mainly for mathematical convenience) that the function ϕ is continuously differentiable, then condition (10.4) implies

(10.5) $\phi_i > 0,$ $i = 1, 2, ..., n,$

where $\phi_i = \partial \phi / \partial x^i$. The function ϕ_i is usually referred to as the *marginal utility* of good i, so that (10.5) can be interpreted as requiring the marginal utilities of all goods to be positive.

Indifference Surface. We stated earlier [in condition (10.2b)] that the utility function must assign the same value to all bundles between which the consumer is indifferent. If we consider one such set of bundles and assign to it the utility index u_0, then this set of bundles is defined by the utility function after replacing u by u_0; that is,

(10.6) $u_0 = \phi(x^1, x^2, ..., x^n).$

Equation (10.6) defines an n-dimensional surface which is called an *indifference surface*. In the special case in which the utility function has only two arguments, the surface is 2-dimensional, and is called an indifference *curve*. In the latter case, (10.6) may be written as

(10.7) $$u_0 = \phi(x^1, x^2),$$

and the indifference curve can be stated in an explicit form such as

(10.8) $$x^1 = \psi(x^2; u_0).$$

From the mathematical point of view, the indifference curve is identical to the concept of an isoquant used in the theory of production, and hence the properties of indifference curves can be analyzed by the same method that we followed in Section 3.1, with respect to isoquants. Substituting for x^1 in (10.7) from (10.8), we get

(10.9) $$u_0 = \phi[\psi(x^2; u_0), x^2],$$

which, upon differentiation, yields

(10.10) $$0 = \phi_1 \psi' + \phi_2,$$

where $\psi' = d\psi/dx^2$. From (10.10) we immediately have

(10.11) $$\psi' = -\frac{\phi_2}{\phi_1},$$

which by virtue of (10.5) is negative. Thus, like isoquants, indifference curves have negative slopes. Since the slope of the indifference curve is equal to the rate at which the two goods must be substituted for one another, so as to keep the utility index constant, we refer to it as the *marginal rate of substitution* (MRS).

The fact that the slope of the indifference curve is negative does not, of course, tell us anything about the behavior of the MRS as we move along the indifference curve. In order to study the change in the MRS as we increase the amount of x^2 slightly, we differentiate (10.11). This gives

(10.12) $$\psi'' = \frac{d(-\phi_2/\phi_1)}{dx^2} = -\left[\frac{\phi_{21}\psi' + \phi_{22}}{\phi_1} - \frac{\phi_2(\phi_{11}\psi' + \phi_{12})}{\phi_1^2} \right].$$

Substituting for ψ' in (10.12) from (10.11), and rearranging terms, we get

(10.13) $$\psi'' = -\frac{1}{\phi_1^3}(\phi_{11}\phi_2^2 - 2\phi_{12}\phi_1\phi_2 + \phi_{22}\phi_1^2).$$

Since we have made no assumptions about the signs of the second-order partial derivatives of the utility function, it is clear that the sign of ψ'' is indeterminate. It is not unreasonable, and certainly very convenient, to assume that $\psi'' > 0$. Since $\psi' < 0$, the condition $\psi'' > 0$ implies that, as we move down an indifference curve, its slope becomes less in absolute value. For this reason, the condition $\psi'' > 0$ is referred to as *diminishing marginal rate of substitution*.

If we draw an indifference curve on a 2-dimensional diagram, then diminishing marginal rate of substitution implies that the graph of the indifference curve, like that of the isoquant (Fig. 3.1), is strictly convex to the origin. Another way of describing this property is to say that, if one draws a line between any two distinct points on the indifference curve, then any point on that line segment, except the endpoints, lies above the indifference curve. In other words, points in the interior of the above line segment belong to indifference curves associated with higher levels of utility. If x_0 and x_1 are two distinct points on an indifference curve, and x_2 is a point on the interior of the line segment joining x_0 and x_1, then strict convexity implies $\phi(x_2) > \phi(x_0)$ $[= \phi(x_1)]$. For an illustration, see Fig. 10.1. However, a point between x_0 and x_1 is defined by the expression $\alpha x_0 + (1 - \alpha)x_1$, where $0 < \alpha < 1$, therefore strict convexity holds if for any two distinct points x_0 and x_1 on a given indifference curve the inequality $\phi[\alpha x_0 + (1 - \alpha)x_1] > \phi(x_0)$ is satisfied for all α between zero and one.*

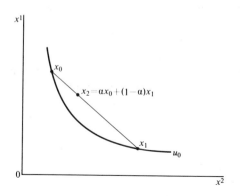

Figure 10.1

If there are n $(n > 2)$ goods in the utility function, then the set of bundles which are associated with the same level of utility constitutes an n-dimensional surface. Of course, for $n > 3$ it becomes quite difficult to present an indifference surface with the aid of a 2-dimensional diagram: however, the condition of strict convexity is easily generalized, and it is in fact the same as that given at the end of the last paragraph, considering x_0 and x_1 as n-dimensional vectors. If $n > 2$, then diminishing marginal rate of substitution is assumed to hold between all possible pairs of goods, but this assumption is not quite

* If x is a vector, and α a scalar (number), then αx means that every component of x is multiplied by α; that is, $\alpha x = (\alpha x^1, \alpha x^2, \ldots, \alpha x^n)$.

sufficient to guarantee strict convexity of the indifference surface. Sufficient conditions for strict convexity are the following determinantal conditions:

$$\begin{vmatrix} \phi_{11} & \phi_{12} & y^1 \\ \phi_{21} & \phi_{22} & y^2 \\ y^1 & y^2 & 0 \end{vmatrix} > 0, \quad \begin{vmatrix} \phi_{11} & \phi_{12} & \phi_{13} & y^1 \\ \phi_{21} & \phi_{22} & \phi_{23} & y^2 \\ \phi_{31} & \phi_{32} & \phi_{33} & y^3 \\ y^1 & y^2 & y^3 & 0 \end{vmatrix} < 0, \ldots,$$

(10.14)

$$(-1)^n \begin{vmatrix} \phi_{11} & \phi_{12} & \cdots & \phi_{1n} & y^1 \\ \phi_{21} & \phi_{22} & \cdots & \phi_{2n} & y^2 \\ \vdots & & & & \vdots \\ \phi_{n1} & \phi_{n2} & \cdots & \phi_{nn} & y^n \\ y^1 & y^2 & \cdots & y^n & 0 \end{vmatrix} > 0,$$

where the y^i are any positive numbers, and the inequalities hold for all x.

10.3 UTILITY MAXIMIZATION

As was pointed out earlier, the assumption that the consumer's preferences are representable by a utility function enables us to construct a fairly simple decision model. Since it is assumed that the consumer always chooses the most preferred bundle from any given set of bundles within his reach, then, given his utility function, the consumer's choice can be determined (predicted) by maximizing his utility function over the feasible set. The feasible set may be described in a number of different ways, depending essentially on how the consumer is assumed to receive his purchasing power. Let us assume that the consumer receives a certain level of income (in dollars) in every period of time, but we shall not concern ourselves at this point with the question of how the level of income is determined; from the point of view of the present model, the consumer's income is considered a parameter. In that case, the feasible set consists of all the bundles that the consumer can purchase with the given level of income. If the market prices, which are also parameters, are denoted by p^i, and income is denoted by m, then the feasible set consists of all bundles satisfying

(10.15)
$$\sum_{i=1}^{n} p_0^i x^i \leqslant m_0.$$

The above inequality is known as the consumer's *budget constraint*. Actually, because of the greediness assumption [A.10.3 and Eq. (10.5)], it is quite obvious that the consumer will always spend his entire income, so that we can safely state the budget constraint in the form

$$(10.16) \qquad \sum_{i=1}^{n} p_0^i x^i = m_0.{}^*$$

The problem, then, is to maximize (10.1) subject to (10.16). The Lagrangian form for this problem is

$$(10.17) \qquad \phi(x) + \lambda\left(\sum_{i=1}^{n} p_0^i x^i - m_0\right),$$

and the first-order conditions, assuming a regular interior maximum, are

$$(10.18) \qquad \phi_i + \lambda p_0^i = 0, \qquad i = 1, 2, ..., n,$$

$$(10.19) \qquad \sum_{i=1}^{n} p_0^i x^i - m_0 = 0.$$

If we eliminate λ from (10.18), we get

$$(10.20) \qquad \frac{\phi_i}{\phi_j} = \frac{p_0^i}{p_0^j}, \qquad i, j = 1, 2, ..., n.$$

These are familiar equations of the type which we have encountered before (e.g., in Chapter 3); they state that the MRS between any two goods must be equal to the ratio of their prices. Geometrically speaking, at the optimal bundle, the highest indifference surface in the feasible set must be tangent to the budget plane.

The second-order conditions for this problem involve a series of bordered Hessian determinants; specifically,

$$(10.21)$$

$$\begin{vmatrix} \phi_{11} & \phi_{12} & p^1 \\ \phi_{21} & \phi_{22} & p^2 \\ p^1 & p^2 & 0 \end{vmatrix} > 0, \qquad \begin{vmatrix} \phi_{11} & \phi_{12} & \phi_{13} & p^1 \\ \phi_{21} & \phi_{22} & \phi_{23} & p^2 \\ \phi_{31} & \phi_{32} & \phi_{33} & p^3 \\ p^1 & p^2 & p^3 & 0 \end{vmatrix} < 0, \dots,$$

$$(-1)^n \begin{vmatrix} \phi_{11} & \phi_{12} & \cdots & \phi_{1n} & p^1 \\ \phi_{21} & \phi_{22} & \cdots & \phi_{2n} & p^2 \\ \vdots & & & & \vdots \\ \phi_{n1} & \phi_{n2} & \cdots & \phi_{nn} & p^n \\ p^1 & p^2 & \cdots & p^n & 0 \end{vmatrix} > 0.$$

---

* This formulation does not necessarily exclude the act of saving. In order to permit the consumer to save part of his income, we merely have to specify that one of the x^i denotes the amount saved in the period in question. Of course, if x^j denotes saving (in the form of cash balances), then $p^j = 1$ (ignoring, for the time being, any interest that may be earned).

It may be pointed out that if conditions (10.14) are satisfied, so are conditions (10.21) (because the p^i are positive numbers); that is, if the indifference surfaces are strictly convex, then any tangency point between an indifference surface and a budget plane represents a utility-maximizing bundle relative to the given budget.

Transforming the Utility Function. In our discussion of the utility function, we pointed out that such a function must possess the order-preserving property. This requires, essentially, that the numbers (that is, functional values) which the utility function attaches to various bundles must reflect the order of these bundles in the consumer's structure of preferences. However, the number which the utility function assigns to a particular bundle has no meaning as such. For example, if bundle x_0 is preferred to bundle x_1, then the utility function may assign to these bundles, respectively, any two distinct numbers, the only requirement being that bundle x_0 be given the larger of the two numbers. In other words, we require the utility function only to indicate the *order* of the consumer's preferences, but not, for instance, their intensity. For this reason, it is sometimes referred to as an *ordinal* utility function. This suggests that a consumer's preferences may be represented by more than one utility function; indeed, it can be shown that if there exists one utility function which correctly represents the preferences of a consumer, then there exist many, literally infinitely many, functions which will do just as well.

Given the utility function $u = \phi(x)$, we form a new function by subjecting u to a positive-monotonic transformation; that is, we take any function ω which is defined on the set of all real numbers, and which is monotonically increasing, that is, $\omega' > 0$, and form $w = \omega(u)$. [Basically, the function ω is an order-preserving function, since $\omega(u_0) > \omega(u_1)$ if and only if $u_0 > u_1$.] Substituting for u, we get the new utility function

$$(10.22) \qquad w = \omega[\phi(x)] = \Omega(x)$$

To show that Ω is a legitimate utility function, we shall show that if the consumer is confronted with a certain level of income and a set of prices, his optimal bundle can be found by maximizing either $\phi(x)$ or $\Omega(x)$.

If prices and income are the same as those given in (10.19), then maximizing $\Omega(x)$ subject to (10.19) leads to the first-order conditions

$$(10.23a) \qquad \Omega_i + \lambda p_0^i = 0, \qquad i = 1, 2, ..., n,$$

$$(10.24) \qquad \sum_{i=1}^{n} p_0^i x^i - m_0 = 0.$$

But differentiation of (10.22) with respect to x^i yields

$$(10.25) \qquad \Omega_i = \omega' \phi_i,$$

so that after substituting for Ω_i in (10.23a) from (10.25), we can write (10.23a) as

(10.23b) $\omega'\phi_i + \lambda p_0^i = 0,$ $i = 1, 2, ..., n.$

Eliminating λ from (10.23b), we get

(10.26) $\dfrac{\omega'\phi_i}{\omega'\phi_j} = \dfrac{\phi_i}{\phi_j} = \dfrac{p_0^i}{p_0^j},$ $i, j = 1, 2, ..., n.$

The optimal levels of the x^i can now be found by solving Eqs. (10.24) and (10.26). Since the equations in (10.24) and (10.26) are identical to those in (10.19) and (10.20), we see that the consumer's choice can be determined by maximizing $\Omega(x)$ just as well as by maximizing $\phi(x)$.*

10.4 DEMAND FUNCTIONS

The objective of the theory of consumer behavior is not only to provide a basic explanation of the choice of an optimal bundle, but also to discover any general laws concerning the changes in the consumer's choice following variations in the parameters which characterize the consumer's environment. One of the immediate goals of this analysis is, therefore, the derivation of the consumer's demand functions, and the study of their properties. In the present model, the demand functions are the solutions to the first-order conditions (10.18) and (10.19), expressed as functions of the parameters p^i and m (where the latter are now considered as variables). These functions may be written as

(10.27) $\bar{x}^j = h^j(p^1, p^2, ..., p^n, m),$ $j = 1, 2, ..., n,$

where the bar indicates that the x^j are evaluated at the point satisfying Eqs. (10.18) and (10.19).

10.4.1 Income Effects

Our first problem is to investigate the signs of the derivatives of the demand functions. To do this, we substitute for the x^i in (10.18) and (10.19) from (10.27), and then differentiate the system of equations implicitly with respect to some parameter. First, we differentiate with respect to m. This yields

(10.28) $\displaystyle\sum_{j=1}^{n} \phi_{ij} h_m^j + p^i \dfrac{\partial\lambda}{\partial m} = 0,$ $i = 1, 2, ..., n,$

(10.29) $\displaystyle\sum_{j=1}^{n} p^j h_m^j = 1,$

---

* The demonstration of the invariance of the second-order conditions to a monotonic transformation of the utility function requires a somewhat larger number of manipulations, and therefore is omitted here.

where $h_m^j = \partial h^j / \partial m$. We can solve for the h_m^j by making use of Cramer's rule, and thus get

$$(10.30) \qquad\qquad h_m^j = \frac{D_{n+1,j}}{D},$$

where D is the determinant of the coefficient matrix of system (10.28) and (10.29), and $D_{n+1,j}$ is a typical cofactor. The determinant D is, of course, the same as the $(n+1) \times (n+1)$ Hessian determinant appearing in (10.21), and so its sign, given n, is known. However, the sign of $D_{n+1,j}$ is indeterminate since conditions (10.21) involve only the principal minors, that is, cofactors of diagonal elements, of D.

The derivative h_m^j indicates the rate of change in the purchase of good j with respect to an (infinitesimal) increase in the consumer's income. Our model, therefore, fails to predict whether or not an increase in his income will make the consumer increase his consumption of a particular good. Since the effect of an increase in income may fall into one of three cases, it is customary to classify goods in accordance with the sign of the income effect. According to this classification we say:

If $h_m^j > 0$, then good j is a superior *good (sometimes also referred to as a* normal *good).*

If $h_m^j = 0$, then good j is a neutral *good.*

If $h_m^j < 0$, then good j is an inferior *good.*

It must be remembered, of course, that the h_m^j are themselves functions of the p^i and m, so that a good may be, say, superior for one particular combination of prices and income, and neutral or inferior for another price-income combination. It may further be pointed out that it is not possible for all goods purchased by the consumer to be either neutral or inferior. Earlier, we argued that a utility-maximizing consumer will always spend all of his income, hence, when income is increased, the increment must be spent on some good, and consequently there must necessarily be at least one superior good in the chosen bundle. This conclusion may be verified formally by inspecting Eq. (10.29): since the prices are assumed to be positive, it is obvious that for the equation to be satisfied, some (that is, at least one) h_m^j must be positive.

10.4.2 Price Effects

Turning now to the effects of a change in one of the prices, we differentiate system (10.18) and (10.19) implicitly with respect to p^i, and thus obtain

$$(10.31a) \qquad \sum_{j=1}^{n} \phi_{kj} h_i^j + p^k \frac{\partial \lambda}{\partial p^i} = 0, \qquad k = 1, 2, \ldots, n, \quad k \neq i,$$

(10.31b) $$\sum_{j=1}^{n} \phi_{ij} h_i^j + p^i \frac{\partial \lambda}{\partial p^i} = -\lambda,$$

(10.32) $$\sum_{j=1}^{n} p^j h_i^j = -\bar{x}^i,$$

where $h_i^j = \partial h^j / \partial p^i$. Using Cramer's rule again, we find

(10.33) $$h_i^j = -\lambda \frac{D_{ij}}{D} - \bar{x}^i \frac{D_{n+1,j}}{D},$$

where D and D_{ij} are defined as in (10.30). The sign of h_i^j is clearly indeterminate since the rhs of (10.33) involves cofactors of D whose signs are not restricted by the conditions for utility maximization. Interestingly enough, the indeterminacy of h_i^j holds also for $i = j$; that is, contrary to what is commonly assumed, an increase in the price of a good need not necessarily lead to a reduction in the demand for it. While we cannot predict the sign of h_i^i, we can say something about those goods for which the inequality $h_i^i > 0$ holds. To do so, we examine the expression in Eq. (10.33), letting $j = i$.

Since $D_{ii}/D < 0$ by (10.21), and since $\lambda < 0$ by (10.5) and (10.18), it follows that $-\lambda D_{ii}/D < 0$. Therefore, $h_i^i > 0$ implies $D_{n+1,i}/D < 0$. In view of (10.30), the preceding inequality states that the income effect of the ith good must be negative, hence the ith good is an inferior good according to the classification introduced earlier. The conclusion, therefore, is that if the own-price demand function of good i (that is, h^i as a function of p^i only, all other prices and income being held constant) has a positive slope, then good i is an inferior good. The converse, however, is not necessarily true, that is, if good i is an inferior good, its own-price demand function need not have a positive slope. The reason for this is that, for the latter case to hold, the income effect must be not only negative, but also large enough to offset the effect of the first term on the rhs of (10.33). Formally, $h_i^i > 0$ implies $D_{n+1,i}/D < 0$ as well as $|\bar{x}^i D_{n+1,i}/D| > \lambda D_{ii}/D$. A good whose own-price effect is positive (that is, $h_i^i > 0$ in some range) is sometimes referred to as a *Giffen good*.*

Goods are also classified on the basis of the signs of the cross-price effects. Thus, if $h_i^j > 0$, then a rise in the price of good i will cause the consumer to purchase more of good j. This may be rationalized as follows. Since a rise in the price of good i will lower the demand for good i (assuming it is not a Giffen good), the consumer purchases more of good j, and thereby he is replacing the forgone units of good i by additional units of good j. In this case, good j can be regarded as a substitute for good i. If $h_i^j < 0$, the decrease

---

* After the English economic statistician Sir Robert Giffen, who allegedly observed that a rise in the price of such staples as bread may strain the budget of low-income families to such an extent that they are forced to forgo the consumption of more expensive (and tastier) foods, and consequently consume (and demand) more bread.

in the purchase of good i following a rise in its price is accompanied by a decrease in the purchase of good j. In this case, the diminished consumption of good i calls for a simultaneous diminishing of the consumption of good j, presumably because good j acts as a complement to good i. Formally, this classification may be stated as follows:

If $h_i^j \geq 0$, then good j is a weak gross substitute for good i.

If $h_i^j < 0$, then good j is a gross complement for good i.

The inclusion of the term "weak" in the above classification is meant to indicate the possibility $h_i^j = 0$. The reason for the adjective "gross" will become evident in Section 10.4.4, when the concepts of net substitutes and net complements will be introduced.

One feature of the above classification which is, perhaps, less than satisfactory is the fact that if, for example, good j is a gross substitute (complement) for good i, then, in general good i need not be a gross substitute (complement) for good j. This follows directly from the lack of symmetry between the h_i^j; thus $h_i^j \geq 0$ ($h_i^j < 0$) does not necessarily imply $h_j^i \geq 0$ ($h_j^i < 0$). Therefore, only if $h_i^j \geq 0$ ($h_i^j < 0$) and $h_j^i \geq 0$ ($h_j^i < 0$) is it possible to say that goods i and j are gross substitutes (complements) for one another.

10.4.3 Homogeneity

Let us now look at the expression

$$(10.34) \qquad \sum_{i=1}^{n} h_i^j p^i + h_m^j \, m.$$

Substituting for the h_i^j from (10.33) and for h_m^j from (10.30), we get

$$(10.35a) \qquad \sum_{i=1}^{n} \left(-p^i \lambda \frac{D_{ij}}{D} - p^i \bar{x}^i \frac{D_{n+1,j}}{D} \right) + m \frac{D_{n+1,j}}{D},$$

which may be rewritten as

$$(10.35b) \qquad -\lambda \sum_{i=1}^{n} p^i \frac{D_{ij}}{D} - \frac{D_{n+1,j}}{D} \left(\sum_{i=1}^{n} p^i \bar{x}^i - m \right).$$

The second term in (10.35b) is clearly zero by (10.19), and the first term is zero because it is equal to λ/D times the quantity which is obtained as a result of expanding the determinant D by using the elements of column $n+1$ together with the cofactors of the elements of column j—the so-called *expansion by alien cofactors*. (See the section on cofactors in Chapter 15.) Therefore, the expression in (10.34) vanishes. It follows from Euler's theorem on homogeneous functions (Proposition 15.16) that the demand functions are homogeneous of degree zero in all prices and income. This result can also be inferred from the first-order conditions: multiplying all prices and income by some common factor k leaves Eq. (10.19) unchanged (because k can be factored out, and then multiplying both sides of the equation by $1/k$ reproduces the original equation), and the equations in (10.20) are likewise invariant under equiproportionate changes in prices and income (since the ratios p^i/p^j remain unchanged when each price is multiplied by the same factor).

Since the values of the demand functions do not change when each argument is multiplied by the same factor, we can write the demand functions in slightly different form by multiplying each argument by $1/m$. Then we get

$$(10.36) \quad h^j(p^1, p^2, ..., p^n, m) = h^j\left(\frac{p^1}{m}, \frac{p^2}{m}, ..., \frac{p^n}{m}, 1\right) = \tilde{h}^j(s^1, s^2, ..., s^n),$$

where $s^i = p^i/m$. The quantity s^i represents the *share* of the consumer's income which he has to pay for one unit of good i. Naturally, the $\tilde{h}^j$ are not homogeneous in *their* arguments; that is, multiplying all the s^i by a common factor will, in general, bring about changes in the composition of the consumer's optimal bundle.

The homogeneity property of the demand functions may also be removed if each argument of h^j is multiplied by the reciprocal of one of the prices, say p^n. Then we have

$$(10.37)$$
$$h^j(p^1, p^2, ..., p^n, m) = h^j\left(\frac{p^1}{p^n}, \frac{p^2}{p^n}, ..., \frac{p^{n-1}}{p^n}, 1, \frac{m}{p^n}\right) = \overset{*}{h}{}^j(\overset{*}{p}{}^1, \overset{*}{p}{}^2, ..., \overset{*}{p}{}^{n-1}, \overset{*}{m}),$$

where $\overset{*}{p}{}^i = p^i/p^n$, and $\overset{*}{m} = m/p^n$. When the prices of goods are expressed in units of a particular good, the latter good is called a *numéraire*. Thus, in the above example, we have assumed good n to be the numéraire, and therefore $\overset{*}{p}{}^i$ represents the price of good i in units of the numéraire; that is, $\overset{*}{p}{}^i$ represents the number of units of the numéraire that can be exchanged for one unit of good i. Likewise, $\overset{*}{m}$ represents the consumer's income in units of the numéraire. Naturally, the price of the numéraire in terms of itself is always unity. The functions $\overset{*}{h}{}^j$, like the $\tilde{h}^j$, are not homogeneous.

10.4.4 Compensated Price Changes

In our discussion of the effects of a change in one of the market prices, we paid no explicit attention to the fact that such a change has a direct effect on the purchasing power of the consumer's income. For example, if p^i increases, all other parameters remaining constant, and the consumer desires to leave unchanged his purchases of all goods except the ith, then the increase in p^i will force him to buy less of good i. The opposite will happen if p^i falls. It is effects of this type that one has in mind when one says that a price change affects the consumer's *real* income. Thus, the effects of price variations which we discussed in Section 10.4.2 may, in part, be explained in terms of the concomitant change in the consumer's real income. In the analysis which follows, we shall isolate the change in real income, and investigate the nature of the effects of variations in a market price under conditions in which the consumer's real income is kept constant.

Unfortunately, there exists no ideal definition of the concept of real income, and we shall, therefore, apply the analysis to each of two different definitions that have been used in the literature. We shall start by constructing an example involving a discrete change in price, and analyze it with the aid of a diagram.

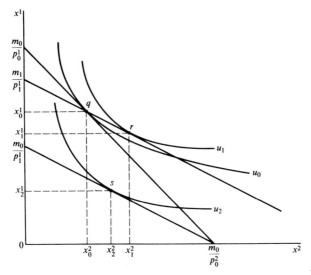

Figure 10.2

In our example, the utility function has only two arguments, x^1 and x^2, and the initial prices and income are p_0^1, p_0^2, and m_0, respectively. The initial optimal bundle is characterized by point q in Fig. 10.2, at which indifference curve u_0 is tangent to the relevant budget line. The price of x^1 is now increased from p_0^1 to p_1^1, causing a shift in the x^1-intercept of the budget line from m_0/p_0^1 to m_0/p_1^1. Consequently, the consumer moves from point q to point s. Now, to determine the change in real income due to the above increase in p^1, we shall say (define) that the consumer's real income is constant so long as he is able to purchase the intial bundle. Obviously, with his income being m_0 dollars, the consumer is no longer in a position to purchase the bundle represented by point q. To offset the loss in real income due to the rise in p^1, the consumer must be given a compensatory increase in nominal income. In the present example, he must be given an amount which is just enough to shift the budget line to the right until it goes through point q. If the consumer's adjusted level of income is denoted by m_1, then the adjusted budget line goes through the intercepts m_1/p_1^1 and m_1/p_0^2.

However, if the increase in p^1 is accompanied by a compensating increase in income, then the consumer will choose the bundle at point r. Thus, the net effect of the *compensated* price change is a decrease in the purchase of x^1 by $x_0^1 - x_1^1$ units, and an increase in the purchase of x^2 by $x_1^2 - x_0^2$ units. The change in x^1 (that is, $x_1^1 - x_0^1$) is called the *own-substitution effect* and the change in x^2 (that is, $x_1^2 - x_0^2$) is called the *cross-substitution effect*. In general, therefore, substitution effects refer to *variations in quantities purchased resulting from a price change which is accompanied by a compensatory change in income*.

What about the move from point r to point s? If we take away from the consumer the compensatory increment in income which accompanied the increase in p^1, that is, $m_1 - m_0$, the consumer will move back from point r to point s. The quantity $m_1 - m_0$ represents, of course, the dollar measure (at the fixed prices p_1^1 and p_0^2) of the loss in real income which the consumer experiences following the increase in p^1 (if he is given no compensation), and therefore the changes $x_2^1 - x_1^1$ and $x_2^2 - x_1^2$ represent *income effects*. We see, then, that the total (uncompensated) price effect is the sum of the substitution and the income effect. In this particular example, we have:

	Total price effect		Own-substitution effect		Income effect
Good x^1	$x_2^1 - x_0^1$	$=$	$x_1^1 - x_0^1$	$+$	$x_2^1 - x_1^1$

	Total price effect		Cross-substitution effect		Income effect
Good x^2	$x_2^2 - x_0^2$	$=$	$x_1^2 - x_0^2$	$+$	$x_2^2 - x_1^2$

Generalizing the analysis to an n-good model, and assuming infinitesimal changes, let us hold all prices constant at p_0^j, except p^i, which will be increased slightly. To allow the consumer to purchase the initial bundle x_0 after p^i is increased, his income must be increased. The change in income depends directly on the change in p^i, and since the budget equation must always be satisfied, the necessary change in income can be found by differentiating the budget equation. Rewriting the latter as

$$(10.38) \qquad m = \sum_{\substack{j=1 \\ j \neq i}}^{n} p_0^j x_0^j + p^i x_0^i = \xi(p^i),$$

and differentiating it with respect to p^i, we obtain

$$(10.39) \qquad \frac{dm}{dp^i} = \xi' = x_0^i.$$

Now, if we consider only compensated price changes, then the consumer's demand functions depend on prices only, since under these conditions, income is no longer an independent parameter, but a variable which depends on the changing price. For a compensated change in p^i, the typical demand function depends only on p^i. It can be written as

$$(10.40) \qquad \bar{x}^j = h^j[p_0^1, p_0^2, \ldots, p_0^{i-1}, p^i, p_0^{i+1}, \ldots, p_0^n, \xi(p^i)].$$

Since, under the present conditions, any change in p^i will automatically bring with it a compensatory change in income, the resulting change in $\bar{x}^j$ represents a compensated price effect, that is, a substitution effect. Differentiating (10.40), we get

$$(10.41) \qquad \frac{d\bar{x}^j}{dp^i} = h_i^j + h_m^j \, \xi' = h_i^j + x_0^i \, h_m^j \qquad \text{by (10.39).}$$

If we denote the term representing the substitution effect (that is, $d\bar{x}^j/dp^i$) by S_i^j, then (10.41) can be written as

$$(10.42) \qquad h_i^j = S_i^j + (-x_0^i \, h_m^j).$$

This, then, is the differential form of the discrete result obtained above; it shows that the rate of change in the purchase of good j following an infinitesimal increase in p^i is the sum of a substitution term and an income term. (The income term is multiplied by the negative quantity $-x_0^i$ because an increase in a price causes a *fall* in real income, and the rate at which real income falls equals x_0^i.)

An Alternative Criterion. We shall now analyze this problem once more, using the second definition of real income. Under this definition, real income is defined in terms of the utility index, and it is said to remain constant so long

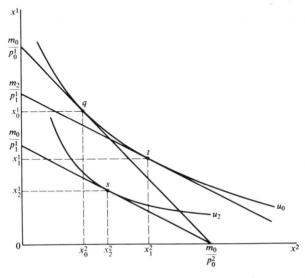

Figure 10.3

as the consumer is in a position to remain on his initial indifference curve. The initial point is represented by point q in Fig. 10.3. If the price of x^1 increases to p_1^1, and the consumer is given no compensation, then, as in the preceding example, he will move from point q to point s. To keep the consumer's real income constant, that is, to permit him to stay on indifference curve u_0, he must be given an increase in his income such that the adjusted budget line forms a tangency with indifference curve u_0. In the present example, this will require an increase of $m_2 - m_0$ dollar. Thus, if the price increase is accompanied by an increase in income of the above amount, the consumer will move from point q to point t, and the resulting changes in quantities purchased represent substitution effects. The move from t to s represents the income effect. As in the first example, the total (uncompensated) price effect is the sum of the substitution and the income effect.

Comparing Figs. 10.2 and 10.3, we see that the only difference between the two cases appears in the manner in which the total price effect (the same in each case) is divided between the substitution and the income effect. The general conclusion which can be drawn from this comparison is that the monetary value of the income effect (loss in real income) is larger under the first definition ($m_1 - m_0 > m_2 - m_0$) because the compensation that is called for under that definition actually makes it possible for the consumer to reach a higher level of utility (indifference curve u_1 in Fig. 10.2). But, as we shall see below, for infinitesimal changes in a price, the two definitions lead to identical results.

The compensation which the consumer is given under the second definition (Fig. 10.3) is governed by two conditions: total income must equal total expenditures (that is, the chosen bundle must lie on the budget plane), and the consumer must be permitted to purchase a bundle lying on the initial indifference surface. These conditions are satisfied by the following equations:

(10.43a)
$$m = \sum_{\substack{j=1 \\ j \neq i}}^{n} p_0^j x^j + p^i x^i,$$

(10.44a)
$$u_0 = \phi(x^1, x^2, ..., x^n).$$

Unlike in Eq. (10.38), the x^j in Eq. (10.43a) are not affixed with subscripts because they are allowed to vary. To emphasize this, and also the fact that income is now a function of p^i, let us replace the x^j by the demand functions, m by $\xi(p^i)$, and write

(10.43b)
$$\xi(p^i) = \sum_{\substack{j=1 \\ j \neq 1}}^{n} p_0^j h^j[p, \xi(p^i)] + p^i h^i[p, \xi(p^i)],$$

(10.44b)
$$u_0 = \phi\{h^1[p, \xi(p^i)], h^2[p, \xi(p^i)], ..., h^n[p, \xi(p^i)]\},$$

where $p = (p_0^1, p_0^2, ..., p_0^{i-1}, p^i, p_0^{i+1}, ..., p_0^n)$. Differentiating each of the above two equations with respect to p^i, we get

(10.45)
$$\xi' = \sum_{j=1}^{n} p_0^j (h_i^j + h_m^j \xi') + x_0^i,$$

(10.46)
$$0 = \sum_{j=1}^{n} \phi_j (h_i^j + h_m^j \xi').$$

Even though the x^j and p^i are variables, in (10.45) they appear with subscripts because the derivative ξ' is evaluated at the initial point (q in Fig. 10.3). Substituting for the ϕ_j in (10.46) from (10.18), we have

(10.47)
$$0 = \lambda \sum_{j=1}^{n} p_0^j (h_i^j + h_m^j \xi'),$$

and since $\lambda \neq 0$, it follows that

$$\sum_{j=1}^{n} p_0^j (h_i^j + h_m^j \xi') = 0.$$

Thus (10.45) and (10.47) imply $\xi' = x_0^i$. This is the same result as that given in (10.39), so that the derivation of the substitution and the total price effect in the present example is exactly the same as in the first example as given by Eqs. (10.40) through (10.42). This completes the demonstration of the fact that in the limiting case (that is, as the change in p^i approaches zero) each of the two definitions of real income, and hence each of the two compensation criteria, leads to the same basic Eq. (10.42), in which the total price effect is expressed as the sum of a substitution and an income effect.

The Slutsky Equation. Equation (10.42), or its equivalent

(10.48)
$$S_i^j = h_i^j + \bar{x}^i h_m^j,$$

is known as the *Slutsky equation*, after the Russian economist who is credited with its derivation. It serves primarily, as was shown above, as a formal illustration of the separation of the total price effect into its two components: the income term, representing the change in quantity demanded because of a change in real income; and the substitution term, representing the change in quantity demanded as a result of changes in relative prices. The separation of the substitution term from the other term in the Slutsky equation is of some importance, because it enables us to make at least one prediction about the effects of a compensated price change. From (10.30), (10.33), and (10.42) it is easily seen that

(10.49)
$$S_i^j = -\lambda \frac{D_{ij}}{D},$$

and as we have already pointed out (in Section 10.4.2) that, for $j = i$, the rhs of (10.49) is negative, we have

(10.50) $S_i^i < 0,$

which may be expressed as follows:

> A compensated change in the price of a good (the compensation being equal to the loss in real income) always causes a decrease in the quantity demanded of that good.

This conclusion is sometimes referred to as the *law of demand*.*

The cross-substitution terms, on the other hand, have indeterminate signs, since the off-diagonal cofactors are not restricted by the conditions for utility maximization. Because of the symmetry of the bordered Hessian matrix, it follows that $D_{ij} = D_{ji}$, and so

(10.51) $S_i^j = S_j^i.$

The signs of the cross-substitution terms give rise to the following classification of goods:

> If $S_i^j \geqslant 0$, then goods i and j are weak net substitutes *for one another.*

> If $S_i^j < 0$, then goods i and j are net complements *for one another.*

This classification is similar to that which is based on the effects of total (uncompensated) price changes (see Section 10.4.2), except that, because of the symmetry property (10.51), any pair of goods must be either weak net substitutes or net complements for one another; in other words, if good i, for example, is a net substitute for good j, then it follows that good j is also a net substitute for good i.

It is also obvious that, since the own-substitution terms are negative, the model places certain restrictions on the extent of complementarity among the goods. Multiplying both sides of (10.48) by p^j, and summing over all j, we get

(10.52) $$\sum_{j=1}^{n} p^j S_i^j = \sum_{j=1}^{n} p^j h_i^j + \bar{x}^i \sum_{j=1}^{n} p^j h_m^j.$$

Now, from (10.32) we see that the first expression on the rhs of (10.52) equals $-\bar{x}^i$, and from (10.29) it is clear that the second expression on the rhs of (10.52) equals $\bar{x}^i$; hence

(10.53) $$\sum_{j=1}^{n} p^j S_i^j = 0, \qquad \text{for all } i.$$

---

* This result is predicated on the assumption that the consumer is being compensated through an appropriate change in his (nominal) income. Real income may also be kept constant by suitable changes in prices. Under the latter method of compensation, a compensated increase in the price of some good need not necessarily lead to a decrease in the quantity demanded of that good.

Since $S_i^i < 0$, it is obvious that some (that is, at least one) S_i^j must be positive, and therefore not all goods can be net complements for one another.

Example 10.1. Suppose that the utility function is of the form

$$u = \sum_{i=1}^{n} a_i \ln x^i = \phi(x), \qquad a_i > 0 \text{ for all } i.$$

This function is not defined at $x^i = 0$, but since we have been assuming interior solutions in most of our problems, we might just as well choose for the present example a utility function which implies that the consumer always purchases some positive amount of every good. Forming the Lagrangian function

$$\sum_{i=1}^{n} a_i \ln x^i + \lambda \left(\sum_{i=1}^{n} p_0^i x^i - m_0 \right),$$

and then taking partial derivatives, we get the first-order conditions

$$\frac{a_i}{x^i} + \lambda p_0^i = 0, \qquad i = 1, 2, \ldots, n,$$

$$\sum_{i=1}^{n} p_0^i x^i - m_0 = 0.$$

The second-order conditions take the form

$$
\begin{vmatrix}
\dfrac{-a_1}{(x^1)^2} & 0 & p^1 \\
0 & \dfrac{-a_2}{(x^2)^2} & p^2 \\
p^1 & p^2 & 0
\end{vmatrix} > 0,
\qquad
\begin{vmatrix}
\dfrac{-a_1}{(x^1)^2} & 0 & 0 & p^1 \\
0 & \dfrac{-a_2}{(x^2)^2} & 0 & p^2 \\
0 & 0 & \dfrac{-a_3}{(x^3)^2} & p^3 \\
p^1 & p^2 & p^3 & 0
\end{vmatrix} < 0, \ldots,
$$

$$
(-1)^n
\begin{vmatrix}
\dfrac{-a_1}{(x^1)^2} & 0 & \cdots & 0 & p^1 \\
0 & \dfrac{-a_2}{(x^2)^2} & \cdots & 0 & p^2 \\
\vdots & & & & \vdots \\
0 & 0 & \cdots & \dfrac{-a_n}{(x^n)^2} & p^n \\
p^1 & p^2 & \cdots & p^n & 0
\end{vmatrix} > 0,
$$

and these are easily verified to hold. Solving the first-order conditions simultaneously, we obtain the demand functions

$$\bar{x}^j = \frac{a_j m}{p^j \sum_{k=1}^{n} a_k} = h^j(p, m), \qquad j = 1, 2, \ldots, n,$$

where p is the vector of the n prices.

We see that, in this example, all goods are superior goods because the income effects (h_m^j) are all positive. As for price effects, the quantity demanded of each good depends only on its own price—quantity and price being inversely related. Since the cross-price effects are zero, all goods are weak gross substitutes for one another. It is also interesting to note that the fraction of his income which the consumer spends on each good is independent of the prices, and is equal to the relative weight of the logarithm of the respective good in the utility function; that is,

$$\frac{p^j \bar{x}^j}{m} = \frac{a_j}{\sum_{k=1}^{n} a_k}.$$

For the own-substitution terms, we get

$$S_i^i = \underset{(h_i^i)}{\frac{-a_i m}{(p^i)^2 \sum_{k=1}^{n} a_k}} + \underset{(x^i h_m^i)}{\frac{(a_i)^2 m}{\left(p^i \sum_{k=1}^{n} a_k\right)^2}} = \frac{-a_i m \sum_{\substack{k=1 \\ k \neq i}}^{n} a_k}{\left(p^i \sum_{k=1}^{n} a_k\right)^2} < 0,$$

and for the cross-substitution terms,

$$S_i^j = \underset{(h_i^j)}{0} + \underset{(x^i h_m^j)}{\frac{a_i a_j m}{p^i p^j \left(\sum_{k=1}^{n} a_k\right)^2}} > 0,$$

so that all goods are net substitutes for one another. It is easy to see that the cross-substitution terms are symmetric, and condition (10.53) may also be verified without much difficulty: we have

$$p^i S_i^i = \frac{-a_i m \sum\limits_{\substack{k=1 \\ k \neq i}}^{n} a_k}{p^i \left(\sum\limits_{k=1}^{n} a_k \right)^2}, \qquad p^j S_i^j = \frac{a_i a_j m}{p^i \left(\sum\limits_{k=1}^{n} a_k \right)^2},$$

and therefore

$$\sum\limits_{j=1}^{n} p^j S_i^j = \frac{-a_i m \sum\limits_{\substack{k=1 \\ k \neq i}}^{n} a_k}{p^i \left(\sum\limits_{k=1}^{n} a_k \right)^2} + \frac{a_i m \sum\limits_{\substack{j=1 \\ j \neq i}}^{n} a_j}{p^i \left(\sum\limits_{k=1}^{n} a_k \right)^2} = 0.$$

10.5 THE INDIRECT UTILITY FUNCTION

10.5.1 Income and Price Effects

So far, we have examined the effects of changes in prices and income on the consumer's demand for the various goods. We now analyze the effects of these changes on his level of utility. For this purpose, we replace the x^i in the utility function by the demand functions, thereby obtaining the indirect utility function

(10.54) $u = \phi[h^1(p, m), h^2(p, m), \ldots, h^n(p, m)] = \Phi(p, m),$

where p denotes the vector of the n prices. Differentiating the indirect utility function with respect to income, we get

(10.55) $\Phi_m = \sum\limits_{j=1}^{n} \phi_j h_m^j.$

Substituting for the ϕ_j from (10.18), we can write

(10.56) $\Phi_m = -\lambda \sum\limits_{j=1}^{n} p^j h_m^j = -\lambda,$

where the second equation in (10.56) follows from (10.29).

The quantity Φ_m indicates the change in the consumer's level of utility due to an infinitesimal increase in his income, and for this reason it is sometimes called the *marginal utility of income*.* Since $\lambda < 0$ [by (10.18)], it follows that

---

* The name is, perhaps, somewhat misleading since it may suggest that income is an argument of the utility function. In the context of the present model, it would be more appropriate to refer to it as the marginal *indirect* utility of income in order to distinguish it from the change in utility resulting from an increment in income occurring in models in which income *is* an argument of the (direct) utility function.

the marginal indirect utility of income is positive. This is precisely what we should expect: an increase in income allows the consumer to purchase a "larger" bundle, and such a bundle, according to the greediness assumption, is always preferred to "smaller" bundles.

From Eqs. (10.18) and (10.56), we see that the marginal indirect utility of income is also equal to ϕ_i/p^i. This relationship may be explained as follows: Suppose that the consumer receives an infinitesimal increment in income, and he decides to spend the entire increment on good i. This will enable him to increase his purchase of good i by $1/p^i$, and consequently the utility index will increase by $1/p^i$ times the marginal utility of good i; that is, ϕ_i/p^i. Furthermore, we see from (10.20) that $\phi_i/p^i = \phi_j/p^j$ for all i and j. Using the preceding interpretation, these equations say that an increment in income spent on good i should increase the consumer's utility index by the same amount by which it would increase if the increment in income were spent on good j, or any other good. The reason for this condition is also intuitively obvious: if the equality failed to hold for a particular pair of goods, say $\phi_i/p^i < \phi_j/p^j$, then the consumer could increase his level of utility by spending a little less on good i and a little more on good j, which means that the original bundle was not the most preferred bundle within the consumer's budget. In other words, the first-order conditions for utility maximization may also be interpreted as requiring that the marginal indirect utility of income be the same for all goods.

To determine the effect on the level of utility of a change in price, we differentiate (10.54) with respect to p^i. This yields

$$(10.57) \qquad \Phi_i = \sum_{j=1}^{n} \phi_j h_i^j,$$

which, after substituting for the ϕ_j from (10.18), becomes

$$(10.58) \qquad \Phi_i = -\lambda \sum_{j=1}^{n} p^j h_i^j = -\lambda(-\bar{x}^i),$$

where the second equation in (10.58) follows from (10.32). Equations (10.56) and (10.58) clearly show the similarity between the two effects; specifically, we see that the effect of a change in price is equivalent to a particular change in income. This is not really surprising in view of the income effect which is part of uncompensated price changes. We saw earlier [in (10.39), for example] that to keep the consumer's real income constant, his nominal income must be increased at a rate of $\bar{x}^i$ (whenever p^i is increased, all other prices remaining constant). This means that, if his nominal income were held constant, his real income would fall at a rate of $\bar{x}^i$, that is, change at a rate of $-\bar{x}^i$. Therefore, the change in utility following an infinitesimal increase in p^i is equal to the concomitant change in real income times the marginal indirect utility of income, which is exactly what Eq. (10.58) says.

A direct corollary to this conclusion is that compensated price changes must leave the consumer's level of utility unchanged. Substituting for the x^j in the utility function from (10.40), and differentiating with respect to p^i, we get

$$(10.59) \qquad \frac{du}{dp^i} = \sum_{j=1}^{n} \phi_j(h_i^j + h_m^j \xi'),$$

which after proper substitutions from (10.18), (10.39), and (10.48) becomes

$$(10.60) \qquad \frac{du}{dp^i} = -\lambda \sum_{j=1}^{n} p^j S_i^j.$$

This expression clearly vanishes by virtue of (10.53).*

Finally, if we eliminate the marginal indirect utility of income from (10.58), the amounts of goods in the optimal bundle can be expressed in terms of the derivatives of the indirect utility function. Dividing each equation in (10.58) by any other, we get

$$(10.61) \qquad \frac{\Phi_i}{\Phi_j} = \frac{\bar{x}^i}{\bar{x}^j}, \qquad i, j = 1, 2, ..., n.$$

According to these equations, the ratio of the amounts of any two goods in the optimal bundle is equal to the ratio of the marginal indirect utilities of the prices of the respective goods.

10.5.2 Minimizing Indirect Utility

It is possible to formulate an interesting problem in which the indirect utility function takes the place of the objective function. It will be recalled that, in the standard consumer model, the consumer is thought of as being confronted with a given set of prices and income, while the decision problem that he tries to solve is concerned with the choice of an optimal bundle from within the feasible set. Suppose that we now reverse the situation, and ask the following question: "Given a predetermined bundle of goods, what set of prices and income will make the consumer choose that particular bundle?" It turns out that the answer to this question is found by *minimizing* the indirect utility function, subject to a budget constraint in which the x^i are fixed at the levels specified by the given bundle. The reason for this is that if a price-income combination is selected which is not minimizing the indirect utility function, the consumer will be able to purchase a bundle that has a higher utility index than the specific bundle. The problem is illustrated in Fig. 10.4, in which it is assumed that x_0 is the prespecified bundle.

---

* However, if the compensated change in price is of discrete magnitude, the consumer will be made better off, provided his income is increased according to the first method of compensation (Fig. 10.2).

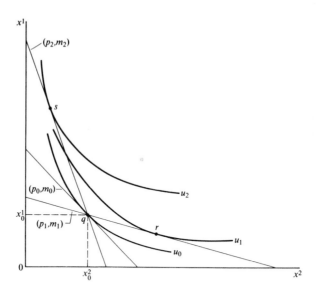

Figure 10.4

Suppose, for example, that the selected price-income combination is given by the vector (p_1, m_1) (which is feasible, because the budget line defined by that combination goes through the specified bundle x_0), then the consumer chooses the bundle represented by point r. Point r, however, does not represent the bundle x_0, hence it is clear that (p_1, m_1) is the wrong combination. For the combination (p_2, m_2) the consumer moves to point s, which is also different from the specified bundle x_0. From the outcomes of these two trials we can easily see that neither of the above price-income combinations minimizes the indirect utility function over the feasible set, since it is obvious that the lowest level of utility that can be attained with a budget line going through point q is u_0. The latter is attained by choosing the combination (p_0, m_0) for which the budget line is tangent to indifference curve u_0 at point q, and which will consequently make the consumer choose the bundle x_0. Moreover, the minimum value of the (constrained) indirect utility function is the same as the highest level of utility that the consumer can reach if he is confronted with the combination (p_0, m_0). We have here, therefore, a case of duality, in which the minimization of the indirect utility function is the *dual* of the standard utility maximization problem. We shall now analyze this problem formally.

Since the indirect utility function is constructed by inserting the demand functions into the direct utility function, and since the demand functions are homogeneous of degree zero in prices and income, it follows that the indirect utility function is also homogeneous of degree zero in prices and income. Consequently, if one particular combination of prices and income minimizes the indirect utility function, then there are infinitely many such combinations, because if each component in the original solution is multiplied by some positive constant k, the value of the indirect utility function will not change, and hence k times the original solution is also a solution.

To avoid multiple solutions, we may do either one of the following:

a) consider m a fixed parameter, and minimize the indirect utility function with respect to the p^i only;

b) normalize the prices.

We shall adopt the second approach, and replace the ordinary prices by the fractions of the consumer's income which correspond to the dollar values of the respective prices. [See (10.36).] If these fractions are denoted by s^i, $s^i = p^i/m$, then the indirect utility function depends only on the s^i. The switch from ordinary to normalized prices is given by the following relations:

$$(10.62) \qquad \Phi(p^1, p^2, ..., p^n, m) = \Phi\left(\frac{p^1}{m}, \frac{p^2}{m}, ..., \frac{p^n}{m}, 1\right) = \tilde{\Phi}(s^1, s^2, ..., s^n).$$

Our problem can now be stated as:

Minimize $\qquad\qquad\qquad\qquad \tilde{\Phi}(s^1, s^2, ..., s^n),$

subject to $\qquad\qquad\qquad\qquad \sum_{i=1}^{n} s^i x_0^i = 1.$

The Lagrangian form is written as

$$(10.63) \qquad\qquad \tilde{\Phi}(s^1, s^2, ..., s^n) + \mu\left(\sum_{i=1}^{n} s^i x_0^i - 1\right),$$

and the first-order conditions are

$$(10.64) \qquad\qquad \tilde{\Phi}_i + \mu x_0^i = 0, \qquad i = 1, 2, ..., n,$$

$$(10.65) \qquad\qquad \sum_{i=1}^{n} s^i x_0^i - 1 = 0,$$

where μ is a Lagrange multiplier, and $\tilde{\Phi}_i = \partial\tilde{\Phi}/\partial s^i$. The second-order conditions for this problem require that all the relevant bordered Hessian determinants be negative. Eliminating μ from (10.64), we get

$$(10.66) \qquad\qquad \frac{\tilde{\Phi}_i}{\tilde{\Phi}_j} = \frac{x_0^i}{x_0^j}, \qquad i, j = 1, 2, ..., n.$$

The primal (original) problem, on the other hand, is:

Maximize $\qquad\qquad\qquad\qquad \phi(x^1, x^2, ..., x^n),$

subject to $\qquad\qquad\qquad\qquad \sum_{i=1}^{n} s_0^i x^i = 1,$

for which the Lagrangian form is

(10.67) $$\phi(x^1, x^2, ..., x^n) + \lambda\left(\sum_{i=1}^{n} s_0^i x^i - 1\right).$$

This problem has the first-order conditions

(10.68) $$\phi_i + \lambda s_0^i = 0, \qquad i = 1, 2, ..., n,$$

(10.69) $$\sum_{i=1}^{n} s_0^i x^i - 1 = 0.$$

We are assuming, of course, that the solution to the primal is the same as the prespecified bundle in the dual; that is,

(10.70) $$\bar{x}^i = x_0^i, \qquad i = 1, 2, ..., n,$$

where the $\bar{x}^i$ are the values of the x^i satisfying (10.68) and (10.69). If we express the amounts of the goods in the optimal bundle as functions of the parameters s^i, we obtain the demand functions which can be written as

(10.71) $$\bar{x}^i = \tilde{h}^i(s^1, s^2, ..., s^n), \qquad i = 1, 2, ..., n.$$

Naturally, since we have normalized the prices, the functions $\tilde{h}^i$, unlike the h^i in (10.27), are not homogeneous.

Now, in our analysis of the effects of changes in prices on the level of utility, we obtained a relationship between the derivatives of the indirect utility function and the quantities in the optimal bundle; namely, Eq. (10.61). The reader should easily be able to convince himself that a similar set of equations is obtained if prices are normalized, so that we can state

(10.72) $$\frac{\tilde{\Phi}_i}{\tilde{\Phi}_j} = \frac{\bar{x}^i}{\bar{x}^j}, \qquad i, j = 1, 2, ..., n.$$

Then it is clear that, in view of (10.70), the equations in (10.66) are the same as those in (10.72), and consequently both sets are satisfied for the same values of the s^i. We have thus shown that the set of (normalized) prices for which the bundle x_0 maximizes the consumer's utility function is also the set which minimizes the consumer's indirect utility function, given the bundle x_0.*

If we solve the first-order conditions (10.64) and (10.65) of the dual for the optimal values of the s^i, the latter can be expressed as functions of the parameters x^i, and may be written as

(10.73) $$\bar{s}^i = g^i(x^1, x^2, ..., x^n), \qquad i = 1, 2, ..., n.$$

---

* We have not shown that the second-order conditions for the minimization of the indirect utility function are implied by the second-order conditions for utility maximization, but Fig. 10.4 should provide the reader with at least an intuitive demonstration of the proposition that the function $\tilde{\Phi}$ attains a constrained minimum (rather than maximum) at (p_0, m_0).

These functions are the counterparts of the demand functions in (10.71). Mathematically speaking, they are the inverse functions of the demand functions. For any given bundle x, the functions g^i indicate the fractions of the consumer's income that he must be required to give up for one unit of the respective good if he is to choose the bundle x. Of course, if the consumer's income is given, or fixed arbitrarily, then each s^i defines a particular market price. The functions g^i may be referred to as *pricing functions*.

The properties of the pricing functions may be investigated by the same method that we applied in the investigation of the demand functions. Differentiating the first-order conditions (10.64) and (10.65) with respect to x^j, after substituting for the s^i from (10.73), we get

(10.74a)
$$\sum_{k=1}^{n} \tilde{\Phi}_{ik} g_j^k + x^i \frac{\partial \mu}{\partial x^j} = 0, \qquad i = 1, 2, \ldots, n, \quad i \neq j,$$

(10.74b)
$$\sum_{k=1}^{n} \tilde{\Phi}_{jk} g_j^k + x^j \frac{\partial \mu}{\partial x^j} = -\mu,$$

(10.75)
$$\sum_{k=1}^{n} x^k g_j^k = -\bar{s}^j.$$

Solving for g_j^i by Cramer's rule, we get

(10.76)
$$g_j^i = -\mu \frac{\tilde{D}_{ji}}{\tilde{D}} - \bar{s}^j \frac{\tilde{D}_{n+1,i}}{\tilde{D}},$$

where $\tilde{D}$ is the determinant of the coefficient matrix of system (10.74) and (10.75), and $\tilde{D}_{ji}$ is a typical cofactor. The term g_j^i indicates the necessary change in $\bar{s}^i$ if, in the bundle which the consumer is to purchase, the amount of good j is increased slightly. In general, the sign of g_j^i is indeterminate, but the terms $-\mu \tilde{D}_{ji}/\tilde{D}$ have properties similar to those of the Slutsky substitution terms. It may also be noted that the functions g^i are not homogeneous.

Finally, we can construct the indirect indirect utility function by replacing the s^i in the indirect utility function by the pricing functions. We then have

(10.77)
$$\Phi[g^1(x), g^2(x), \ldots, g^n(x)] = \Psi(x).$$

We shall now show that the function Ψ is the original utility function. Differentiating $\Psi(x)$ with respect to x^j, we get

(10.78)
$$\Psi_j = \sum_{k=1}^{n} \tilde{\Phi}_k g_j^k.$$

Substituting for the $\tilde{\Phi}_k$ in (10.78) from (10.64), we obtain

(10.79)
$$\Psi_j = -\mu \sum_{k=1}^{n} x_0^k g_j^k = -\mu(-\bar{s}^j) \qquad \text{by (10.75).}$$

Now, if, in the original problem, we had used the same type of price normalization as in the dual, and consequently written the demand functions as $\tilde{h}^j(s^1, s^2, \ldots, s^n)$, and the indirect utility function as $\tilde{\Phi}(s^1, s^2, \ldots, s^n)$, then Eq. (10.58) would assume the form

$$(10.80) \qquad\qquad \tilde{\Phi}_j = -\lambda(-\bar{x}^j).$$

Then, comparing (10.80) and (10.64), and recalling (10.70), it is clear that

$$(10.81) \qquad\qquad \mu = -\lambda.$$

In words, the Lagrange multiplier in the dual problem is the negative of the Lagrange multiplier in the primal. Or, put differently, the Lagrange multiplier of the dual is equal to the marginal indirect utility of income multiplied by -1. Then, if we substitute for μ in (10.79) from (10.81), we get

$$(10.82) \qquad\qquad \Psi_j = -\lambda \bar{s}^j = \phi_j,$$

where the second equality follows from (10.68), and the fact that the solutions to both the primal and the dual are obtained for the same values of the s^j; that is, $\bar{s}^j = s_0^j$. Since, according to (10.82), the functions Ψ and ϕ have the same derivatives, the two functions are one and the same (except, possibly, for a constant).

We have thus come full circle, demonstrating the complete duality relationship between maximizing utility and minimizing indirect utility. It may also be pointed out that it is formally quite appropriate, if one wishes to do so, to regard the minimization of indirect utility as the primal problem, and the maximization of utility as the dual. In general, one may start with either of the two problems, and proceed from there to derive the indirect objective function. Constructing the indirect version of the indirect objective function always leads back to the original objective function, regardless of whether that happens to be the direct or the indirect utility function.

Example 10.2. Using the same utility function as in Example 10.1, that is,

$$u = \sum_{j=1}^{n} a_j \ln x^j,$$

we construct the indirect utility function by replacing the x^i in the utility function by the demand functions (which we have derived in Example 10.1). We obtain

$$\sum_{j=1}^{n} a_j \ln \left(\frac{a_j m}{p^j \sum_{k=1}^{n} a_k} \right) = \Phi(p, m).$$

Differentiating with respect to m, we get

$$\Phi_m = \sum_{j=1}^{n} \frac{a_j}{m},$$

which represents the marginal indirect utility of income. Differentiating with respect to p^i, we see that

$$\Phi_i = - \frac{a_i}{p^i},$$

which, being negative, shows that an (uncompensated) increase in a price forces the consumer to a lower level of utility. On the other hand, if we wish to keep the consumer's real income constant, we must increase his nominal income at a rate of $\bar{x}^i$ for an infinitesimal increase in p^i. Thus, the marginal indirect utility of a compensated price change is given by

$$\Phi_i + \bar{x}^i \Phi_m = - \frac{a_i}{p^i} + \bar{x}^i \sum_{j=1}^{n} \frac{a_j}{m}.$$

Replacing $\bar{x}^i$ by its demand function (that is, by the term in parentheses in the indirect utility function given above), we get

$$\Phi_i + \bar{x}^i \Phi_m = \frac{-a_i}{p^i} + \frac{a_i m}{p^i \sum_{k=1}^{n} a_k} \sum_{j=1}^{n} \frac{a_j}{m} = 0.$$

Turning now to the dual problem, we wish to find a combination (p, m) such that the consumer, when confronted with it, will choose the prespecified bundle x_0. In this problem, prices will be expressed in fractions of the consumer's income which are equal to the respective prices; that is, $s^i = p^i/m$, where s^i represents the fraction of the consumer's income that he has to give up for one unit of good i. The optimal s^i are found by minimizing the indirect utility function $\tilde{\Phi}(s^1, s^2, ..., s^n)$, subject to the appropriate budget constraint. The Lagrangian form in this example is

$$\sum_{j=1}^{n} a_j \ln\left(\frac{a_j}{s^j \sum_{k=1}^{n} a_k} \right) + \mu\left(\sum_{i=1}^{n} s^i x_0^i - 1 \right),$$

and the first-order conditions are

$$\frac{-a_j}{s^j} + \mu x_0^j = 0, \qquad j = 1, 2, ..., n,$$

$$\sum_{i=1}^{n} s^i x_0^i - 1 = 0.$$

The second-order conditions for this problem are given by

$$
\begin{vmatrix}
\dfrac{a_1}{(s^1)^2} & 0 & x^1 \\
0 & \dfrac{a_2}{(s^2)^2} & x^2 \\
x^1 & x^2 & 0
\end{vmatrix} < 0,
\qquad
\begin{vmatrix}
\dfrac{a_1}{(s^1)^2} & 0 & 0 & x^1 \\
0 & \dfrac{a_2}{(s^2)^2} & 0 & x^2 \\
0 & 0 & \dfrac{a_3}{(s^3)^2} & x^3 \\
x^1 & x^2 & x^3 & 0
\end{vmatrix} < 0, \ldots,
$$

$$
\begin{vmatrix}
\dfrac{a_1}{(s^1)^2} & 0 & \cdots & 0 & x^1 \\
0 & \dfrac{a_2}{(s^2)^2} & \cdots & 0 & x^2 \\
\vdots & & & \vdots & \vdots \\
0 & 0 & \cdots & \dfrac{a_n}{(s^n)^2} & x^n \\
x^1 & x^2 & \cdots & x^n & 0
\end{vmatrix} < 0,
$$

which are clearly satisfied. Solving the first-order conditions, we obtain the pricing functions

$$
\bar{s}^i = \frac{a_i}{x^i \displaystyle\sum_{k=1}^{n} a_k} = g^i(x^1,\, x^2,\, \ldots,\, x^n).
$$

It is easily seen that

$$
g^i_i = \frac{-a_i}{(x^i)^2 \displaystyle\sum_{k=1}^{n} a_k} < 0, \qquad \text{for all} \;\; i,
$$

and
$$
g^i_j = 0, \qquad \text{for all} \;\; i \;\; \text{and} \;\; j, \qquad i \neq j.
$$

Finally, replacing the s^i in the indirect utility function by their respective pricing functions, we have

$$
\sum_{i=1}^{n} a_i \ln \left[\frac{x^i a_i \displaystyle\sum_{k=1}^{n} a_k}{a_i \displaystyle\sum_{k=1}^{n} a_k} \right] = \sum_{i=1}^{n} a_i \ln x^i,
$$

which is the original utility function used in this example.

BIBLIOGRAPHICAL NOTES

General

The origins of the modern theory of consumer behavior are to be found in the early theories of utility, such as those of H. Gossen, S. Jevons, C. Menger, and L. Walras. Especially influential were the ideas of Walras' successor V. Pareto. The elements of contemporary theory, as we know it today, have first been formulated rigorously by E. Slutsky in his celebrated article "On the Theory of the Budget of the Consumer," first published (in Italian) in 1915 and reprinted in K. E. Boulding and G. S. Stigler (eds.), *Readings in Price Theory*, Chicago: Irwin, 1952, pp. 27–56. R. G. D. Allen and J. R. Hicks, working independently of Slutsky, have developed a similar formulation. This was published in J. R. Hicks, "A Reconsideration of the Theory of Value, Part I," *Economica*, **1**, 52–76 (1934), and R. G. D. Allen, "A Reconsideration of the Theory of Value, Part II," *Economica*, **1**, 196–219 (1934). A comparison of Slutsky's work with that of Allen and Hicks is given in R. G. D. Allen's article "Professor Slutsky's Theory of Consumers' Choices," *Review of Economic Studies*, **3**, 120–129 (1935–36), reprinted in A. N. Page (ed.), *Utility Theory*, New York: Wiley, 1968, pp. 183–195. Further elaborations and refinements of these early ideas were undertaken by J. R. Hicks in his *Value and Capital*, Oxford: Oxford University Press, 2nd edition, 1946, Chapters 1-3, and the respective mathematical appendixes. A summary of the theory of the consumer, along the lines of Hicks, is in J. L. Mosak, *General Equilibrium Theory in International Trade* (Cowles Foundation Monograph No. 7), Chicago: Cowles Commission, 1941, Chapter 1. A more complete mathematical treatment may be found in P. A. Samuelson, *Foundations of Economic Analysis*, Cambridge: Harvard University Press, 1947, Chapters 5 and 7. Two recent works on the theory of consumer behavior are: S. Wu and J. A. Pontney, *Modern Demand Theory*, New York: Random House, 1967, and D. Katzner, *Static Demand Theory*, New York: Macmillan, 1970.

From a mathematical point of view, the most important recent development is the set-theoretic approach to consumer behavior. A fairly complete exposition of this approach is in G. Debreu, *Theory of Value* (Cowles Foundation Monograph No. 17), New York: Wiley, 1959, Chapter 4.

Readers interested in a general overview of various aspects of consumer behavior may consult survey articles on this subject. Two such articles, each containing an extensive bibliography, are H. S. Houthakker, "The Present State of Consumption Theory," *Econometrica*, **29**, 704–740 (1961), and P. C. Fishburn, "Utility Theory," *Management Science*, **14**, 335–378 (1968).

Special Topics

Several aspects of consumer behavior have not been treated adequately in this chapter, and some have been omitted altogether. Of the latter, the most important is the theory of revealed preference, originally formulated by Samuelson. A selected list of articles on this subject are the following (in chronological order): P. A. Samuelson, "A Note on the Pure Theory of Consumer's Behavior," *Economica*, **5**, 61–71 (1938); P. A. Samuelson, "Consumption Theory in Terms of Revealed Preference," *Economica*, **15**, 243–253 (1948), reprinted in A. N. Page, *Utility Theory*, New York: Wiley, 1968, pp. 149–159; I. M. D. Little, "A Reformulation of the Theory of Consumer's Behavior," *Oxford Economic Papers*, **1**, 90–99 (1949); H. S. Houthakker, "Revealed Preference and the Utility Function," *Economica*, **17**, 159–174 (1950), reprinted in P. Newman (ed.), *Readings in Mathematical Economics*, Volume 1, Baltimore: The Johns Hopkins Press, 1968, pp. 281–296; P. Newman, "The Foundations of Revealed Preference Theory," *Oxford Economic Papers*, **7**, 151–169 (1955); H. Uzawa, "Preference and Rational Choice in the Theory of Consumption," in K. J. Arrow, S. Karlin, and P. Suppes (eds.), *Mathematical Methods in the Social Sciences, 1959*, Stanford: Stanford University Press, 1960, pp. 129–148, reprinted in P. Newman (ed.), *Readings in Mathematical Economics*, Volume 1, Baltimore: The Johns Hopkins Press, 1968, pp. 297–316; and M. K. Richter, "Revealed Preference Theory," *Econometrica*, **34**, 635–645 (1966).

The concept of the indirect utility function, and the duality relationship between direct and indirect utility, have been explored by several writers. One of the first to do so was R. Roy in his article "La Distribution du Revenu entre les Divers Biens," *Econometrica*, **15**, 205–225 (1947). Other works dealing with indirect utility are H. S. Houthakker, "Compensated Changes in Quantities and Qualities Consumed," *Review of Economic Studies*, **19**, 155–164 (1952), and P. A. Samuelson, "Using Full Duality to Show that Simultaneously Additive Direct and Indirect Utilities Implies Unitary Price Elasticity of Demand," *Econometrica*, **33**, 781–796 (1965).

A special class of utility functions, one in which goods are grouped according to their use, has been proposed by R. Strotz. The properties and implications of such utility functions are discussed in the following articles: R. Strotz, "The Empirical Implications of a Utility Tree," *Econometrica*, **25**, 269–280 (1957); W. M. Gorman, "Separable Utility and Aggregation," *Econometrica*, **27**, 469–481 (1959); and R. Strotz, "The Utility Tree—A Correction and Further Appraisal," *Econometrica*, **27**, 482–488 (1959). Related problems are explored by I. F. Pearce in *A Contribution to Demand Analysis*, Oxford: Oxford University Press, 1964.

The question of the invariance of the Slutsky substitution term, and some aspects of the compensatory mechanism for maintaining the consumer's real income, are dealt with in the following articles: H. W. Folk and J. N. Wolfe, "The Ambiguity of the Substitution Term," *Economica*, **31**, 288–293 (1964); R. G. D. Allen and E. J. Mishan, "Is the Substitution Term Ambiguous?" *Economica*, **32**, 215–222 (1965); and J. Hadar, "The Substitution Term *is* Ambiguous," *Economica*, **34**, 428–430 (1967). Also of some relevance to these issues is J. L. Mosak, "On the Interpretation of the Fundamental Equation of Value Theory," in O. Lange, F. McIntyre, and T. Yntema (eds.), *Studies in Mathematical Economics and Econometrics*, Chicago: Chicago University Press, 1942, pp. 69–74.

Since this chapter was devoted primarily to a thorough examination of the standard model of consumer behavior, it provides no examples of applications of the theory to other contexts of consumer choice. One problem which can easily be analyzed by means of the standard theory is the choice between leisure and work. Two papers on this topic are: G. Cooper, "Taxation and Incentive in Mobilization," *Quarterly Journal of Economics*, **66**, 43–66 (1952), reprinted in R. A. Musgrave and C. S. Shoup (eds.), *Readings in the Economics of Taxation*, Homewood: Irwin, 1959, pp. 470–492, and C. T. Brehm and T. R. Saving, "The Demand for General Assistance Payments," *American Economic Review*, **54**, 1002–1018 (1964).

While most theoretical works on consumer behavior are based on the conceptual framework developed by Slutsky, Allen, and Hicks, some attempts have been made to develop theories of consumer behavior from a somewhat different set of premises. Two examples are G. S. Becker, "A Theory of the Allocation of Time," *Economic Journal*, **75**, 493–517 (1965), and K. Lancaster, "A New Approach to Consumer Theory," *Journal of Political Economy*, **74**, 132–157 (1966).

Finally, we have avoided any discussion in this chapter of problems of statistical estimation of economic relationships relevant to consumer behavior. As an introduction into this area the reader may consult H. Wold, *Demand Analysis*, New York: Wiley, 1953.

CHAPTER 11

INTERTEMPORAL UTILITY MAXIMIZATION

In this chapter we consider certain extensions of the standard model of consumer behavior presented in Chapter 10. These extensions consist essentially of considering explicitly two aspects of consumer behavior from which we abstracted in the preceding chapter. These aspects are:

a) the fact that the goods purchased by the consumer may not only be *consumed* (i.e., destroyed), but may also be *held* (i.e., kept intact) as inventory;

b) the possibility that the consumer's plan for his economic activities may cover more than just one period of time.

These two aspects of consumer behavior are closely related. For example, if one wants to analyze the consumption pattern of a consumer over two successive periods of time, then it is important to know whether, at the end of the first period, the consumer possesses any inventories of goods; if he does, these goods are available to him in the second period, and this will determine, in part, his desired purchases in the latter period.

Even though the models presented here are labeled as consumer models, this chapter may very well serve as an introduction to intertemporal optimization in general, since the basic concepts and techniques to be discussed are not necessarily unique to consumer behavior. For instance, by suitably redefining the variables (and possibly making other minor changes), the models can easily be interpreted as models of the firm, especially if one takes the more general approach to the theory of the firm, and assumes that, instead of maximizing profit, the firm maximizes a utility function whose arguments include other target variables besides profit. It is, of course, true that certain features of intertemporal optimization are of a rather specialized nature, and hence may be applicable to either the firm, or the consumer, but not to both; nevertheless, we feel that the objectives of this introductory discussion are adequately served by confining the exposition to consumer models. Before beginning with the construction of models, we introduce a number of basic concepts and terms.

When a quantity of some good is consumed over a period of time, this act represents a flow of consumption, and the good is then referred to as a *flow* good; when, on the other hand, the consumer holds a good in stock as inventory, the good in question is a *stock* good. The consumption of a flow good is measured in *rates per period of time* (or possibly in rates at a point of time), while holdings of stock goods are always measured *at a point of time*. Some goods (such as services) are flow goods by nature, since they normally cannot be stored, and hence are called *pure flow* goods; some goods (such as cash balances) cannot be consumed (although they can be destroyed by acts other than consumption), and hence are called *pure stock* goods; goods that are capable of being consumed *and* held as inventory are called *stock-flow* goods. Thus, when dealing with models of intertemporal behavior, it is imperative to distinguish between flows and stocks, because the latter may be carried from one period to the next, and this establishes a link between the consumer's behavior in different periods of time.

11.1   MULTIPERIOD MODELS OF CONSUMER BEHAVIOR

In order to simplify the notation, we shall formulate the model *as though* all goods represented in the model were stock-flow goods. The symbol x_t^i will denote the amount of good i consumed (or to be consumed) in period t, and v_t^i the amount of good i held (or to be held) as stock at the beginning of period t, exclusive of the amount x_t^i earmarked to be consumed in period t. To be more precise, assume that all transactions are carried out on the first "day" of each period of time, then v_t^i represents the amount of good i available to the consumer for inventory purposes *at the end* of the transaction "day." Thus, the above simplifying assumption implies that our model will have an x_t^i and v_t^i for all i. This simply means that if the ith good is, in fact, a pure flow good, then $v_t^i = 0$ for all t, and if the ith good is a pure stock good, then $x_t^i = 0$ for all t. Therefore, the above assumption entails no loss of generality, whereas the device of occasionally denoting a zero by such symbols as x_t^i and v_t^i will permit us to apply to various expressions involving x_t^i and v_t^i the same limits of summation.

11.1.1   The Static Structure of the Model

It is assumed that the consumer's planning horizon extends over s periods; by which we mean that the consumer plans for each of s successive periods of time. To put it still more explicitly, a typical decision problem is assumed to consist of choosing optimal levels for the x_t^i and v_t^i in s successive periods of time. If we use the vector notation $x_t = (x_t^1, x_t^2, ..., x_t^n)$ and $v_t = (v_t^1, v_t^2, ..., v_t^n)$, where n represents the number of goods, then the consumer's utility function can be stated as

$$(11.1) \qquad u = \phi(x_1, x_2, ..., x_s, v_1, v_2, ..., v_s).$$

Before formulating the consumer's budget constraint, we must make some provisions for the possibility of changes in the consumer's stock holdings during a typical period of time. Basically, there are two reasons for such changes. One of these is a physical change in the goods held in stock, such as depreciation. If the change in one unit of the stock of good i during period t is given by $\alpha_t^i - 1$, then an initial amount of v_t^i will change by $(\alpha_t^i - 1)v_t^i$, so that at the end of period t (that is, the beginning of period $t + 1$) the stock of good i will be equal to $v_t^i + (\alpha_t^i - 1) v_t^i = \alpha_t^i v_t^i$. In the case of depreciation, we have, of course, $\alpha_t^i - 1 < 0$. Even if no physical depreciation occurs, the stock of a typical good may nevertheless suffer a loss in market value. For example, if the market price of one unit of good i in period t is p_t^i, it is conceivable that the consumer will not be able to sell a stock carried over from period $t - 1$ at more than $p_t^i \alpha_{t-1}^i$ per unit, $\alpha_{t-1}^i < 1$ (the stock now being considered "second hand"), so that at the end of period $t - 1$, the market value of the stock holdings is equal to $p_t^i \alpha_{t-1}^i v_{t-1}^i$. Of course, a stock of goods may also appreciate in value, in which case we have $\alpha_{t-1}^i > 1$. Examples are bonds, or other interest-bearing assets. If, say, the ith good is a perpetuity whose market price is one dollar, and which pays r dollars in interest in each period of time, then an initial stock of v_{t-1}^i perpetuities will at the end of period $t - 1$ be worth $\alpha_{t-1}^i v_{t-1}^i$ dollars, where $\alpha_{t-1}^i = 1 + r$. In general, then, we assume that $\alpha_t^i > 0$ for all i and t.* (If $\alpha_t^i = 0$, then good i may be considered a pure flow good.)

Another departure from the general procedure followed in Chapter 10 is the identification of one particular good; specifically, x^n will denote leisure time (hence $v^n = 0$). Our reason for doing so is that the introduction of leisure time makes the consumer's income a decision variable, so that (unlike in Chapter 10) we no longer need to assume that income is a parameter determined by factors outside the model. We define leisure time as any time during which the consumer is not engaged in remunerative work. If leisure time is measured in hours, and the typical period (all periods being of equal length) has δ hours, then a choice on the part of the consumer of x_t^n hours of leisure in period t, implies a willingness to work $\delta - x_t^n$ hours. Assuming that the consumer is paid p_t^n dollars for every hour worked during period t, then his earned income in that period is equal to $p_t^n(\delta - x_t^n)$ dollars.

The consumer's expenditures in each period of time can be determined just as easily. If in period t he wishes to consume x_t^i units of good i, and in

---

* A stock may also change as a result of consumption. For example, the consumer may decide to hold at the beginning of period $t + 1$ and inventory of good i which is less than that which he holds in period t. In that case, he may either sell the undesired surplus at the beginning of period $t + 1$, or consume it during period $t + 1$. What we rule out in this model is the unexpected consumption of v_t^i, or part of it, *during* period t. A systematic analysis of such a possibility would require us to deal explicitly with the question of uncertainty, but we do not plan to do this in the present chapter.

addition hold v_t^i units as inventory, then on the transaction "day" of period t he must purchase $x_t^i + v_t^i - \alpha_{t-1}^i v_{t-1}^i$ units of good i at a cost of $p_t^i (x_t^i + v_t^i - \alpha_{t-1}^i v_{t-1}^i)$. Thus, the s budget constraints which the consumer must obey are given by

$$(11.2) \quad \sum_{i=1}^{n-1} p_t^i (x_t^i + v_t^i - \alpha_{t-1}^i v_{t-1}^i) = p_t^n (\delta - x_t^n), \qquad t = 1, 2, ..., s.$$

We shall again assume that the optimal bundle lies in the interior of some subset of the relevant space, except that in the present model this subset is not the nonnegative orthant. We have already indicated the possibility that the consumer may wish to hold certain financial assets, such as bonds. If the consumer does acquire financial assets, he is in fact lending some of his cash balances (or other form of purchasing power). On the other hand, if he is also allowed to borrow, then the consumer is issuing his own bonds (I.O.U.s), so that if he is a net borrower, his bond holdings are negative. Therefore, the optimal amounts of goods such as bonds may lie in the interior of the entire real line. Finally, to avoid economic nonsense, it is also necessary to assume that $\bar{x}_t^n \leqslant \delta$, but to have an interior solution, we assume $0 < \bar{x}_t^n < \delta$.

Having assumed the existence of an interior solution, we can state the first-order conditions. They are:

$$(11.3a) \quad \phi_{it} + \lambda_t p_t^i = 0, \quad i = 1, 2, ..., n,$$

$$(11.3b) \quad \phi_{it} + \lambda_t p_t^i - \lambda_{t+1} p_{t+1}^i \alpha_t^i = 0, \quad i = n+1, n+2, ..., 2n,$$

$$(11.4a) \quad \sum_{i=1}^{n} p_t^i (x_t^i + v_t^i - \alpha_{t-1}^i v_{t-1}^i) - p_t^n \delta = 0,$$

$$\left. \right\} \quad t = 1, 2, ..., s,$$

where $\phi_{it} = \partial\phi/\partial x_t^i$ for $i = 1, 2, ..., n$; $\phi_{it} = \partial\phi/\partial v_t^{i-n}$ for $i = n+1$, $n+2, ..., 2n$; $p_t^i = p_t^{i+n}$ for $i = 1, 2, ..., n$; $p_t^i = p_t^{i-n}$ for $i = n+1$, $n+2, ..., 2n$; $\alpha_t^i = \alpha_t^{i-n}$ for $i = n+1, n+2, ..., 2n$; and $\lambda_{s+1} = 0$. As usual, prices are considered to be parameters; the fact that they are affixed with time subscripts merely indicates that they may assume different values in each of the s periods. Of course, at the time at which the consumer draws up his plans (that is, at the beginning of the transaction "day" of the first period in the horizon) he can observe only the prices of the first (current) period, and consequently the p_t^i for $t > 1$ must be interpreted as the consumer's expectations of future prices. The other parameters in the model are the α_t^i and v_0^i.

Conditions (11.3) indicate that the (absolute value of the) marginal rate of substitution (MRS) between any two flows in the same period of time must equal the ratio of their prices. Thus, as in the one-period model, we have

(11.5) $$\frac{\phi_{it}}{\phi_{jt}} = \frac{p_t^i}{p_t^j}, \qquad i = 1, 2, \ldots, n, \quad t = 1, 2, \ldots, s.$$

However, the MRSs between flows in two different periods of time must not, in general, equal the ratio of their prices in the respective periods; rather, they must equal the ratio of their prices multiplied by the ratio of the marginal indirect utilities of income in the respective periods. Thus, instead of (11.5), we have the general conditions for the MRSs between flows:

(11.6) $$\frac{\phi_{it}}{\phi_{j\tau}} = \frac{p_t^i \lambda_t}{p_\tau^j \lambda_\tau}, \qquad i, j = 1, 2, \ldots, n, \quad t, \tau = 1, 2, \ldots, s.$$

The MRS between a flow and a stock, or between two stocks, must be equal to quantities that do not lend themselves to such simple interpretations, because of the extra terms appearing in (11.3b).

The MRS between goods consumed (or held) in different periods of time is sometimes referred to as the consumer's *time preference*. For example, the expression $\phi_{it}/\phi_{i\tau}$ represents the rate at which the amount of good i available in period τ must be decreased for a small increase in the amount of good i available in period t if the consumer is to remain on the same indifference surface. This ratio, therefore, is a measure of the consumer's preference for consuming (or holding) good i in period τ rather than in period t, and vice versa. On the other hand, the expression $\phi_{i\tau}/\phi_{j\tau}$ is simply the MRS between goods i and j in period τ; it measures the desirability of good i relative to that of good j. To distinguish the latter measure from that of time preference, we may call it *commodity preference*. Hence, a general expression such as $\phi_{it}/\phi_{j\tau}$ measures the desirability of good i available in period t relative to that of good j in period τ. This measure is compounded of the consumer's time preference and his commodity preference with respect to the time periods and goods in question. Formally,

$$\frac{\phi_{it}}{\phi_{j\tau}} = \underbrace{\frac{\phi_{it}}{\phi_{i\tau}}}_{\substack{\text{time} \\ \text{preference}}} \cdot \underbrace{\frac{\phi_{i\tau}}{\phi_{j\tau}}}_{\substack{\text{commodity} \\ \text{preference}}}.$$

The second-order conditions for the present maximization problem, like those which appeared in Chapter 10, involve a series of bordered Hessian determinants with alternating signs, except that, since in the present problem there are s constraints, the "border" of each determinant consists of s rows and s columns. To simplify the statement of the conditions, we shall adopt the following notation: We shall assume that the arguments of ϕ are numbered from 1 to $2ns$ (including those that are identically equal to zero, such as v''), so that ϕ_{ij} will represent the second-order partial derivative of ϕ with respect to the ith and jth arguments. We shall also represent the budget constraints in the following general functional form:

$$\sum_{i=1}^{n} p_t^i (x_t^i + v_t^i - \alpha_{t-1}^i v_{t-1}^i) - p_t^n \delta$$
$$= f_t (x_1, x_2, ..., x_s, \ v_1, v_2, ..., v_s)$$
$$= 0,$$
$$t = 1, 2, ..., s.$$

Here, we have represented the budget constraints *as if* each of them depended on *all* the $2ns$ arguments of the utility function. This, of course, is true only in a trivial sense, and it simply means that some (in fact, most) derivatives of each function f_t are identically zero. It is also assumed that the numbering of the arguments of the functions f_t is the same as that which is applied to the arguments of the utility function, so that f_{ti} will denote the first-order partial derivative of f_t with respect to its ith argument.

Unlike in problems which are subject to only one constraint, the first (that is, smallest) determinant in the series of determinants relevant to the present problem need not necessarily be positive (for a maximum); it must be positive if the number of constraints is odd, negative if the number of constraints is even. If there are s constraints, and if the number of goods (arguments) is $2ns$, the first determinant is of order $2s + 1$, and the last one of order $2ns + s$. (See Section 15.1.5.)

To state the second-order conditions in as compact a form as possible, we use the following notation for a typical principal minor:

$$D^r = \begin{vmatrix} \phi_{11} & \phi_{12} & \cdots & \phi_{1r} & f_{11} & f_{21} & \cdots & f_{s1} \\ \phi_{21} & \phi_{22} & \cdots & \phi_{2r} & f_{12} & f_{22} & \cdots & f_{s2} \\ \vdots & & & & & & & \vdots \\ \phi_{r1} & \phi_{r2} & \cdots & \phi_{rr} & f_{1r} & f_{2r} & \cdots & f_{sr} \\ f_{11} & f_{12} & \cdots & f_{1r} & 0 & 0 & \cdots & 0 \\ f_{21} & f_{22} & \cdots & f_{2r} & 0 & 0 & \cdots & 0 \\ \vdots & & & & & & & \vdots \\ f_{s1} & f_{s2} & \cdots & f_{sr} & 0 & 0 & \cdots & 0 \end{vmatrix} .$$

Then the second-order conditions can be stated as

(11.7) $(-1)^r D^r > 0, \qquad r = s + 1, s + 2, ..., 2ns.$

It may be helpful to rewrite the budget constraints as

(11.4b)

$$\sum_{i=1}^{n} p_t^i (x_t^i + v_t^i) = w_t,$$

where

$$t = 1, 2, ..., s.$$

(11.8a)

$$w_t = p_t^n \delta + \sum_{i=1}^{n-1} p_t^i \alpha_{t-1}^i v_{t-1}^i,$$

The quantity w_t represents the consumer's potential wealth at the beginning of period t, and it consists of two distinct parts. The first term on the rhs of (11.8a) represents the maximum income that the consumer can earn in period t, the maximum being realized if he chooses to consume zero hours of leisure (that is, if he spends δ hours at work during period t). The second expression in (11.8a) represents the market value of the consumer's initial stock holdings in period t. The notion of wealth employed here is, therefore, equivalent with purchasing power, and the wealth equation shows that the consumer's purchasing power derives from his capacity for work, as well as his ownership of stock goods.

The consumer's demand functions, which, as usual, are the solutions to the first-order conditions (11.3) and (11.4), can be stated as

(11.9a) $$\bar{x}_t^i = h_t^i (p, w_1),$$

(11.9b) $$\bar{v}_t^i = g_t^i (p, w_1),$$

$$i = 1, 2, ..., n, \quad t = 1, 2, ..., s,$$

where p denotes the vector of prices. The optimal values given by these functions constitute the consumer's economic plan for the horizon extending over the periods 1, 2, ..., s; they indicate the amounts of the various goods that the consumer plans to consume and hold in each of the s periods. The demand functions depend on the ns prices (observed and expected), and on the consumer's holdings of stocks at the beginning of the horizon. (They also depend on the α_t^i, but the effects of changes in these coefficients will not be studied in this work.) The form in which the demand functions are stated also indicates that the initial stock holdings exert their influence only through their effect on the consumer's wealth in the first period of the horizon. This means that if, for example, the amount of v_0^i were increased slightly, and that of v_0^j were decreased so as to leave the market value of the initial stock holdings unchanged, then the consumer's economic plan for the horizon would also remain unchanged, and hence the demand functions depend only on w_1. It hardly seems necessary to comment on the absence, from the demand functions, of the w_t for $t > 1$, the reason for this being that the latter quantities are themselves a part of the consumer's plan for the horizon, rather than predetermined parameters. The determinants of the consumer's desired levels of consumption and stocks in each period are the prices and the initial wealth, and consequently these parameters also determine the consumer's planned level of wealth for each period in the horizon (except that for the first period, which is already given).

The signs of the derivatives of the demand functions may be determined by differentiating the first-order conditions (11.3) and (11.4). We shall omit this analysis here, the basic method by which it is done having already been demonstrated in Chapter 10, and, as was shown there, the results are largely indeterminate. Ambiguities of sign may also be encountered in the study of compensated price changes, because in the present model the method of compensation is itself ambiguous. Thus, a price increase may be compensated, for example, by an increase in one of the stock goods, or by giving the consumer a certain amount of income (possibly in the form of credit). Furthermore, the compensation may be made available in either one of the s periods of the horizon, and, to keep the real income constant, it need not necessarily be given in the period in which the price increase goes into effect. Each method of compensation gives rise to a different definition of a substitution term, and, in general, we cannot expect that these will have the same properties as the Slutsky substitution terms introduced in the previous chapter.

As for uncompensated changes in prices and wealth, we may observe the following: An increase in the consumer's initial wealth is equivalent to an increase in income in the standard consumer model. Symbolically,

$$
(11.10a) \qquad \frac{\partial \bar{x}_t^i}{\partial w_1} = h_{tw}^i, \left.\begin{array}{c} \\ \\ \\ \\ \\ \end{array}\right\}
$$

$$
i = 1, 2, ..., n, \quad t = 1, 2, ..., s,
$$

$$
(11.10b) \qquad \frac{\partial \bar{v}_t^i}{\partial w_1} = g_{tw}^i,
$$

where $h_{tw}^i = \partial h_t^i / \partial w_1$, and $g_{tw}^i = \partial g_t^i / \partial w_1$. The effects of price changes, on the other hand, are given by

$$
(11.11a) \qquad \frac{\partial \bar{x}_t^i}{\partial p_1^j} = h_{tj1}^i + \alpha_0^j v_0^j h_{tw}^i, \qquad j = 1, 2, ..., n - 1, \left.\begin{array}{c} \\ \\ \\ \end{array}\right.
$$

$$
i = 1, 2, ..., n,
$$
$$
t = 1, 2, ..., s,
$$

$$
(11.11b) \qquad \frac{\partial \bar{x}_t^i}{\partial p_1^n} = h_{tn1}^i + \delta h_{tw}^i,
$$

$$
(11.11c) \qquad \frac{\partial \bar{x}_t^i}{\partial p_\tau^j} = h_{tj\tau}^i, \qquad i, j = 1, 2, ..., n, \quad t = 1, 2, ..., s, \quad \tau = 2, 3, ..., s,
$$

$$(11.11\mathrm{d}) \quad \frac{\partial \bar{v}_t^i}{\partial p_1^j} = g_{tj1}^i + \alpha_0^j v_0^j g_{tw}^i, \qquad j = 1, 2, ..., n - 1,$$

$$i = 1, 2, ..., n,$$
$$t = 1, 2, ..., s,$$

$$(11.11\mathrm{e}) \quad \frac{\partial \bar{v}_t^i}{\partial p_1^n} = g_{tn1}^i + \delta g_{tw}^i,$$

$$(11.11\mathrm{f}) \quad \frac{\partial \bar{v}_t^i}{\partial p_\tau^j} = g_{tj\tau}^i, \qquad i, j = 1, 2, ..., n, \quad t = 1, 2, ..., s, \quad \tau = 2, 3 ..., s,$$

where $h_{tj\tau}^i = \partial \bar{x}_t^i / \partial p_\tau^j$, and $g_{tj\tau}^i = \partial \bar{v}_t^i / \partial p_\tau^j$. What is interesting to note here is that the effects of changes in current prices (that is, changes in the prices of the first period of the horizon) are the sum of three distinct components. The first term on the rhs of (11.11a) and (11.11d) represents the effect of a change in p_1^j *if* the consumer's initial wealth were unaffected by this change; this term represents what, in Chapter 10, has been called the total price effect, and it can, in general, be decomposed into a substitution effect, and an income effect. The second term in (11.11a) and (11.11d) represents the effect of the change in the value of the consumer's initial stock holdings which is brought about by the change in p_1^j. We see, therefore, that changes in current prices carry with them a built-in compensation. In general, however, this compensation [that is, the second term in (11.11a) and (11.11d)] is not equal in magnitude to the income effect which is part of the first term in the above equations, so that the sum of these three components is, in general, not equal to the substitution effect. Of course, changes in the prices of pure flow goods (except leisure) produce no such wealth effects, nor are there any wealth effects associated with changes in expected prices.

If all prices (current and expected) change by the same proportion, the consumer will not adjust his plan. This is obvious from an inspection of conditions (11.3) and (11.4), which can be shown (after eliminating the λ_t) to be invariant to such equiproportionate changes. Hence the consumer's demand functions are homogeneous of degree zero in all prices.

11.1.2 Dynamic Aspects

When the consumer arrives at the end of period s of his horizon (or at the beginning of period 1 of the new horizon), he repeats the process of maximizing his multiperiod utility function in order to plan his economic activities for the new horizon. Under certain conditions we can say something about the relationship between the consumer's plans for the two horizons. One such condition is the assumption that the consumer's relative preferences for the various goods (that is, his commodity preferences) remain unchanged, and that his time preference should depend only on the distance between the time at which he makes his plans and the time at which the various goods are to be consumed or held (and not, for instance, on the calendar date as such). In other words, we may assume that the form of the consumer's utility function remains the same as he moves from one horizon to the next. In that case, we need not go through the process of maximizing his utility function (at the end of each horizon) in order to predict what he will plan for the next horizon; so long as the utility function remains unchanged, the form of the demand functions will also remain constant. Consequently, the plan for the next horizon can be determined directly from the consumer's demand functions by inserting into them the appropriate values of their arguments.

Of course, this being a model of an individual consumer (rather than a general equilibrium model), it cannot tell us anything about the manner in which the market prices change over time; thus, knowing the values of the p_1^j gives us no information about the values of the p_{s+1}^j. This points out one limitation of analyzing economic behavior over time in as partial a setting as a model of an individual decision maker. Nevertheless, certain characteristics of dynamic models of individual consumers (or producers) can shed some light on the dynamic properties of more general models. For instance, we may ask the following question: Given that all prices remain constant over time (and the above assumption that the utility function is fixed over time), and assuming perfect knowledge on the part of the consumer about future prices, will the consumer's plan for the new horizon be the same as that for the preceding horizon? This question is of some interest, because if the answer is in the negative, it will provide us with some indication that the equilibrium in markets for goods and services may be disrupted not only by factors outside the model (such as, say, changes in technology or government actions), but also as a result of changes in the plans of consumers (or producers) that are part of the adjustment of moving from one horizon to the next.

To find the answer to the above question, we proceed as follows: We shall denote the periods of a typical horizon by $\tau, \tau + 1, \ldots, \tau + s - 1$. Now, if the first horizon is identified by the periods $1, 2, \ldots, s$, then the periods of the second horizon must bear the labels $s + 1, s + 2, \ldots, 2s$, and so on. Therefore, τ takes the values $1, s + 1, 2s + 1, 3s + 1, \ldots$. Hence the demand functions for a typical horizon will be written as

(11.12a) $\bar{x}_t^i = h_t^i(p, w_\tau),$

(11.12b) $\bar{v}_t^i = g_t^i(p, w_\tau),$ $i = 1, 2, \ldots, n, \quad t = \tau, \tau + 1, \ldots, \tau + s - 1.$

For $t = \tau + s - 1$, we can write

(11.12b') $\bar{v}_{\tau+s-1}^i = g_{\tau+s-1}^i(p, w_\tau),$

and shifting subscripts back by s periods (which is permissible, since the demand functions for the respective periods in each horizon are the same), we have

(11.12b'')
$$\bar{v}_{\tau-1}^i = g_{\tau-1}^i(p, w_{\tau-s}).$$

Finally, setting $t = \tau$ in (11.8a), we obtain

(11.8b)
$$w_\tau = p^n\delta + \sum_{i=1}^{n-1} p^i\alpha_{\tau-1}^i v_{\tau-1}^i,$$

and substituting for the $v_{\tau-1}^i$ in (11.8b) from (11.12b''), we get

(11.13)
$$w_\tau = p^n\delta + \sum_{i=1}^{n-1} p^i\alpha_{\tau-1}^i g_{\tau-1}^i(p, w_{\tau-s}) = G(w_{\tau-s}).$$

Prices are no longer affixed with time subscripts because they are assumed to be constant, and, in fact, the same in each period of time. Equation (11.13) indicates how the consumer's initial wealth changes from one horizon to the next. For example, given the consumer's wealth in period 1 (setting $\tau = s + 1$), one can compute his wealth in period $s + 1$, the latter period being the first period of the succeeding horizon. The changes in the consumer's initial wealth in each horizon are, of course, crucial to the question on hand, since with prices assumed fixed, the consumer's plan will change only if his initial wealth changes. In general, there is no reason to expect that G is the identity function, and therefore we can, indeed, conclude that the consumer's initial wealth, and therefore his entire economic plan, will change from one horizon to another, even if all prices are constant.

Equation (11.13) may be regarded as defining the basic dynamic structure of the model; if the behavior over time of w_τ is given, then the time paths of the $\bar{x}_t^i$ and $\bar{v}_t^i$ are also determined, as can be seen from an inspection of Eq. (11.12). It is, therefore, of interest to study the type of behavior embodied in the function G, and in particular its stability properties. For this purpose, we may use the same conditions as those which we applied to the dynamic model in Chapter 8 [condition (8.67)]. The present dynamic model [that is, Eq. (11.13)] is actually much simpler than that of Chapter 8, since it consists of only one function (first-order difference equation), which has only one argument. Therefore, the stability condition takes the following simple form:

If there exists a number $k < 1$ such that

(11.14)
$$|G'| \leqslant k \quad \text{for all } w,$$

where $G' = \dfrac{dG}{dw_{\tau-s}}$, then $\lim\limits_{\tau\to\infty} G(w_{\tau-s}) = \bar{w}$ for all w_1.

It may be pointed out that if G is linear, then condition (11.14) can be replaced by "$|G'| < 1$ for all w," which is not only a sufficient condition, but also a necessary one. Naturally, if condition (11.14) is satisfied, then not only w_τ, but also the $\bar{x}^i_t$ and $\bar{v}^i_t$ will converge to some equilibrium values; the convergence of the latter variables follows directly from the continuity of the functions h^i_t and g^i_t.

To see what restrictions have to be imposed on the model if condition (11.14) is to hold, let us first of all differentiate (11.13). This gives

$$(11.15) \qquad G' = \sum_{i=1}^{n-1} p^i \alpha^i_{\tau-1} g^i_{\tau-1, w}.$$

Let us also assume

$$(11.16) \qquad\qquad \alpha^i_t \leqslant 1 \qquad \text{for all } i \text{ and } t.$$

This assumption is not quite necessary, but it simplifies the analysis, and at the same time it gives us some idea about the nature of the restrictions which will make the model stable. Differentiating (11.4b) with respect to w_τ, after replacing the x^i_t and v^i_t by their demand functions, and letting t equal τ and $\tau + 1$ alternately, we get

$$(11.17) \qquad\qquad \sum_{i=1}^{n} p^i (h^i_{\tau w} + g^i_{\tau w}) = 1,$$

$$(11.18) \qquad \frac{dw_{\tau+1}}{dw_\tau} = \sum_{i=1}^{n} p^i (h^i_{\tau+1, w} + g^i_{\tau+1, w}) = \sum_{i=1}^{n} p^i \alpha^i_\tau g^i_{\tau w} \leqslant \sum_{i=1}^{n} p^i g^i_{\tau w},$$

where the first equation in (11.18) follows from (11.4b) for $t = \tau + 1$, the second equation from (11.8a) for $t = \tau + 1$, and the inequality from (11.16).

Then it follows from (11.17) and (11.18) that

$$(11.19) \qquad \sum_{i=1}^{n} p^i g^i_{\tau+1, w} \leqslant 1 - \sum_{i=1}^{n} p^i (h^i_{\tau w} + h^i_{\tau+1, w}).$$

If one proceeds to differentiate the remaining budget equations, substituting for the rhs of each differentiated equation in the same fashion as that which led to the inequality given in (11.19), then it can be shown that

$$(11.20a) \quad \sum_{i=1}^{n} p^i \alpha^i_{\tau+s-1} g^i_{\tau+s-1, w} \leqslant \sum_{i=1}^{n} p^i g^i_{\tau+s-1, w} \leqslant 1 - \sum_{i=1}^{n} p^i \sum_{t=\tau}^{\tau+s-1} h^i_{tw},$$

or, shifting subscripts back by s periods,

$$(11.20b) \quad \sum_{i=1}^{n} p^i \alpha^i_{\tau-1} g^i_{\tau-1, w} \leqslant \sum_{i=1}^{n} p^i g^i_{\tau-1, w} \leqslant 1 - \sum_{i=1}^{n} p^i \sum_{t=\tau-s}^{\tau-1} h^i_{tw}.$$

In view of (11.14) and (11.15), it is clear that if all the g^i_{tw} are non-negative, and if all the h^i_{tw} are bounded away from zero, then condition

(11.14) will be satisfied. Formally, if there exists a positive number a (no matter how small) such that

(11.21a) $\qquad\qquad h^i_{tw} \geqslant a \qquad$ for all i, t, and w,

and if

(11.21b) $\qquad\qquad g^i_{tw} \geqslant 0 \qquad$ for all i, t, and w,

then

(11.22) $\quad 0 \leqslant \sum_{i=1}^{n} p^i \alpha^i_{\tau-1} g^i_{\tau-1,\,w} \leqslant 1 - \sum_{i=1}^{n} p^i \sum_{t=\tau-s}^{\tau-1} h^i_{tw} \leqslant 1 - sa \sum_{i=1}^{n} p^i < 1,$

in which case it follows from (11.15) that (11.14) is satisfied with

$$k = 1 - sa \sum_{i=1}^{n} p^i.$$

The essence of these conditions requires that the goods in the model be predominantly superior. The reason for this is not difficult to detect. Suppose, for example, that the consumer's initial wealth in some horizon is given an increase. Then, if all the flows were neutral goods (that is $h^i_{tw} = 0$ for all i, t, and w), and stocks neither depreciated nor appreciated (that is, $\alpha^i_t = 1$ for all i and t), then the entire increase in wealth would be carried over to the next horizon in the form of stocks, and cause an increase in the initial wealth of that horizon. This increase would, in turn, be carried over the the following horizon, and so on. Under these conditions, the level of wealth will never approach a stationary state. The situation in the example just described would be further exacerbated (as far as stability is concerned) if stock goods tended, on the whole, to appreciate over time. In that case, the initial increase in wealth would grow steadily over time, resulting in an "explosive" situation. It is precisely to prevent the latter situation that we did not permit the α^i_t to exceed unity.

However, it is clear that restrictions (11.16) and (11.21) are somewhat stronger than necessary. What is required for stability is that if the initial (equilibrium) wealth in some horizon is given an autonomous increase, then the incremental amount by which stock goods appreciate over the horizon must be more than offset by additional consumption and/or depreciation, so that only a portion of the original increase in wealth is passed on to the succeeding horizon. If this is true for all horizons, then the effect of the original increase will eventually wear off, resulting in a return to the initial equilibrium. Thus, the inclusion in the model of appreciating stocks and inferior goods is not necessarily incompatible with stability, provided the model also includes depreciating stocks, and goods that are sufficiently superior.

11.1.3 Revisability

There is one implicit assumption in the formulation of the above model which we wish to reconsider at this point: this is the assumption that the consumer executes his plan for each horizon exactly as he planned it at the beginning of the horizon. It is, however, not difficult to think of several arguments which suggest that this assumption should be relaxed so as to permit the consumer to revise his original plan, should he wish to do so, at various points during the horizon. Perhaps the most important point to be made in connection with this issue is the fact that the consumer is subject to uncertainty when he draws up a plan for an entire horizon. Thus, at the beginning of the first period of a typical horizon, the consumer may be assumed to have perfect knowledge of his initial wealth, and of the market prices prevailing on the transaction "day" of the first period; prices for future periods are, in general, not known with certainty, and so the values that the consumer assigns to these parameters are in the nature of expectations. Therefore, when the consumer arrives at later points of time within his horizon, he may find that his expectations were not fulfilled, and this may necessitate a revision in the plan for the remaining periods of the horizon.

Of course, unless something is known (or assumed) about the behavior of prices over time, we cannot say anything about the manner in which the consumer will revise his plan, and therefore we cannot establish a functional relationship between the original plan and the revised one. In fact, in the dynamical version of our model, we assumed that all prices were constant, and that the consumer had perfect knowledge of their constancy. The question, then, is whether there are reasons other than uncertainty which might induce the consumer to reconsider his original plan. There are two such reasons that are relevant in the context of our model. One of these is that, as time goes on, and the consumer moves through his horizon, the calendar dates of the different periods in the horizon come closer to the consumer, and consequently he may view them in a different light than he did when he was at the beginning of the horizon. It may then be the case that the plan, as viewed at the later date, is no longer optimal from the point of view of the consumer's time preference, thus justifying a revision. Of course, in the special case of absence of time preference (that is, if the consumer's utility index depends only on the total amount consumed and held of each good, and not at all on the distribution of the total amounts over the horizon), the utility of a given plan is independent of the date on which the plan is evaluated; in this case, the change in the consumer's (time) position within the horizon will in itself not require a reevaluation of the original plan.

As the consumer moves through time, however, he not only changes his position within his horizon, he is also in a sense moving the entire horizon with him. For example, if the consumer's planning horizon spans s periods, then his original plan may cover, say, periods $1 - s$. Now, when the consumer arrives at the beginning of period 2, his "vision" extends one period farther into the future than it did when he was at the beginning of period 1, so that his new planning horizon encompasses periods $2 - (s + 1)$. Since the original plan includes no provisions for period $s + 1$ (except an initial wealth position), the consumer may now wish to draw up a new plan which will specify, among other things, his desired levels of consumption and stock holdings for that period. We thus see that, even if we remove uncertainty and time preference from the model, periodic revisions of the consumer's plans may still be justified on the ground that the consumer's horizon is itself constantly shifting through time.

While it is not absolutely necessary to assume that the consumer revises his plans after *every* period, this assumption simplifies the analysis to some extent. As we shall see, the introduction of revisability causes few, if any, complications. Whereas in the absence of revisability the consumer draws up a plan once every s periods, under revisability he does so after every single period. This means, among other things, that only the provisions for the first period of each horizon are carried out as originally planned, while those for the remaining $s - 1$ periods are subject to revision. Whether the revised levels of the desired flows and stocks are in fact different from the original ones depends, of course, on the properties of the utility function.

Planning dates \ Consumption dates	τ	$\tau+1$	$\tau+2$	$\cdots$	$\tau+s-1$	$\tau+s$	$\tau+s+1$
τ	$_\tau\bar{x}_\tau$ $_\tau\bar{v}_\tau$	$_\tau\bar{x}_{\tau+1}$ $_\tau\bar{v}_{\tau+1}$	$_\tau\bar{x}_{\tau+2}$ $_\tau\bar{v}_{\tau+2}$	$\cdots$	$_\tau\bar{x}_{\tau+s-1}$ $_\tau\bar{v}_{\tau+s-1}$		
$\tau+1$		$_{\tau+1}\bar{x}_{\tau+1}$ $_{\tau+1}\bar{v}_{\tau+1}$	$_{\tau+1}\bar{x}_{\tau+2}$ $_{\tau+1}\bar{v}_{\tau+2}$	$\cdots$	$_{\tau+1}\bar{x}_{\tau+s-1}$ $_{\tau+1}\bar{v}_{\tau+s-1}$	$_{\tau+1}\bar{x}_{\tau+s}$ $_{\tau+1}\bar{v}_{\tau+s}$	
$\tau+2$			$_{\tau+2}\bar{x}_{\tau+2}$ $_{\tau+2}\bar{v}_{\tau+2}$	$\cdots$	$_{\tau+2}\bar{x}_{\tau+s-1}$ $_{\tau+2}\bar{v}_{\tau+s-1}$	$_{\tau+2}\bar{x}_{\tau+s}$ $_{\tau+2}\bar{v}_{\tau+s}$	$_{\tau+2}\bar{x}_{\tau+s+1}$ $_{\tau+2}\bar{v}_{\tau+s+1}$

Figure 11.1

The behavioral pattern emerging under these circumstances is depicted schematically in Fig. 11.1 for three consecutive horizons. The top row of the table represents the horizon confronting the consumer when he is at the beginning of period τ, and the entries in that row are the planned flows and stocks for the horizon spanning periods τ to $(\tau + s - 1)$. The additional subscript placed at the lower left side of each x and v indicates the date at which the respective quantity was planned. At the beginning of period $\tau + 1$, the consumer draws up a new plan for the periods $(\tau + 1)$ to $(\tau + s)$, which is shown by the entries in the second row. A similar process is repeated at the beginning of period $\tau + 2$, and in each succeeding period. The quantities in the shaded rectangles are those actually consumed and held by the consumer.

So long as it is assumed that the consumer's utility function undergoes no changes through time, we need not repeat the maximization process in every period in order to determine the consumer's revised plan; it can be obtained directly from the demand functions by inserting into them the consumer's level of wealth at the end of the preceding period (since that quantity constitutes his initial wealth for the new horizon). Formally, the actual amounts consumed and held are still given by (11.12), with $t = \tau$, and τ taking the values 1, 2, 3, ... As for the time path of wealth, it is described correctly by (11.13) for $s = 1$. The stability conditions are essentially the same as those which apply in the absence of revisability, and it is easy to see that under assumptions (11.16) and (11.21), condition (11.14) is satisfied with

$$k = 1 - a \sum_{i=1}^{n} p^i.$$

11.1.4 Collapsibility

One of the consequences of the policy under which the consumer revises his plans after every period of time is the fact that he acts *as if* his planning horizon extended over just one period. Of course, a consumer whose planning horizon does in fact extend over only one period draws up a new plan at the beginning of every period, not because he is revising plans made in the past, but because he never enters into a new period with a previously prepared plan. Thus, the behavior, on the one hand, of a consumer who has a multiperiod planning horizon and who revises his plans after every period, and the behavior, on the other hand, of a consumer with a single-period horizon have the following common characteristics:

a) Plans for the future are always made at the beginning of every period of time.

b) The *actual* levels of consumption and stock holdings are the same as those planned for the first period of each horizon.

Since there exists such a striking similarity between the behavior of a "short-sighted" consumer, and that of a consumer whose decision making is characterized by foresightedness as well as willingness to revise plans made in the past, one may wonder whether or not the above two approaches to intertemporal utility maximization can be represented by one basic model. This, as it turns out, can indeed be done, and in the remainder of this section we shall prove the following proposition:

If a consumer maximizes a multiperiod utility function which is constrained by a set of appropriate budget equations, and if the optimal plans are subject to revision after every period, then there exists a one-period utility function which, when maximized subject to a single budget constraint, yields a set of dynamical demand functions that trace out the time paths of the actual amounts consumed and held by the consumer in question.

Let us first restate the decision problem of a consumer with a multiperiod planning horizon. The problem is to maximize

(11.23) $u = \phi(x_\tau, x_{\tau+1}, ..., x_{\tau+s-1}, v_\tau, v_{\tau+1}, ..., v_{\tau+s-1})$,

subject to

(11.24) $\sum_{i=1}^{n} p_t^i(x_t^i + v_t^i) = w_t$,

where

(11.25) $w_t = p_t^n \delta + \sum_{i=1}^{n-1} p_t^i \alpha_{t-1}^i v_{t-1}^i$,

$\qquad\qquad\qquad t = \tau, \tau + 1, ..., \tau + s - 1.$

The first-order conditions for this problem are given by (11.24) and (11.25), and the following equations:

(11.26a) $\phi_{it} + \lambda_t p_t^i = 0, \quad i = 1, 2, ..., n,$

(11.26b) $\phi_{it} + \lambda_t p_t^i - \lambda_{t+1} p_{t+1}^i \alpha_t^i = 0,$
$\qquad\qquad i = n + 1, n + 2, ..., 2n,$

$\qquad\qquad\qquad t = \tau, \tau + 1, ..., \tau + s - 1,$

where $\phi_{it} = \partial\phi/\partial x_t^i$ for $i = 1, 2, ..., n$; $\phi_{it} = \partial\phi/\partial v_t^{i-n}$ for $i = n + 1$, $n + 2, ..., 2n$; $p_t^i = p_t^{i+n}$ for $i = 1, 2, ..., n$; $p_t^i = p_t^{i-n}$ for $i = n + 1$, $n + 2, ..., 2n$; $\alpha_t^i = \alpha_t^{i-n}$ for $i = n + 1, n + 2, ..., 2n$; and $\lambda_{\tau+s} = 0$. We shall also note that, after appropriate substitutions for λ_τ and $\lambda_{\tau+1}$ from (11.26a), the equations in (11.26b) for $t = \tau$ can be written as

(11.26b′) $\phi_{i\tau} - \phi_{j\tau} + \dfrac{\phi_{n,\tau+1} p_{\tau+1}^i \alpha_\tau^i}{p_{\tau+1}^n} = 0,$

$\qquad\qquad\qquad i = n + 1, n + 2, ..., 2n, \quad j = i - n.$

The solution to the problem is given by the demand functions

(11.27a) $\bar{x}_t^i = h_t^i(p, w_\tau),$

(11.27b) $\bar{v}_t^i = g_t^i(p, w_\tau),$

$\qquad\qquad i = 1, 2, ..., n, \quad t = \tau, \tau + 1, ..., \tau + s - 1,$

where p denotes the vector of prices in the horizon as they are seen (that is, observed for $t = \tau$, and expected for $t > \tau$) by the consumer at the beginning of period τ. If plans are revised after every period, the actual levels of flows and stocks are given by (11.27) with $t = \tau$, and $\tau = 1, 2, 3, \ldots$ (see Fig. 11.1, and accompanying explanation).

We shall now substitute the demand functions for the flows and stocks in periods $\tau + 1, \tau + 2, \ldots, \tau + s - 1$, except the demand function for $x_{\tau+1}^n$, into the utility function and the budget constraints. Then the utility function becomes

$$(11.28) \quad u = \phi\,[x_\tau, v_\tau, x_{\tau+1}^n, h_{\tau+1}(p, w_\tau), \ldots, h_{\tau+s-1}(p, w_\tau), g_{\tau+1}(p, w_\tau), \ldots$$
$$\ldots, g_{\tau+s-1}(p, w_\tau)],$$

where the $h_t(p, w_\tau)$ and $g_t(p, w_\tau)$ denote the vectors of the h_t^i and g_t^i, except that, in the former set of vectors, one component, namely, $h_{\tau+1}^n$, has been removed. Solving for $x_{\tau+1}^n$ explicitly from (11.24) and (11.25) for $t = \tau + 1$, and substituting into (11.28), we obtain

$$(11.29) \quad u = \phi\,[x_\tau, v_\tau, \xi(v_\tau;\ p, w_\tau), h_{\tau+1}(p, w_\tau), \ldots$$
$$\ldots, h_{\tau+s-1}(p, w_\tau), g_{\tau+1}(p, w_\tau), \ldots, g_{\tau+s-1}(p, w_\tau)]$$
$$= \Phi\,(x_\tau, v_\tau),$$

where

$$x_{\tau+1}^n = \frac{p_{\tau+1}^n \delta + \displaystyle\sum_{i=1}^{n-1} p_{\tau+1}^i [\alpha_\tau^i v_\tau^i - h_{\tau+1}^i(p, w_\tau) - g_{\tau+1}^i(p, w_\tau)]}{p_{\tau+1}^n}$$
$$= \xi\,(v_\tau;\ p, w_\tau).$$

What is important to note here is that, as a result of the substitutions, the only unknowns left in the function ϕ are x_τ and v_τ, the remaining ones being fully determined by the given parameters p and w_τ; hence the representation of the original utility function by $\Phi(x_\tau, v_\tau)$.

Consider now the following problem:
Maximize the utility function

$$(11.30) \qquad\qquad \Phi(x_\tau, v_\tau),$$

subject to

$$(11.31) \qquad \sum_{i=1}^{n} p_\tau^i(x_\tau^i + v_\tau^i) = p_\tau^n \delta + \sum_{i=1}^{n-1} p_\tau^i \alpha_{\tau-1}^i v_{\tau-1}^i = w_\tau.$$

Suppose that the solution to this problem can be stated as

$$(11.32a) \qquad \bar{x}_\tau^i = \hat{h}_\tau^i\,(p_\tau, w_\tau),$$

$$(11.32b) \qquad \bar{v}_\tau^i = \hat{g}_\tau^i\,(p_\tau, w_\tau),$$

$$i = 1, 2, \ldots, n,$$

then what the above proposition asserts is that the functions in (11.32) are identical with those given in (11.27) for $t = \tau$.

The first-order conditions for the above problem are given by (11.31) and the following equations:

$$(11.33) \qquad \Phi_{i\tau} + \mu p_\tau^i = 0, \qquad i = 1, 2, ..., 2n,$$

where $\Phi_{i\tau} = \partial \Phi / \partial x_\tau^i$ for $i = 1, 2, ..., n$; $\Phi_{i\tau} = \partial \Phi / \partial v_\tau^{i-n}$ for $i = n + 1, n + 2, ..., 2n$; μ is a Lagrange multiplier; and the notation p_τ^i has the same meaning as that given to the p_t^i in Eq. (11.26). Differentiating (11.29), and making use of the definition of the function $\xi(v_\tau; p, w_\tau)$, we get

$$(11.34a) \qquad \Phi_{i\tau} = \phi_{i\tau}, \qquad i = 1, 2, ..., n,$$

$$(11.34b) \qquad \Phi_{i\tau} = \phi_{i\tau} + \frac{\phi_{n,\tau+1} p_{\tau+1}^i \alpha_\tau^i}{p_{\tau+1}^n}, \qquad i = n + 1, n + 2, ..., 2n,$$

where the $\phi_{i\tau}$ and α_τ^i are defined as in (11.26). Substituting for $\Phi_{i\tau}$ in (11.33) from (11.34), we get

$$(11.35a) \qquad \phi_{i\tau} + \mu p_\tau^i = 0, \qquad i = 1, 2, ..., n,$$

$$(11.35b) \qquad \phi_{i\tau} + \frac{\phi_{n,\tau+1} p_{\tau+1}^i \alpha_\tau^i}{p_{\tau+1}^n} + \mu p_\tau^i = 0, \qquad i = n + 1, n + 2, ..., 2n.$$

Eliminating μ from the equations in (11.35), we have

$$(11.36) \qquad \phi_{i\tau} - \phi_{j\tau} + \frac{\phi_{n,\tau+1} p_{\tau+1}^i \alpha_\tau^i}{p_{\tau+1}^n} = 0,$$

$$i = n + 1, n + 2, ..., 2n, \qquad j = i - n,$$

which are the same equations as those given in (11.26b').

Now, it may be pointed out that maximizing Φ subject to the constraint in (11.31) is equivalent to maximizing ϕ subject to the constraints given in (11.24) and (11.25) while holding $(n - 1)(s - 1)$ of its arguments constant at the levels at which ϕ attains its constrained maximum if it is maximized over *all* its arguments. This relationship between the two maximization problems follows from the fact that Φ is constructed by inserting into ϕ the maximizing values (that is, demand functions) of $(n - 1)(s - 1)$ of its arguments. It should also be noted that all the constraints given in (11.24) and (11.25) are satisfied in the problem given in (11.30) and (11.31): the budget constraint for $t = \tau$ is reproduced in (11.31); that for $t = \tau + 1$ is satisfied because the term $x_{\tau+1}^n$ in the utility function is replaced by making use of the budget equations for period $\tau + 1$; and the budget constraints for the periods $\tau + 2, \tau + 3, ..., \tau + s - 1$ are automatically satisfied because the replacement of the x_t^i and v_t^i in these equations by their demand functions transforms these constraints into identities which hold for all p and w_τ. From this it follows that the constrained maximum of Φ equals the constrained maximum of ϕ, and, moreover, the values of the x_τ and v_τ which maximize Φ are the same as those that maximize ϕ. We can see this by observing that the first-order conditions (11.31) and (11.35) are a subset of the first-order conditions (11.24) through (11.26), and with $(n-1)(s-1)$ variables taking the same values in both problems, the solutions to the above two sets of first-order conditions must be the same for the corresponding variables. Hence the functions $\hat{h}_\tau^i$ and $\hat{g}_\tau^i$ in (11.32) are the same as the h_t^i and g_t^i in (11.27) for $t = \tau$, and thus the proposition is proved.

The possibility of collapsing the multiperiod optimization problem into a single-period problem is of some significance, because it provides us with a justification for simplifying the structure of models dealing with intertemporal optimization. Obviously, the multiperiod model is potentially richer than the single-period model because it can deal with problems and aspects of intertemporal optimization for which the one-period model is too narrow. On the other hand, the assumption that plans are revised, if necessary, after each period of time seems to be quite reasonable. If so, then under the assumptions made in this section, it is possible to analyze intertemporal behavior with a single-period model without assuming that the decision maker's planning horizon consists of only one period.

11.2 LIFETIME MODELS

A special class of intertemporal utility maximization models are those in which the planning horizon of the consumer extends over his entire economic life. Models in this class may be regarded as special cases of the type of models discussed in the preceding section; thus, if in the model given in Section 11.1 the symbol s (the number of periods in the planning horizon) is assumed to be equal to the total number of periods during which the consumer expects to make economic decisions, then the latter model becomes a so-called *lifetime model*. Of course, in the context of such a model, we cannot talk about a moving horizon (and associated problems) because one of the endpoints of the horizon is (by definition) fixed.* But the issue of revisability is still relevant, since there is nothing in the nature of a lifetime model that rules out the possibility, or rationality, of subjecting plans to periodic revisions.

In the analysis of a particular lifetime model presented below, we take a simplified approach to the problem and assume that the consumer's plan for a typical period of time consists not of vectors of flows and stocks of all the different goods, but only of the total amount of leisure, and the sum of all expenditures in each period of time. This assumption results in considerable

---

* An exception to this case is a model in which the end of the economic lifetime (e.g., the date of retirement) is itself a decision variable. The introduction of this variable into the model will not necessarily lead to a moving horizon, but it allows for changes in both endpoints of the horizon.

(notational) simplification, but at the same time it is not all that unreasonable. After all, a consumer who draws up a plan for as long a span of time as his economic life may not be concerned, in such a plan, with such fine details as the amounts of the various goods to be consumed and held in the different periods of his economic life; but he may very well confine himself to such major decisions as the total amounts of leisure and purchasing power to be made available in each period. Having made these long-run decisions, the consumer will then be faced with a series of short-run problems of allocating his income in each period among the different goods; which problems may be solved by using either a one-period model of the type analyzed in Chapter 10, or a multiperiod model of the type presented in Section 11.1.

We shall make another assumption about the utility function of the consumer in order to facilitate the analysis of certain aspects of the model: it will be assumed that the utilities of the bundles of goods in the different periods of the horizon are independent of one another. This assumption enables us to express the consumer's utility index as a sum of independent utility functions. Each of these functions (except one) depends on the two variables that constitute the consumer's plan for the respective period: total expenditures and leisure time. As for stocks, we will introduce one stock variable into the utility function of the last period of the horizon, and this variable will represent the value (in dollars) of the consumer's assets at the end of his economic life. This assumption by no means implies that the consumer will not hold stocks during his lifetime, but only that his utility index is not affected by changes in his stock holdings except those which constitute his terminal wealth.

11.2.1   The Static Structure of the Model

If x_t denotes total expenditures in period t, y_t leisure time in period t, and v_T the consumer's wealth at the end of period T, T being the last period in his economic life, then the utility index is written as

$$(11.37) \qquad u = \sum_{t=1}^{T-1} \phi^t(x_t, y_t) + \phi^T(x_T, y_T, v_T),$$

where, in general, the form of the functions ϕ^t may be different for each particular value of t. Since the consumer's stock holdings in periods other than the last do not appear in the utility function, we need not subject the consumer's choices in each period to a periodic budget constraint. Naturally, the consumer must keep his books balanced, so to speak, which means that spending in excess of the available purchasing power in any period of time must be offset by borrowing, while income not spent is assumed to be lent, and thereby converted into a financial asset. It is, however, necessary to impose on the consumer an overall budget constraint, relating his final assets to his receipts and expenditures during his lifetime. This constraint may be constructed in the following manner: If the consumer starts out with an initial asset position of v_0 dollars, then the value of his assets at the end of the first period is given by

$$[v_0 + w(\delta - y_1) - x_1](1 + r) = v_1,$$

where δ again denotes the length of a typical period of time, w denotes the prevailing wage rate, and r the prevailing rate of interest. If the consumer spends less than his total purchasing power, then $v_1 > 0$, whereas if he spends in excess of his purchasing power, then $v_1 < 0$, in which case v_1 indicates the consumer's debt.

This construction is based on a number of assumptions. First, it is assumed that the consumer may spend his earnings in the same period in which they are received; consequently, his purchasing power in period 1 is is given by $v_0 + w(\delta - y_1)$. Second, if the consumer wishes to spend more than the available purchasing power, he must borrow the difference at the beginning of the period, and pay interest on the amount borrowed for the full period; similarly, if he intends to spend less than the available amount of purchasing power, he may invest the remainder at the beginning of the period, and he will earn one period's worth of interest on that amount. Third, it is assumed that he can borrow and lend at the same rate of interest. Finally, to make things simple, we assume that the rate of interest and wage rate are constant throughout the horizon.

Moving subscripts ahead by one period in the above equation, we get

$$[v_1 + w(\delta - y_2) - x_2](1 + r) = v_2,$$

which, after substituting for v_1 from the preceding equation, and rearranging terms, becomes

$$v_0(1 + r)^2 + [w(\delta - y_1) - x_1](1 + r)^2 + [w(\delta - y_2) - x_2](1 + r) = v_2.$$

If one repeats this iterative process sufficiently, one obtains an equation involving the consumer's terminal assets v_T. This equation is given by

$$v_0(1 + r)^T + \sum_{t=1}^{T} [w(\delta - y_t) - x_t](1 + r)^{T-t+1} = v_T.$$

We may rearrange this into the form of a standard budget equation, showing total expenditures on one side, and total receipts on the other. Accordingly, we write the above equation as

$$(11.38a) \qquad \sum_{t=1}^{T} (x_t + wy_t)(1+r)^{T-t+1} + v_T = v_0(1+r)^T + w\delta \sum_{t=1}^{T} (1+r)^{T-t+1}.$$

A few observations are now in order. Perhaps the first thing to point out is that, as in the standard budget constraint, the lhs of (11.38a) consists of a sum of price-quantity products. Of course, one of the goods (x_t) is not a good in the common sense of the word, but one which is expressed in monetary (rather than physical) units. But since the market price of one unit of x_t (that is, one dollar's worth of goods purchased in period t) is obviously equal to one dollar, the reader may wonder why in Eq. (11.38a) the price assigned to x_t is different from unity. The reason for this is that the quantity $(1 + r)^{T-t+1}$ represents not the market price of x_t, but the *opportunity cost* of one unit of x_t. Thus, if the consumer invested one dollar in period t, and reinvested it (together with the earned interest) after each period, the original dollar would at the end of period T have grown to $(1 + r)^{T-t+1}$ dollars. This quantity, therefore, represents the value of final assets which the consumer forgoes when he spends, rather than saves, one dollar in period t. Hence the quantity $(1 + r)^{T-t+1}$ represents the opportunity cost of one dollar's worth of x_t in terms of final assets.

In the case of leisure, we see that its opportunity cost is compounded of two factors: w represents the income which the consumer gives up in period t when he consumes one unit of leisure time in period t instead of spending that time at work, and this forgone amount of income is multiplied by $(1 + r)^{T-t+1}$, since the latter is the quantity of final assets which he could make available to himself if he invested a dollar of income earned in period t. Thus, the quantity $w(1 + r)^{T-t+1}$ represents the opportunity cost of one unit of y_t in terms of final assets. The opportunity cost of one dollar's worth of final assets (in terms of final assets) is, of course, just equal to one, as can be verified from (11.38a).

The lhs of the budget constraint may also be interpreted in terms of capitalized values. Since the quantity $(1 + r)^{T-t+1}$ is equal to the capitalized value (at the end of period T) of one dollar in period t, the lhs of (11.38a) represents the capitalized value of the consumer's purchases over his entire horizon. This quantity should be equal to the capitalized value of the consumer's income, which is precisely what (11.38a) says; the first expression on the rhs of the equation represents the capitalized value of the consumer's initial assets, and the second expression represents the capitalized value of a constant stream of receipts consisting of $w\delta$ dollars per period. Thus, the rhs of (11.38a) may be referred to as the capitalized value of the consumer's (potential) wealth over his economic lifetime. (The reference to "potenial " in the last sentence is in recognition of the fact that the quantity $w\delta$ represents the *maximum*, rather than the *actual*, amount that the consumer can earn in wages in each period.)

The budget constraint may equally well be formulated in terms of present values. This may be done by dividing both sides of (11.38a) by $(1 + r)^T$, thus obtaining

$$(11.38b) \qquad \sum_{t=1}^{T} (x_t + wy_t)(1+r)^{1-t} + v_T(1+r)^{-T} = v_0 + w\delta \sum_{t=1}^{T} (1+r)^{1-t}.$$

Clearly, the present value (that is, at the beginning of period 1) of one dollar received at the end of period $t - 1$ (or at the beginning of period t) is equal to $(1 + r)^{1-t}$, and that of one unit of leisure in period $t - 1$ is $w(1 + r)^{1-t}$. The latter quantity is the product of two components: the opportunity cost of a unit of leisure time in period $t - 1$ and the present value of one dollar received at the end of period $t - 1$. Therefore, the lhs of (11.38b) represents the present value of the consumer's purchases over the horizon, while the rhs equals the present value of the consumer's (potential) wealth; the latter is the sum of his initial endowment, and the present value of a constant stream of receipts, $w\delta$ dollars per period of time.

Our problem can now be stated as maximizing (11.37) subject to (11.38). If the problem has an interior solution (that is, $\bar{x}_t > 0$ for all t, and $0 < \bar{y}_t < \delta$ for all t), then the first-order conditions are given by (11.38a) and the following equations:

(11.39a) $\qquad \phi_x^t + \lambda(1 + r)^{T-t+1} = 0,$ $\left.\begin{array}{l} \\ \\ \end{array}\right\}$ $t = 1, 2, ..., T,$

(11.39b) $\qquad \phi_y^t + \lambda w(1 + r)^{T-t+1} = 0,$

(11.39c) $\qquad \phi_v^T + \lambda \qquad\qquad\qquad = 0,$

where $\phi_x^t = \partial\phi^t/\partial x_t$, $\phi_y^t = \partial\phi^t/\partial y_t$, and $\phi_v^T = \partial\phi^T/\partial v_T$. These equations give rise to the familiar conditions equating marginal rates of substitution with price (opportunity cost) ratios. For example, from (11.39a) we get

$$\frac{\phi_x^t}{\phi_x^\tau} = \frac{(1 + r)^{T-t+1}}{(1 + r)^{T-\tau+1}} = (1 + r)^{\tau-t},$$

according to which the MRS between spending in period t and spending in period τ must equal the ratio of the respective opportunity costs. This ratio reduces to $(1 + r)^{\tau-t}$, which represents (as does any price ratio) the terms at which the respective goods can be exchanged (or transformed into one another) in the market. If $\tau > t$, then the quantity $(1 + r)^{\tau-t}$ is simply the capitalized value, at the end of period τ, of one dollar invested at the end of period t; if $\tau < t$, then $(1 + r)^{\tau-t}$ represents the present value, at the beginning of period τ, of one dollar received at the beginning of period t. Similar interpretations may be given to the conditions involving the marginal rates of substitution between spending and leisure time, leisure time in different periods, and so on.

The second-order conditions, as in any constrained optimization problem, involve a series of bordered Hessian determinants. Taking into account the fact the certain cross-partial derivatives of the utility function are zero, we can state the conditions as

(11.40)

$$
\begin{vmatrix}
\phi^1_{xx} & \phi^1_{xy} & (1+r)^T \\
\phi^1_{yx} & \phi^1_{yy} & w(1+r)^T \\
(1+r)^T & w(1+r)^T & 0
\end{vmatrix} > 0,
\quad
\begin{vmatrix}
\phi^1_{xx} & \phi^1_{xy} & 0 & (1+r)^T \\
\phi^1_{yx} & \phi^1_{yy} & 0 & w(1+r)^T \\
0 & 0 & \phi^2_{xx} & (1+r)^{T-1} \\
(1+r)^T & w(1+r)^T & (1+r)^{T-1} & 0
\end{vmatrix} < 0, \dots;
$$

$$
\begin{vmatrix}
\phi^1_{xx} & \phi^1_{xy} & 0 & 0 & \cdots & 0 & 0 & 0 & (1+r)^T \\
\phi^1_{yx} & \phi^1_{yy} & 0 & 0 & \cdots & 0 & 0 & 0 & w(1+r)^T \\
0 & 0 & \phi^2_{xx} & \phi^2_{xy} & \cdots & 0 & 0 & 0 & (1-r)^{T-1} \\
0 & 0 & \phi^2_{yx} & \phi^2_{yy} & \cdots & 0 & 0 & 0 & w(1+r)^{T-1} \\
\vdots & & & & & & & & \vdots \\
0 & 0 & 0 & 0 & \cdots & \phi^T_{xx} & \phi^T_{xy} & \phi^T_{xv} & (1+r) \\
0 & 0 & 0 & 0 & \cdots & \phi^T_{yx} & \phi^T_{yy} & \phi^T_{yv} & w(1+r) \\
0 & 0 & 0 & 0 & \cdots & \phi^T_{vx} & \phi^T_{vy} & \phi^T_{vv} & 1 \\
(1+r)^T & w(1+r)^T & (1+r)^{T-1} & w(1+r)^{T-1} & \cdots & (1+r) & w(1+r) & 1 & 0
\end{vmatrix} < 0.
$$

11.2.2 Revisability and Consistent Planning

At this stage of the analysis, we would normally turn to an examination of the properties of the demand functions (the solution to the first-order conditions), but this time we shall omit this particular exercise, it being assumed that the reader is by now able to do this by himself. Instead, we intend to look at certain implications of the possibility that the consumer may revise his original plan as he moves through his horizon. A rationalization for introducing revisability, even under conditions of perfect knowledge, has already been given in Section 11.1.3. In this section, we wish to address ourselves specifically to the following question: Given an optimal plan made at some initial time period τ, under what conditions will the consumer abide by his original plan even if he reevaluates it at some later points of time? More formally, if the maximization of the utility function over the periods τ to T yields the optimal plan P, under what conditions will the maximization of the utility function over the periods $(\tau + s)$ to T, where $1 \leqslant s \leqslant T - \tau$, yield a plan identical with those provisions of plan P that pertain to the periods $(\tau + s)$ to T?

To carry out this investigation, it is convenient to affix additional superscripts to the various components of the utility function. Consequently, we rewrite (11.37) as

$$(11.41) \qquad u_\tau = \sum_{t=\tau}^{T-1} {}^\tau\phi^t(x_t, y_t) + {}^\tau\phi^T(x_T, y_T, v_T),$$

where ${}^\tau\phi^t(x_t, y_t)$ represents the utility of the bundle (x_t, y_t) *as viewed by the consumer at the beginning of period* τ. Period τ may or may not represent the first period in the consumer's economic life. It is important to realize that the superscript τ is not merely a device for helping us keep track of the dates at which the consumer may reassess his plans, but it actually is an integral part of the functional notation. Thus, ${}^\tau\phi^t$ and ${}^{\tau+1}\phi^t$ are, in general, two different functions. Of course, when the consumer draws up a plan for his horizon at some initial period τ, he is presumably already taking into consideration certain changes in his preferences that he expects to experience in future periods of time. These expected changes in preferences are allowed for by the presence of the superscript t, which, like τ, serves here as an economical device for denoting different functional forms. However, expectations about future preferences formed at one point of time may not necessarily be realized, so that at subsequent points of time the consumer may find himself with a preference structure different from what he expected it to be. These changes may be caused by the fact that, as the consumer moves through time, he is constantly changing his point of vantage relative to the different calendar dates, as well as the end of his horizon. Second, as the consumer moves through time, he is accumulating an ever-growing stock of past consumption experience on which he may draw in forming, and consequently changing, his expectations about future preferences. It is these changes in the expected preference structure of the consumer which the superscript τ is meant to make possible.

The maximization of u_τ is constrained by a budget equation which may be stated as

$$(11.42) \quad \sum_{t=\tau}^{T} (x_t + wy_t)(1+r)^{T-t+1} + v_T = v_{\tau-1}(1+r)^{T-\tau+1} + w\delta \sum_{t=\tau}^{T} (1+r)^{T-t+1}.$$

The first-order conditions are, therefore, given by (11.42), plus the equations

$$
\begin{aligned}
(11.43a) \qquad & {}^\tau\phi_x^t + \lambda(1+r)^{T-t+1} && = 0, \\
(11.43b) \qquad & {}^\tau\phi_y^t + \lambda w(1+r)^{T-t+1} && = 0,
\end{aligned}
\right\} \quad t = \tau, \tau+1, ..., T,
$$

$$(11.43c) \qquad {}^\tau\phi_v^T + \lambda \qquad\qquad\qquad = 0,$$

where ${}^\tau\phi_x^t = \partial{}^\tau\phi^t/\partial x_t$, ${}^\tau\phi_y^t = \partial{}^\tau\phi^t/\partial y_t$, and ${}^\tau\phi_v^T = \partial{}^\tau\phi^T/\partial v_T$. The second-order conditions are the same as those in (11.40) (after adding the superscript τ). We shall make no further references to these conditions in this or the following analysis, but assume that they are satisfied for all the problems that will be discussed.

We assume that the consumer is free to revise the above plan (that is, the solution to the first-order conditions) in any subsequent period. Whether the revision takes place in period $\tau + 1$ or at a later date is not really essential to the present analysis, so that the date of revision may, without loss of generality, be denoted by $\tau + s$, where $1 \leqslant s \leqslant T - \tau$. When the consumer arrives at that date, he maximizes his new utility function over the remaining period of his lifetime, subject to an appropriate budget constraint. In other words, revising the original plan at the beginning of period $\tau + s$ is equivalent to maximizing

$$(11.44) \qquad u_{\tau+s} = \sum_{t=\tau+s}^{T-1} {}^{\tau+s}\phi^t(x_t, y_t) + {}^{\tau+s}\phi^T(x_T, y_T, v_T),$$

subject to

$$(11.45) \qquad \sum_{t=\tau+s}^{T} (x_t + wy_t)(1 + r)^{T-t+1} + v_T$$
$$= v_{\tau+s-1}(1 + r)^{T-\tau-s+1} + w\delta \sum_{t=\tau+s}^{T} (1 + r)^{T-t+1}.$$

Now, the value of the consumer's assets at the beginning of period $\tau + s$, that is, $v_{\tau+s-1}$, may be expressed in terms of his initial endowment $v_{\tau-1}$, his income during the periods τ to $(\tau + s - 1)$, and his expenditures in those periods. (The construction of such a relationship is possible because the consumer must balance his books in each period of time.) It can be shown that

$$(11.46)$$
$$v_{\tau+s-1} = v_{\tau-1}(1+r)^s + w\delta \sum_{t=\tau}^{\tau+s-1} (1+r)^{\tau+s-t} - \sum_{t=\tau}^{\tau+s-1} (x_t+wy_t)(1+r)^{\tau+s-1}.$$

If we substitute for $v_{\tau+s-1}$ in (11.45) from (11.46), and rearrange terms, we obtain Eq. (11.42). Thus, the maximization of $u_{\tau+s}$ is constrained by exactly the same budget equation as is the maximization of u_τ, except that when maximizing $u_{\tau+s}$ (at the beginning of period $\tau + s$), the quantities x_t and y_t for $t = \tau, \tau + 1, \ldots, \tau + s - 1$ are in the nature of historical data, rather than unknown variables. Consequently, the first-order conditions for the maximization of $u_{\tau+s}$ are given by (11.42) (with the x_t and y_t for periods τ through $\tau + s - 1$ already known), and the following:

$$(11.47a) \quad {}^{\tau+s}\phi_x^t + \mu(1 + r)^{T-t+1} = 0, \quad \Bigg\} $$
$$(11.47b) \quad {}^{\tau+s}\phi_y^t + \mu w(1 + r)^{T-t+1} = 0, \quad \Bigg\} \quad t = \tau + s, \tau + s + 1, \ldots, T,$$
$$(11.47c) \quad {}^{\tau+s}\phi_v^T + \mu \qquad\qquad\quad = 0,$$

where μ is a Lagrange multiplier.

Consumption dates →

Planning dates ↓

	τ	$\tau+1$	$\tau+2$	$\tau+3$	$\tau+4$	$\cdots$	T
τ	$_{\tau}\bar{x}_{\tau}$ $_{\tau}\bar{y}_{\tau}$	$_{\tau}\bar{x}_{\tau+1}$ $_{\tau}\bar{y}_{\tau+1}$	$_{\tau}\bar{x}_{\tau+2}$ $_{\tau}\bar{y}_{\tau+2}$	$_{\tau}\bar{x}_{\tau+3}$ $_{\tau}\bar{y}_{\tau+3}$	$_{\tau}\bar{x}_{\tau+4}$ $_{\tau}\bar{y}_{\tau+4}$	$\cdots$	$_{\tau}\bar{x}_{T}$ $_{\tau}\bar{y}_{T}$
$\tau+1$		$_{\tau+1}\bar{x}_{\tau+1}$ $_{\tau+1}\bar{y}_{\tau+1}$	$_{\tau+1}\bar{x}_{\tau+2}$ $_{\tau+1}\bar{y}_{\tau+2}$	$_{\tau+1}\bar{x}_{\tau+3}$ $_{\tau+1}\bar{y}_{\tau+3}$	$_{\tau+1}\bar{x}_{\tau+4}$ $_{\tau+1}\bar{y}_{\tau+4}$	$\cdots$	$_{\tau+1}\bar{x}_{T}$ $_{\tau+1}\bar{y}_{T}$
$\tau+2$			$_{\tau+2}\bar{x}_{\tau+2}$ $_{\tau+2}\bar{y}_{\tau+2}$	$_{\tau+2}\bar{x}_{\tau+3}$ $_{\tau+2}\bar{y}_{\tau+3}$	$_{\tau+2}\bar{x}_{\tau+4}$ $_{\tau+2}\bar{y}_{\tau+4}$	$\cdots$	$_{\tau+2}\bar{x}_{T}$ $_{\tau+2}\bar{y}_{T}$

Figure 11.2

Before proceeding with the formal analysis, it might be helpful to describe the nature of the problem with the aid of the diagram given in Fig. 11.2. The entries in the first row represent the consumer's optimal plan when he is at the beginning of the initial time period τ. (Subscripts on the rhs of a symbol represent consumption dates, those on the lhs denote planning dates.) If we assume that the consumer revises his plans at the beginning of every period, the first revision will take place at the beginning of period $\tau + 1$. The result of this revision, that is, the consumer's optimal plan at the beginning of period $\tau + 1$, is given by the entries in the second row of the diagram. Now, in general, we have no reason to expect that the new plan will be consistent with the original plan; that is, we should not necessarily expect that

$$_{\tau}\bar{x}_{\tau+1} = {}_{\tau+1}\bar{x}_{\tau+1}, \quad _{\tau}\bar{y}_{\tau+1} = {}_{\tau+1}\bar{y}_{\tau+1}, \quad _{\tau}\bar{x}_{\tau+2} = {}_{\tau+1}\bar{x}_{\tau+2}, \quad _{\tau}\bar{y}_{\tau+2} = {}_{\tau+1}\bar{y}_{\tau+2},$$

and so on. However, if these equations *do* hold, then we shall refer to such a situation as *consistent planning*. However, as the consumer is free to revise his plans whenever he sees fit, and as frequently as he wishes, we will say that he is a consistent planner only if his planning is consistent with respect to *any two* plans; that is, only if

$$_{\tau+t-1}\bar{x}_{\tau+s} = {}_{\tau+t}\bar{x}_{\tau+s}, \text{ and } _{\tau+t-1}\bar{y}_{\tau+s} = {}_{\tau+t}\bar{y}_{\tau+s} \text{ for } s = 1, 2, ..., T - \tau,$$

and $t = 1, 2, ..., s$. In terms of Fig. 11.2, if the table were complete, that is, if it had $T - \tau + 1$ rows (the number of columns in each row being one less than that in the preceding row), then we would say that the consumer's plans were consistent if in each column all the pairs $(\bar{x}, \bar{y})$ had the same values. (While for consistent planning we insist that the values of the chosen bundles be uniform within each column of Fig. 11.2, they need not, of course, be the same from one column to another.) To express this idea in words, consistent planning means that the optimal bundle for any particular period of time is independent of the planning date.

If we eliminate λ from (11.43), then the first-order conditions may be stated as

$$(11.48a) \qquad \frac{{}^{\tau}\phi_x^t}{{}^{\tau}\phi_v^T} = (1 + r)^{T-t+1},$$

$$(11.48b) \qquad \frac{{}^{\tau}\phi_y^t}{{}^{\tau}\phi_v^T} = w(1 + r)^{T-t+1}, \qquad \left.\right\} \quad t = \tau, \tau + 1, ..., T,$$

while the elimination of μ from (11.47) enables us to write

$$(11.49a) \qquad \frac{{}^{\tau+s}\phi_x^t}{{}^{\tau+s}\phi_v^T} = (1 + r)^{T-t+1},$$

$$(11.49b) \qquad \frac{{}^{\tau+s}\phi_y^t}{{}^{\tau+s}\phi_v^T} = w(1 + r)^{T-t+1} \qquad \left.\right\} \quad t = \tau + s, t + s + 1, ..., T.$$

Thus, the conditions for consistent planning will be satisfied if the above two sets of first-order conditions have the same solution. More precisely, planning will be consistent if the optimal values of the x_t and y_t for periods $\tau + s$, $\tau + s + 1$, ..., T, obtained by solving the system (11.48) and (11.42), are the same as the solution to the system (11.49) and (11.42). In view of (11.48) and (11.49), and the fact that the two sets of first-order conditions share the same budget equation, it follows that planning is consistent if and only if

$$(11.50a) \qquad \frac{{}^{\tau}\phi_x^t}{{}^{\tau}\phi_v^T} = \frac{{}^{\tau+s}\phi_x^t}{{}^{\tau+s}\phi_v^T},$$

$$(11.50b) \qquad \frac{{}^{\tau}\phi_y^t}{{}^{\tau}\phi_v^T} = \frac{{}^{\tau+s}\phi_y^t}{{}^{\tau+s}\phi_v^T}, \qquad \left.\right\} \begin{array}{l} t = \tau + s, \tau + s + 1, ..., T, \\ s = 1, 2, ..., T - \tau. \end{array}$$

Essentially, what these conditions say is that all the MRSs (not only those between spending and terminal assets, and leisure and terminal assets) must be the same on all planning dates. Notationally speaking, the MRSs must be independent of the superscripts τ and $\tau + s$, so that the latter may be removed from Eqs. (11.50). Each MRS is then simply a constant which does not change as the consumer moves through time. Certainly, these conditions are satisfied in the special case in which the utility function itself is independent of τ. Then, the utility of a particular bundle depends solely on the date on which it is to be consumed, and not at all on the date on which the consumer plans, or contemplates, that particular act of future consumption. The absence of τ from the utility function means, therefore, that the structure of the consumer's preferences, time and commodity preferences, remains unchanged as the consumer moves through time.

However, the independence of the utility function of the planning date is not a necessary condition for consistent planning. Since the MRSs are ratios of marginal utilities (MUs), the conditions for consistent planning will still be satisfied if each MU changes by the same percentage when the consumer moves from one period to the next. This condition is not as strong as the complete absence of τ from the utility function, but it, too, implies that the consumer's time and commodity preferences remain unchanged over time. Let us write one particular MRS, say that between x_t and v_T, as the consumer perceives it at the beginning of period τ, in the form

$$\frac{{}^\tau\phi_x^t}{{}^\tau\phi_x^T} \cdot \frac{{}^\tau\phi_x^T}{{}^\tau\phi_v^T} .$$

Here, the expression to the left of the multiplication dot represents the consumer's time preference between spending in period t and spending in period T, and the expression on the right represents his commodity preference between spending and terminal assets (in period T). Clearly, if all the MUs change by the same percentage (as τ takes on successive values), each of the above ratios will retain its initial value. This must, of course, be true for all MRSs. Therefore, we may conclude that the constancy over time of the consumer's time and commodity preferences is a necessary, as well as a sufficient, condition for consistent planning.

11.2.3 Consistent Planning and Explicit Discounting

In this section, we reexamine the problem of consistent planning by using a model with a utility function which has one of the conditions for consistent planning built into it. This type of utility function, however, is of more general interest because of its similarity to objective functions encountered in other contexts of intertemporal decision making.

As in the preceding model, we assume that the utility of a particular bundle depends (aside from the *amounts* of the goods in the bundle) on two factors: the calendar date on which the bundle will become available and the planning (or contemplation) date. In the present approach, however, we assume that the effects of these two factors can be separated from one another. The effect of the consumption date is again represented by the superscript t, and is considered to be part of the functional notation. The planning date, on the other hand, is assumed to affect the consumer's preference for the various bundles only inasmuch as it determines the time distance between the present (the planning date) and the date on which the bundle under consideration is to be consumed. This makes it possible to think of the consumer as attaching different weights to the utilities of various goods, the weights depending on the relative distances of the consumption dates from the present. The function which determines these weights is called a *discount function*, and we shall denote it by $\theta(t - \tau)$.

Our formal assumption, then, is that the utility of a particular bundle (x_t, y_t) is given by $\theta(t - \tau) \phi^t(x_t, y_t)$, so that the utility function for the entire horizon is written as

$$(11.51) \qquad u_\tau = \sum_{t=\tau}^{T-1} \theta(t - \tau) \phi^t(x_t, y_t) + \theta(T - \tau) \phi^T(x_T, y_T, v_T).$$

One implication of this type of utility function should be pointed out. If we form the ratio of, say, the weighted marginal utilities of spending and leisure, respectively, in some period t, we get

$$\frac{\theta(t - \tau)}{\theta(t - \tau)} \cdot \frac{\phi^t_x}{\phi^t_y} = \frac{\phi^t_x}{\phi^t_y} \qquad \text{for all } \tau.$$

These equations show that the MRSs between different goods consumed in the same period of time are independent of the present. This means, of course, that these MRSs remain unchanged as the consumer moves through time. Put differently, the consumer's structure of commodity preference is constant over time, and so we see that the type of utility function given in (11.51) satisfies one of the conditions for consistent planning.

On the other hand, the MRSs between goods consumed in different periods of time are subject to change. For example, the MRS between x_t and y_{t+1}, that is,

$$\frac{\theta(t - \tau)}{\theta(t + 1 - \tau)} \cdot \frac{\phi^t_x}{\phi^{t+1}_y},$$

is not necessarily constant over time, since the ratio $\theta(t - \tau)/\theta(t + 1 - \tau)$ is, in general, not independent of τ.

Maximizing the above utility function subject to the budget constraint in (11.42), we obtain the following conditions:

$$(11.52a) \quad \theta(t - \tau) \phi^t_x + \lambda(1 + r)^{T-t+1} = 0, \left.\begin{array}{l}\\\\\end{array}\right\}$$
$$(11.52b) \quad \theta(t - \tau) \phi^t_y + \lambda w(1 + r)^{T-t+1} = 0, \quad t = \tau, \tau + 1, ..., T,$$

$$(11.52c) \quad \theta(T - \tau) \phi^T_v + \lambda = 0.$$

Eliminating λ from (11.52), we can write

$$(11.53a) \qquad \frac{\theta(t - \tau)}{\theta(T - \tau)} \frac{\phi^t_x}{\phi^T_v} = (1 + r)^{T-t+1}, \left.\begin{array}{l}\\\\\\\\\end{array}\right\}$$

$$\qquad\qquad\qquad\qquad\qquad\qquad\qquad\qquad t = \tau, \tau + 1, ..., T.$$

$$(11.53b) \qquad \frac{\theta(t - \tau)}{\theta(T - \tau)} \frac{\phi^t_y}{\phi^T_v} = w(1 + r)^{T-t+1},$$

Conditions (11.53) imply, among other things, that the optimal bundles depend only on the *ratios* of the discount function evaluated at different points, so that it is possible to normalize this function. Without loss of generality, we may assume

$$(11.54) \qquad\qquad\qquad \theta(0) = 1.$$

Consistent planning requires that the maximization of (11.51) at the beginning of period $\tau + s$ yield a solution which coincides with the solution to (11.53) and (11.42) for the periods $(\tau + s)$ through T. First-order conditions for the revised plan consist of (11.42) and a set of equations similar to those in (11.53). These equations are given by

$$(11.55a) \qquad \frac{\theta(t - \tau - s)}{\theta(T - \tau - s)} \frac{\phi_x^t}{\phi_v^T} = (1 + r)^{T-t+1},$$

$$(11.55b) \qquad \frac{\theta(t - \tau - s)}{\theta(T - \tau - s)} \frac{\phi_y^t}{\phi_v^T} = w(1 + v)^{T-t+1},$$

$$t = \tau + s, \tau + s + 1, ..., T,$$
$$s = 1, 2, ..., T - \tau.$$

It is clear from (11.53) and (11.55) that the two problems will have consistent solutions if

$$(11.56a) \qquad \frac{\theta(t - \tau)}{\theta(T - \tau)} \frac{\phi_x^t}{\phi_v^T} = \frac{\theta(t - \tau - s)}{\theta(T - \tau - s)} \frac{\phi_x^t}{\phi_v^T},$$

$$(11.56b) \qquad \frac{\theta(t - \tau)}{\theta(T - \tau)} \frac{\phi_y^t}{\phi_v^T} = \frac{\theta(t - \tau - s)}{\theta(T - \tau - s)} \frac{\phi_y^t}{\phi_v^T},$$

which, in turn, implies

$$(11.57) \qquad \frac{\theta(t - \tau)}{\theta(T - \tau)} = \frac{\theta(t - \tau - s)}{\theta(T - \tau - s)}, \qquad \begin{array}{l} t = \tau + s, \tau + s + 1, ..., T, \\ s = 1, 2, ..., T - \tau. \end{array}$$

Since these equations must hold for all s, it follows that the relative discount factor must be constant. In other words, the weights attached to the various MRSs must be the same on all planning dates. Obviously, in the trivial case, in which the discount function is itself constant (that is, if the weights attached to the ϕ^t are all the same, and independent of τ), the relative discount factor will also be constant, and so planning will be consistent. This is the case in which the consumer's preferences do not undergo any changes whatsoever as the consumer moves through time. However, planning may be consistent even if the discount function is not constant, as will be shown below.

Let us take the case of $t = T - 1$, and some fixed initial period τ such that $\tau < t$. Then the original plan for the future period t may be revised in any of the periods $\tau + 1, \tau + 2, ..., t$. Thus, if $\tau + s$ is a typical revision date, then the variable s can take the values $s = 1, 2, ..., t - \tau$. Now, as s varies, the lhs of (11.57) remains constant, hence the rhs of that equation must also remain constant. Consequently, there exists a constant k such that

(11.58) $\theta(T - \tau - s) = k\theta(t - \tau - s)$ for $s = 1, 2, ..., t - \tau$.

Evaluating the function in this equation for each admissible value of s, beginning with the highest value $t - \tau$, we get the following equations:

(11.59a)   when $s = t - \tau$ $\theta(T - t) = k\theta(0)$

   or (since $T - t = 1$) $\theta(1) = k$ by (11.54),

(11.59b)   when $s = t - \tau - 1$ $\theta(2) = k\theta(1) = k^2$ by (11.59a),

(11.59c)   when $s = t - \tau - 2$ $\theta(3) = k\theta(2) = k^3$ by (11.59b),

$$\vdots$$

(11.59d)   when $s = 1$ $\theta(T - \tau - 1) = k\theta(t - \tau - 1) = k^{T - \tau - 1}$

   by induction.

By inspecting these equations, we see that the function θ is obviously an exponential function. Specifically, if the argument of the function θ is denoted by z, then we have

(11.60) $\theta(z) = k^z.$

Even though we used fixed values of t and τ in the derivation of this function, we can easily verify that this function satisfies conditions (11.57) for all admissible values of t, τ, and s. Rewriting (11.57), using the exponential function given in (11.60), we get

(11.61) $\dfrac{k^{t-\tau}}{k^{T-\tau}} = \dfrac{k^{t-\tau-s}}{k^{T-\tau-s}} = k^{t-T}$ for all admissible t, τ, and s.

We see that each ratio in (11.57) is equal to k^{t-T}. This means that ratios of the discount function evaluated at different planning (or revision) dates $\tau + s$ are independent of the planning date, and depend only on the consumption date of the bundle being discounted. This implies, of course, that the consumer's structure of time preference does not change as he moves from one planning date to the next, and it is this condition which, together with the constancy of commodity preference, guarantees consistent planning. Thus, if the consumer's discount function is of the form given in (11.60), then any plan that he draws up at some initial period τ will be found to be optimal at any subsequent period in the horizon, and therefore the plan will be carried out as originally planned.

In conclusion, it should be remarked that a consumer may conceivably behave in a way which might suggest to an outside observer (assuming that such observation is possible) that the consumer is a consistent planner, when in fact he is not; in other words, the fact that the consumer is seen never to revise his plan does not necessarily prove that changes in his time preference are determined by an exponential discount function. What this may mean is that the consumer simply neglects to revise his plan for lack of concern over intertemporal optimality. In which case, the consumer draws up a plan which is optimal at some initial period of time, and decides to abide by it without subjecting it to periodic revisions. In other words, the consumer commits himself in advance to follow his plan to the letter, and, as far as he is concerned, the issue of consistent planning simply does not arise.

11.3   CONTINUOUS MODELS

At this point, it may be in order to construct a continuous version of an intertemporal utility maximization model. Not that continuous models are necessarily more realistic than discrete models, but it seems that this is a suitable place for an introduction to continuous models in general. Indeed, for many problems, continuous models are basically simpler than discrete ones, and often they are more amenable to the analysis of certain aspects that are of interest to the researcher. In such cases, continuous models are likely to result in a better understanding of the problem being modelled.

In a continuous model, time is regarded as a continuous variable, and the consumer is assumed to make decisions continuously, instead of at discrete intervals. In the context of intertemporal utility maximization, the consumer draws up a plan at every single point of time in his horizon. More-over, unlike in the discrete case, a plan consists not of a finite set of bundles, but of rates of consumption and spending at each single point in the horizon. Typically, the locus of the chosen points for each decision variable (in the commodity-time space) is some continuous function of time. Hence, instead of choosing a set of bundles such as (x_t, y_t), under continuous decision making the consumer chooses *functions* such as $x = h(t)$ and $y = g(t)$. Here, $h(t)$ denotes the rate of spending at the *point* of time t, and similarly $g(t)$ denotes the rate of consuming leisure time at the *point* of time t. Of course, the actual amount spent or consumed at a single point of time is zero; how-ever, if spending or consumption goes on continuously at certain rates over a finite interval of time, then the amounts spent and consumed over that interval are some finite quantities (unless the rates of spending and consump-tion are zero over the entire interval). Since these finite quantities are cal-culated by integrating the spending and consumption functions over the relevant interval of time, it is only natural that, in this model, the utility function should take the form of an integral. Thus, the continuous version of (11.51) is written as

$$(11.62) \qquad u_\tau = \int_\tau^T \theta(t - \tau)\,\phi[h(t), g(t), t]\,dt + \theta(T - \tau)\,\phi^T(v_T).$$

The role of the function ϕ in this model is to assign a number to any given combination of spending and leisure rates at any given calendar date t. As in the discrete case, we assume that the MUs of spending and leisure (ϕ_x and ϕ_y) are positive, but we place no restrictions on the partial derivative of ϕ with respect to t. The discount function, as in the discrete model, attaches weights to the various combinations of spending and leisure rates, so that the integral appearing in (11.62) can be interpreted as a weighted "sum" of all the rates of spending and rates of leisure over the consumer's horizon. Formally, such an expression is called a *functional* because its value depends on the *form* of the functions h and g (unlike a function whose value depends on the *values* of its variables). The second expression on the rhs of (11.62) is an ordinary utility function which attaches a number to the consumer's asset position at the last point in his horizon. Thus, the utility index in this particular model is the sum of a functional and a function.

The budget constraint which the consumer must obey may be constructed in a manner similar to that which we used in the construction of the budget equation—(11.38)—for the discrete model in Section 11.2.1. First, let us note that if the rate of consuming leisure time at the point t is equal to $g(t)$, then the rate at which the consumer is willing to work at that point must be equal to $1 - g(t)$. Then, if the wage rate is given by w (assumed to be constant throughout the horizon), the consumer's rate of earning at point t equals $w[1 - g(t)]$. The consumer's rate of saving can now be obtained by subtracting the rate of spending from the rate of earning; that is, $w[1 - g(t)] - h(t)$. Assuming that the consumer can lend and borrow at a fixed rate of interest, with interest being compounded continuously on both savings and debts, then his asset position at the end of the time interval $t_0 - t_1$ is given by

$$\int_{t_0}^{t_1} \{w[1 - g(t)] - h(t)\} e^{r(t_1 - t)} dt,$$

given that his initial asset position is zero. (We remind the reader that, here, the symbol e refers to the base of natural logarithms.) If the consumer starts out at the point t_0 with initial asset holdings equal to v_0, then these holdings, if invested, will have grown to $v_0 e^{r(t_1 - t_0)}$ by the end of the interval, so that his total asset position at the end of the above interval is given by

$$v_1 = \int_{t_0}^{t_1} \{w[1 - g(t)] - h(t)\} e^{r(t_1 - t)} dt + v_0 e^{r(t_1 - t_0)}.$$

The consumer's budget constraint for the entire horizon is simply an equation of the above type for a time interval beginning at some initial point τ (the planning date), and spanning the consumer's economic lifetime up to the endpoint T. Consequently, the consumer's budget constraint can be stated as

$$(11.63a) \qquad v_T = \int_\tau^T \{w[1 - g(t)] - h(t)\}\, e^{r(T-t)}\, dt + v_\tau e^{r(T-\tau)},$$

or, equivalently,

$$(11.63b) \qquad \int_\tau^T [h(t) + wg(t)]\, e^{r(T-t)}\, dt + v_T = v_\tau e^{r(T-t)} + w \int_\tau^T e^{r(T-t)}\, dt.$$

The latter equation may be given an interpretation similar to that given to the budget equation in (11.38a): the lhs of (11.63b) represents the capitalized value of the consumer's stream of purchases (of goods and leisure time) over his horizon; the rhs represents the capitalized value of his (potential) wealth over his horizon. The coefficients of the spending and leisure rates in the budget constraint represent prices (opportunity costs): $e^{r(T-t)}$ represents the price of spending at a rate of one dollar at the point t, and $we^{r(T-t)}$ is the price of consuming leisure time at the maximum rate (one) at the point t.

The consumer's optimal plan is obtained by maximizing (11.62) subject to (11.63). In this maximization process, the consumer chooses optimal functions h and g, and an optimal value for v_T. Mathematically speaking, this is a problem in the calculus of variations (or, to be more precise, it is a mixed problem, using techniques of calculus of variations as well as those of ordinary calculus). As usual, we shall assume that a solution exists, and that it is in the interior of some appropriate space; that is, $\bar{h}(t) > 0$ and $0 < \bar{g}(t) < 1$ for $\tau \leqslant t \leqslant T$. In that case, the necessary conditions for a maximum—the so-called *Euler equations*—take the form

$$(11.64a) \qquad \theta(t - \tau)\, \phi_x + \lambda e^{r(T-t)} = 0,$$
$$(11.64b) \qquad \theta(t - \tau)\, \phi_y + \lambda w e^{r(T-t)} = 0, \qquad \left.\right\} \quad \tau \leqslant t \leqslant T,$$
$$(11.64c) \qquad \theta(T - \tau)\, \phi_v^T + \lambda = 0,$$

where $\phi_x = \partial\phi/\partial x$, $\phi_y = \partial\phi/\partial y$, $\phi_v^T = \partial\phi^T/\partial v_T$, and λ is a Lagrange multiplier. These conditions are the counterpart of conditions (11.52), which are the necessary conditions for the discrete version of the present model. Like the latter conditions, those in (11.64) equate various MRSs with the ratios of the respective prices.

Revisability can now be introduced without much difficulty. Let us assume that the consumer reevaluates his original plan at some later point of time, say τ'. This means that, at time τ', he maximizes the functional given in (11.62) (after replacing τ by τ'), subject to a budget constraint such as (11.63). In fact, for the analysis of this problem, we can continue to use Eq. (11.63), since the consumer's behavior over the interval $\tau - \tau'$ must be consistent with the budget equation—(11.63)— for $T = \tau'$. (The invariance of the budget constraint with respect to the revision dates has already been shown in the context of the discrete model discussed in Section 11.2.2.)

Hence, the necessary conditions for the revised plan are given by (11.63) and the following equations:

(11.65a) $\quad\quad \theta(t - \tau')\, \phi_x + \mu e^{r(T-t)} \;\; = 0,$

(11.65b) $\quad\quad \theta(t - \tau')\, \phi_y + \mu w e^{r(T-t)} = 0,$ $\tau' \leqslant t \leqslant T,$

(11.65c) $\quad\quad \theta(T - \tau')\, \phi_v^T + \mu \quad\quad\; = 0,$

    Consistent planning, it will be recalled, requires that the solution to (11.63) and (11.65) coincide with the solution to (11.63) and (11.64) for the interval $\tau' - T$. Furthermore, such consistency should obtain for *any* revision date; that is, Eqs. (11.64) and (11.65) should be identical for all τ and τ'. It is easily seen that this requires that the equation

$$\frac{\theta(t - \tau')}{\theta(T - \tau')} = \frac{\theta(t - \tau)}{\theta(T - \tau)}$$

should hold for all t and τ' such that $\tau \leqslant \tau' \leqslant t \leqslant T$. If we let $z = t - \tau'$, and $z' = T - \tau'$, then we can write

$$\frac{\theta(z)}{\theta(z')} = \frac{\theta(t - \tau)}{\theta(T - \tau)}.$$

For fixed t and τ, the rhs of the above equation is a constant. Therefore, by differentiating the equation with respect to τ', and rearranging terms, we get

$$\frac{\theta'(z)}{\theta(z)} = \frac{\theta'(z')}{\theta(z')}.$$

Now, for z' fixed, the rhs of the last equation is a constant, say, k. Then by integrating the latter equation, we get

$$\ln \theta(z) = kz,$$

where we have used (11.54) to determine that the constant of integration is zero. Then it follows immediately that

(11.66) $\quad\quad\quad\quad\quad\quad \theta(z) = e^{kz},$

which is of the same general form as the function in (11.60). Thus, we see that the conditions for consistent planning require the discount function to be exponential, regardless of whether decisions are made at discrete intervals or continuously.

Example 11.1 In this example, we shall use a utility function which is independent of the planning date τ; specifically,

$$u_0 = \int_0^T [a \ln x - b \ln (1 - y)]\, dt + cv_T, \quad\quad a, b, c > 0,$$

where $x = h(t)$, $y = g(t)$, and the present (the date at which plans are made) is denoted by 0. The above functional is to be maximized subject to the budget constraint

$$v_T = \int_0^T \{w[1 - g(t)] - h(t)\} \, e^{r(T-t)} \, dt + v_0 e^{rT}.$$

The Euler equations for this problem take the form

$$
\left.
\begin{aligned}
\frac{a}{x} + \lambda e^{r(T-t)} &= 0, \\[2mm]
\frac{b}{1-y} + \lambda w e^{r(T-t)} &= 0, \\[2mm]
c + \lambda \phantom{e^{r(T-t)}} &= 0.
\end{aligned}
\right\} \quad 0 \leqslant t \leqslant T,
$$

Using the third equation, we can easily eliminate the Lagrange multiplier, and this yields at once the optimal rates of spending and leisure. These are

$$\bar{x} = \frac{a e^{r(t-T)}}{c} = \bar{h}(t; r), \qquad \bar{y} = 1 - \frac{b e^{r(t-T)}}{cw} = \bar{g}(t; w, r), \qquad 0 \leqslant t \leqslant T,$$

where bars denote optimal values (and functions). The optimal level of terminal assets may now be obtained by inserting the optimal rates of spending and leisure into the budget equation, and integrating it. We thus have

$$\bar{v}_T = \int_0^T \left\{ w\left[1 - 1 + \frac{b e^{r(t-T)}}{cw}\right] - \frac{a e^{r(t-T)}}{c} \right\} e^{r(T-t)} \, dt + v_0 \, e^{rT},$$

$$= \int_0^T \left[\frac{(b-a)}{c} \, e^{r(t-T)}\right] e^{r(T-t)} \, dt + v_0 \, e^{rT},$$

$$= \frac{(b-a)}{c} \int_0^T dt + v_0 e^{rT},$$

$$= \frac{(b-a)}{c} T + v_0 e^{rT}.$$

   A few comments on the nature of the solution may be in order. We see, first of all, that the optimal rate of spending is always positive, and that it grows at an exponential rate as the consumer moves through his horizon. Furthermore, spending, in this model, does not depend on the wage rate, but it does depend on the rate of interest; clearly, $\bar{h}_r < 0$ (since $t < T$), hence an increase in the rate of interest decreases the rate of spending at every point in the horizon (except at the endpoint T).

The rate of consuming leisure time, as we have already pointed out, must lie between zero and one, as any other value would not make sense. This requires us to place a restriction on the coefficients of the model. The necessary restriction is

$$0 \leqslant 1 - \frac{be^{r(t-T)}}{cw} \leqslant 1,$$

which is satisfied if

$$\frac{be^{r(t-T)}}{cw} \leqslant 1.$$

Now, since

$$\frac{be^{r(t-T)}}{cw} \leqslant \frac{b}{cw},$$

it follows that if we assume $b/cw \leqslant 1$, then the necessary restriction will be satisfied.

It is easily seen that the rate of leisure decreases with time and increases with an increase in either the wage rate or the rate of interest. Since the consumer's rate of *work* is given by $1 - \bar{y} = be^{r(t-T)}/cw$, it follows immediately that the effects of changes in the parameters t, w, and r on his willingness to work are of opposite signs, respectively, to those of the effects on his demand for leisure. Multiplying the rate of work by the wage rate, we get the consumer's rate of *earning* at any point of time, which in this particular example equals $be^{r(t-T)}/c$. The rate of earning, therefore, is independent of the wage rate, increases exponentially with time, and decreases when the rate of interest increases. Finally, subtracting the rate of spending from the rate of earning, we get the consumer's rate of *saving*. This is given by

$$\frac{(b - a)\, e^{r(t-T)}}{c},$$

which is also independent of the wage rate. The sign of the rate of saving is the same as the sign of $b - a$.

The consumer's asset position at any point of time t may be obtained from the solution for $\bar{v}_T$ given above after replacing T by t. We see that the asset equation has two terms: the first term is the capitalized value of the consumer's flow of saving, and it may be of either sign; the second term is the capitalized value of the consumer's initial asset holdings, and it, too, may be of either sign.

Example 11.2 We now modify the preceding example by introducing into the utility function a variable planning date. We shall do this by writing the utility function as

$$u_\tau = \int_\tau^T \frac{\tau}{t} \left[a \ln x - b \ln (1 - y) \right] dt + \frac{\tau}{T} cv_T, \qquad a, b, c > 0, \quad \tau, t \geqslant 1,$$

where the ratio τ/t may be interpreted as a discount function. According to this discount function, the weights attached to the rates of spending and leisure diminish with the distance between the planning and consumption dates. On the other hand, as the consumer moves from one planning date to another, the entire discount function undergoes an upward shift.

The budget constraint is essentially the same as in the preceding example, except that the present is denoted by τ. Thus,

$$v_T = \int_\tau^T \{ w[1 - g(t)] - h(t) \} e^{r(T-t)} dt + v_\tau e^{r(T-\tau)}.$$

The Euler equations now take the following forms:

$$\left.
\begin{aligned}
\frac{\tau a}{t x} + \lambda e^{r(T-t)} &= 0, \\[2em]
\frac{\tau b}{t(1 - y)} + \lambda w e^{r(T-t)} &= 0, \\[2em]
\frac{\tau}{T} c + \lambda &= 0,
\end{aligned}
\right\} \qquad 1 \leqslant \tau, t \leqslant T.$$

It is clear that, although the MUs depend on the planning date τ, the MRSs do not, so that the utility function in this particular example satisfies the conditions for consistent planning. This is obvious from the solution itself. which is given by

$$\left.
\begin{aligned}
\bar{x} &= \frac{aT}{ct} e^{r(t-T)} &= \bar{h}(t; r), \\[2em]
\bar{y} &= 1 - \frac{Tb}{cwt} e^{r(t-T)} = \bar{g}(t; w, r),
\end{aligned}
\right\} \qquad 1 \leqslant t \leqslant T.$$

$$\bar{v}_T = \frac{(b - a)}{c} T \ln T + v_1 e^{r(T-1)}.$$

This example also illustrates the fact that the conditions for consistent planning do not necessarily require the discount function to be an exponential function; such was the case in Section 11.2.3. only because there the discount function was assumed to depend on the argument $z = t - \tau$.

BIBLIOGRAPHICAL NOTES

One of the early works on intertemporal optimization is F. P. Ramsey's article, "A Mathematical Theory of Saving," *Economic Journal,* **37,** 543–559 (1928), reprinted in K. J. Arrow and T. Scitovsky (eds.), *Readings in Welfare Economics,* Chicago: Irwin, 1969, pp. 619–633. Even though Ramsey did not address himself in this paper to the behavior of a single consumer, his model may very well be interpreted as such. A later paper, explicitly concerned with consumer behavior, is G. Tintner, "The Maximization of Utility over Time," *Econometrica,* **6,** 154–158 (1938). F. Modigliani and R. Brumberg have concerned themselves with intertemporal consumption and saving behavior, considering especially the relationship between theoretical models and empirical data. This appeared in "Utility Analysis and the Consumption Function: An Interpretation of Cross-Section Data," in K. K. Kurihara (ed.), *Post-Keynesian Economics,* New Brunswick: Rutgers University Press, 1954, pp. 388–436. The concept of consistent planning was first formulated by R. Strotz in "Myopia and Inconsistency in Dynamic Utility Maximization," *Review of Economic Studies,* **23,** 165–180 (1956). This paper was commented on by R. A. Pollack, in "Consistent Planning," *Review of Economic Studies,* **35,** 201–208 (1968). More recent examples of lifetime models of consumer behavior are M. Yaari, "On the Consumer's Lifetime Allocation Process," *International Economic Review,* **5,** 304–317 (1964); T. C. Koopmans, P. A. Diamond, and R. E. Williamson, "Stationary Utility and Time Preference," *Econometrica,* **32,** 82–100 (1964); and H. Uzawa, "Time Preference, the Consumption Function, and Optimum Asset Holdings," in J. N. Wolfe (ed.), *Value, Capital, and Growth* (*Papers in honor of Sir John Hicks*), Chicago: Aldine, 1968, pp. 485–504. Comparative static properties of multiperiod models of the consumer are examined in J. Hadar, "Comparative Statics of Stock-Flow Equilibrium," *Journal of Political Economy,* **73,** 304–309 (1965).

The literature on intertemporal behavior of the firm is at least as rich as that relating to the consumer. The following is a selected sample: A. Smithies, "The Maximization of Profits over Time with Changing Cost and Demand Functions," *Econometrica,* **7,** 312–318 (1939); F. Modigliani and F. E. Hohn, "Production Planning over Time and the Nature of the Expectation and Planning Horizon," *Econometrica,* **23,** 46–66 (1955); K. J. Arrow and S. Karlin, "Production over Time with Increasing Marginal Costs," in K. J. Arrow, S. Karlin, and H. Scarf, *Studies in the Mathematical Theory of Inventory and Production,* Stanford: Stanford University Press, 1958, pp. 61–69; D. W. Jorgenson, "The Theory of Investment Behavior," in R. Ferber (ed.), *Determinants of Investment Behavior,* New York: National Bureau of Economic Research, 1967, pp. 129–155; K. J. Arrow, "Optimal Capital Policy with Irreversible Investment," in J. N. Wolfe (ed.), *Value, Capital, and Growth* (*Papers in honor of Sir John Hicks*), Chicago: Aldine, 1968, pp. 1–19; and J. P. Gould, "Adjustment Costs in the Theory of Investment of the Firm," *Review of Economic Studies,* **35,** 47–55 (1968).

CHAPTER 12

BEHAVIOR UNDER UNCERTAINTY

In all the preceding chapters we have assumed, almost without exception, that the decision maker had complete information about the nature of his environment; that is, we assumed that the decision maker knew (or thought he knew) the exact form of such relations as the cost, production, and demand functions. Aside from the fact that in an introductory work such as this the emphasis on full-information models is a pedagogical necessity, we may offer the following observations in support of the approach taken in the preceding chapters:

a) In certain situations, the decision maker may have enough information about his environment to make the assumption of full knowledge a satisfactory approximation to the real state of nature.

b) Some models in which uncertainty is treated in an explicit fashion have formal structures that are quite similar to those of standard full-information models.

But there is, of course, no doubt that in numerous situations the decision maker is fully aware of the fact that he is operating under conditions of incomplete information. Moreover, in many such instances he may be able to characterize the state of uncertainty in quantitative terms taking the form of probability statements about the outcomes of alternative courses of action. Thus, our exposition of microeconomic theory would certainly not be complete without some formal discussion of the basic methods of modelling decision making under conditions of incomplete information.

The standard consumer model will serve as our point of departure (but other models will also be considered). We choose this model because it is sufficiently general to suggest possible applications of the basic method to other decision-making contexts. For instance, one may without difficulty think of the utility function as representing some general objective function which depends on certain decision variables, and in what follows, the reader may replace the word "consumer" by the word "decision maker"; this in itself, will not invalidate the method that will be discussed in this chapter. Without risking an undue loss of generality, we will confine ourselves mostly to choice situations in which the outcomes of the consumer's choices are in the form of monetary receipts, such as income. What is essential in the situations to be considered here is that, while each action taken by the consumer will eventually yield one particular level of income, he does not know in advance exactly what the level of income will be. We do assume, however, that the consumer can attach probabilities to all possible levels (or intervals) of income. Each action is, therefore, associated with a "bundle" consisting of various levels of income and their respective probabilities (or densities), and so, when the consumer decides on a particular action, he is really choosing a particular probability distribution. One of the main purposes of this chapter is to explain the principles underlying this choice.

12.1 PREFERENCES FOR UNCERTAIN PROSPECTS

It is obvious that, in the present scheme, the objects of choice—the "uncertain bundles"—are different entities from the bundles of commodities and levels of expenditure that constituted the decision variables of the models in Chapters 10 and 11. It is therefore necessary, first of all, to make some assumptions concerning the structure of the consumer's preferences for uncertain bundles. But before we do so, a few words about terminology and notation.

Throughout the chapter we shall use the terms "uncertain bundle," "uncertain prospect," and "probability distribution" as synonymous. As for notation, occasionally we will denote uncertain bundles by capital letters such as A, B, C, etc. At other times, we will represent an uncertain bundle by the probability distribution itself; i.e., by the various levels of income and their probabilities. For example, a bundle A may be denoted by the vector $(x_1, x_2, ..., x_n; \alpha_1, \alpha_2, ..., \alpha_n)$, where the x_i denote the levels of income, and the α_i the respective probabilities. At some points in the discussion, we will also encounter *compound bundles*; that is, bundles whose outcomes, or payoffs, are not levels of income, but other uncertain bundles. For example, an uncertain bundle offering bundle A with probability α, and bundle B with probability $1 - \alpha$, is a compound bundle, and will be denoted by $(A, B; \alpha, 1 - \alpha)$.

The first assumption which we are making is essentially the same as Assumptions A.10.1 and A.10.2 in Chapter 10, concerning preferences under conditions of complete certainty. Recalling that those assumptions imply the existence of a complete preordering, we may, for simplicity, collapse them into one composite assumption as follows:

A.12.1 Complete Preordering.

a) Given any set of uncertain bundles, then for any two bundles A and B in that set, either $A \succeq B$, or $B \succeq A$.

b) For any three bundles A, B, and C, if $A \succeq B$, and $B \succeq C$, then $A \succeq C$.

The symbol $\succeq$, as well as the symbols $\succ$ and $\sim$, is used here in the same sense as we defined it in Section 10.1, of Chapter 10. It may be pointed out that the assumption concerning the existence of a complete preordering on the set of all uncertain bundles also implies the existence of a complete preordering on the set of all certain bundles (i.e., bundles of the type encountered in Chapters 10 and 11). This follows immediately from the simple fact that certain bundles are merely special cases of uncertain bundles: if in some uncertain bundle we set the probability of a particular level of income equal to one, and those of all other incomes at zero, then if the consumer chooses this bundle, the outcome (i.e., the resulting income) of that choice is known with certainty. Hence we see that certain bundles are (trivial) special cases of uncertain bundles.

We now make two additional assumptions about the consumer's preferences for uncertain bundles.

A.12.2 Continuity. *For any three uncertain bundles A, B, and C, if $A \succsim B$, and $B \succsim C$, then there exists a number $\alpha, 0 < \alpha < 1$, such that $B \sim (A, C; \alpha, 1 - \alpha)$.*

To explain the meaning of this, it may help to think of A, B, and C as certain bundles, each offering only one level of income with probability one. In order to rule out the trivial case, we assume that each bundle consists of a different level of income, A having the highest of the three incomes. Then it is clear that, as between bundles A and B, the consumer will choose A, but given the choice between B and C, he will choose B. Now, if the consumer is offered a choice between bundle B and the uncertain bundle offering A with a probability very close to one, and C with a probability very close to zero, then the consumer will probably still prefer the uncertain bundle over the certain bundle B. Likewise, if the probability of A in the uncertain bundle is very small, and that of C very large, then the consumer may possibly choose the certain bundle B. What the continuity assumption says, in effect, is that as the parameter α—the probability of A in the uncertain bundle—varies continuously from zero to one, it is bound to take on a value at which the consumer will be indifferent between the certain bundle B and the uncertain bundle containing both A and C.

Of course, the bundles A, B, and C need not necessarily be regarded as certain bundles with only one income per bundle. Suppose, for example, that A is an uncertain bundle consisting of the income levels $x_1, x_2, \ldots, x_m$, and their respective probabilities $\alpha_1, \alpha_2, \ldots, \alpha_m, \sum_{i=1}^{m} \alpha_i = 1$, while C consists of the incomes $y_1, y_2, \ldots, y_n$, with probabilities $\gamma_1, \gamma_2, \ldots, \gamma_n, \sum_{i=1}^{n} \gamma_i = 1$. Then if B is an uncertain bundle offering A with probability α, and C with probability $1 - \alpha$, bundle B is in effect offering the income levels x_i with probabilities $\alpha\alpha_i$, and the income levels y_i with probabilities $(1 - \alpha)\gamma_i$. In this case, B may be regarded as an uncertain bundle with $m + n$ levels of income, such that their respective probabilities add up to unity. Assumption A.12.1 thus asserts that the consumer is capable of comparing (and expressing preference for) not only *simple* uncertain bundles, but also *compound* uncertain bundles.

The last assumption about the consumer's preferences is:

A.12.3 Independence. *For any two uncertain bundles A and B such that A* $\}$ *B, and any third bundle C, it is true that* $(A, C;\ \alpha, 1 - \alpha)\ \} \ (B, C;\ \alpha, 1 - \alpha)$.

The reason why the above is referred to as an independence assumption is that it rules out any interrelationship, such as substitutability or complementarity, between the various bundles. More precisely, if A is preferred to B, then the independence assumption requires that this preference should not be changed just because both A and B are offered in conjunction with a third bundle C; that is, the fact that C is offered jointly with A and jointly with B in two uncertain bundles should not diminish the desirability of A relative to B (or enhance the attractiveness of B relative to A). Hence, given the preference of A over B, an uncertain bundle offering both A and C should be preferred to an uncertain bundle offering both B and C, provided the probability of C is the same in each of the two bundles.

The independence assumption has some interesting implications, which may be illustrated with simple examples. Note that the bundle C appearing in the statement of Assumption A.12.3 can be any arbitrary bundle. Suppose we let bundle C be the same as bundle A. Then, given that $C = A$, the uncertain bundle $(A, C;\ \alpha, 1 - \alpha) = (A, A;\ \alpha, 1 - \alpha)$ is, in fact, offering bundle A with certainty. Thus, according to the independence assumption, if $A\ \}\ B$, then also $A\ \}\ (B, A;\ \alpha, 1 - \alpha)$. Now, suppose, that $A\ \}\ B$ and the consumer chooses the uncertain bundle. In that case, one of the following will be true:

a) The actual outcome is bundle A, in which case the consumer is as well off as he would have been had he chosen the certain bundle A in the first place.

b) The actual outcome is bundle B, in which case the consumer is either as well off or, in the case of strict preference, worse off than he would have been had he chosen the certain bundle A.

Therefore, one of the implications of the independence assumption is that it rules out a desire for "gambling for the sake of gambling." As we have just shown, the consumer should never prefer an uncertain bundle to a certain bundle if the choice of the uncertain bundle cannot, even under the best of circumstances, make the consumer better off than he would be if he chose the certain bundle; if, that is, none of the payoffs of the uncertain bundle is preferred to the certain bundle. To put it slightly differently, the consumer is allowed to prefer an uncertain bundle to a certain bundle only if there exists some chance, possibly very small, that the choice of the uncertain bundle will yield a payoff which is preferred to the certain bundle.

Interestingly enough, while the above assumption rules out "irrational" *preferences* for risky prospects, it also excludes, at the same time, equally irrational *rejections* of uncertain bundles. Suppose we let bundle C in Assumption A.12.3 be the same as bundle B. Then, according to the assumption, $A\ \}\ B$

implies $(A, B; \alpha, 1 - \alpha) \} B$. Here we see that if the consumer chooses the uncertain bundle, there is some chance (a probability of α) that he will receive a bundle which he prefers to the certain bundle B, and no chance at all of receiving anything inferior to B. Thus, the independence assumption requires, in effect, that the consumer should not pass up any opportunity of engaging in a gamble when to do so cannot make him worse off than he would be if he refrained from taking the gamble. In other words, the consumer may reject an uncertain bundle only if it contains at least one payoff that is inferior to the bundle offered with certainty.

12.2 THE EXPECTED UTILITY FUNCTION

If the consumer's preferences satisfy Assumptions A.12.1 through A.12.3, then his preferences are *representable*; that is, there exists a function which assigns a real number to each possible bundle in such a way as to reflect the consumer's preferences. If we think of a general bundle A as having income levels $x_1, x_2, ..., x_n$ with associated probabilities $\alpha_1, \alpha_2, ..., \alpha_n$, then the above assumptions imply the existence of a real-valued function $\phi(x_i)$ such that the expression $\sum_{i=1}^{n} \alpha_i \phi(x_i)$ constitutes a rule for assigning a number to any bundle A. This number, as we can see, depends on the income levels x_i as well as on the probabilities α_i. Hence, given the function ϕ (which is an ordinary utility function), we can write

$$(12.1a) \qquad \sum_{i=1}^{n} \alpha_i \phi(x_i) = \Phi(x_1, x_2, ..., x_n; \alpha_1, \alpha_2, ..., \alpha_n),$$

or, more compactly,

$$(12.1b) \qquad \sum_{i=1}^{n} \alpha_i \phi(x_i) = \Phi(A).$$

Here, the symbol A represents the vector of the x_i and α_i. The expression on the lhs of (12.1) can be viewed as a linear function in the utility levels of the incomes contained in the bundle in question; more precisely, the lhs of (12.1) is nothing but the mathematical expectation (or expected value) of utility, and therefore the function Φ is referred to as the *expected utility function*.

It is clear that the existence of an expected utility function implies the existence of an ordinary utility function (but not vice versa). Furthermore, in the case in which the bundle under consideration is certain in nature, the two functions coincide. That is, if, for example, $\alpha_j = 1$, and $\alpha_i = 0$ for all $i \neq j$, then (12.1a) reduces to

$$\phi(x_j) = \Phi(x_1, x_2, ..., x_j, ..., x_n; 0, 0, ..., 1, ..., 0).$$

Like any ordinary utility function, the expected utility function is order-preserving. This means that for any two uncertain bundles A and B, the following statements hold.

(12.2a) $\Phi(A) > \Phi(B)$ if and only if $A \} B$;

(12.2b) $\Phi(A) = \Phi(B)$ if and only if $A \sim B$.

Combining the two statements, we can also write

(12.2c) $\Phi(A) \geqslant \Phi(B)$ if and only if $A \} B$.

The order-preserving property (12.2) indicates that of any two uncertain bundles, the consumer always prefers that bundle whose expected utility is higher. Thus, while under conditions of complete certainty we explain the behavior of the consumer in terms of *utility maximization,* under the present approach to behavior under uncertainty, the consumer's choices are assumed to be the result of the *maximization of expected utility.* This approach, however, is not unique to the theory of consumer behavior; it is merely an application of a general rule for behavior under uncertainty according to which choices are the result of maximizing the expected value of the relevant objective function. An example from the theory of the firm is given in Section 12.4.1.

Now that the existence of the expected utility function has been established, it may be helpful to restate Assumption A.12.2 in terms of the expected utility function.

A.12.2′ Continuity. *For any three uncertain bundles A, B, and C, if $\Phi(A) \geqslant \Phi(B)$ and $\Phi(B) \geqslant \Phi(C)$, then there exists a number α, $0 < \alpha < 1$, such that $\Phi(B) = \alpha\Phi(A) + (1 - \alpha)\,\Phi(C)$.*

The continuity condition may be used to "construct" the utility function (and hence the expected utility function) for any consumer who satisfies Assumptions A.12.1 through A.12.3. In other words, condition A.12.2′ suggests a method for assigning numbers to as many different bundles as one may wish, in such a way that these numbers correctly reflect the order of the consumer's preferences. Let us again consider the special case of certain bundles; that is, let us assume that each of the bundles in A.12.2′ consists of one level of income—x_1, x_2, and x_3, respectively—and $x_1 > x_2 > x_3$. Then we have $\phi(x_1) > \phi(x_2) > \phi(x_3)$. Since we are free to choose the origin of the utility function, as well as its scale, we can, for example, assume that $\phi(x_1) = 10$, and $\phi(\bar{x}_3) = 0$. Then, according to A.12.2′, there exists α_1, $0 < \alpha_1 < 1$, such that

$$\phi(x_2) = \alpha_1\phi(x_1) + (1-\alpha_1)\phi(x_3) = 10\alpha_1.$$

We have thus assigned a number to the utility of the income level x_2.

Similarly, suppose that $x_4 > x_1$, then there exists an uncertain bundle offering income x_4 with probability α_2 and income x_3 with probability $1 - \alpha_2$ such that the consumer is indifferent between the latter uncertain bundle and the income x_1 offered with certainty; in other words, we can find a number α_2, $0 < \alpha_2 < 1$, such that

$$\phi(x_1) = \alpha_2 \phi(x_4) + (1 - \alpha_2) \phi(x_3),$$

or

$$10 = \alpha_2 \phi(x_4) + 0,$$

hence

$$\phi(x_4) = \frac{10}{\alpha_2}.$$

Such "experiments" can, in principle, be repeated as often as is necessary to assign numbers to the utilities of any desired levels of income. Once the levels of utility are given, the expected utility of any uncertain bundle can be computed in a straightforward fashion by performing the operation of expectation, that is, by combining the levels of utility according to the rule given in (12.1).

Uniqueness of the Expected Utility Function. So far, we have not said much about the utility function ϕ (and the expected utility function Φ) except that it is monotonically increasing. In Chapter 10, however, we saw that the utility function was not unique; it was shown that if we subject the utility function to a monotonic transformation, we obtain another legitimate utility function [Eq. (10.22)]. Let us perform such a transformation on the utility function of the present model. The original utility index is denoted by u, that is, $u = \phi(x)$, where x denotes the income variable. The new utility index will be denoted by w, and the transformation by ω, that is,

$$(12.3) \qquad\qquad w = \omega(u), \qquad \omega' > 0.$$

It will be convenient here to use subscripts to denote the level of income at which the utility function is evaluated. For example, if the income level is x_1, the original index corresponding to that level of income will be denoted by u_1, and the new index by w_1.

We now apply the continuity condition A.12.2′ to the three income levels $x_1 > x_2 > x_3$. Accordingly, there exists a probability α such that

$$(12.4) \qquad\qquad u_2 = \alpha u_1 + (1 - \alpha)u_3.$$

Since the consumer's system of preferences is independent of the method by which we happen to choose to number the utilities of the various bundles, the state of indifference described by Eq. (12.4) must also hold if we use the index w instead of u; that is, we must also have

$$(12.5) \qquad\qquad w_2 = \alpha w_1 + (1 - \alpha)w_3.$$

Substituting for the three values of w in (12.5) from (12.3), we get

$$(12.6) \qquad\qquad \omega(u_2) = \alpha\omega(u_1) + (1 - \alpha)\,\omega(u_3),$$

and substituting for u_2 in (12.6) from (12.4), we get

(12.7) $\omega[\alpha u_1 + (1 - \alpha)u_3] = \alpha\omega(u_1) + (1 - \alpha)\omega(u_3).$

It is clear that condition (12.7) will be satisfied only if ω is a linear function. Therefore, any utility index w must be related to the original index u by a relation such as $w = a + bu, b > 0$.

What the above analysis has shown is that, under conditions of expected utility minimization, the utility function is in some sense more unique than under conditions of complete certainty. Specifically, the class of transformations which preserves the consumer's preferences is narrower than the class of all monotonically increasing transformations: only linear (increasing) transformations are admissible. We therefore say that under conditions of expected utility maximization, the utility function is *unique up to a linear (increasing) transformation.*

One property of order-preserving functions that are unique up to a linear transformation is the invariance of *differences* between functional values. What this means is that admissible transformations preserve not only the ordering of preferences, but also the ordering of differences between preferences. This can be demonstrated as follows: Suppose that $A \} B \} C$, so that $\Phi(A) > \Phi(B) > \Phi(C)$. Assume, also, that the consumer's preference for A to B is stronger than his preference for B to C; that is, assume that

(12.8) $\Phi(A) - \Phi(B) > \Phi(B) - \Phi(C).$

What we want to show is that this inequality is preserved if we replace the original utility function by a linear transformation. For this purpose, we replace $u = \phi(x)$ by $\omega(u) = \omega[\phi(x)]$, where $\omega(u) = a + bu$, $b > 0$. Then the expected utility of bundle A, $\Omega(A)$, can be computed by using rule (12.1), which yields

$$\Omega(A) = \sum_{i=1}^{n} \alpha_i[a + b\phi(x_i)] = a + b\sum_{i=1}^{n} \alpha_i \phi(x_i) = a + b\Phi(A),$$

or

(12.9) $$\Phi(A) = \frac{\Omega(A) - a}{b}.$$

Similar transformations can be carried out for bundles B and C. If we then replace the terms in the inequality in (12.8) by their equivalents as given in (12.9), we get

(12.10) $$\left[\frac{\Omega(A)}{b} - \frac{a}{b}\right] - \left[\frac{\Omega(B)}{b} - \frac{a}{b}\right] > \left[\frac{\Omega(B)}{b} - \frac{a}{b}\right] - \left[\frac{\Omega(C)}{b} - \frac{a}{b}\right],$$

from which it follows that

(12.11) $\Omega(A) - \Omega(B) > \Omega(B) - \Omega(C).$

Thus, the ranking of differences between utility levels is not changed when the utility function is subjected to a linear transformation.

The invariance of utility differences under linear transformations is one aspect of the present model which sets it apart from the theory of consumer behavior under complete certainty. In the latter theory, it will be recalled, the shape of the marginal utility function plays no role whatsoever in determining the behavior of the consumer, because marginal utility is *not* necessarily invariant under any *arbitrary* monotonic transformation. This means, for example, that if marginal utility is decreasing in a given interval, it is, in general, possible to find a monotonic transformation of the utility function such that marginal utility will be constant, or increasing, in the same interval. The consumer's choice, on the other hand, is not affected by a monotonic transformation, as we saw in Chapter 10. From this it follows that, if we confront the consumer with a change in one of his environmental parameters (such as a change in a price or income), knowledge of the general shape of the marginal utility function will, by itself, be of no help whatsoever in predicting the effect of the parameter change on the consumer's behavior.

However, under the conditions of expected utility maximization, which require the utility function to be unique up to a linear transformation, the sign of the change in marginal utility is invariant to all admissible transformations. By way of an illustration, suppose the utility function is given by $u = \phi(x)$, and the monotonically increasing transformation is given by $w = \omega[\phi(x)] = \Omega(x)$. Then we have

$$\Omega' = \omega'\phi' \qquad\qquad \text{marginal utility,}$$
$$\Omega'' = \omega'\phi'' + \omega''(\phi')^2 \qquad \text{change in marginal utility.}$$

If the transformation ω is linear, then $\omega'' = 0$, in which case Ω'' has the same sign as ϕ''. In fact, since ω' is a positive constant here, it is clear that when the utility function is subjected to a linear transformation, the marginal utility of the new utility function is proportional to that of the original utility function. Thus, under the conditions of expected utility maximization, the general shape (i.e., slope) of the marginal utility function *is* an invariant property of the utility function, and therefore it does indeed reflect certain characteristics of the individual's preference structure. We shall return to this point in Section 12.3.4.

12.3 THE RELATIONSHIP BETWEEN EXPECTED UTILITY AND PROBABILITY DISTRIBUTIONS

Suppose we consider any two uncertain prospects with a view of determining which of them will be preferred (chosen) by a typical consumer. By "typical" we mean any consumer who fulfills the assumptions of expected utility maximization, but whose utility function is not known to us. Essentially, what we are trying to do here is to make some statements about preference for uncertain prospects which will be true for any expected-utility-maximizing consumer, regardless of the particular specifications of his utility function. Or, to put it differently, we are trying to establish some general relationship between the characteristics of uncertain bundles, and preference for these bundles. In the context of complete certainty, it will be recalled, the greediness axiom permits us to say that, between any two (certain) bundles, the "larger" (in the vectorial sense) bundle is always preferred. It is the purpose of this section to explore the possibilities of making similar statements concerning preference for uncertain bundles.

12.3.1   Expected Utility and the Moments of a Distribution

Probability distributions are often characterized by a set of specifications that embody a great deal of descriptive content; these are the *moments* of the distribution. We will show that it is possible to express the expected utility of an uncertain bundle in terms of the moments of the bundle; this will give us an alternative formulation of the expected utility function.

Let us expand the utility function $\phi(x)$ around the point $x = 0$; in other words, let us assume that the utility functions may be represented by Maclaurin's series. (See the last two paragraphs of Section 15.1.2.) This expansion takes the form

$$(12.12a) \qquad \phi(x) = \phi(0) + \phi'(0)x + \frac{\phi''(0)x^2}{2!} + \frac{\phi'''(0)x^3}{3!} + \cdots,$$

or, more compactly,

$$(12.12b) \qquad \phi(x) = \sum_{r=0}^{\infty} \frac{\phi^r(0)x^r}{r!},$$

where ϕ^r denotes the rth derivative of ϕ, and $\phi^0 = \phi$. If we consider the class of, say, all n-payoff bundles, then x_i (the ith payoff) is itself a variable, and so, of course, is the probability α_i. In that case, the utility of the ith payoff may be represented by an expression such as (12.12). Letting $x = x_i$, we have the following n expressions:

$$(12.13) \qquad \phi(x_i) = \sum_{r=0}^{\infty} \frac{\phi^r(0)(x_i)^r}{r!}, \qquad i = 1, 2, \ldots, n.$$

Substituting for the $\phi(x_i)$ in (12.1) from (12.13), we get

$$(12.14a) \qquad \Phi(A) = \sum_{r=0}^{\infty} \frac{\phi^r(0)}{r!} \sum_{i=1}^{n} \alpha_i(x_i)^r.$$

This expression may be simplified in two ways. First, since we are free to choose the origin of the utility function, we may assume $\phi(0) = 0$. Second, we see that the terms $\sum_{i=1}^{n} \alpha_i(x_i)^r$ appearing in (12.14a) are the moments around zero of the uncertain bundle A. Hence we can write (12.14a) as

$$(12.14b) \quad \Phi(A) = \phi'(0)\, m^1 + \frac{\phi''(0)\, m^2}{2!} + \frac{\phi'''(0)\, m^3}{3!} + \cdots,$$

where m^i denotes the ith moment around zero, and primes denote derivatives. Of course, m^1 is the same as the *mean* of the distribution, that is, the expected payoff.

The last equation shows that expected utility is a weighted (infinite) sum of all the moments of the probability distribution, the weights depending on the derivatives of the utility function. While this equation provides us with a direct and explicit relationship between expected utility and certain characteristics of the probability distribution, we can see that this equation is of only limited use for comparisons of different distributions. First, in order to compare any two distributions, one would, in general, have to know the values of *all* the moments of the two distributions. Second, one also needs to know the values of all the derivatives of the utility function at the origin. However, Eq. (12.14) may possibly be applied to cases involving special types of utility functions. For example, if the utility function is a kth-degree polynomial, then all derivatives of order $k + 1$ or higher are identically zero, so that the rhs of (12.14) reduces to a sum of k terms involving only the first k moments of the distribution. In the special case of a quadratic utility function, the situation is fairly simple; expected utility depends only on the first two moments, or (equivalently) on the mean and the variance of the distribution. In that case, pairs of distributions may be ordered (compared), at least partially, as soon as one specifies the sign of the second derivative of the utility function.

12.3.2 Expected Utility and the Parameters of a Distribution

In the case of discrete distributions with a finite number of payoffs, statements about preference may be deduced not from a comparison of moments, but from a comparison of the parameters of the distributions. If an uncertain prospect has n payoffs, then it has $n + (n - 1)$ independent parameters—n payoffs, and $n - 1$ probabilities. We may, therefore, consider pairs of uncertain prospects in which one prospect is constructed by changing some of the parameters in the other given prospect. Then, by virtue of the positivity of marginal utility, we can state the following proposition:

> ***Proposition 12.1.*** *For any two uncertain prospects A and B with identical probabilities, if some or all of the payoffs in A are larger, and none is smaller, than the respective payoffs in B, then A is preferred to B.*

In the above proposition, "respective payoffs" means payoffs with the same probabilities. A similar proposition can be made with respect to uncertain prospects in which the probabilities are different, the payoffs being the same.

Except that (since probabilities have to add up to unity) an increase in one probability always entails a corresponding decrease in some other probability. Consequently, the second proposition takes the following form:

> **Proposition 12.2.** *For any two uncertain prospects A and B with payoffs x_i and probabilities α_i and β_i, respectively, if $\alpha_j > \beta_j$ and $\alpha_k < \beta_k$, all other probabilities being equal, then A is preferred to B if and only if $x_j > x_k$, and B is preferred to A if and only if $x_j < x_k$.*

In some sense, the above two propositions are manifestations of the consumer's greediness. Under the conditions of Proposition 12.1, given that the payoffs of the two prospects have identical probabilities, prospect A is preferred because its vector of payoffs is "larger" than that of prospect B. The conditions of Proposition 12.2 are slightly different, and, to clarify the case, let us assume that A and B are two-payoff prospects: $A = (x_k, x_j; \alpha_k, \alpha_j)$, and $B = (x_k, x_j; \beta_k, \beta_j)$. If $x_k > x_j$, and $\alpha_k < \beta_k$, then B is preferred to A, the explanation for this being that the probability of receiving the larger of the two payoffs (that is, x_k) is higher in prospect B (that is, $\beta_k > \alpha_k$), and this preference may be regarded as a probabilistic version of greediness. The conditions of the above two propositions can be described by a more general property of probability distributions, which we introduce in the next section.

12.3.3 Stochastic Dominance

Stochastic dominance is a condition that relates pairs of probability distributions. Two types of dominance seem to be useful for the analysis of a variety of decision problems under uncertainty. The stronger of these conditions is referred to as *first-degree stochastic dominance* (FSD), and it holds whenever one cumulative distribution lies, at least partly, under the other cumulative distribution. When this conditions holds between any two distributions, the dominant distribution is said to be larger than the other distribution in the sense of FSD. To develope this condition formally, let us consider all distributions defined on the interval $I = [x_1, x_n]$. Then for any two cumulative distributions $F(x_i)$ and $G(x_i)$ we say:

> *If $G(x_i) \leqslant F(x_i)$ for all $x_i \in I$, the strict inequality holding for at least one x_i, then G is larger than F in the sense of FSD.*

It should be pointed out that it is not necessary for any two distributions to satisfy the FSD conditions; that is, given any two distributions F and G, it is quite possible that neither of the two distributions is larger than the other in the sense of FSD. In that case, the two distributions are noncomparable from the point of view of FSD. It is, therefore, obvious that by means of the FSD relation one can, in general, obtain only a partial ordering of the distributions in some given set.

The relevance of the FSD condition to the subject matter of this chapter is that, by means of this condition, it is possible to make a prediction about preference for uncertain prospects (probability distributions) without any knowledge of the utility function. This result is stated in the following proposition:

Proposition 12.3. For any two uncertain prospects A and B, if A is larger than B in the sense of FSD, then A is preferred to B by all expected-utility maximizers.

It should be clear now that the reason why in Propositions 12.1 and 12.2 we were able to make statements (predictions) about preference without any knowledge of the utility function is that, in both these cases, the preferred prospect is larger than the other prospect in the sense of FSD. Hence, the above two propositions are merely special cases of Proposition 12.3.

Of still greater significance is the fact that FSD is not only a sufficient, but also a necessary, condition for preference. This means that the converse of Proposition 12.3 also holds; thus

Proposition 12.4. If prospect A is preferred to prospect B by all expected-utility maximizers, then A is larger than B in the sense of FSD.

Propositions 12.3 and 12.4 taken together imply that FSD and preference are equivalent relations; that is, the statement "*A* is larger than *B* in the sense of FSD" is *equivalent* to the statement "*A* is preferred to *B* by all expected-utility maximizers."

The weaker dominance condition is called *second-degree stochastic dominance* (SSD), and it holds whenever the area under one cumulative distribution is smaller than that under the other distribution. More precisely, considering all distributions defined on the interval $I = [x_1, x_n]$ we say:

$$\text{If } \sum_{i=1}^{r} G(x_i)(x_{i+1} - x_i) \leqslant \sum_{i=1}^{r} F(x_i)(x_{i+1} - x_i), \qquad r = 1, 2, ..., n-1,$$

the strict inequality holding for at least one r, then G is larger than F in the sense of SSD.

For continuous distributions, the above inequality is replaced by

$$\int_{x_1}^{x} G(t)dt \leqslant \int_{x_1}^{x} F(t)dt \qquad \text{for all } x \in I.$$

It is clear that FSD implies SSD, but not vice versa, hence SSD is a weaker condition than FSD. As in the case of FSD, the SSD relation is only a partial ordering, except that the set of distributions that can be ordered by means of SSD is, in general, larger than that which is orderable by means of FSD.

The SSD condition enables us to make statements like those in Propositions 12.3 and 12.4, but only for utility functions with nonincreasing marginal utility everywhere. For simplicity, let us confine ourselves to utility functions with strictly decreasing marginal utility everywhere. Then we can state the following:

Proposition 12.5. *For any two uncertain prospects A and B, if A is larger than B in the sense of* SSD, *then A is preferred to B by all expected-utility maximizers whose utility functions have decreasing marginal utility.*

For the class of utility functions that we are considering here, the SSD condition is also necessary, and so we have the converse of Proposition 12.5:

Proposition 12.6. *If prospect A is preferred to prospect B by all expected-utility maximizers whose utility functions have decreasing marginal utility, then A is larger than B in the sense of* SSD.

We see that SSD and preference are equivalent conditions for all utility functions with decreasing marginal utility. The latter assumption about marginal utility is made quite frequently in the literature because, among other things, it has certain implications concerning the behavior of the consumer. These implications are discussed in the next section.

12.3.4 Attitude toward Risk

In considering choices among uncertain prospects, we distinguish between *aversion to risk*, and *attraction to risk*. Roughly speaking, a consumer who rejects a fair bet is said to be averse to risk, while the consumer who accepts a fair bet is said to be attracted to risk. To define these concepts more rigorously, let us consider an uncertain bundle A whose expected payoff is given by m; that is, $\sum_{i=1}^{n} \alpha_i x_i = m$. Then we say (define):

The consumer shows aversion *to risk if and only if* $\Phi(A) < \phi(m)$.

The consumer shows attraction *to risk if and only if* $\Phi(A) > \phi(m)$.

If $\Phi(A) = \phi(m)$, we may say that the consumer has a *neutral attitude* toward risk. We see from the above definition that the consumer's attitude toward risk is revealed by his preference (or choice) between an uncertain bundle and a certain bundle whose income is equal to the expected payoff of the uncertain bundle: preference for the certain payoff reveals aversion to risk; preference for the gamble reveals attraction to risk.

What is the relationship between a particular attitude toward risk, and the utility function? To investigate this question, we make use of Taylor's expansion with a remainder. Expanding the utility function around the mean (m) of the probability distribution, we have

$$(12.15) \qquad \phi(x) = \phi(m) + \phi'(m)(x - m) + \frac{\phi''(\xi)}{2!}(x - m)^2,$$

where ξ is a properly chosen point between x and m. If the bundle under consideration has n payoffs, then the utility of each of these payoffs can be represented by an expansion such as (12.15). We thus have

$$(12.16) \qquad \phi(x_i) = \phi(m) + \phi'(m)(x_i - m) + \frac{\phi''(\xi_i)}{2!} (x_i - m)^2,$$

$$i = 1, 2, ..., n,$$

where ξ_i is a properly chosen point between x_i and m. If we now substitute for the $\phi(x_i)$ in (12.1) from (12.16), we get

$$(12.17) \qquad \Phi(A) = \phi(m) + \sum_{i=1}^{n} \frac{\phi''(\xi_i)}{2!} \alpha_i(x_i - m)^2.$$

In the case of aversion to risk we have, by definition,

$$\phi(m) + \sum_{i=1}^{n} \frac{\phi''(\xi_i)}{2!} \alpha_i(x_i - m)^2 < \phi(m),$$

or

$$\sum_{i=1}^{n} \frac{\phi''(\xi_i)}{2!} \alpha_i(x_i - m)^2 < 0.$$

Clearly, the only terms in the above summation of cross-products that can take negative values are the $\phi''(\xi_i)$. We can, therefore, conclude that at least at one point in the interval between the smallest and the largest payoff of the uncertain bundle, the marginal utility must be decreasing; that is, at one of the ξ_i we must have $\phi''(\xi_i) < 0$. Obviously, if the marginal utility is decreasing at *every* point in some interval, the consumer shows aversion to risk with respect to all bundles whose payoffs lie entirely in this interval. Needless to say, this result applies also to cases of attraction to risk; then the above inequalities are reversed, and the conditions for attraction to risk involve increasing, rather than decreasing, marginal utility.

In Section 12.3.1, we pointed out that in the special case of a quadratic utility function, it is possible to order pairs of uncertain prospects if the sign of the second derivative of the utility function is specified. We can, therefore, make the following statement:

> *If the consumer has a quadratic utility function, and he is globally averse to risk, then between any two uncertain prospects he will always prefer the one with the higher mean, given that the variances are the same, or prefer the prospect with the smaller variance, given identical means.*

Similar statements can be made for individuals who are attracted to risk.

Of course, if it is assumed that all individuals are averse to risk, then it is not necessary to restrict consideration to the special case of quadratic utility functions in order to make predictions about preference. Instead, we can then make use of the SSD condition which applies to *all* utility functions with decreasing marginal utility, not only to those that are quadratic. Indeed, since the SSD condition is both necessary and sufficient, it enables us to make a general statement about preference, given that the only known information about utility functions is that all consumers are averse to risk.

12.3.5   Two-Payoff Prospects

In this section, we take a brief look at two-payoff prospects. Because of the simple form of such prospects, a study of their properties will provide additional insight into various aspects of behavior under uncertainty in general.

Two-payoff prospects depend on three independent parameters: the two payoffs, and one probability. We shall denote a typical prospect by $A = (x_1, x_2; \alpha)$, where x_1 and x_2 are the two payoffs, and α is the probability of payoff x_1. Expected utility is then given by

$$(12.18) \qquad \Phi(A) = \alpha\phi(x_1) + (1 - \alpha)\phi(x_2) = \alpha[\phi(x_1) - \phi(x_2)] + \phi(x_2).$$

One property of two-payoff bundles is that, if the payoffs are held fixed, so that only the probability α is allowed to vary, then expected utility depends only on the expected payoff of the prospect, regardless of the form of the utility function; in fact, under these conditions, expected utility is a linearly increasing function of the expected payoff. Applying the Theorem of the Mean to the utility function, we get

$$(12.19) \qquad\qquad \phi(x_1) - \phi(x_2) = \phi'(\xi)(x_1 - x_2),$$

where ξ is a properly chosen point between x_1 and x_2. Substituting for $\phi(x_1) - \phi(x_2)$ in (12.18) from (12.19), we can write

$$(12.20) \qquad\qquad \Phi(A) = \alpha k(x_1 - x_2) + \phi(x_2),$$

where $k = \phi'(\xi)$. But the expected payoff (the mean of the probability distribution) is given by $m = \alpha x_1 + (1 - \alpha)x_2$, so that $\alpha(x_1 - x_2) = m - x_2$. Using the latter equation, we can write (12.20) as

$$(12.21) \qquad\qquad \Phi(A) = [\phi(x_2) - kx_2] + km = \hat{\Phi}(m).$$

Equation (12.21) expresses expected utility as a linear function of the expected payoff m. Since the expected payoff always lies between the two (fixed) payoffs of the prospect, the domain of definition of $\hat{\Phi}$ is the interval $[x_1, x_2]$.

The case is illustrated in Fig. 12.1. In this diagram, the horizontal axis has a dollar scale, since both x and m represent levels of income. On the other hand, the values taken by the utility function and the expected utility function, respectively, are measured by some real valued index, denoted here by u. As the diagram clearly shows, given the expected payoff of a particular prospect (with fixed payoffs x_1 and x_2), say m_0, the corresponding utility index can be read off the u-axis in the usual manner. It is clear, therefore, that the set of all

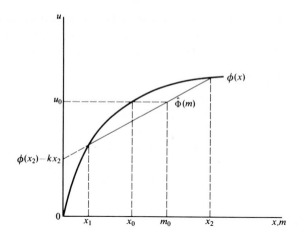

Figure 12.1

prospects having the same two payoffs can be completely ordered according to preference; furthermore, this ordering depends only on the expected payoff of the prospect, and not on any other characteristics of the probability distribution. It is easy to verify that, between any two distinct prospects with identical payoffs, one prospect is always larger than the other in the sense of FSD. The orderability of such prospects follows, therefore, directly from Proposition 12.3.

Insurance Premium. Since the utility function in Fig. 12.1 is everywhere strictly concave, the diagram represents an example of a consumer who is globally averse to risk. As we have defined it in Section 12.3.4, this implies that the consumer will prefer the income m_0 offered with certainty to the uncertain prospect whose expected payoff is m_0. This can easily be seen to be true in Fig. 12.1. In fact, the consumer will even prefer incomes smaller than m_0 to the uncertain prospect represented in Fig. 12.1. At the limit, when he is confronted with the choice between x_0 dollars offered with certainty and the uncertain prospect with expected income m_0, the consumer is indifferent between the two. And if the income that is offered with certainty is less than x_0, he will choose the uncertain prospect rather than the certain income. Thus, the difference $m_0 - x_0$ can be interpreted as the maximum amount of mean income that the consumer is willing to forgo in order not to be exposed to uncertainty. Essentially, when he chooses a certain income $x < m_0$ rather than the uncertain prospect, he may be thought of as insuring himself against a possible loss that he might incur if he chooses the uncertain bundle. For this reason, the amount $m_0 - x_0$ is sometimes referred to as an *insurance premium.*

It may be observed that the magnitude of the insurance premium depends on the expected payoff. If the probability α is very close to either one or zero, so that the expected payoff is very close to either x_1 or x_2, then the insurance premium is relatively small; when α is in the neighborhood of $1/2$, the insurance premium is relatively large. This may be explained by the fact that the variance of the uncertain prospect may be regarded as an approximate measure of the riskiness of the prospect, Hence, a risk averter will be attracted to prospects with small variances. Since the variance of two-payoff prospects is greatest when the probability is $1/2$, and smallest when the probability is either zero or one, we can say that the magnitudes of different insurance premiums reflect the relative magnitudes of the variances of the prospects under consideration.

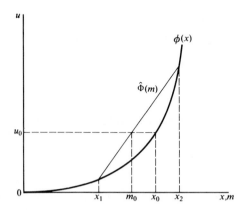

Figure 12.2

What happens to the insurance premium under conditions of attraction to risk? An individual who is attracted to risk will be willing to forgo a certain amount of mean income in order to expose himself to risk, rather than to insure himself against it. In that case, the insurance premium is negative, as is shown in Fig. 12.2 .Given the uncertain prospect with expected payoff m_0, the consumer is willing to give up a maximum of $x_0 - m_0$ dollars in mean income for the privilege of engaging in a gamble. It is also clear that the magnitude of the opportunity cost that the individual is ready to bear is related directly to the riskiness of the gamble: when the variance of the gamble is large, he is willing to bear a relatively high cost, and the opposite for small-variance gambles.

12.4 CHOICE SITUATIONS WITH CONTINUOUS DISTRIBUTIONS

In most economic models, it is customary to assume that variables such as output, price, income, profit, etc., may vary continuously, and hence take on infinitely many values. If some of these are random variables, the discrete probability function must be replaced by a probability density function, and expected values are computed by integrating, rather than summing, the appropriate functions. However, while the mechanics of optimization in the continuous case are somewhat different from those that apply to the discrete case, the fundamental principles underlying the two approaches are essentially the same. We will illustrate the continuous case with choice situations from the theory of the firm and the theory of consumer behavior.

12.4.1 Expected Profit Maximization

The first case is a fairly simple application of decision making under uncertainty to the standard model of the firm. We think here of a firm selling a single product in some market, but we ignore any interrelationships with rival firms. We make the customary assumption about market demand by postulating that the quantity demanded of the firm's product is inversely related to the price charged by the firm. However, whereas under conditions of complete certainty we would have expressed this assumption in the form of a deterministic downward-sloping demand function, we shall now introduce an element of uncertainty, and consequently we characterize the demand relation in stochastic terms. The simplest approach to this problem is to assume the following:

a) For every price set by the firm, quantity demanded is governed by some probability density function.

b) The expected value of quantity demanded varies inversely with price.

To formalize this model, we introduce the density function $\theta(x; p)$, where x denotes all possible levels of demand, and p is the price chosen by the firm. The latter is a parameter of the density function. We shall assume that quantity demanded is always nonnegative regardless of the price. Since θ is a density function, it must satisfy the following conditions:

$$(12.22a) \qquad \theta(x; p) \geqslant 0 \qquad \text{for all } x \text{ and } p,$$

$$(12.22b) \qquad \int_0^\infty \theta(x; p)dx = 1 \qquad \text{for all } p.$$

If we apply the definition of expected value to the present density function (assuming the expected value exists and is finite), we have

$$(12.23) \qquad \bar{x} = \int_0^\infty x\theta(x; p)dx = h(p),$$

where $\bar{x}$ denotes the expected level of demand. Since p is a parameter of the density function, it is clear that expected demand depends on the level of price, and the relationship between these two quantities is defined by the function h. In condition (b) we assumed this to be an inverse relationship, so that we have

$$(12.24) \qquad h' = \int_0^\infty x\theta_p(x; p)dx < 0 \qquad \text{for all } p,$$

where $h' = dh/dp$, and $\theta_p = \partial\theta/\partial p$. It is clear from (12.24) that we must have $\theta_p < 0$ over some range of x.

Since the seller operates under conditions of uncertainty, he cannot know in advance how much he can sell at various prices, and thus he is also unable to compute the level of profit associated with various price levels. Maximization of profit is, therefore, not a feasible objective under the present circumstances. In analogy with our approach to the behavior of the consumer under conditions of uncertainty, we assume that the firm attempts to maximize *expected* profit. If π denotes the possible levels of profit, and $\bar{\pi}$ is expected profit, then we have

$$(12.25a) \qquad \bar{\pi} = \int_0^\infty \pi\theta(x;\ p)dx.$$

Replacing π by its usual definition of TR $-$ TC, we get

$$(12.25b) \qquad \bar{\pi} = \int_0^\infty [px - f(x) - c]\theta(x;\ p)dx,$$

where $f(x)$ is the TVC function (which is known with certainty).This equation may, in turn, be written as a difference between two quantities, namely

$$(12.25c) \qquad \bar{\pi} = p\int_0^\infty x\theta(x;\ p)dx - \left[\int_0^\infty f(x)\theta(x;\ p)dx + c\right],$$

which shows that expected profit is simply the difference between expected revenue and expected cost. It should, however, be pointed out that in the present model, the function $f(x)$ refers to the cost of quantity demanded, and not to the cost of quantity produced. Since the level of demand is not known with certainty, the cost of the quantity demanded is also a random variable (even though the form of the function f is known with certainty), and hence the above reference to expected cost. The definition of expected profit in terms of expected *demand*, rather than expected *sales*, is, perhaps, not the best definition; it is adopted here mainly for the sake of simplification. The possibility that sales may fall short of demand follows, of course, from the fact that, under conditions of uncertainty, the firm's level of production, plus existing inventory, may, in any given period, fall short of demand. Thus, if the model is to be formulated in terms of expected sales, production as well as inventory must be considered. In this model, we simplify matters by assuming that the pricing decision is related only to expected demand.

The equation in (12.25) represents the objective function of the model, and the problem is to maximize it with respect to the decision variable p. To do this, we apply the standard mathematical technique for maximizing a one-variable function. Assuming that the expected profit function has an interior maximum, then the first derivative must be equal to zero; that is,

(12.26a) $\bar{x} + p \int_0^\infty x\theta_p(x; \ p)dx - \int_0^\infty f(x)\theta_p(x; \ p)dx = 0,$

or, using the notation introduced earlier,

(12.26b) $h(p) + ph' - \int_0^\infty f(x)\theta_p(x; \ p)dx = 0.$

This condition may be interpreted as equating expected marginal revenue with expected marginal cost. (Of course, the marginal quantities in this model are not the same as those which we normally denote by MR and MC. The latter, it will be recalled, are functions of x, whereas in the above conditions, expected revenue and cost are defined as functions of p.)

The second-order condition for a maximum requires the second derivative to be negative. Hence we have

(12.27) $2h' + ph'' - \int_0^\infty f(x)\theta_{pp}(x; \ p)dx < 0,$

where $\theta_{pp} = \partial^2\theta/\partial p^2$.

The solution to the first-order condition given in (12.26) is the price the firm should charge. But what about the level of production? The reader will recall that in a complete-information model, the first-order condition yields either the optimal price or the optimal level of output; having found one of these, the firm then computes the other by making a substitution in the demand function. Under the present conditions, however, price and output must be determined separately, since the demand function is not known. The decision process by which the level of production may be determined will not be discussed here at great length, since that process can (although it need not) be modeled in deterministic, rather than stochastic, terms. For example, as soon as the firm has chosen a price, it can compute expected demand. The level of production may then be related in some fashion to expected demand, allowing, of course, for the possibility that actual demand will be different from expected demand. In general, when operating under conditions of uncertainty, the firm will maintain a certain level of inventory as protection against unforeseen increases in demand (or as a means of minimizing fluctuations in production). Thus, it is reasonable that the rule for the determination of the level of production should involve expected demand as well as the given stock of inventory. An example of such a production model is given in the context of a nonstochastic decision model in Section 12.5.2.

Example 12.1. Let us suppose that the firm believes its demand to be a random variable with an exponential distribution, that is,

$$\theta(x; \ p) = \alpha e^{-\alpha x}, \qquad \text{where } \alpha = ap^2, \quad a > 0.$$

To simplify the arithmetic, we assume a linear cost function, namely $TC = bx + c$, $b, c > 0$. Since the mean of the above exponential distribution is given by $1/\alpha$, we have

$$\bar{x} = \frac{1}{ap^2} = h(p),$$

which satisfies our assumption that expected demand is a decreasing function of price. Expected cost can also be computed without difficulty because of the linearity of $f(x)$. We have,

$$\text{expected cost of demand} = b\bar{x} + c = \frac{b}{ap^2} + c.$$

Given the above expected values, the expected profit function takes the form

$$\bar{\pi} = p\bar{x} - b\bar{x} - c = \frac{p-b}{ap^2} - c.$$

First- and second-order conditions can now be derived directly by differentiation:

$$\bar{\pi}' = \frac{2b-p}{ap^3} = 0, \qquad \bar{\pi}'' = \frac{2(p-3b)}{ap^4} < 0.$$

From the first-order condition we get $p = 2b$, and a substitution for p in the second-order condition shows that the latter is satisfied for all optimal prices.

12.4.2   Intertemporal Expected Utility

In this section, we construct and analyze a stochastic model for a decision problem confronting a consumer with a multiperiod planning horizon. The general framework in which the problem will be cast is similar to that discussed in Chapter 11; specifically, we consider a problem in which the consumer is concerned with planning the levels of total expenditures for each period in his horizon, as well as the amount of terminal assets. (The end of the horizon may or may not represent the end of the consumer's economic life.) In other words, the utility function is of the form $u = \phi(x_1, x_2, \ldots, x_T, v_T)$, where x_t denotes total expenditures in period t, and v_T denotes the amount (in dollars) of assets at the end of period T. In this model, we do not consider the choice between leisure and working hours, and consequently we regard the income in each period as a parameter. In fact, it is this aspect of the model that we assume to be stochastic in nature.

  If there exists complete certainty, then the consumer's budget constraint for the present model is given by

$$(12.28a) \qquad v_T = v_0(1+r)^T + \sum_{t=1}^{T} m_t(1+r)^{T-t+1} - \sum_{t=1}^{T} x_t(1+r)^{T-t+1},$$

where v_0 denotes the value of the consumer's initial stock of assets, m_t denotes the income in period t, and r the rate at which money can be lent and borrowed in each of the T periods. Equation (12.28a) is essentially the same as Eq. (11.38a), in Chapter 11, and we are making assumptions similar to those underlying the construction of the budget constraint given by (11.38a). For convenience, we rewrite (12.28a) as

$$(12.28b) \qquad v_T = v_0(1+r)^T + m - x,$$

where $m = \sum_{t=1}^{T} m_t(1 + r)^{T-t+1}$, and $x = \sum_{t=1}^{T} x_t(1 + r)^{T-t+1}$. At this point, we are making the assumption that the m_t are random variables, so that the weighted sum m is also a random variable. We shall assume that the possible values of m range from $-\infty$ to $+\infty$. If m is a random variable, v_T is also a random variable, and since v_T is an argument of the utility function, utility itself is a random variable. It is therefore appropriate to assume that the consumer wishes to maximize expected utility.

If the probability density function of m is denoted by $\theta(m)$, expected utility (assumed to exist and finite) is given by

$$(12.29a) \qquad \bar{u} = \int_{-\infty}^{+\infty} \phi(x_1, x_2, ..., x_T, v_T)\theta(m)\,dm,$$

or, making use of (12.28b),

$$(12.29b) \qquad \bar{u} = \int_{-\infty}^{+\infty} \phi[x_1, x_2, ..., x_T, v_0(1+r)^T + m - x]\theta(m)\,dm$$

$$= \Phi(x_1, x_2, ..., x_T).$$

Thus, under the present formulation, the expenditure levels are parameters of the expected utility function, and they are, of course, the decision variables with respect to which the expected utility function is to be maximized. What this implies is that the consumer carries out his consumption plans exactly as originally planned, and hence there is no uncertainty about the actual levels of expenditure in each period of the horizon. What *is* uncertain is the consumer's actual income in each period, and therefore the amount that he will lend or borrow; consequently, terminal assets are also not known with certainty.

Assuming that the expected utility function has a regular interior maximum, the first-order conditions take the form

$$(12.30a) \qquad \Phi_t = \int_{-\infty}^{+\infty} [\phi_t - \phi_v(1+r)^{T-t+1}]\theta(m)\,dm = 0, \qquad t = 1, 2, ..., T,$$

where $\Phi_t = \partial\Phi/\partial x_t$, $\phi_t = \partial\phi/\partial x_t$, and $\phi_v = \partial\phi/\partial v_T$. The above equations can also be written as

$$(12.30b) \qquad \int_{-\infty}^{+\infty} \phi_t\theta(m)\,dm = (1+r)^{T-t+1}\int_{-\infty}^{+\infty} \phi_v\theta(m)\,dm, \qquad t = 1, 2, ..., T.$$

These conditions have an obvious interpretation: the expected marginal utility of expenditure in each period must be proportional to the expected marginal utility of terminal assets, where in each case the factor of proportionality is the opportunity cost of one dollar of expenditure in the respective period. The interpretation of $(1+r)^{T-t+1}$ as the opportunity cost of one dollar spent in period t has already been explained and justified in the discussion of Eq. (11.38a), in Section 11.2.1 of Chapter 11. In fact, the similarity between the first-order conditions of the present model and those of the model in Section 11.2.1 becomes even more apparent if we divide the equations in (12.30b) by one another. This gives

$$(12.31) \quad \frac{\int_{-\infty}^{+\infty} \phi_t \theta(m)\, dm}{\int_{-\infty}^{+\infty} \phi_\tau \theta(m)\, dm} = \frac{(1+r)^{T-t+1}}{(1+r)^{T-\tau+1}} = (1+r)^{\tau-t} \qquad \text{for all } t \text{ and } \tau.$$

According to these equations, the ratios of expected marginal utilities must be equal to the ratio of the respective opportunity costs. Not surprisingly, these conditions are essentially of the familiar type equating MRSs with price ratios. The solutions to these conditions constitute the consumer's demand (consumption) functions, and they depend, in this case, on the parameters v_0 and r. We may write them as

$$(12.32) \qquad x_t = h_t(v_0, r), \qquad t = 1, 2, \ldots, T.$$

Even though the level of terminal assets is not known with certainty, the consumer can compute their expected value. This may be done with the aid of the demand functions given in (12.32), the density function, and Eq. (12.28b). This yields

$$(12.33) \qquad \bar{v}_T = v_0(1 + r)^T + \bar{m} - h,$$

where bars denote expected values, and

$$h = \sum_{t=1}^{T} h_t(v_0, r)(1 + r)^{T-t+1}.$$

The second-order conditions for this problem are:

$$\Phi_{11} < 0, \quad \begin{vmatrix} \Phi_{11} & \Phi_{12} \\ \Phi_{21} & \Phi_{22} \end{vmatrix} > 0, \ldots, \quad (-1)^T \begin{vmatrix} \Phi_{11} & \Phi_{12} & \cdots & \Phi_{1T} \\ \Phi_{21} & \Phi_{22} & \cdots & \Phi_{2T} \\ \vdots & & & \vdots \\ \Phi_{T1} & \Phi_{T2} & \cdots & \Phi_{TT} \end{vmatrix} > 0.$$

Example 12.2. For the purpose of illustrating the above model, we shall assume a two-period planning horizon, and use a multiplicative utility function; that is,

$$u = x_1 x_2 v_2 = \phi(x_1, x_2, v_2).$$

Terminal assets are given by

$$v_2 = v_0(1 + r)^2 + m - x,$$

where $m = (1 + r)^2 m_1 + (1 + r) m_2$, and $x = (1 + r)^2 x_1 + (1 + r) x_2$.

If $\theta(m)$ denotes the density function of m, then

$$\bar{u} = \int_{-\infty}^{+\infty} \{x_1 x_2 [v_0(1 + r)^2 + m - x]\} \theta(m) dm$$

$$= x_1 x_2 [v_0(1 + r)^2 + \bar{m} - x] = \Phi(x_1, x_2),$$

where $\bar{m}$ is the expected value of m. We may draw attention here to the fact that because of the simple form of the utility function ϕ, the only characteristic of the probability distribution of m that has any effect on expected utility is the expected value of m. In other words, the only specification about the probability distribution that the consumer needs to know (or speculate about) in this particular example is the expected value of the random variable. If the utility function is of a more complicated form, expected utility may depend also on the higher moments of the distribution.

First-order conditions for the maximization of $\Phi(x_1, x_2)$ are

$$\Phi_1 = x_2 v_0(1 + r)^2 + x_2 \bar{m} - 2(1 + r)^2 x_1 x_2 - (1 + r) x_2^2 = 0,$$

$$\Phi_2 = x_1 v_0(1 + r)^2 + x_1 \bar{m} - (1 + r)^2 x_1^2 - 2(1 + r) x_1 x_2 = 0,$$

and for the second-order conditions we have

$$- 2(1 + r)^2 x_2 < 0, \quad \begin{vmatrix} - 2(1 + r)^2 x_2 & v_0(1 + r)^2 + \bar{m} - 2x \\ v_0(1 + r)^2 + \bar{m} - 2x & - 2(1 + r) x_1 \end{vmatrix} > 0.$$

Solving the first-order conditions, we find the consumer's optimal expenditure levels in the two periods of the horizon:

$$x_1 = \frac{v_0(1 + r)^2 + \bar{m}}{3(1 + r)^2} = h_1(v_0, r; \bar{m}),$$

$$x_2 = \frac{v_0(1 + r)^2 + \bar{m}}{3(1 + r)} = h_2(v_0, r; \bar{m}).$$

In order to guarantee an interior solution we must, of course, assume that $v_0(1 + r)^2 + \bar{m} > 0$; that is, it is necessary to assume that the capitalized value of the consumer's expected wealth is positive. In this particular example, the demand functions depend on two different types of parameter: the *objective* parameters v_0 and r, and the *subjective* parameter $\bar{m}$. Hence, the consumer's expenditure levels will change whenever there is a change in his initial assets or the rate of interest, and also when the consumer changes his view about the mean of the probability function $\theta(m)$.

The expected value of the consumer's terminal assets is given by

$$\bar{v}_2 = \frac{v_0(1 + r)^2 + \bar{m}}{3}.$$

Finally, it is easy to verify that the second order conditions are satisfied for x_1 and x_2 evaluated at their optimal levels.

Unequal Rates of Interest. An interesting, and somewhat more realistic, version of the model given in (12.28) and (12.29) may be constructed by assuming that the interest payable on loans is different from that payable on savings. If we let α denote the borrowing rate, and β the lending rate, then it is reasonable to assume that $\alpha > \beta$. Unfortunately (but predictably), the introduction of two different rates of interest complicates matters considerably. We will, therefore, illustrate this case in the context of a one-period model, involving only total spending in that period, x, initial and terminal assets, v_0 and v, respectively, and income m.

To clarify the situation, let us plot the consumer's terminal asset position, v, against the amount borrowed (lent), $v_0 + m - x$, assuming m is known with certainty. This is done in Fig. 12.3. We see that if the consumer spends x' dollars, then he lends (invests) the unspent part of his income, and at the end of the period his asset position equals $(1 + \beta)$ times the amount lent. If, on the other hand, the consumer chooses to spend x'' dollars, then he is forced to borrow, and by the end of the period he will have incurred a debt which equals $(1 + \alpha)$ times the amount borrowed. The important point to

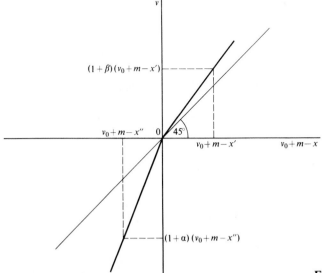

Figure 12.3

note is that the functional relationship between v and $v_0 + m - x$ consists of two linear segments (with different slopes) joined at the origin.

Now, if income is a random variable, so is v, and we can compute its expected value $\bar{v}$. Because of the discontinuity (at the origin) in the slope of the function shown in Fig. 12.3, however, the computation of $\bar{v}$ calls for piecewise integration (summation). Specifically,

$$(12.34) \qquad \bar{v} = \int_{-\infty}^{x-v_0} (1 + \alpha)(v_0 + m - x)\,\theta(m)dm$$

$$+ \int_{x-v_0}^{+\infty} (1 + \beta)(v_0 + m - x)\,\theta(m)dm.$$

It follows that if the utility function is of the general form $u = \phi(x, v)$, expected utility is given by

$$(12.35) \qquad \bar{u} = \int_{-\infty}^{x-v_0} \phi[x, (1 + \alpha)(v_0 + m - x)]\,\theta(m)dm$$

$$+ \int_{x-v_0}^{+\infty} \phi[x, (1 + \beta)(v_0 + m - x)]\,\theta(m)dm = \Phi(x).$$

Notice that in Eq. (12.35), the limits of integration, as well as the integrand, depend on the decision variable x. According to the rules for differentiating expressions such as the above (see the last section of Chapter 15), we have

$$(12.36) \qquad \Phi' = \int_{-\infty}^{x-v_0} [\phi_x - \phi_v(1 + \alpha)]\,\theta(m)\,dm + \phi(x, 0)$$

$$+ \int_{x-v_0}^{+\infty} [\phi_x - \phi_v(1 + \beta)]\,\theta(m)dm - \phi(x, 0).$$

Consequently, the first-order condition for the maximization of $\bar{u}$ is

$$(12.37a) \qquad \int_{-\infty}^{x-v_0} [\phi_x - \phi_v(1 + \alpha)]\,\theta(m)dm$$

$$+ \int_{x-v_0}^{+\infty} [\phi_x - \phi_v(1 + \beta)]\,\theta(m)dm = 0,$$

or

$$(12.37b) \qquad \int_{-\infty}^{+\infty} \phi_x\,\theta(m)dm = (1 + \alpha)\int_{-\infty}^{x-v_0} \phi_v\,\theta(m)dm$$

$$+ (1 + \beta)\int_{x-v_0}^{+\infty} \phi_v\,\theta(m)dm.$$

Comparing (12.37b) with (12.30b), we can see the similarity as well as the difference between the two models: in the preceding model, the expected marginal utility of expenditure is proportional to the expected marginal utility of terminal assets; in the present model, the expected marginal utility of expenditure is equal to a *weighted* expected marginal utility of terminal assets, where the two weights depend on the borrowing and lending rates of interest.

The solution to (12.37) is the consumer's demand function for spending which may be written as $x = h(v_0, \alpha, \beta)$. The second-order condition for the problem is simply $\Phi'' < 0$.

Example 12.3. To simplify the illustration of this model, we assume a partially exponential utility function:

$$u = - ae^{-x} + v = \phi(x, v), \qquad a > 0.$$

We further assume that income may take on any value from zero to infinity, and that the density function is exponential with mean one; that is,

$$\theta(m) = e^{-m}.$$

The expected utility function takes the form

$$\bar{u} = - \int_0^{x - v_0} [ae^{-x} - (1 + \alpha)(v_0 + m - x)]e^{-m} dm$$

$$- \int_{x - v_0}^{+\infty} [ae^{-x} - (1 + \beta)(v_0 + m - x]e^{-m} dm = \Phi(x),$$

and the counterpart of the first-order condition (12.37a) is

$$\Phi' = ae^{-x} - (1 + \alpha)[1 - e^{-(x - v_0)}] - (1 + \beta)e^{-(x - v_0)} = 0.$$

Collecting and rearranging terms, we get

$$[a + (\alpha - \beta)e^{v_0}]e^{-x} = 1 + \alpha,$$

so that

$$x = - \ln\left[\frac{1 + \alpha}{a + (\alpha - \beta)e^{v_0}}\right] = h(v_0, \alpha, \beta).$$

We must, of course, assume that the parameter a is sufficiently large; specifically, to ensure the positivity of x, we require $a + (\alpha - \beta)e^{v_0} > 1 + \alpha$. Finally, we see that

$$\Phi'' = -[a + (\alpha - \beta)e^{v_0}]e^{-x} < 0,$$

hence the solution indeed furnishes a maximum.

12.5   A NONSTOCHASTIC APPROACH TO UNCERTAINTY

In the preceding sections, we dealt with various cases in which situations of incomplete information were defined in stochastic terms; that is, we considered cases in which the outcome of a decision was assumed to be governed by a probability distribution the properties of which were, at least partially, known (or believed to be known) by the decision maker. In some sense, then, we really dealt with cases of *partial* lack of information. Clearly, we may think of situations in which decision makers hold other views about the nature of their environment, and possess (objectively or subjectively) less information about it than we assumed in the preceding sections. It is the purpose of this section to model behavior of decision makers who have "almost" no information whatsoever about certain aspects of their environment. In particular, we consider the decision process of a firm which possesses no information whatsoever about its demand environment, except (and even this qualification could be dispensed with) that the firm assumes demand to be inversely related to price.

12.5.1 Price Adjustment

The crucial step in the construction of the present model is the formulation of a rational basis for the pricing and production decisions of the firm. The approach taken in Section 12.4.1 (that is, maximizing expected profit) is obviously not applicable in the present model, because we are now assuming that the firm is unable (or perhaps unwilling) to attach probabilities to the outcomes (quantities demanded) associated with any given course of action. Therefore, a nonstochastic approach is called for. We take as our point of departure the condition from which the firm determines its optimal plan when it does have full information. Under the latter circumstances, it will be recalled, the firm chooses a price (and output) which equates MC and MR. That is, if the demand function is known, the firm's optimal price is the solution to the equation

$$(12.38) \qquad\qquad f' = p\left(1 + \frac{1}{e}\right),$$

where $f(x)$ is the firm's (known) TVC function, p is the price set by the firm, and e the elasticity of the demand function $x = h(p)$. Since we normally assume that $e < 0$, it follows that $f' < p$. This simply says that when the firm faces a downward-sloping demand function, it charges a price that exceeds the MC of the quantity demanded. It is therefore not unreasonable to assume that, in the absence of information about the exact form of the demand function, the firm will adopt a decision rule which has the same qualitative characteristic as condition (12.38). Accordingly, in our model we assume that the firm adopts the general principle of setting its price above MC. Formally, we assume that the firm sets its price so as to satisfy the condition

$$(12.39) \qquad\qquad f' = \eta p, \qquad 0 < \eta < 1.$$

There are two problems with this approach; one has to do with the choice of η. First, we may point out that a comparison of Eqs. (12.38) and (12.39) suggests that η may be interpreted as the firm's estimate of the quantity $1 + 1/e$; consequently, the rhs of (12.39) may be referred to as *estimated* MR. (In the present context, the term "estimated" has no statistical connotation.) For our present purposes, we regard the estimate of the quantity $1 + 1/e$ as a given parameter. Conceivably, the firm may experiment with different magnitudes of η, and finally choose a value which yields satisfactory results. Such a search for an optimal η can, of course, also be modeled formally, but doing so will add an entirely new dimension to the present model. Since this will complicate the analysis further, we prefer the simpler approach in which η is regarded as given.

The other difficulty with condition (12.39) is that, even when η is already chosen, the firm will, in general, not be able to fulfill this condition, for the simple reason that quantity demanded, and hence the MC of quantity demanded, is not known in advance. This is, of course, the essence of what the present model is all about. But while the firm has no way of knowing whether any particular choice of price will, in fact, result in the fulfillment of condition (12.39), it does have complete knowledge of the outcomes of the decisions it has taken in preceding periods, and it is reasonable to assume that it will draw on that information when choosing an optimal price in any given period. For example, if the price chosen in the preceding period resulted in a difference between MC and estimated MR, then the firm is likely to change its price in the current period in a manner which is designed to eliminate the "error" committed in the previous period.

It is also quite clear in what direction the adjustments should be made. If, for example, MC exceeded estimated MR in some period, then the price should be raised in the following period. Such a change will have two effects: first, it raises estimated MR, and this in itself is a step toward closing the gap between MC and estimated MR; second, if demand is inversely related to price, a rise in the price will reduce demand, and if MC is an increasing function (as we shall assume), then the rise in the price will at the same time bring about a fall in MC. Thus, a change in price in the right direction generates two different corrective forces. It is also clear, therefore, that the *magnitude* of the change in price should be less than the observed gap between MC and estimated MR.

To formalize this price adjustment process, we use time subscripts to identify the time periods. Since the observed difference between MC and estimated MR in period t is given by $f'(x_t) - \eta p_t$, and since the change in price (between periods t and $t + 1$) is given by $p_{t+1} - p_t$, the adjustment process that we have discussed above takes the form

(12.40) $p_{t+1} = p_t + k[f'(x_t) - \eta p_t]$, $0 < k < 1$.

What (12.40) clearly shows is that, in choosing its price in a particular period

of time, the firm makes use only of data from the preceding period, all of
which are, of course, known. Formally, (12.40) represents a recursive system,
and as such it describes the entire time path of the firm's price. We should,
therefore, also be able to investigate whether the price will ever reach a
stationary state (equilibrium), and determine the properties that characterize
this state. Before we do so, we have to deal with another aspect of the model.

12.5.2 Production and Inventory Adjustment

So far we have not said anything about the firm's level of production. Under
conditions of full information, this problem need not be discussed separately,
for if the demand function is known, price and output are determined simultaneously. If the firm has no knowledge of its demand function, however, it
is unable to associate any determinate level of demand with a particular price;
hence the need for a separate decision on the level of production.

It must be remembered that, under conditions of unknown demand, the
realized level of demand may exceed or fall short of the level of production.
In the latter event, the excess production constitutes an inventory of unsold
output. Inventory therefore constitutes an integral element of the unknown-
demand model. In fact, because of the state of uncertainty, the firm will wish
to maintain some desired level of inventory at all times, so as to be able to
fulfill unanticipated increases in demand. The production decision, then, is
designed to achieve two objectives: (a) to provide an adequate supply of output to meet expected demand, and (b) to bring the inventory to its desired
level. We now formalize these aspects.

If the firm keeps some inventory on hand, production to meet expected
demand can be made equal to some rough estimate of expected demand. As
the demand function is not known, such an estimate may be computed by
taking a weighted average of past demands, where the weights in the averaging formula diminish with the distance between the weighted demand and the
present. For greater clarity, we shall use a specific weighting function. If y_t^x
denotes production to meet expected demand in period t, we may write

$$(12.41) \qquad y_t^x = (1 - c) \sum_{\tau=1}^{t-1} c^{\tau-1} x_{t-\tau} + c^{t-1} x_0, \qquad 0 < c < 1/2.$$

The assumption is that expected demand is computed by averaging all
demands back to some initial period $t = 0$. This means that, as time goes on,
the number of demand levels used in the construction of the average increases
steadily. Nevertheless, the sum of the weights is always unity; that is,

$$(1 - c) \sum_{\tau=1}^{t-1} c^{\tau-1} + c^{t-1} = 1 \qquad \text{for all } t \geqslant 1.$$

The second component of production is geared to the inventory requirement. It is customary to assume that the desired level of inventory is some

fraction of expected demand. In lieu of expected demand (which is unknown) we may use the above weighted average, so that the desired inventory can be defined by $\delta y_t^x, 0 < \delta < 1$. Consequently, the difference between *desired* and *actual* inventory is given by $\delta y_t^x - v_{t-1}$, where v_{t-1} denotes actual inventory at the end of period $t - 1$ (and beginning of period t). Of course, a given shortage or excess of inventory need not be eliminated in one period. (In fact, since the change in y_t^x from one period to another is not known in advance, the firm will, in general, not be able to reach the desired level of inventory in one step even if it tried to.) It is, therefore, reasonable to assume that (except for a special case) production for inventory is some *fraction* of the difference between desired and actual inventories. Letting y_t^v denote production for inventory in period t, we write

$$(12.42) \qquad y_t^v = \max \left[\gamma(\delta y_t^x - v_{t-1}), \, -y_t^x \right], \qquad 0 < \gamma < 1.$$

To explain this equation, we first introduce the self-explanatory identity

$$(12.43) \qquad\qquad y_t = y_t^x + y_t^v,$$

where y_t denotes total production in period t. Now, when the firm has excess inventory, that is, when $\delta y_t^x < v_{t-1}$, the reduction of this excess requires production for inventory to be negative. This means, in effect, that production for purposes of satisfying expected demand, as determined by (12.41), should be reduced by a fraction of the inventory surplus, that is, by $\gamma(\delta y_t^x - v_{t-1})$. But there is a limit to the amount by which y_t^x can be reduced, since total production cannot be negative. Clearly, this limit is y_t^x, and hence the requirement, as stated in (12.42), that y_t^v be bounded from below by $-y_t^x$.

To complete the description of the production model, we have to introduce two additional relations; one of which is the inventory identity given by

$$(12.44) \qquad\qquad v_t = v_{t-1} + y_t - s_t,$$

where s_t denotes the amount sold in period t. This identity merely states the accounting fact that the change in inventory equals (is defined as) the difference between production and sales. But the latter variable calls for a few words of explanation. Like the inventory variable, sales, as distinct from demand, is a variable typically found in models dealing with uncertainty. If demand is known with certainty, production can always be adjusted so as to make it possible to satisfy demand in its entirety. If demand is unknown, however, the firm may find itself unable to meet demand in certain periods; in other words, in spite of the firm's efforts to estimate expected demand, and in spite of the existing stock of inventory, we cannot rule out the possibility that in some period t the firm will be confronted with a level of demand x_t such that $x_t > y_t + v_{t-1}$. But since sales can never exceed the current level of production plus inventory on hand, they are defined by

$$(12.45) \qquad\qquad s_t = \min(x_t, y_t + v_{t-1}).$$

This completes the specification of the entire production model. The reader will be able to verify that Eqs. (12.41) through (12.45) constitute a self-contained system. Furthermore, the determination of the current values for the decision variables by the decision maker requires him to know only past values of these variables, all of which are, of course, known.

12.5.3   Dynamic Properties

We return now to the price adjustment process (12.40) in order to investigate its dynamic properties. If we replace x_t in that equation by the demand function $h(p_t)$, we get

(12.46) $p_{t+1} = p_t + k\{f'[h(p_t)] - \eta p_t\} = H(p_t)$,

which is a first-order difference equation in p_t. To guarantee the stability of this process, we may use the theorem which we applied to the dynamic system (8.65), in Chapter 8. According to that theorem, the infinite sequence $H(p_t)$ converges to some limit if there exists some number less than one, say c, such that $|H'| \leqslant c$ for all p_t. Since $H' = 1 + k(f''h' - \eta)$, it is obvious that to satisfy the condition of the above theorem, certain restrictions have to be imposed on k, f'', and h'. The following restrictions are sufficient:

a) There exists a positive number a such that $0 \leqslant f'' \leqslant a$.
b) There exists a positive number b such that $-b \leqslant h' < 0$.
c) The speed-of-adjustment coefficient k satisfies $0 < k \leqslant 1/(ab + \eta)$.

If these restrictions hold, then $|H'| = 1 - k|f''h' - \eta| < 1 - k\eta < 1$, in which case the condition of the theorem is satisfied for $c = 1 - k\eta$.

The proof of the stability of the production model (12.41) through (12.45) is more complicated; here, we will only outline the major steps of the proof. The first point to note is that the convergence of the price (for which we have just given sufficient conditions) implies the convergence of quantity demanded (by virtue of the continuity of the demand function). This, in turn, implies the convergence of production for sales, y_t^x, to the same limit as quantity demanded. One can then show that sales, s_t, also converge to the same limit. The convergence of the above variables implies, of course, that the fluctuations in these variables (to the extent that such fluctuations exist) steadily diminish in magnitude. Then it follows (as we would intuitively expect) that changes in the stock of inventory also become smaller over time; in fact, the inventory converges to its desired level, and production for inventory goes to zero.

BIBLIOGRAPHICAL NOTES

The hypothesis that choice under uncertainty is based on expected utility was first proposed by the mathematician Daniel Bernoulli in a paper published (in Latin) in 1738. An English translation of this work appeared as "Exposition of a New

Theory on the Measurement of Risk," in *Econometrica*, **22**, 23–36 (1954), and is reprinted in A. N. Page, *Utility Theory*, New York: Wiley, 1968, pp. 199–214. It was not until the first half of the present century, however, that Bernoulli's ideas stimulated further developments in this area. In 1934, K. Menger published a paper (in German) which contains an extensive discussion of Bernoulli's work, with particular reference to those aspects of uncertainty which Bernoulli did not settle satisfactorily. An English translation of Menger's paper is published as "The Role of Uncertainty in Economics," in M. Shubik (ed.), *Essays in Mathematical Economics*, Princeton: Princeton University Press, 1967, pp. 211–231. A major impetus to the growth of the modern theory of behavior under uncertainty was the publication of the work of J. von Neumann and O. Morgenstern, *Theory of Games and Economic Behavior*, Princeton: Princeton University Press, 1943. Among other things, the authors provided an axiomatic system for the maximization of expected utility. Somewhat different axiomatic systems were constructed by J. Marschak, in "Rational Behavior, Uncertain Prospects, and Measurable Utility," *Econometrica*, **18**, 111–141 (1950), and by I. N. Herstein and J. Milnor, in "An Axiomatic Approach to Measurable Utility," *Econometrica*, **21**, 291–297 (1953), reprinted in P. Newman (ed.), *Readings in Mathematical Economics*, Volume 1, Baltimore: The Johns Hopkins Press, 1968, pp. 264–297. A still different approach is given by K. J. Arrow in his *Aspects of the Theory of Risk-Bearing*, Helsinki: Yrjö Johnssonin Säätiö, 1965. J. W. Pratt, in his paper, "Risk Aversion in the Small and in the Large," *Econometrica*, **32**, 122–136 (1964), deals with the concept of risk premium and develops measures of risk aversion. As for general texts on uncertainty, two fairly recent examples are W. Fellner, *Probability and Profit*, Chicago: Irwin, 1965, and K. H. Borch, *The Economics of Uncertainty*, Princeton: Princeton University Press, 1968.

Choice situations under uncertainty occur in many areas of economics, one of which is the selection of optimal portfolios. This problem is dealt with in the following: J. Tobin, "Liquidity Preference as Behavior Towards Risk," *Review of Economic Studies*, **25**, 65–86 (1958), reprinted in M. G. Mueller (ed.), *Readings in Macroeconomics*, New York: Holt, Rinehart and Winston, 1966, pp. 173–191; H. M. Markowitz, *Portfolio Selection* (Cowles Foundation Monograph No. 16), New York: Wiley, 1959; M. K. Richter, "Cardinal Utility, Portfolio Selection, and Taxation," *Review of Economic Studies*, **27**, 152–166 (1960); D. E. Farrar, *The Investment Decision under Uncertainty*, Englewood Cliffs, N.J.: Prentice-Hall, 1962; J. Tobin, "The Theory of Portfolio Selection," in F. H. Hahn and F. P. R. Brechling (eds.), *The Theory of Interest Rates*, London: Macmillan, 1965, pp. 3–51; and J. Mossin, "Taxation and Risk-Taking: An Expected Utility Approach," *Economica*, **35**, 74–82 (1968). A paper which combines portfolio choice with consumption decisions is A. Sandmo, "Capital Risk, Consumption, and Portfolio Choice," *Econometrica*, **37**, 586–599 (1969).

An example of a lifetime model with a stochastic element is provided by M. Yaari, "Uncertain Lifetime, Life Insurance, and the Theory of the Consumer," *Review of Economic Studies*, **32**, 137–150 (1965).

The application of stochastic dominance to utility theory under conditions of uncertainty was first shown by J. P. Quirk and R. Saposnik in "Admissibility and Measurable Utility Functions," *Review of Economic Studies*, **29**, 140–146 (1962). Further extensions of this approach may be found in P. C. Fishburn, *Decision and Value Theory*, New York: Wiley, 1964, Chapter 8; J. Hadar and W. R. Russell, "Rules for Ordering Uncertain Prospects," *American Economic Review*, **59**, 25–34 (1969); and G. Hanoch and H. Levy, "The Efficiency Analysis of Choices Involving

Risk," *Review of Economic Studies*, **36**, 335–346 (1969). Stochastic dominance has also been used by S. Karlin in "Dynamic Inventory Policy with Varying Stochastic Demands," *Management Science*, **6**, 231–258 (1960).

Models of behavior under uncertainty dealing with various aspects of the firm may be found in K. J. Arrow, T. Harris, and J. Marschak, "Optimal Inventory Policy," *Econometrica*, **19**, 250–272 (1951); S. Karlin "One Stage Inventory Models with Uncertainty," in K. J. Arrow, S. Karlin, and H. Scarf, *Studies in the Mathematical Theory of Inventory and Production*, Stanford: Stanford University Press, 1958, pp. 109–134; A. Charnes and W. W. Cooper, "Chance-Constrained Programming," *Management Science*, **6**, 73–79 (1959); E. S. Mills, "Uncertainty and Price Theory," *Quarterly Journal of Economics*, **73**, 116–130 (1959); C. A. Tisdell, *The Theory of Price Uncertainty, Production, and Profit*, Princeton: Princeton University Press, 1968; and E. Zabel, "Monopoly and Uncertainty," *Review of Economic Studies*, **37**, 205–219 (1970). A discussion of several different approaches to investment under uncertainty is presented by J. Hirshleifer in "Investment Decision under Uncertainty: Choice-Theoretic Approaches," *Quarterly Journal of Economics*, **79**, 509–536 (1965).

Finally, a few examples of nonstochastic approaches to uncertainty. These are: R. W. Clower, "Some Theory of an Ignorant Monopolist," *Economic Journal*, **69**, 705–716 (1959); R. H. Day, "Profits, Learning and the Convergence of Satisficing to Marginalism," *Quarterly Journal of Economics*, **81**, 302–311 (1967); and J. Hadar and C. Hillinger, "Imperfect Competition with Unknown Demand," *Review of Economic Studies*, **36**, 519–523 (1969).

CHAPTER 13

GENERAL EQUILIBRIUM

A general equilibrium model is a model which in some sense represents the workings of an entire economic system. Although the degree of aggregation (or disaggregation) is not an essential part of the definition of a general equilibrium model, the material that one finds in the literature under such headings as "General Equilibrium Theory" is invariably concerned with disaggregated models. Since such models have their foundations in micro-theory, a brief examination of some disaggregated general equilibrium models is not out of place in a work such as this. Indeed, it might well be argued that one of the primary functions of models of individual (consumer or firm) behavior is to serve as building blocks for the construction of general equilibrium models.

In this chapter, we consider two classes of general equilibrium models: (a) pure exchange models, and (b) production and exchange models. In models of the first class, it is assumed that individuals in the economy are in the possession of quantities of various goods, and the only activity that individuals engage in is the exchange of goods. Thus, goods are neither produced nor consumed. Production and exchange models, on the other hand, are of a more general nature inasmuch as they deal with the production, consumption, as well as the exchange of goods. Pure competition is assumed throughout.

13.1 PURE EXCHANGE

13.1.1 The Model

We assume that the economy consists of J individuals identified by the superscript j, $j = 1, 2, ..., J$, and $n + 1$ goods identified by the superscript i, $i = 0, 1, 2, ..., n$. The preferences of each individual are represented by a utility function which depends on the (final) bundle of goods available to the individual. If we let $x^{\cdot j} = (x^{0j}, x^{1j}, ..., x^{nj})$ denote the bundle of goods of individual j, we can write the utility function of individual j as $u^j = \phi^j(x^{\cdot j})$. Each individual also possesses a bundle of goods representing his initial endowment, the latter bundle being denoted by $x_0^{\cdot j} = (x_0^{0j}, x_0^{1j}, ..., x_0^{nj})$.

Since there is no production or consumption in a pure exchange model, the only economic activity that individuals perform in such a model is the trading of goods with one another; in other words, given a set of prices for the $n + 1$ goods, each individual will wish to attain an optimal bundle of goods, and toward this end he may offer to purchase from, as well as to sell to, the other individuals certain amounts of the $n + 1$ goods. Our first task, therefore, is to determine the amounts that will be offered for purchase and sale by each individual.

As usual, we assume that each individual selects his optimal bundle by maximizing his utility function subject to an appropriate budget constraint. In the present set-up, the individual's "income" is the value of his initial endowment, that is,

$$\sum_{i=0}^{n} \hat{p}^i x_0^{ij},$$

where $\hat{p}^i$ denotes the price of good i. Consequently, each individual's budget constraint is of the form

$$(13.1a) \qquad \sum_{i=0}^{n} \hat{p}^i x^{ij} = \sum_{i=0}^{n} \hat{p}^i x_0^{ij},$$

or

$$(13.1b) \qquad \sum_{i=0}^{n} \hat{p}^i (x^{ij} - x_0^{ij}) = 0.$$

It will be recalled that, in the standard consumer model, the demand functions are homogeneous of degree zero in prices and income. In the present model, as we have described it above, income is not an independent parameter, but a function of market prices; hence, maximizing the utility function subject to the constraint given in (13.1), yields demand functions that are homogeneous of degree zero in prices. To avoid certain implications of the homogeneity property, we shall formulate our model in terms of *relative* (or normalized) prices. To do this, we assume that the price of one good, say 0, is fixed (in terms of some unit of account, e.g., the dollar), and then express the prices of all other goods in terms of the price of good 0. The good whose price is held fixed (0 in our model) is said to be the *numéraire*. Without loss of generality, we may set the price of the numéraire equal to unity, that is, $\hat{p}^0 = 1$, so that the remaining n prices $\hat{p}^i$ can now be regarded as relative prices. The budget constraint may therefore be written as

$$(13.2) \qquad \sum_{i=1}^{n} \hat{p}^i (x^{ij} - x_0^{ij}) + x^{0j} - x_0^{0j} = 0.$$

Assuming, for simplicity, that the optimal bundle is strictly positive for all $\hat{p}^i$ and x_0^{ij}, we write the demand functions as

$$(13.3) \qquad x^{ij} = \hat{h}^{ij}(\hat{p}, x_0^{\cdot j}), \qquad i = 0, 1, ..., n, \quad j = 1, 2, ..., J,$$

where $\hat{p} = (\hat{p}^1, \hat{p}^2, ..., \hat{p}^n)$. It must be pointed out, of course, that x^{ij} in (13.3) represents the quantity that an individual wishes to possess at the conclusion of the trade, and *not*, in general, the amount he wishes to purchase (or sell). The latter amount is given by $x^{ij} - x_0^{ij}$, and is referred to as *excess demand*. It should also be clear that, even though we assumed that the desired (final) bundle is always strictly positive, excess demand may be positive, negative, or zero.

13.1.2 Existence and Stability of the Equilibrium

The main object of interest in general equilibrium analysis is, first of all, the existence of an equilibrium, as well as the properties of the equilibrium. In some sense, this kind of investigation is similar in nature to that which we carried out in most of the preceding chapters. For instance, when we derived individual demand and supply functions, and subjected them to a comparative static analysis, in effect we examined the equilibrium position of an individual decision maker (consumer or producer), and determined its properties. Our analysis of models of monopolistic competition was also of this type: we investigated the possibility of the convergence of prices and quantities to an equilibrium point, and the effects on the equilibrium of changes in certain shift parameters. In this chapter, we address ourselves to the same kind of questions, except that we now deal with models which (by definition) encompass and interrelate *all* the participants in the economic system.

From a strictly formal point of view, it is undoubtedly more elegant to treat the issue of existence separately from that of stability. On the other hand, it might be argued that interest in the existence of an equilibrium arises (except, perhaps, in a purely mathematical context) primarily from an attempt to answer a question such as the following: "Given that the individuals in an economic system are engaged in mutual trading, will the prices and quantities exchanged (or offered for exchange) tend to reach some stationary state?" According to this view, the existence of an equilibrium is an integral part of the question of the stability of the trading process, and this is how we shall approach the problem here. Consequently, we first formulate the process by which market prices are determined.

Since the system is assumed to be purely competitive, we are, of course, faced with a slight contradiction: on the one hand, a competitive system postulates that every individual in the system regards prices as given parameters; on the other hand, it is clear that prices will remain fixed unless they are changed by someone. So, *who* changes the prices? This contradiction may be resolved by viewing the trading process as an auction in which (relative) prices are set by an auctioneer. This scheme, however, gives rise to the following problem: since the auctioneer has no information about the individuals' preferences, or their excess demands, he has no way of knowing whether any particular set of prices will satisfy all traders simultaneously, that is, whether any particular set of prices will match quantities demanded with quantities supplied in each market. Indeed, the entire auction may be regarded as a mechanism designed to solve this very problem; that is, to find a set of prices such that all markets will be cleared at the same time. Such a search procedure is referred to as a *tâtonnement process*, and may be described as follows: The auctioneer announces a set of prices, but no goods are exchanged *unless* prices happen to clear all markets simultaneously. If the announced prices do not clear all markets (that is, if there exists nonzero excess demand in at least one market), all bids and offers are withdrawn, and the auctioneer announces a new set of prices. The general rule by which prices are changed is this: in each market, the change in price is some sign-preserving function of excess demand in the respective market. We now turn to the formulation of this rule.

We shall use a somewhat unorthodox formulation of the tâtonnement process inasmuch as it will be defined in terms of *logarithms* of prices and quantities. We introduce the following definitions:

$$(13.4) \qquad p^i = \ln \hat{p}^i,$$
$$(13.5) \qquad h^i(p;\ x_0) = \ln \hat{h}^i(\hat{p}, x_0) - \ln x_0^i, \qquad \left. \right\} \quad i = 1, 2, ..., n,$$

where $\quad p = (p^1, p^2, ..., p^n)$, $\hat{h}^i(\hat{p}, x_0) = \sum\limits_{j=1}^{J} \hat{h}^{ij}(\hat{p}, x_0^j);\qquad x_0^i = \sum\limits_{j=1}^{J} x_0^{ij};$

and $\quad x_0 = (x_0^{\cdot 1}, x_0^{\cdot 2}, ..., x_0^{\cdot J}).$

Since we have assumed that the optimal bundles are strictly positive, the logarithm of $\hat{h}^i(\hat{p}, x_0)$ is defined for all $\hat{p}$ and x_0; we must, however, add the assumption that the total initial endowment of each good (x_0^i) is also strictly positive.

To demonstrate that no loss of generality is incurred by using the logarithmic excess demand functions, we show that the derivatives of the functions h^i are of the same signs as those of the respective derivatives of the functions $\hat{h}^i$. From (13.4) and (13.5) we have

$$h^i(\ln \hat{p};\ x_0) = \ln \hat{h}^i(\hat{p}, x_0) - \ln x_0^i,$$

where $\ln \hat{p} = (\ln \hat{p}^1, \ln \hat{p}^2, ..., \ln \hat{p}^n)$. Differentiating the above equation with respect to $\hat{p}^r$, and rearranging terms, we get

$$(13.6) \qquad h_r^i = \hat{h}_r^i \frac{\hat{p}^r}{\hat{h}^i(\hat{p}, x_0)},$$

where $h_r^i = \partial h^i / \partial p^r$, and $\hat{h}_r^i = \partial \hat{h}^i / \partial \hat{p}^r$. Clearly, sign $h_r^i =$ sign $\hat{h}_r^i$, since both $\hat{p}^r$ and $\hat{h}^i(\hat{p}, x_0)$ are positive. But more important, the derivatives (with respect to the p^r) of the logarithmic market excess demand function $h^i(p; x_0)$ are the price elasticities of the ordinary market demand function $\hat{h}^i(\hat{p}, x_0)$. This property of the present formulation will play a significant role in the analysis.

If we assume that prices are announced at discrete time intervals, then the rule that determines the adjustments in prices in each period can be stated as a discrete dynamic process, as shown below:

$$(13.7) \qquad p_{t+1}^i = p_t^i + k^i h^i(p_t; x_0) = H^i(p_t), \qquad k^i > 0, \quad i = 1, 2, ..., n,$$

where p_t^i is the logarithm of the price of good i in period t. The elements of the vector x_0 do not appear as arguments of the mapping H, since in the absence of trade, the distribution of the goods among the traders remains unchanged. It should be noted that, even though the above process is defined in terms of the logarithms of prices and quantities, it is consistent with the general rule described earlier. For example, if in period t there is positive excess demand in market i, that is, if $\hat{h}^i(\hat{p}_t, x_0) - x_0^i > 0$, then we also have $h^i(p_t; x_0) > 0$, which implies $\ln \hat{p}_{t+1}^i > \ln \hat{p}_t^i$; hence the price in market i is raised; and similarly for negative excess demand. As for the formal structure of the above mapping, it is of the type already discussed in Chapter 8, and so we once again use a condition such as (8.67) as a sufficient condition for the existence and stability of an equilibrium. Applied to the present model, this condition takes the form

$$(13.8) \qquad\qquad \sum_{r=1}^{n} |H_r^i| \leqslant c < 1, \qquad i = 1, 2, ..., n,$$

where $H_r^i = \partial H^i / \partial p_t^r$.

In order to satisfy condition (13.8), certain restrictions have to be imposed on the excess demand functions, as well as the adjustment coefficients k^i. The purpose of these restrictions is to impose bounds on certain magnitudes, and to restrict the degree of interrelationship between the demands (supplies) of the various goods. The following restrictions constitute a set of sufficient conditions:

a) There exists a positive number a such that for all p_t and x_0

$$- a \leqslant h_i^i < 0, \qquad i = 1, 2, ..., n.$$

This condition assumes (by implication) that each market demand function is downward sloping (with respect to its own price), and that the magnitude of its own-price elasticity is bounded away from infinity.

b) There exists a positive number b such that for all p_t and x_0

$$|h_i^i| - \sum_{\substack{r=1 \\ r \neq i}}^{n} |h_r^i| \geqslant b, \qquad i = 1, 2, ..., n.$$

This condition requires own-price elasticities to dominate the sum of cross elasticities. It implies that the matrix of elasticities $[h_r^i]$ has a dominant diagonal.

c) $$0 < k^i \leqslant 1/a, \qquad i = 1, 2, ..., n.$$

The last condition defines the allowed range for the adjustment coefficients.

We now prove that conditions (a) through (c) imply the existence of a positive number c satisfying condition (13.8). Differentiating (13.7) with respect to p_t^i, we get

(13.9a) $$H_i^i = 1 + k^i h_i^i.$$

However, from conditions (a) and (c) it follows that $-1 \leqslant k^i h_i^i < 0$; therefore we have

(13.9b) $$|H_i^i| = 1 - k^i |h_i^i|.$$

Differentiating (13.7) with respect to p_t^r, $r \neq i$, we obtain

(13.10a) $$H_r^i = k^i h_r^i,$$

and hence,

(13.10b) $$|H_r^i| = k^i |h_r^i|.$$

Consequently,

(13.11) $$\sum_{r=1}^{n} |H_r^i| = 1 - k^i |h_i^i| + \sum_{\substack{r=1 \\ r \neq i}}^{n} k^i |h_r^i| = 1 - k^i \left(|h_i^i| - \sum_{\substack{r=1 \\ r \neq i}}^{n} |h_r^i| \right).$$

Using condition (b) in conjunction with (13.11), we obtain the inequalities

(13.12) $$\sum_{r=1}^{n} |H_r^i| \leqslant 1 - k^i b \leqslant 1 - k^* b < 1,$$

where $k^* = \min k^i$. Thus, condition (13.8) is satisfied with $c = 1 - k^* b$, and therefore the convergence of the tâtonnement process to a (unique) equilibrium is proved. In other words, if conditions (a) through (c) are satisfied, then the logarithms of the prices converge to a set of limit values at which the excess demand functions vanish simultaneously. Hence, if the vector of these limit (equilibrium) values is denoted by $\bar{p} = (\bar{p}^1, \bar{p}^2, ..., \bar{p}^n)$, we have

(13.13) $$h^i(\bar{p}; x_0) = 0, \qquad i = 1, 2, ..., n.$$

Walras' Law. At this point, the following question may be raised: "Will the vector $\bar{p}$ also guarantee the clearing of the market for the numéraire good?" We know, of course, that even though the price of the numéraire is (by definition) fixed, the demand for the numéraire good, like that of any other good, depends in general on all prices, so that during the tâtonnement process, the excess demand for the numéraire good is free to change from one period to another. Nevertheless, it can be shown that the equilibrium price vector $\bar{p}$ clears all the $n + 1$ markets simultaneously.

This result follows directly from the fact that, regardless of whether or not goods are exchanged, every trader is assumed to satisfy his budget constraint. Substituting the demand functions given by (13.3) into the budget equation (13.2) and evaluating the latter at the equilibrium prices $\bar{p}^i$, where $\bar{p}^i = \ln \tilde{p}^i$, we have

$$(13.14) \quad \sum_{i=1}^{n} \tilde{p}^i [\hat{h}^{ij}(\tilde{p}, x_0^j) - x_0^{ij}] + \hat{h}^{0j}(\tilde{p}, x_0^j) - x_0^{0j} = 0, \quad j = 1, 2, \ldots, J,$$

where $\tilde{p} = (\tilde{p}^1, \tilde{p}^2, \ldots, \tilde{p}^n)$. Summing the above equations over all individuals, and using the notation for market demand and supply, respectively, introduced in Eq. (13.5), we get

$$(13.15) \quad \sum_{i=1}^{n} \tilde{p}^i [\hat{h}^i(\tilde{p}, x_0) - x_0^i] + \hat{h}^0(\tilde{p}, x_0) - x_0^0 = 0.$$

Now, each of the n terms $[\hat{h}^i(\tilde{p}, x_0) - x_0^i]$ is zero by (13.5) and (13.13), hence the term $[\hat{h}^0(\tilde{p}, x_0) - x_0^0]$ also vanishes, as is obvious from (13.15). In fact, (13.15) implies the following general conclusion: Given a system of $n + 1$ markets, if any n markets are in equilibrium (cleared), the remaining market must also be in equilibrium (cleared). This result is known as *Walras' law*.

The Relationship between Stability and Consumer Behavior. Having proved the sufficiency, for stability, of conditions (a) through (c), it may be instructive to examine the relationship between condition (b)—the strongest of the three conditions—and the basic results of consumer behavior theory. We indicated earlier in the chapter that when the consumer's income derives entirely from his initial endowment, his demand functions are homogeneous of degree zero in all prices (if prices are not normalized). Let us denote the homogeneous demand functions by $\overset{*}{h}{}^{ij}(\overset{*}{p})$, where $\overset{*}{p}$ is the vector of the $n + 1$ (nonnormalized) prices $\overset{*}{p}{}^r$. Then, by virtue of Euler's equation, we have

$$(13.16) \quad \sum_{r=0}^{n} \overset{*}{h}{}^{ij}_r \overset{*}{p}{}^r = 0,$$

where $\overset{*}{h}{}^{ij}_r = \partial \overset{*}{h}{}^{ij}/\partial \overset{*}{p}{}^r$. Suppose now that good 0 is designated as the numéraire, and $\overset{*}{p}{}^0$ is fixed, say, at $\overset{*}{p}{}^0 = 1$; then we have

$$\hat{h}^{ij}(\hat{p}^1, \hat{p}^2, \ldots, \hat{p}^n) = \overset{*}{h}{}^{ij}(1, \overset{*}{p}{}^1, \overset{*}{p}{}^2, \ldots, \overset{*}{p}{}^n),$$

where $\hat{p}^r = \overset{*}{p}{}^r$, and it is clear that

$$(13.17) \quad \hat{h}^{ij}_r = \overset{*}{h}{}^{ij}_r.$$

Combining (13.16) and (13.17), we get

(13.18a)
$$\sum_{r=1}^{n} \hat{h}_r^{ij} \hat{p}^r = - \overset{*}{h}_0^{ij},$$

and dividing both sides of (13.18a) by x^{ij}, we get

(13.18b)
$$\sum_{r=1}^{n} \hat{h}_r^{ij} \frac{\hat{p}^r}{x^{ij}} = \frac{- \overset{*}{h}_0^{ij}}{x^{ij}},$$

or

(13.18c)
$$\sum_{r=1}^{n} e_r^{ij} = \frac{- \overset{*}{h}_0^{ij}}{x^{ij}},$$

where the e_r^{ij} denote the price elasticities of the (nonhomogeneous) demand functions.

Clearly, if $\overset{*}{h}_0^{ij} > 0$ for all $\overset{*}{p}$, i, and j, that is, if (when the price of the numéraire good is changed) all goods are strict gross substitutes for the numéraire good, then the sum of all the price elasticities of the demand for each good is negative. However, since we have assumed that own-price demand functions are downward sloping (that is, $e_i^{ij} < 0$), then if all the remaining n goods are weak gross substitutes (that is, if $e_r^{ij} \geqslant 0$, $i \neq r$), then the elasticity matrix $[e_r^{ij}]$ of each individual has a dominant diagonal. Roughly speaking, therefore, gross substitutability implies elasticity matrixes with dominant diagonals. On the other hand, if some goods are complements, that is, if $e_r^{ij} < 0$ for some i and r, $i \neq r$, then the diagonal dominance condition does not follow from (13.18), and must be introduced as an independent assumption. In which case, the assumption of a dominant diagonal places a restriction on the extent of complementarity among the goods.

It remains to investigate whether the above conclusions carry over to the market demand functions. Since market demand functions are simply sums of individual demand functions, each market elasticity is a weighted sum of individual elasticities; that is,

(13.19)
$$h_r^i = \sum_{j=1}^{J} s^{ij} e_r^{ij},$$

where s^{ij} is the proportion of total market demand desired by individual j; that is,

$$s^{ij} = \frac{\hat{h}^{ij}(\hat{p}, x_0^j)}{\hat{h}^i(\hat{p}, x_0)}.$$

Summing (13.19) over all r, we write

(13.20)
$$\sum_{r=1}^{n} h_r^i = \sum_{j=1}^{J} \sum_{r=1}^{n} s^{ij} e_r^{ij}.$$

To simplify matters, let us assume that all the $\overset{*}{h}{}_0^{ij}/x^{ij}$ are bounded away from zero; in other words, that there exists a positive number b' (possibly very small) such that

(13.21) $$\frac{\overset{*}{h}{}_0^{ij}}{x^{ij}} \geqslant b' \qquad \text{for all } \overset{*}{p}, i, \text{ and } j.$$

Then, since $\sum_{r=1}^{n} s^{ij}e_r^{ij} = -s^{ij}\dfrac{\overset{*}{h}{}_0^{ij}}{x^{ij}}$ by (13.18c), and since $\sum_{j=1}^{J} s^{ij} = 1$

by definition, we have

(13.22) $$\sum_{r=1}^{n} h_r^i \leqslant -\sum_{j=1}^{J} s^{ij}b' = -b' \qquad \text{for all } i.$$

It is thus clear that, if all the n goods $i = 1, 2, ..., n$ are weak gross substitutes for all individuals, and condition (13.21) also holds, then the matrix of market elasticities has a dominant diagonal; that is, condition (b) holds with $b = b'$. If, however, for some individuals certain goods are complements, then condition (b) must be assumed, thereby restricting the degree of complementarity in the system.

13.1.3 A Continuous Adjustment Process

The rule for the adjustment of prices given by system (13.7) can also be formulated as a continuous process. While discrete adjustment processes are often more realistic, continuous processes are frequently used in the literature. Since the analysis of continuous processes requires a slightly different set of tools, reformulating the process in (13.7) will not be entirely a repetition.

The basic assumption underlying a continuous price adjustment process is that prices may change continuously (instead of at discrete intervals); formally, each price is regarded as some continuous (and possibly also differentiable) function of time. In this approach, then, the counterpart to the adjustment rule given in (13.7) is a statement about the rate of change of each price at a typical point of time; specifically, the continuous version of (13.7) postulates that the rate of change in the logarithm of $\overset{*}{p}{}^i$ at any point of time is proportional to the logarithmic excess demand in market i at the same point of time. This rule is expressed by the following set of differential equations:

(13.23) $$\dot{p}^i = k^i h^i[p(t); x_0] = H^i[p(t)], \qquad k^i > 0, \quad i = 1, 2, ..., n,$$

where $\dot{p}^i = dp^i/dt$; $p(t) = [p^1(t), p^2(t), ..., p^n(t)]$; and t denotes time.

Since the existence of an equilibrium price vector $\bar{p}$ has already been demonstrated, in the preceding section, we confine ourselves here to the question of stability. In view of the assumptions that we have already made, it is most convenient to examine the stability properties of the above system by applying to it the method of Liapunov. To this end we construct the following function:

$$(13.24) \qquad L(q) = \sum_{i=1}^{n} \frac{(q^i)^2}{2k^i},$$

where $q^i = p^i - \bar{p}^i$, and $q = (q^1, q^2, ..., q^n)$. It is easy to see that $L(q)$ satisfies the following conditions:

(13.25a) $L(q) > 0$ for $q \neq 0$ (that is, $q^i \neq 0$ for at least one i),

(13.25b) $L(0) = 0.$

What remains to be examined is the derivative $\dot{L} = dL/dt$. Differentiating (13.24) with respect to t, we get

$$(13.26) \qquad \dot{L} = \sum_{i=1}^{n} \frac{q^i}{k^i}\, \dot{p}^i.$$

We now apply the Theorem of the Mean to the functions $H^i(p)$, and write

$$(13.27) \qquad H^i(p) - H^i(\bar{p}) = \sum_{r=1}^{n} k^i h_r^i q^r, \qquad i = 1, 2, ..., n,$$

where the h_r^i are evaluated at a suitably chosen point between p and $\bar{p}$. Since $H^i(\bar{p}) = 0$ for all i, combining (13.23) and (13.27), we get

$$(13.28) \qquad \dot{p}^i = \sum_{r=1}^{n} k^i h_r^i q^r, \qquad i = 1, 2, ..., n,$$

and substituting for the $\dot{p}^i$ in (13.26) from (13.28), we have

$$(13.29a) \qquad \dot{L} = \sum_{i=1}^{n} \sum_{r=1}^{n} q^i h_r^i q^r,$$

where the rhs of (13.29a) may be recognized as a quadratic form in the n variables q^i. Using matrix notation, we rewrite (13.29a) as

$$(13.29b) \qquad \dot{L} = qHq',$$

where H denotes the matrix $[h_r^i]$, and q' represents the transpose of the row vector q.

To evaluate $\dot{L}$, it is clear that some assumptions about the matrix H are necessary. We assume that H has a negative dominant diagonal. This means that we are retaining condition (b) of the preceding section, but conditions (a) and (c) may be weakened; all we need here is $h_i^i < 0$, and $k^i > 0$ for all i. But it is known that a (square) matrix with a negative dominant diagonal is the matrix of a negative definite quadratic form, which, in conjunction with (13.29), implies

(13.30a) $\dot{L} < 0$ for $q \neq 0,$

(13.30b) $\dot{L} = 0$ for $q = 0.$

According to Liapunov's theorem, the existence of such a function implies that the system is asymptotically stable; that is, the p^i converge to the $\bar{p}^i$ as t goes to infinity. Since in our example, conditions (13.25) and (13.30) hold for all q, the result is global; that is, the system converges regardless of where it starts. The reason for this result is not difficult to see. The function $L(q)$ is nothing but the square of a weighted Euclidian distance between the points p and $\bar{p}$ (the weights being the terms $1/2k^i$). The fact that the time-derivative of this distance function is negative whenever the price in any market is different from its equilibrium level means that the distance between the vector p and $\bar{p}$ diminishes over time; and this, after all, is what is meant by convergence.

13.1.4 Comparative Statics

In the context of models of individual decision makers (consumers or producers) comparative static analysis is concerned with the effects on the equilibrium (optimal) levels of the decision variables resulting from changes in certain shift parameters (such as prices, incomes, tax rates, etc.). Applied to general equilibrium models, comparative static analysis deals with changes in the equilibrium levels of the system due to changes in certain shift parameters. It must be pointed out, of course, that a comparative static analysis is meaningful only if the model is stable: if the model is unstable, a displacement from some initial equilibrium position will place the system in a state of constant motion, and thus prevent its convergence to another equilibrium position; in which case, the initial equilibrium point cannot be subjected to any comparison.

We now introduce the shift parameter α to represent the "taste" for the various goods. We may define an increase in α as representing an "increase" in taste, but it should be quite clear that such an increase cannot, given fixed prices and initial endowments, bring about an increase in the demand for every good. If we introduce α into the market demand functions, then the aggregate budget equation [Eq. (13.15), in Section 13.1.2] takes the form

(13.31) $\sum\limits_{i=1}^{n} \hat{p}^i [\hat{h}^i(\hat{p}, \alpha, x_0) - x_0^i] + \hat{h}^0(\hat{p}, \alpha, x_0) - x_0^0 = 0.$

Differentiating the above equation with respect to α, we get

(13.32) $\sum\limits_{i=1}^{n} \hat{p}^i \hat{h}_\alpha^i + \hat{h}_\alpha^0 = 0,$

where $\hat{h}_\alpha^i = \partial \hat{h}^i / \partial \alpha$. Clearly, the $\hat{h}_\alpha^i$ cannot all take the same sign (except zero); in general, some may be positive, others negative. It is, therefore, more correct to say that a change in α represents a change in the *structure* of tastes for the various goods. For simplicity, we assume that the levels of taste for the n goods $i = 1, 2, ..., n$ always move in the same direction, and hence in an opposite direction from that of the change in the level of taste for the numéraire good; more precisely, we assume

(13.33a) $\hat{h}_\alpha^i \geqslant 0$ for $i = 1, 2, ..., n$,   the strict inequality holding for
at least one i,

(13.33b) $\hat{h}_\alpha^0 < 0$.

Having introduced α into the market demand functions, we see that the equilibrium price vector $\tilde{p}$ depends on α, and the relationship between $\tilde{p}$ and α is defined implicitly by the equations

(11.34) $\hat{h}^i(\tilde{p}, \alpha, x_0) - x_0^i = 0$, $i = 1, 2, ..., n$.

Using a logarithmic transformation such as in (13.5), we can write (13.34) in terms of the logarithmic market excess demand functions. Thus

(13.35) $h^i(\bar{p}; \alpha, x_o) = 0$, $i = 1, 2, ..., n$,

and it should be obvious that the derivatives $h_\alpha^i = \partial h^i / \partial \alpha$ have the same signs as the respective derivatives $\hat{h}_\alpha^i$. If we now apply the Implicit Function Theorem to (13.35), we can express each $\bar{p}^r$ as some function of α; in other words, according to the Implicit Function Theorem (which is applicable here since the dominant diagonal condition implies that the Jacobian matrix of the above system is nonsingular), there exist n functions, say $\theta^r(\alpha)$, such that

(13.36) $\bar{p}^r = \theta^r(\alpha)$, $r = 1, 2, ..., n$.

The comparative static analysis with which we are concerned in this section can now be stated in more precise terms, namely: to determine the signs of the derivatives of the functions $\theta^r(\alpha)$. To this end, we substitute for the $\bar{p}^r$ in (13.35) from (13.36), and then differentiate each of the n equations in (13.35) with respect to α. This gives

(13.37)
$$\begin{aligned}
h_1^1 \theta^{1\prime} + h_2^1 \theta^{2\prime} + \cdots + h_n^1 \theta^{n\prime} &= -h_\alpha^1, \\
h_1^2 \theta^{1\prime} + h_2^2 \theta^{2\prime} + \cdots + h_n^2 \theta^{n\prime} &= -h_\alpha^2, \\
\vdots \qquad\qquad\qquad &\quad \vdots \\
h_1^n \theta^{1\prime} + h_2^n \theta^{2\prime} + \cdots + h_n^n \theta^{n\prime} &= -h_\alpha^n,
\end{aligned}$$

where $\theta^{r\prime} = d\theta^r / d\alpha$. The above may be regarded as a system of linear equations in the unknowns $\theta^{r\prime}$. Denoting the determinant of the matrix $[h_r^i]$

by D, and its cofactors by D_{ir}, then according to Cramer's rule we have

$$(13.38) \qquad \theta^{r\prime} = -\sum_{i=1}^{n} h_\alpha^i \frac{D_{ir}}{D}.$$

Since the matrix $[h_r^i]$ has a negative dominant diagonal, it follows that $D_{ii}/D < 0$ for all i. This enables us to deduce a conclusive result for the special case in which the change in α increases the demand for one good only. For example, if $h_\alpha^s > 0$, and $h_\alpha^i = 0$ for all i, $i \neq s$ (and $h_\alpha^0 < 0$), then the equilibrium price of good s will rise, while the changes in the equilibrium prices of all other goods are indeterminate. However, if $h_\alpha^i > 0$ for at least two goods, the signs of all the $\theta^{r\prime}$ are indeterminate.

We can, of course, increase the predictive content of the model by imposing on it (in addition to the negative dominant diagonal) the assumption of weak gross substitutability; that is, $h_r^i \geqslant 0$ for all i and r, $i \neq r$. In that case, it can be shown that the D_{ir}/D satisfy, among others, the following conditions:

$$(13.39a) \qquad \frac{D_{ir}}{D} \leqslant 0 \qquad \text{for all } i \text{ and } r,$$

$$(13.39b) \qquad \frac{D_{ii}}{D} < 0 \quad \cdot \quad \text{for all } i.$$

Then it is clear from (13.38) that an increase in the parameter α will bring about an increase, or no change, in the equilibrium price of every good, even if several or all of the h_α^i (except h_α^0) are positive.

13.2 PRODUCTION AND EXCHANGE

A general equilibrium model of an economy in which the economic units produce, exchange, and consume goods is a model in which the desires of consumers to sell and buy factors and goods, respectively, are allowed to interact with the desires of producers to buy and sell factors and goods, respectively. To formulate such a model in its fullest generality gives rise to various difficulties, substantive as well as notational. Consequently, we consider here a simplified version of such a model, one in which only a single factor of production—labor—is introduced explicitly. Even though such a simplified model ignores many of the interrelationships that characterize more complicated general equilibrium models, it does provide for a minimum degree of interdependence between the consumer sector and the producer sector.

13.2.1 The Model

As in Section 13.1, it is assumed that each consumer maximizes a utility function, except that one of its arguments will now be designated as leisure time. We will dispense with initial endowments, and assume that the income of each consumer derives from two sources: (a) wages earned from the sale of labor services, and (b) shares of the profits earned by the producing units in the preceding period. The producing sector, on the other hand, consists of n markets, or industries, each of which produces one good (including the numéraire). Each market consists of a number of firms, each of which produces only one good. The levels of output are determined by profit maximization, and the profit earned by each firm is distributed among the consumers who own shares in the firm.

If the nth good is leisure time, the budget constraint of a typical individual takes the form

$$(13.40a) \qquad \sum_{i=1}^{n-1} \hat{p}^i x^{ij} + x^{0j} = \hat{p}^n(\delta - x^{nj}) + \sum_{i=0}^{n-1} \sum_{s=1}^{mi} \sigma^{isj} \pi^{is},$$

where δ is the length of the time period, $\delta - x^{nj}$ represents the number of labor hours sold (or offered for sale) by individual j, σ^{isj} denotes the share of individual j of the profit earned by the sth firm in industry i, m^i is the number of firms in industry i, and π^{is} is the profit of firm s in market i. Of course, since no goods are produced or exchanged when the system is in disequilibrium, the π^{is} remain constant during the tâtonnement process. The σ^{isj} satisfy the condition

$$(13.41) \qquad \sum_{j=1}^{J} \sigma^{isj} = 1 \qquad \text{for all } i \text{ and } s.$$

Transposing one term in (13.40a), we can also write

$$(13.40b) \qquad \sum_{i=1}^{n} \hat{p}^i x^{ij} + x^{0j} = \hat{p}^n \delta + \sum_{i=0}^{n-1} \sum_{s=1}^{mi} \sigma^{isj} \pi^{ij}.$$

We may note that $\hat{p}^n$ can be interpreted as either the wage rate, or the (opportunity) price of leisure. Finally, we write the demand functions as

$$(13.42) \qquad x^{ij} = \hat{h}^{ij}(\hat{p}), \qquad i = 0, 1, ..., n, \quad j = 1, 2, ..., J,$$

which, like those given in (13.3), are not homogeneous, the $\hat{p}^i$ being normalized prices. We assume again that $x^{ij} > 0$ for all i and j, and also that $x^{nj} < \delta$ for all j.

The technological environment of a typical firm is described by the production function $y^{is} = \psi^{is}(z^{is})$, where y^{is} is the quantity of product i produced by firm s, and z^{is} is the amount of labor employed in market i by firm s. (The labor provided by the consumers is assumed to be a homogeneous factor of production that may be used in any of the $n + 1$ industries). We write the profit function of a typical firm as

$$(13.43) \qquad \pi^{is} = \hat{p}^i \psi^{is}(z^{is}) - \hat{p}^n z^{is}.$$

Normally, a profit function also includes a component of fixed cost. However, since, in the present model, we assume that the consumers are the owners of all the factors of production that are not introduced explicitly into the production functions, we may assume that the owners of these resources are compensated for the use of these resources directly through their respective shares of "gross" profit. The labor demand functions, which are derived from the maximization of the profit functions, are given by

(13.44a) $\quad z^{is} = \hat{\eta}^{is}(\hat{p}^i, \hat{p}^n),$

(13.44b) $\quad z^{0s} = \hat{\eta}^{0s}(\hat{p}^n),$

$\left.\begin{array}{l} \\ \\ \end{array}\right\}$ $\begin{array}{l} i = 1, 2, ..., n - 1, \\ s = 1, 2, ..., m^i. \end{array}$

If we substitute the labor demand function into the production function, we obtain the firms' generalized supply functions. These are given by

(13.45a) $\quad y^{is} = \psi^{is}[\hat{\eta}^{is}(\hat{p}^i, \hat{p}^n)] = \hat{g}^{is}(\hat{p}),$

(13.45b) $\quad y^{0s} = \psi^{0s}[\hat{\eta}^{0s}(\hat{p}^n)] = g^{0s}(\hat{p}),$

$\left.\begin{array}{l} \\ \\ \end{array}\right\}$ $\begin{array}{l} i = 1, 2, ..., n - 1, \\ s = 1, 2, ..., m^i. \end{array}$

(For the sake of uniformity in notation, each supply function is shown to depend on the entire vector $\hat{p}$. In fact, none of the supply functions has more than two arguments.)

13.2.2 Existence and Stability of the Equilibrium

For the construction of the price adjustment process, we shall again use logarithms of prices, as defined in (13.4), and logarithmic excess demand functions similar to those given in (13.5). Accordingly, we define

(13.46a) $\quad h^i(p) = \ln \hat{h}^i(\hat{p}) - \ln \hat{g}^i(\hat{p}), \quad i = 1, 2, ..., n - 1,$

(13.46b) $\quad h^n(p) = \ln \hat{\eta}(\hat{p}) - \ln[J\delta - \hat{h}^n(\hat{p})],$

where $\hat{h}^i(\hat{p}) = \sum_{j=1}^{J} \hat{h}^{ij}(\hat{p}), \hat{g}^i(\hat{p}) = \sum_{s=1}^{m^i} \hat{g}^{is}(\hat{p}),$ and $\hat{\eta}(\hat{p}) = \sum_{i=0}^{n-1} \sum_{s=1}^{m^i} \hat{\eta}^{is}(\hat{p}).$

The price adjustment process then takes a form similar to that in (13.7), namely,

(13.47) $\quad p_{t+1}^i = p_t^i + k^i h^i(p_t) = H^i(p_t), \quad k^i > 0, \quad i = 1, 2, ..., n.$

It is clear that prices will converge to a unique limit if the functions H^i satisfy a condition such as (13.8), which, in turn, will be satisfied if conditions (a) through (c) in Section 13.1.2 hold. We saw that, in a pure exchange model, gross substitutability implies the dominant diagonal condition (b). In the present model, however, the situation is somewhat more complicated, since underlying the system of the excess demand functions $h^i(p)$ there are *two* microstructures: one representing the behavior of consumers, the other representing the behavior of producers. Therefore, the dominant diagonal condition can no longer be deduced from as simple a set of assumptions as those which we used in Section 13.1.2. It will be more convenient to impose conditions (a) through (c) directly on the market excess demand function.

The assumption that the market excess demand functions satisfy the dominant diagonal condition says, in effect, that a price change has a stronger impact on the market whose price is changed than on the other markets. Differentiating (13.46), we see that $h_i^i = {}^d e_i^i - {}^s e_i^i$, where ${}^d e_i^i$ is the own-price elasticity of the market demand for product i, and ${}^s e_i^i$ is the own-price elasticity of the market supply of product i. (Note that h_i^i is *not* the same as the elasticity of the market excess demand function.) But since ${}^d e_i^i < 0$, and ${}^s e_i^i > 0$, we can write $|h_i^i| = |{}^d e_i^i| + {}^s e_i^i$, which indicates that $|h_i^i|$ represents the sum of the magnitudes of the percentage changes in demand and supply. Similarly, $|h_r^i| = |{}^d e_r^i - {}^s e_r^i|$, which represents the magnitude of the sum (or difference) of the cross elasticities of demand and supply. What the dominant diagonal condition requires is that the sum of the cross effects always be smaller than the own-price effect.

13.2.3 Comparative Statics

In Section 13.1.4, we investigated the effects on equilibrium prices of a change in a parameter representing tastes; here, we carry out a similar analysis with respect to a parameter representing technological change. Specifically, we introduce the parameter α into the production functions of the firms in market r, and assume that an increase in α shifts the production functions upward, and also increases their slopes. Writing the production functions as $y^{rs} = \psi^{rs}(z^{rs}; \alpha)$, we assume

$$(13.48) \qquad \psi_\alpha^{rs} = \frac{\partial \psi^{rs}}{\partial \alpha} > 0,$$

$$(13.49) \qquad \psi_{z\alpha}^{rs} = \frac{\partial^2 \psi^{rs}}{\partial z \, \partial \alpha} > 0, \qquad \Big\} \quad \text{for all } z^{rs} \text{ and } \alpha.$$

The parameter α may, therefore, be interpreted as a measure of labor productivity. The profit functions of the firms in market r are now written as

$$(13.50) \qquad \pi^{rs} = \hat{p}^r \psi^{rs}(z^{rs}; \alpha) - \hat{p}^n z^{rs},$$

the input demand functions as

$$(13.51) \qquad z^{rs} = \hat{\eta}^{rs}(\hat{p}; \alpha),$$

and the supply functions as

$$(13.52) \qquad y^{rs} = \psi^{rs}[\hat{\eta}^{rs}(\hat{p}; \alpha), \alpha] = \hat{g}^{rs}(\hat{p}; \alpha).$$

First, we establish the effect of an increase in α on the amount supplied.

Differentiating (13.52) with respect to α, we have

$$(13.53) \qquad \hat{g}_\alpha^{rs} = \psi_z^{rs}\hat{\eta}_\alpha^{rs} + \psi_\alpha^{rs} > 0 \qquad \text{for all } p \text{ and } \alpha,$$

where $\hat{g}_\alpha^{rs} = \partial\hat{g}^{rs}/\partial\alpha$, $\psi_z^{rs} = \partial\psi^{rs}/\partial z^{rs}$, and $\hat{\eta}_\alpha^{rs} = \partial\hat{\eta}^{rs}/\partial\alpha$. The above inequality follows from the fact that $\psi_z^{rs} > 0$ and $\psi_\alpha^{rs} > 0$ (by assumption), and $\hat{\eta}_\alpha^{rs} > 0$ by the first- and second-order conditions for profit maximization, and assumption (13.49).

As for the consumer sector, we must remember that equilibrium prices are the prices at which plans for production, consumption, and exchange become final. Thus, when the economy moves from one equilibrium to another, the profits distributed to the consumers change, and hence they can no longer be regarded as constant. Consequently, in considering equilibrium prices, the budget constraints of the consumers must be written as

$$(13.54) \qquad \sum_{i=1}^{n} \tilde{p}^i x^{ij} + x^{0j} = \tilde{p}^n\delta + \sum_{i=0}^{n-1}\sum_{s=1}^{mi} \sigma^{isj}[\tilde{p}^i\hat{g}^{is}(\tilde{p}; \alpha) - \tilde{p}^n\hat{\eta}^{is}(\tilde{p}; \alpha)],$$

where the $\tilde{p}^i$, as well as the vector $\tilde{p}$, denote equilibrium prices. (To simplify notation, we are introducing the parameter α into all the demand and supply functions. It should, of course, be understood that $\hat{g}_\alpha^{is} = 0$ and $\hat{\eta}_\alpha^{is} = 0$ for all i except $i = r$.) The consumers' demand functions (evaluated at equilibrium prices) are, therefore, given by

$$(13.55) \qquad x^{ij} = \hat{h}^{ij}(\tilde{p}; \alpha).$$

We now define logarithmic transformations similar to those in (13.46)

$$(13.56a) \qquad h^i(\tilde{p}; \alpha) = \ln \hat{h}^i(\tilde{p}; \alpha) - \ln \hat{g}^i(\tilde{p}; \alpha),$$

$$(13.56b) \qquad h^n(\tilde{p}; \alpha) = \ln \hat{\eta}(\tilde{p}; \alpha) - \ln [J\delta - \hat{h}^n(\tilde{p}; \alpha)],$$

where $\hat{h}^i(\tilde{p}; \alpha) = \sum_{j=1}^{J} \hat{h}^{ij}(\tilde{p}; \alpha)$, $\hat{g}^i(\tilde{p}; \alpha) = \sum_{s=1}^{mi} \hat{g}^{is}(\tilde{p}; \alpha)$,

$\hat{\eta}(\tilde{p}; \alpha) = \sum_{i=0}^{n-1}\sum_{s=1}^{mi} \eta^{is}(\tilde{p}; \alpha)$, and $\bar{p}^i = \ln \tilde{p}^i$.

Thus, when the economy is in equilibrium, we have

$$(13.57) \qquad h^i(\bar{p}; \alpha) = 0, \qquad i = 1, 2, ..., n.$$

Invoking the Implicit Function Theorem, we can assert the existence of n functions $\theta^r(\alpha)$ such that

$$(13.58) \qquad \bar{p}^r = \theta^r(\alpha), \qquad r = 1, 2, ..., n,$$

and the purpose of the analysis is to determine the signs of the first derivatives of the functions θ^r. Substituting for the $\bar{p}^r$ in (13.57) from (13.58), and then differentiating the equations in (13.57) with respect to α, we obtain

(13.59)
$$h_1^1 \theta^{1'} + h_2^1 \theta^{2'} + \cdots + h_n^1 \theta^{n'} = -h_\alpha^1,$$
$$h_1^2 \theta^{1'} + h_2^2 \theta^{2'} + \cdots + h_n^2 \theta^{n'} = -h_\alpha^2,$$
$$\vdots \qquad\qquad\qquad\qquad \vdots$$
$$h_1^n \theta^{1'} + h_2^n \theta^{2'} + \cdots + h_n^n \theta^{n'} = -h_\alpha^n,$$

where $\theta^{r'} = d\theta^r/d\alpha$.

To determine the signs of the $\theta^{r'}$, it is clear that we must, among others, know the signs of the h_α^i. The latter, unfortunately, turn out to be ambiguous. For example, partial differentiation of (13.56a) for $i = r$, gives

$$h_\alpha^r = \frac{\hat{h}_\alpha^r}{\hat{h}^r(\tilde{p};\ \alpha)} - \frac{\hat{g}_\alpha^r}{\hat{g}^r(\tilde{p};\ \alpha)}.$$

Since $\hat{g}_\alpha^r$ is equal to the sum of the $\hat{g}_\alpha^{rs}$, it follows from (13.53) that $\hat{g}_\alpha^r > 0$. The term $\hat{h}_\alpha^r$, on the other hand, represents the effect of an increase in α on market demand. This effect operates through the changes in the amounts of profit distributed to the consumers. It is easy to show, using the conditions for profit maximization and assumption (13.48), that the firms in market r experience higher profits as a result of the higher productivity of labor. Hence, each consumer who holds shares in some firm in market r will receive larger dividend payments. Now, we know that it is impossible for all goods to be inferior, so that for some consumers, good r may be a superior good. Consequently, the increase in dividend payments may bring about an increase in the demand for good r, in which case we have $\hat{h}_\alpha^r > 0$. This makes h_α^r ambiguous. In the market for good i, $i \neq r$, n, we have $h_\alpha^i = \hat{h}_\alpha^i/\hat{h}^i(\tilde{p};\ \alpha)$, which is also of indeterminate sign, for the reasons just discussed. Hence we are unable to deduce any conclusive result.

The reader may wonder why the present model fails to predict the effects of changes in a shift parameter, especially since the results of similar changes in the context of standard models of the firm, or even markets, can usually be demonstrated with minimum assumptions. The answer to this is that models of single firms, or markets, are in the nature of *partial equilibrium* models. Essentially, what is missing from most partial equilibrium market models are the repercussions from the consumer sector due to changes in the prices of the various goods. When prices change, consumers rearrange their purchases not only because of changes in the structure of relative prices, but also because of the concomitant changes in incomes. The latter may result from changes in the wage rate, as well as in the level of dividends paid to share holders. These income effects are usually not accounted for in partial equilibrium models. From a formal point of view, a partial equilibrium model may be regarded as an *open* system since it imposes no overall balancing requirement on the system. A general equilibrium model, on the other hand, represents a *closed* system, not unlike a closed circuit: every outflow of payments from any economic unit in the system is also represented as an inflow of payments to some other unit, and vice versa. Because of this network of interrelationships, the actions of a typical economic unit create effects that spread out through the entire system, and ultimately impinge on the original actor himself in the form of a feedback. It is this mutual interdependence among the components of a general equilibrium model that is the source of the difficulty of obtaining determinate comparative static results.

BIBLIOGRAPHICAL NOTES

General

The theory of general equilibrium is usually associated with the name of Leon Walras, since he was the first to conceive and formulate a truly integrated model of an entire economy. This pioneering work was first published (in French) in 1874, and is now available in an English translation by W. Jaffe, under the title *Elements of Pure Economics*, Homewood, Ill.: Irwin 1954. The more technical aspects of general equilibrium, however, were not fully analyzed by Walras, and it was not until quite recently that the existence and stability of a general equilibrium were proved. Most intermediate and advanced texts on microtheory currently in use contain some discussion of general equilibrium, but for more specialized treatments the reader may consult the following: R. E. Kuenne, *The Theory of General Economic Equilibrium*, Princeton: Princeton University Press, 1963; P. Newman, *The Theory of Exchange*, Englewood Cliffs, N.J.: Prentice-Hall, 1965; and J. Quirk and R. Saposnik, *Introduction to General Equilibrium Theory and Welfare Economics*, New York: McGraw-Hill, 1968.

Existence

The first rigorous analysis of the existence of a general equilibrium was carried out by A. Wald in a series of papers published in German. One of these has been published in an English translation under the title "On Some Systems of Equations of Mathematical Economics," *Econometrica*, **19**, 368–403 (1951). Later on, several articles appeared in which existence was proved under less restrictive assumptions and by using different methods of proof. Examples of these are: K. J. Arrow and G. Debreu, "Existence of an Equilibrium for a Competitive Economy," *Econometrica*, **22**, 265–290 (1954); D. Gale, "The Law of Supply and Demand," *Mathematica Scandinavica*, **33**, 155–169 (1955), reprinted in P. Newman (ed.), *Readings in Mathematical Economics*, Volume 1, Baltimore: The Johns Hopkins Press, 1968, pp. 87–101; L. W. McKenzie, "On the Existence of General Equilibrium for a Competitive Market," *Econometrica*, **27**, 54–71 (1959); G. Debreu, *Theory of Value* (Cowles Foundation Monograph No. 17), New York: Wiley, 1959, Chapter 5; and K. Kuga, "Weak Gross Substitutability and the Existence of Competitive

Equilibrium," *Econometrica*, **33**, 593–599 (1965). The case of imperfect competition is examined by T. Negishi in "Monopolistic Competition and General Equilibrium," *Review of Economic Studies*, **28**, 196–201 (1961).

Stability

Discussions of general aspects of stability analysis are presented in the following: P. Newman, "Some Notes on Stability Conditions," *Review of Economic Studies*, **27**, 1–9 (1959); P. Newman, "Approaches to Stability Analysis," *Economica*, **28**, 12–29 (1961); and H. Uzawa, "The Stability of Dynamic Processes," *Econometrica*, **29**, 617–631 (1961). A comprehensive analysis of the stability of the competitive equilibrium is given in the following two papers: K. J. Arrow and L. Hurwicz, "On the Stability of the Competitive Equilibrium, I," *Econometrica*, **26**, 522–552 (1958), and K. J. Arrow, H. D. Block, and L. Hurwicz, "On the Stability of the Competitive Equilibrium, II," *Econometrica*, **27**, 82–109 (1959). Other papers dealing with the stability of general equilibrium models are: H. Uzawa, "Walras' Tâtonnement in the Theory of Exchange," *Review of Economic Studies*, **27**, 182–194 (1960); H. Nikaido and H. Uzawa, "Stability and Non-negativity in a Walrasian Tâtonnement Process," *International Economic Review*, **1**, 50–59 (1960); H. Uzawa, "On the Stability of Edgeworth's Barter Process," *International Economic Review*, **3**, 218–232 (1962); and K. J. Arrow and L. Hurwicz, "Nonlinear Price Adjustment and Adaptive Expectations," *International Economic Review*, **3**, 233–255 (1962). The entire area of the stability of competitive models is reviewed by T. Negishi in "The Stability of a Competitive Economy: A Survey Article," *Econometrica*, **30**, 635–669 (1962); it is reprinted in P. Newman (ed.), *Readings in Mathematical Economics*, Volume 1, Baltimore: The Johns Hopkins Press, 1968, pp. 213–247.

Comparative Statics

The literature on the comparative static properties of general equilibrium models is not very large. J. R. Hicks discusses the problem in his *Value and Capital*, Oxford: Oxford University Press, 1946, Chapter 5 and corresponding appendix. A later work is the paper by M. Morishima, "On Three Hicksian Laws of Comparative Statics," *Review of Economic Studies*, **27**, 195–201 (1960). The area of comparative statics has recently been reexamined rather carefully, especially with reference to models in which the environment is almost completely unspecified. Analysis of this type has come to be known as *qualitative economics*. Some of the important papers on this topic are: K. Lancaster, "The Scope of Qualitative Economics," *Review of Economic Studies*, **29**, 99–123 (1962), and "Partionable Systems and Qualitative Economics," *Review of Economic Studies*, **31**, 69–72 (1964); W. M. Gorman, "More Scope for Qualitative Economics," *Review of Economic Studies*, **31**, 65–68 (1964); G. C. Archibald, "The Qualitative Content of Maximizing Models," *Journal of Political Economy*, **73**, 27–36 (1965); L. Bassett, H. Habibagahi, and J. Quirk, "Qualitative Economics and Morishima Matrixes," *Econometrica*, **35**, 221–233 (1967); and L. Bassett, J. Maybee, and J. Quirk, "Qualitative Economics and the Scope of the Correspondence Principle," *Econometrica*, **36**, 544–563 (1968).

CHAPTER 14

WELFARE ECONOMICS

14.1 THE NATURE OF WELFARE ECONOMICS

From a general point of view, welfare economics may best be defined as that branch of economic theory in which formal propositions contain adjectives such as "good," "bad," "better," "worse," etc. Because of this, it is also referred to as *normative economics*. Welfare economics is thus distinctly different from *positive economics*, which, by definition, is completely devoid of normative content. On a more concrete level, the subject matter of welfare economics deals with social welfare rather than individual welfare, which is the subject of models of individual behavior. As for the formal analysis of welfare economics, it is concerned mainly with comparisons of different social states, as well as the derivation of the conditions that characterize states of maximum welfare. In the context of welfare economics, the term "social state," or simply "state," means essentially a particular organizational scheme for the economic system. For example, a state may specify the amounts of the various goods to be produced by the firms in the economy, as well as the amounts placed at the disposal of each consumer. However, the concept of a state is quite general, and its precise definition may vary from one problem (model) to another. In this chapter, we shall consider two different types of problem, each using a different definition of state.

The most crucial aspect of welfare economics is the choice of an acceptable criterion for the comparison and ordering of different social states. The difficulty in making this choice stems from the fact that, when considering any two distinct states, it will most likely be the case that some individuals are better off under one state (compared to the other), while other individuals are worse off under the same state. Since economists (or anyone else, for that matter) have as yet not found a method for comparing gains (in utility) enjoyed by one individual with the losses (in utility) suffered by another individual, there is no way of combining the utility levels (or changes in these levels) of different individuals into a scalar index that will order social states according to the level of the collective welfare. Thus, given the inadmissibility of interpersonal comparison of utilities, it is impossible to construct a social utility index capable of performing the same task as that performed by an individual utility function in models of individual behavior. Hence, when two states are such that moving from one to the other will make some individuals better off, and others worse off, the states are said to be *noncomparable.*

This leaves us with those states which, when compared to some given state, make some individuals better off, and none worse off, as well as those under which some individuals are worse off, and none is better off. In the framework of modern welfare economics, such states are regarded as comparable, and in ordering such states, use is made of a set of criteria first suggested by Vilfredo Pareto. The basic idea (or ethical judgment) behind the Pareto criteria is that society should be regarded as being better off whenever some individuals are better off, and none is worse off; similarly, society is deemed worse off whenever some individuals are worse off, and none is better off. While these criteria do indeed have a strong appeal, it must nevertheless be remembered that they are only value judgments, and therefore any formal results derived from them can have any significance at all only to the extent that society's value judgment agrees with these criteria.

We now define the Pareto criteria formally.

Definition 14.1. *For any two states S and S', S is said to be* Pareto-superior *to S' if and only if under S at least one individual is better off, and none is worse off, than under S'.*

Definition 14.2. *For any two states S and S', S is said to be* Pareto-inferior *to S' if and only if under S at least one individual is worse off, and none is better off, than under S'.*

It may be observed that the relation "Pareto-superior," as well as the relation "Pareto-inferior," is transitive, but not reflexive. Furthermore, neither of the above two relations must necessarily hold between any two given states since, as was pointed out earlier, pairs of states may be noncomparable. Hence, neither of these relations constitutes a complete ordering of social states.

Definition 14.3. *A state S is said to be* Pareto-optimal *if and only if the following two conditions hold:*

   a) *S is a feasible state;*

   b) *there exists no feasible state which is Pareto-superior to S.*

Note that in examining the optimality of a given state, consideration is confined to feasible states, i.e., states that are attainable with the available resources; clearly, it would make little sense to define something that is not attainable as being optimal.

Since the Pareto criteria do not imply the existence of a complete social preference ordering of all states, it is, of course, meaningless to talk about the maximization of social welfare in the usual sense of the term. To put it differently, given the limitations imposed by the Pareto criteria, there exists no state that can be said to represent at least as high a level of social welfare as that of any other feasible state. It is, however, clear that the welfare of society can always be increased if society has an opportunity to move away from a nonoptimal state to a superior state. Since such a move is always possible (at least theoretically) whenever the current state is not optimal, the maximization of social welfare can be interpreted as the attainment of a Pareto-optimal state, i.e., under the Pareto scheme, society can be thought of as having maximized its welfare whenever it has attained a Pareto-optimal state. Consequently, most of the formal analysis in welfare economics is addressed to either one of the following general classes of problems:

a) The establishment of conditions that characterize a Pareto-optimal state;

b) The examination of given economic systems in order to determine whether or not they have a tendency to attain a Pareto-optimal state.

In this chapter, we shall discuss some examples from each of the above two classes of problems.

14.2   CONDITIONS FOR PARETO-OPTIMALITY

The problems to be examined in this section are of the type that normally arise in planning contexts. For example, we may think of a planning board that is charged with planning the organization of an economic system, or certain aspects of such a system, so as to ensure the attainment of a Pareto-optimal state. We shall first consider a very simple problem of this type, namely that of distributing fixed amounts of certain goods among the individuals in the economy. In this simplified context, a state is simply a particular distribution, and the purpose of our analysis is to find conditions that characterize a Pareto-optimal distribution.

14.2.1   The Distribution Problem

The general set-up is quite similar to that of Section 13.1, in Chapter 13. There are J individuals denoted by the superscript j, $j = 1, 2, ..., J$, and n goods denoted by the superscript i, $i = 1, 2, ..., n$. The preferences of each individual are represented by a utility function $u^j = \phi^j(x^{\cdot j})$, where $x^{\cdot j} = (x^{1j}, x^{2j}, ..., x^{nj})$ denotes a bundle of goods allocated to individual j. The available amounts of the n goods are denoted by $x_0^i, i = 1, 2, ..., n$.

Let us now consider a Pareto-optimal distribution (assuming, of course, that one exists), and suppose that the utility levels attained by the individuals under this distribution are given by $u_0^j, j = 1, 2, ..., J$. Then it is, in general, possible to redistribute the goods among the J individuals in such a way as to keep the utility levels of any $J - 1$ individuals constant at the levels u_0^j, while allowing the utility level of the remaining individual, say individual r, to vary. However, since the initial distribution is assumed to be Pareto-optimal, a redistribution such as the one just mentioned cannot increase the utility level of individual r. Therefore, given the utility levels u_0^j, the utility level of individual r must attain its maximum at the optimal distribution. Thus, a Pareto-optimal distribution can be described as the solution to the problem of maximizing the utility level of one individual, subject to given fixed utility levels for the remaining individuals. This problem can formally be stated as follows:

Maximize $\phi^r(x^{.r})$

subject to: 1) $u_0^j = \phi^j(x^{.j})$, $j = 1, 2, ..., J, \quad j \neq r$,

$\quad\quad$ 2) $\sum_{j=1}^{J} x^{ij} = x_0^i$, $i = 1, 2, ..., n$,

where the u_0^j are prespecified utility levels, and all the nJ quantities x^{ij} are considered as variables. The purpose of the second set of constraints is to ensure that the solution is a feasible distribution. The Lagrangian form for this problem is given by

$$(14.1)\quad \phi^r(x^{.r}) + \sum_{\substack{j=1 \\ j\neq r}}^{J} \lambda^j[\phi^j(x^{.j}) - u_0^j] + \sum_{i=1}^{n} \mu^i\left(\sum_{j=1}^{J} x^{ij} - x_0^i\right),$$

where the λ^j and μ^i are Lagrange multipliers. If we assume the existence of an interior maximum, we get the following first-order conditions:

$(14.2)\quad \phi_i^r + \mu^i = 0$, $i = 1, 2, ..., n$,

$(14.3)\quad \lambda^j\phi_i^j + \mu^i = 0$, $i = 1, 2, ..., n, \quad j = 1, 2, ..., J, \quad j \neq r$,

$(14.4)\quad u_0^j = \phi^j(x^{.j})$, $j = 1, 2, ..., J, \quad j \neq r$,

$(14.5)\quad \sum_{j=1}^{J} x^{ij} = x_0^i$, $i = 1, 2, ..., n$,

where $\phi_i^j = \partial\phi^j/\partial x^{ij}$. The two sets of equations in (14.2) and (14.3) can be combined by eliminating the μ^i; this gives

$(14.6)\quad \phi_i^r = \lambda^j\phi_i^j$, $i = 1, 2, ..., n, \quad j = 1, 2, ..., J, \quad j \neq r$.

We may now divide pairs of equations in (14.6) by one another, and obtain

$(14.7)\quad \dfrac{\phi_i^r}{\phi_k^r} = \dfrac{\phi_i^j}{\phi_k^j}$, $i, k = 1, 2, ..., n, \quad j = 1, 2, ..., J$.

The expressions in the equations given by (14.7) may be recognized as marginal rates of substitution (MRSs) between pairs of goods for the respective individuals. We can, therefore, state the following conclusion:

In order to obtain a Pareto-optimal distribution, the goods must be distributed in a fashion such that the MRS between any two goods is the same for all individuals.

The Contract Curve. In general, there will be infinitely many distributions that satisfy the above conditions. This lack of uniqueness derives directly from the partial character of the Pareto ordering. On a more formal level, we can detect the reason for this in the structure of the above maximization problem. Specifically, since the fixed utility levels u_0^j were chosen arbitrarily, it is clear that we can (in general) obtain a Pareto-optimal distribution for each choice of the u_0^j. (Provided, of course, that the chosen levels u_0^j are feasible; that is, there must exist at least one feasible distribution under which these utility levels can be attained.) To put it differently, the u_0^j constitute parameters of the problem, so that the solution (the optimal distribution) can be represented as a function of these parameters.

For example, in the special case of two goods and two individuals, the first-order conditions consist of seven equations. These equations contain the four quantities x^{ij} that make up the optimal distribution, three Lagrange multipliers, and the utility level of one individual, say u_0^2. By eliminating the three multipliers and the amounts of goods allocated to individual 2, we reduce the first-order conditions to a system of two equations containing the variables x^{11} and x^{21}, and the parameter u_0^2. Hence the optimal bundle of individual 1 can be written as a function of the parameter u_0^2. Thinking of the latter parameter as a variable, we can write

$$\bar{x}^{11} = h^1(u^2), \qquad \bar{x}^{21} = h^2(u^2),$$

where the variables with bars indicate values that are part of a Pareto-optimal distribution. The bundle of individual 2 that corresponds to any given value of u^2 can be computed by substituting the values $h^1(u^2)$ and $h^2(u^2)$ into equations (14.5).

In general, the functions h^1 and h^2 are invertible, so that we can eliminate u^2 and write, for example,

$$\bar{x}^{11} = h^1[\hat{h}^2(\bar{x}^{21})] = H(\bar{x}^{21}),$$

where $\hat{h}^2$ denotes the inverse function of h^2. The function H gives us the optimal bundle of individual 1 for any choice of x^{21}. The domain of definition of the function H is the interval $[0, x_0^2]$, and its range is the interval $[0, x_0^1]$. Plotted in the $x^{11}x^{21}$-plane, the graph of the function H may look like the positively sloped curve shown in Fig. 14.1. To each bundle on the function H, there corresponds a particular value of u^2. For example, the distribution that allocates to individual 1 the bundle $(\bar{x}_1^{11}, \bar{x}_1^{21})$ makes it possible for individual 2 to attain the utility level u_1^2. It is clear that the two functions $h^1(u^2)$ and $h^2(u^2)$ are nothing but the parametric representation of the curve $H(x^{21})$, with u^2 serving as the parameter.

With each point on $H(x^{21})$ we can also associate a bundle of individual 2. But to facilitate the graphical determination of the bundles of individual 2, we use a slightly different construction: we superimpose the indifference map of individual 2 on Fig. 14.1 in such a way that its axes coincide with the dotted lines in Fig. 14.1. The resulting construction, shown in Fig. 14.2, is commonly referred to as an *Edgeworth box*. The dimensions of this box correspond to the total available amounts of the goods to be distributed, and the box has the property that any point in it (including the boundaries) represents a feasible distribution, the four coordinates of each point indicating the amounts of the two goods allocated to the two individuals. As was already pointed out, points on the curve $H(x^{21})$ represent Pareto-optimal distributions, and the curve itself is referred to as the *contract curve* (or *conflict curve*). Geometrically speaking, the contract curve is the locus of points at which pairs of indifference curves are tangent to each other. This follows directly from condition (14.7), which states that at interior Pareto-optimal distributions, the MRSs of the two individuals must be equal.

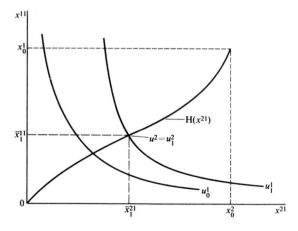

Figure 14.1

Figure 14.2 clearly shows the lack of uniqueness of the solution to the welfare maximization problem. The solution to the simple distribution problem says, in effect, that whoever is charged with choosing an optimal distribution should select a distribution from among those represented by points on the contract curve. However, there is nothing in the solution to indicate which of the distributions on the contract curve should be chosen. Indeed, according to the Pareto criteria, no two distributions on the contract curve can be compared. For example, distributions D_1 and D_2 are clearly non-comparable: individual 1 is better off under D_1 than under D_2, but individual 2 prefers D_2. It is quite clear that this is true with respect to *any two* distributions on the contract curve. Hence the following general result: *the set of Pareto-optimal distributions is a set of noncomparable distributions.*

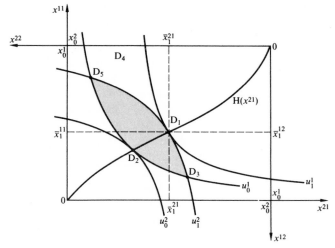

Figure 14.2

The application of the Pareto criteria can essentially be thought of as a method for the elimination of inferior distributions. For example, in the context of the present model, the solution can be interpreted as saying: "Don't choose a distribution which is represented by a point off the contract curve." However, this does not mean that *any* distribution on the contract curve is better than *any* distribution not on that curve. This will not be true, in general, because of the possibility of noncomparability. Thus, D_2 is a Pareto-optimal distribution, while D_4 is not; but it is not valid to conclude that D_2 is better than (i.e., Pareto-superior to) D_4: D_2 and D_4 are noncomparable. What the injunction in quotation marks does imply is the following: for each distribution not on the contract curve there exists at least one distribution that is Pareto-superior to it. For example, distribution D_3 is non-optimal, and all the distributions represented by points in the shaded region (except D_5, which is just as good as D_3) are Pareto-superior to D_3. Thus, choosing D_3 is certainly not optimal. It is the elimination of choices such as D_3 which is one of the main purposes of the use of the Pareto criteria.

In our analysis we have not made any reference to second-order conditions. Of course, the derivation of the first-order conditions assumed that an interior solution exists. This means that certain second-order conditions must also be satisfied. As in all constrained maximization problems, these conditions involve sign restrictions on a series of bordered Hessian determinants. In the present problem, these determinants have a somewhat complicated structure (because of the relatively large number of constraints), and therefore we omit these conditions in the present exposition.

14.2.2 Production and Distribution

We now broaden the scope of the problem by removing the assumption that the amounts of the goods to be distributed are fixed. Instead, we assume that the economy can produce different quantities of the n goods within certain limits imposed by the available resources and the technology. In this enlarged framework, a state is a plan which specifies how much of each good is to be produced, and how much of each good is allocated to each individual in the economy. As before, the different states will be evaluated on the basis of the utility levels attained by the individuals.

For simplification, it is assumed that the rate of utilization of all the factors of production, except one, are predetermined; hence the fixed factors need not be introduced explicitly. The variable factor is labor, and we assume it to be a homogeneous service provided by the individuals in the economy. The technological environment of the economy may then be described by the implicit multiproduct production function $\psi(x^0, x^1, ..., x^{n-1}; z) = 0$, where z denotes the total quantity of labor hours used. (We have made a slight change in the numbering of goods.) The preferences of the individuals are again represented by the utility functions $u^j = \phi^j(x^{\cdot j})$, except that each bundle $x^{\cdot j}$ now has the $n + 1$ components $(x^{0j}, x^{1j}, ..., x^{nj})$, with x^{nj} denoting leisure time of individual j.

An optimal plan may again be described as the solution to the problem of maximizing the utility of one individual, given the utility levels of the remaining individuals. The present problem can be stated as:

Maximize $\phi^r(x^{\cdot r})$

subject to

1) $u_0^j = \phi^j(x^{\cdot j})$, $j = 1, 2, ..., J$, $j \neq r$,

2) $\displaystyle\sum_{j=1}^{J} x^{ij} = x^i$, $i = 0, 1, ..., n-1$,

3) $\psi\left(x^0, x^1, ..., x^{n-1};\ \delta J - \displaystyle\sum_{j=1}^{J} x^{nj}\right) = 0$,

where δ denotes the length of the time period under consideration. The

Lagrangian form for the above problem is given by

$$(14.8) \quad \phi^r(x^{\cdot r}) + \sum_{\substack{j=1 \\ j \neq r}}^{J} \lambda^j [\phi^j(x^{\cdot j}) - u_0^j] + \sum_{i=0}^{n-1} \mu^i \left(\sum_{j=1}^{J} x^{ij} - x^i \right)$$

$$+ v\psi \left(x^0, x^1, \ldots, x^{n-1}; \delta J - \sum_{j=1}^{J} x^{nj} \right),$$

where the λ^j, μ^i, and v are Lagrange multipliers. The variables with respect to which the above form is to be maximized are the $(n+1)J$ variables x^{ij}, and the n variables x^i. Assuming the existence of an interior maximum, the first-order conditions are:

$$(14.9a) \quad \phi_i^r + \mu^i = 0, \qquad i = 0, 1, \ldots, n-1,$$

$$(14.9b) \quad \phi_n^r - v\psi_z = 0,$$

$$(14.10a) \quad \lambda^j \phi_i^j + \mu^i = 0, \quad \left. \begin{array}{l} \\ \end{array} \right\} \quad \begin{array}{l} i = 0, 1, \ldots, n-1, \\ j = 1, 2, \ldots, J, \quad j \neq r, \end{array}$$

$$(14.10b) \quad \lambda^j \phi_n^j - v\psi_z = 0,$$

$$(14.11) \quad -\mu^i + v\psi_i = 0, \qquad i = 0, 1, \ldots, n-1,$$

where $\psi_i = \partial\psi/\partial x^i$, and $\psi_z = \partial\psi/\partial z$.

To interpret the above conditions, let us first review the meaning of the partial derivatives of the implicit production function. (See Section 3.5.) Taking the total differential, we have

$$\psi_0 dx^0 + \psi_1 dx^1 + \cdots + \psi_{n-1} dx^{n-1} + \psi_z dz = 0.$$

Setting all the differentials, except dx^i and dx^k, equal to zero, we have

$$\frac{dx^i}{dx^k} = -\frac{\psi_k}{\psi_i}.$$

Thus, ratios of partial derivatives with respect to products indicate the rate at which one product can be transformed into another product (by a suitable reallocation of inputs), holding all other products and the total amounts of inputs constant. A ratio such as the above is therefore called a *marginal rate of product transformation* (MRPT). Computing the ratio of dx^i to dz, setting all the remaining differentials equal to zero, we have

$$\frac{dx^i}{dz} = -\frac{\psi_z}{\psi_i},$$

which we easily recognize as the marginal product (MP) of labor in the production of good x^i. We also observe that the (absolute value of) MRPT between any two products is equal to the ratio of the MPs of labor in the production of the respective products, all the relevant functions being evaluated at the same point.

If we eliminate the μ^i from the equations in (14.9a) and (14.10a), using (14.11), we get

(14.12) $\qquad \dfrac{\phi_i^j}{\phi_k^j} = \dfrac{\psi_i}{\psi_k}, \qquad i, k = 0, 1, \ldots, n-1, \quad j = 1, 2, \ldots, J.$

These equations state that at the optimal plan, each individual's MRS between any two goods must be equal to the MRPT between the same goods. We also have

(14.13) $\qquad \dfrac{\phi_n^j}{\phi_i^j} = -\dfrac{\psi_z}{\psi_i}, \qquad i = 0, 1, \ldots, n-1, \quad j = 1, 2, \ldots, J,$

which says that for each individual, the MRS between leisure time and any other good must be equal to the MP of labor in the production of that good. Of course, Eqs. (14.12) and (14.13) also imply conditions similar to those in (14.7); namely

(14.14) $\qquad \dfrac{\phi_i^r}{\phi_k^r} = \dfrac{\phi_i^j}{\phi_k^j}, \qquad i, k = 0, 1, \ldots, n, \quad j = 1, 2, \ldots, J.$

Thus, in the production-distribution problem, as in the distribution problem, a Pareto-optimal state is characterized by an equality of all the MRSs between any two goods, including leisure time. It is important to note, however, that the present problem imposes more restrictive conditions: not only must the MRSs between any two goods be equal for all individuals, each MRS must also be equal to the respective MRPT or MP, as the case may be. This means that when the total amounts of the goods can be varied through production or transformation, it is no longer true that any distribu-

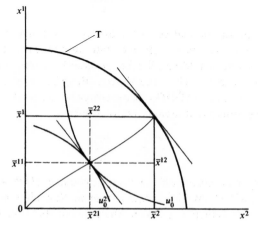

Figure 14.3

tion on the contract curve is as good as any other; only those that satisfy the conditions in (14.12) and (14.13) are optimal. This point may be illustrated with the aid of a diagram.

Let us consider the case of two individuals and two goods, all inputs being fixed. The set of all feasible production combinations is given by the transformation curve, which is shown in Fig. 14.3 as the curve labeled T. This curve is the explicit form of the implicit production function; that is, if we solve the equation $\psi(x^0, x^1, ..., x^{n-1}; z) = 0$ explicitly for x^1 in terms of x^2, holding the remaining arguments constant, then the form of the functional relationship between x^1 and x^2 may be represented by the T curve. The slope of this curve is the MRPT between x^1 and x^2 which, as we have already pointed out, is given by the term $-\psi_2/\psi_1$. The two parallel lines are tangent lines. The optimal production mix, and the components of the optimal distribution, are indicated on the diagram by the barred symbols.

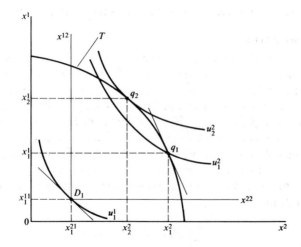

Figure 14.4

To clarify the situation further, we can show that if a plan fails to satisfy the equality between the MRSs and the MRPT, then it is not a Pareto-optimal plan. Consider state S_1 (in Fig. 14.4), which consists of the product mix (x_1^1, x_1^2), and the distribution D_1, which is assumed to lie on the contract curve. However, since the two tangent lines are not parallel to each other, it follows that the MRSs at the distribution D_1 are not equal to the MRPT at the production point q_1. Now, in Fig. 14.4, the origin of the indifference map of individual 2 is placed at the point D_1 instead of q_1, hence indifference curve u_1^2 must *intersect* the T curve, as is shown in the diagram.

Consider now state S_2, which calls for choosing production point q_2 on the T curve, and the distribution that allocates to individual 1 the same amounts as D_1, that is, the amounts x_1^{11} and x_1^{21}, while giving the remaining amounts to individual 2. This will place individual 2 on indifference curve u_2^2, making him better off than he is under state S_1. Consequently, S_2 is Pareto-superior to S_1, and therefore S_1 is not optimal.

14.3 PARETO-OPTIMALITY AND PURE COMPETITION

We now leave the planning problems, and turn to an examination of the optimality properties of some economic systems. In particular, we wish to determine whether the systems under consideration will bring about the attainment of a Pareto-optimal state. To do so, the systems to be examined must, of course, be fully specified, and especially with respect to the environmental conditions under which decision makers are assumed to operate. In this section, we assume that decision makers operate under purely competitive conditions, and therefore it is most convenient to consider the competitive models presented in Chapter 13. First, we examine the pure exchange model.

14.3.1 Pure Exchange

When examining the optimality properties of a given economic system, one is usually concerned with the optimality of the *equilibrium* position of the system. Thus, what we wish to do in this section is to determine whether the equilibrium distribution of the competitive exchange model is Pareto-optimal. Of course, this presumes that the dynamic process which describes the workings of the model will converge to an equilibrium distribution.* A pure exchange model, it will be recalled, consists of J individuals each of whom maximizes a utility function $u^j = \phi^j(x^{\cdot j})$, where $x^{\cdot j} = (x^{0j}, x^{1j}, ..., x^{nj})$, and good 0 is the numéraire. The maximization of utility is restricted by the budget constraint

$$(14.15) \qquad \sum_{i=0}^{n} p^i(x^{ij} - x_0^{ij}) = 0,$$

where the p^i are (normalized) market prices, $p^0 = 1$, and x_0^{ij} denotes the jth individual's initial endowment of good i. If the optimal bundle is in the interior of the feasible set for all p^i and x_0^{ij}, then the necessary conditions for a maximum consist of (14.15) and

$$(14.16) \qquad \phi_i^j + \lambda^j p^i = 0, \qquad i = 0, 1, ..., n, \quad j = 1, 2, ..., J,$$

where the λ^j are Lagrange multipliers, and $\phi_i^j = \partial \phi^j / \partial x^{ij}$. Eliminating the

---

* While conventional analysis in the area of welfare economics is concerned only with the optimality of static states (such as equilibrium positions), the basic idea embodied in the Pareto criteria may also serve as a basis for ordering time series, or time paths, of economic states.

λ^j from the above equations, we can write

(14.17) $$\frac{\phi_i^j}{\phi_k^j} = \frac{p^i}{p^k}, \qquad i = 0, 1, \ldots, n, \quad j = 1, 2, \ldots, J.$$

Now, the equilibrium distribution is simply the set of bundles chosen by the individuals when market prices are equal to their equilibrium values. Interpreting the p^i as denoting equilibrium values, we see that condition (14.17) characterizes the equilibrium distribution. But, since under conditions of pure competition the prices are the same for all individuals, we can eliminate the prices from (14.17) and write

(14.18) $$\frac{\phi_i^r}{\phi_k^r} = \frac{\phi_i^j}{\phi_k^j}, \qquad i, k = 0, 1, \ldots, n, \quad j, r = 1, 2, \ldots, J.$$

These conditions are obviously the same as those in (14.7), and so we conclude that the equilibrium distribution of the competitive exchange model is indeed a Pareto-optimal distribution.

An Alternative Proof. The optimality of the competitive equilibrium may be proved under conditions that are more general than those assumed in the preceding section. Specifically, it is possible to remove the assumption of the differentiability of the utility function, and to admit noninterior distributions. To present this result as a formal proposition, we define a competitive equilibrium (for a pure exchange model) as follows:

Definition 14.4. *A competitive equilibrium is a nonnegative distribution* $\bar{x} = (\bar{x}^{\cdot 1}, \bar{x}^{\cdot 2}, \ldots, \bar{x}^{\cdot J})$ *and a nonnegative price vector* $\bar{p}$ *satisfying the following conditions:*

a) For each j, the $n + 1$ dimensional vector $\bar{x}^{\cdot j}$ constitutes a unique maximum of the function $\phi^j(x^{\cdot j})$ over the feasible set of individual j; that is,

$$\phi^j(\bar{x}^{\cdot j}) > \phi^j(x^{\cdot j}) \text{ for all } x^{\cdot j} \text{ satisfying } \sum_{i=0}^{n} \bar{p}^i(x^{ij} - x_0^{ij}) = 0.$$

b) $$\sum_{j=1}^{J} \bar{x}^{ij} \leqslant \sum_{j=1}^{J} x_0^{ij}, \qquad i = 0, 1, \ldots, n.$$

This definition is perfectly consistent with the way we described an equilibrium distribution in Section 13.1, except that we make no reference whatsoever here to any dynamic process. We now prove the following:

Proposition 14.1. *If $\bar{x}$ and $\bar{p}$ constitute a competitive equilibrium, then $\bar{x}$ is a Pareto-optimal distribution.*

To demonstrate the validity of this proposition, we shall use a proof by contradiction. Thus, suppose that the proposition is false; that is, assume that $\bar{x}$ is not Pareto-optimal. Then there must exist another feasible distribution, say $\hat{x}$, that is Pareto-superior to $\bar{x}$; that is, there exists $\hat{x}$ such that $\phi^j(\hat{x}^{\cdot j}) \geqslant \phi^j(\bar{x}^{\cdot j})$ for all j, and $\phi^k(\hat{x}^{\cdot k}) > \phi^k(\bar{x}^{\cdot k})$ for at least one k, and

$$(14.19) \qquad \sum_{j=1}^{J} \hat{x}^{ij} \leqslant \sum_{j=1}^{J} x_0^{ij} \qquad \text{for all } i.$$

However, from the definition of a competitive equilibrium, it is quite clear that we must have

$$\sum_{i=0}^{n} \bar{p}(\hat{x}^{ik} - x_0^{ik}) > 0$$

for all k: since the hypothesis of the proposition postulates that the function $\phi^k(x^{\cdot k})$ takes its maximum over the feasible set of individual k at the point $\bar{x}^{\cdot k}$, then if $\phi^k(x^{\cdot k})$ assumes a still higher value at the point $\hat{x}^{\cdot k}$, the latter point must be outside the feasible set, that is, outside the budget of consumer k. For the remaining individuals, whose utility levels have not changed, we have

$$\sum_{i=0}^{n} \bar{p}^i(\hat{x}^{ij} - x_0^{ij}) \geqslant 0.$$

This inequality must hold, for if the cost of the bundle $\hat{x}^{ij}$ (at the equilibrium prices $\bar{p}^i$) is less than the cost of bundle $\bar{x}^{\cdot j}$ (and hence less than the cost of $x_0^{\cdot j}$), bundle $\bar{x}^{\cdot j}$ cannot possibly maximize the utility of individual j, as hypothesized by the proposition. Therefore, summing the above J inequalities, we have

$$\sum_{i=0}^{n} \bar{p}^i \sum_{j=1}^{J} (\hat{x}^{ij} - x_0^{ij}) > 0.$$

Since the $\bar{p}^i$ are nonnegative, it follows that at least one of the sums

$$\sum_{j=1}^{J} (\hat{x}^{ij} - x_0^{ij})$$

must be positive, thus violating the feasibility conditions (14.19). Hence a distribution such as $\hat{x}$ does not exist, thereby establishing the optimality of $\bar{x}$.

14.3.2 Production and Distribution

Turning now to a model in which goods are produced and distributed, we briefly summarize the model presented in Section 13.2.1. Each consumer maximizes $u^j = \phi^j(x^{\cdot j})$ subject to

$$(14.20) \qquad \sum_{i=0}^{n} p^i x^{ij} = \delta p^n + \sum_{i=0}^{n-1} \sum_{s=1}^{mi} \sigma^{isj} \pi^{is},$$

where the p^i are market prices, $p^0 = 1$, x^n is leisure time, the π^{is} are profits, and the σ^{isj} are profit shares. Assuming interior maxima, we see that the first-order conditions are (14.20) and

(14.21) $\qquad \phi_i^j + \lambda^j p^i = 0, \qquad i = 0, 1, \ldots, n, \quad j = 1, 2, \ldots, J.$

Eliminating the Lagrange multipliers, we have

(14.22) $\qquad \dfrac{\phi_i^j}{\phi_k^j} = \dfrac{p^i}{p^k}, \qquad i = 0, 1, \ldots, n, \quad j = 1, 2, \ldots, J.$

On the production side, each firm maximizes the profit function $\pi^{is} = p^i \psi^{is}(z^{is}) - p^n z^{is}$, where the $\psi^{is}(z^{is})$ are production functions, and z^{is} denotes the amount of labor employed by firm s in industry i. If each firm always uses a positive amount of labor, then the first-order conditions for profit maximization are given by

(14.23) $\qquad p^i \psi_z^{is} - p^n = 0, \qquad i = 0, 1, \ldots, n-1, \quad s = 1, 2, \ldots, m^i,$

where $\psi_z^{is} = \partial \psi^{is}/\partial z^{is}$. Consequently, conditions (14.22) and (14.23) characterize the equilibrium of the production-distribution model, the p^i being evaluated at their equilibrium values.

Eliminating p^n from (14.23), we have

(14.24) $\qquad \dfrac{\psi_z^{ks}}{\psi_z^{is}} = \dfrac{p^i}{p^k}, \qquad i, k = 0, 1, \ldots, n-1, \quad s = 1, 2, \ldots, m^i.$

But ratios of MPs are equal to the (absolute value of) MRPT; that is, $\psi_z^{ks}/\psi_z^{is} = \psi_i/\psi_k$ for all i, k, and s, the ψ_i as defined in Section 14.2.2. Therefore, combining (14.22) and (14.24), we obtain the conditions

(14.25) $\qquad \dfrac{\phi_i^j}{\phi_k^j} = \dfrac{\psi_i}{\psi_k}, \qquad i, k = 0, 1, \ldots, n-1, \quad j = 1, 2, \ldots, J,$

which are identical to the optimality conditions in (14.12). Furthermore, we can also write (14.23) as

(14.26) $\qquad \psi_z^{is} = \dfrac{p^n}{p^i}, \qquad i = 0, 1, \ldots, n-1, \quad s = 1, 2, \ldots, m^i,$

and, since $\psi_z^{is} = -\psi_z/\psi_i$ for all i and s (as was shown in Section 14.2.2), we can combine (14.22) and (14.26) to yield

(14.27) $\qquad \dfrac{\phi_n^j}{\phi_i^j} = -\dfrac{\psi_z}{\psi_i}, \qquad i = 0, 1, \ldots, n-1, \quad j = 1, 2, \ldots, J.$

The latter equations are the same as those in (14.13), and so we have shown that the equilibrium position of the competitive production-distribution model is Pareto-optimal.

An Alternative Proof. We now prove the above result by following the same approach taken in the alternative proof of the result in Section 14.3.1. First, we provide a formal definition of a competitive equilibrium for a production-distribution model.

> **Definition 14.5.** *A competitive equilibrium is a nonnegative vector of labor inputs $\bar{z} = (\bar{z}^{0\cdot}, \bar{z}^{1\cdot}, ..., \bar{z}^{n-1\cdot})$ where $\bar{z}^{i\cdot} = (\bar{z}^{i1}, \bar{z}^{i2}, ..., \bar{z}^{imi})$, a nonnegative distribution $\bar{x} = (\bar{x}^{\cdot 1}, \bar{x}^{\cdot 2}, ..., \bar{x}^{\cdot J})$, and a nonnegative price vector $\bar{p}$ satisfying the following conditions:*
>
> *a) For each i and s, the labor input $\bar{z}^{is}$ uniquely maximizes the profit of firm s in market i, given $\bar{p}$, that is,*
>
> $$\bar{\pi}^{is} = \bar{p}^i \psi^{is}(\bar{z}^{is}) - \bar{p}^n \bar{z}^{is} > \pi^{is} = \bar{p}^i \psi^{is}(z^{is}) - \bar{p}^n z^{is} \text{ for all nonnegative } z^{is}.$$
>
> *b) For each j, the vector $\bar{x}^{\cdot j}$ uniquely maximizes the utility of individual j over his feasible set; that is, $\phi^j(\bar{x}^{\cdot j}) > \phi^j(x^{\cdot j})$ for all $x^{\cdot j}$ satisfying*
>
> $$\sum_{i=0}^{n} \bar{p}^i x^{ij} - \delta \bar{p}^n - \sum_{i=0}^{n-1} \sum_{s=1}^{mi} \sigma^{isj} \bar{\pi}^{is} = 0.$$
>
> *c)* $\displaystyle \sum_{i=0}^{n-1} \sum_{s=1}^{mi} \bar{z}^{is} \leqslant \delta J - \sum_{j=1}^{J} \bar{x}^{nj}.$
>
> *d)* $\displaystyle \sum_{j=1}^{J} \bar{x}^{ij} \leqslant \sum_{s=1}^{mi} \psi^{is}(\bar{z}^{is}),$ $\quad i = 0, 1, ..., n - 1.$

The counterpart of Proposition 14.1 is:

> **Proposition 14.2.** *If $\bar{z}$, $\bar{x}$, and $\bar{p}$ constitute a competitive equilibrium, then $(\bar{z}, \bar{x})$ is a Pareto-optimal production-distribution state.*

Suppose that the state $(\bar{z}, \bar{x})$ is not optimal. In that case, there exists another feasible state, say $(\hat{z}, \hat{x})$, that is Pareto-superior to $(\bar{z}, \bar{x})$; that is, $\phi^j(\hat{x}^{\cdot j}) \geqslant \phi^j(\bar{x}^{\cdot j})$ for all j, and $\phi^k(\hat{x}^{\cdot k}) > \phi^k(\bar{x}^{\cdot k})$ for at least one k, and

$$\text{(14.28)} \qquad \sum_{i=0}^{n-1} \sum_{s=1}^{mi} \hat{z}^{is} \leqslant \delta J - \sum_{j=1}^{J} \hat{x}^{nj},$$

$$\text{(14.29)} \qquad \sum_{j=1}^{J} \hat{x}^{ij} \leqslant \sum_{s=1}^{mi} \psi^{is}(\hat{z}^{is}), \qquad i = 0, 1, ..., n-1.$$

Since $\bar{x}$ is an equilibrium distribution, we must have

$$\sum_{i=0}^{n} \bar{p}^{ik} \hat{x}^{ik} - \delta \bar{p}^n - \sum_{i=0}^{n-1} \sum_{s=1}^{mi} \sigma^{isk} \bar{\pi}^{is} > 0.$$

Furthermore, since $\bar{\pi}^{is} > \hat{\pi}^{is}$ by condition (a) of Definition 14.5, we have

$$\sum_{i=0}^{n} \bar{p}^{i} \hat{x}^{ik} - \delta \bar{p}^{n} - \sum_{i=0}^{n-1} \sum_{s=1}^{mi} \sigma^{isk} \hat{\pi}^{is} > 0.$$

For the remaining individuals, that is, $j \neq k$, we have

$$\sum_{i=0}^{n} \bar{p}^{i} \hat{x}^{ij} - \delta \bar{p}^{n} - \sum_{i=0}^{n-1} \sum_{s=1}^{mi} \sigma^{isj} \hat{\pi}^{is} \geq 0.$$

Substituting for the $\hat{\pi}^{is}$ in the preceding inequalities, we can write

$$(14.30) \qquad \sum_{i=0}^{n-1} p^{i} [\hat{x}^{ij} - \sum_{s=1}^{mi} \sigma^{isj} \psi^{is}(\hat{z}^{is})] + p^{n} \left(\hat{x}^{nj} + \sum_{i=0}^{n-1} \sum_{s=1}^{mi} \sigma^{isj} \hat{z}^{is} - \delta \right) \geq 0,$$

the strict inequality holding for $j = k$. Summing the inequalities in (14.30) over all individuals, we get

$$(14.31) \qquad \sum_{i=0}^{n-1} \bar{p}^{i} \sum_{j=1}^{J} \left[\hat{x}^{ij} - \sum_{s=1}^{mi} \psi^{is}(\hat{z}^{is}) \right] + \bar{p}^{n} \left(\sum_{j=1}^{J} \hat{x}^{nj} + \sum_{i=0}^{n-1} \sum_{s=1}^{mi} \hat{z}^{is} - \delta J \right) > 0,$$

where we have made use of the condition

$$\sum_{j=1}^{J} \sigma^{isj} = 1$$

for all i and s. Since prices are nonnegative, condition (14.31) implies that at least one of the feasibility conditions in either (14.28) or (14.29) is violated. Therefore, the state $(\hat{z}, \hat{x})$ does not exist, which establishes the optimality of the state $(\bar{z}, \bar{x})$.

Proposition 14.2 (of which Proposition 14.1 is a special case) is one of two fundamental results of modern welfare economics. The other result is in some sense a converse of Proposition 14.2 (or 14.1); stated loosely, the converse says that with any Pareto-optimal state one can associate a competitive equilibrium. More precisely, given a state S which is Pareto-optimal, then, given the available resources and technology, there exists a nonnegative price vector p, and initial endowments, such that S and p constitute a competitive equilibrium. Thus, roughly speaking, Proposition 14.2 tells us that when an economic system operates under competitive conditions, then, given stability, it will lead to the attainment of a Pareto-optimal state; the converse says that any Pareto-optimal state may be attained under competitive conditions, provided the system starts from an appropriate initial position (and is stable). The proof of the converse proposition is quite a bit more complicated than that of Proposition 14.2, and requires more restrictive assumptions; it will not be presented here. If a system satisfies both Proposition 14.2 and the converse proposition, then it is said to be *Pareto-satisfactory*.

14.4 OPTIMALITY OF IMPERFECT COMPETITION

The reader should be careful to note that, even though the competitive mechanism has the property of being a Pareto-satisfactory mechanism, there is nothing in Proposition 14.2 or the converse proposition which asserts, or implies, that the competitive system is the only market mechanism capable of bringing about the attainment of a Pareto-optimal state. As a matter of fact, noncompetitive systems may also lead to Pareto-optimal states, and in this section we provide one such example. Our example is concerned with a pure distribution problem, but here, unlike in Section 13.1, we no longer assume that every trader is a price taker. For our purpose, it will suffice if we assume that all traders, except one, are price takers, while one trader — to be referred to as the *monopolist* — is given the power to set all (relative) prices. We may, incidentally, also think of the scheme to be set out here as an auction, but one in which the auctioneer is himself a trader. However, as will be indicated presently, the "rules of the game" which govern this auction are different in certain respects from those which apply to the auction described in Section 13.1.2.

As before, each competitive trader is assumed to maximize a utility function, subject to an appropriate budget constraint. Since the trading process of the present model is of a dynamic nature, we make use of time subscripts. Thus, in period t the jth competitive trader maximizes $u_t = \phi^j(x_t^{,j})$, subject to

$$(14.32) \qquad \sum_{i=0}^{n} p_t^i(x_t^{ij} - x_{t-1}^{ij}) = 0, \qquad j = 2, 3, ..., J,$$

where p_t^i is the price of good i chosen by the monopolist in period t ($p_t^0 = 1$, for all t), and x_{t-1}^{ij} denotes the jth trader's initial holding of good i at the beginning of period t. Assuming interior maxima for all prices and initial holdings, then in each period t we have

$$(14.33) \qquad \frac{\phi_i^j}{\phi_0^j} = p_t^i, \qquad i = 1, 2, ..., n, \quad j = 2, 3, ..., J.$$

The solutions to the first-order conditions constitute the desired bundles of the competitive traders, and if we subtract from these desired amounts the initial holdings, we obtain the excess demand (supply) functions

$$(14.34) \qquad x_t^{ij} - x_{t-1}^{ij} = h^{ij}(p_t; x_{t-1}^{,j}), \qquad i = 0, 1, ..., n, \quad j = 2, 3, ..., J.$$

Summing the above over all competitive traders, we obtain the market excess demand functions

(14.35) $\qquad x_t^i - x_{t-1}^i = h^i(p_t; \; x_{t-1}^c), \qquad i = 0, 1, ..., n,$

where the absence of the superscript j indicates summation over the $J-1$ competitive traders, and x_{t-1}^c denotes the distribution of the competitive sector, that is, the vector of the $J-1$ vectors $x_{t-1}^{\cdot j}$.

What remains to be specified is the method by which the monopolist (identified by the superscript $j = 1$) chooses the n (relative) prices in each period. Since the monopolist is also a trader, it will be consistent with our general approach to assume that in his choice of prices, he is guided by his desire to maximize his utility (just as a monopolistic producer sets prices so as to maximize profit). This means, of course (so long as we are excluding uncertainty), that the monopolist has full information about the market excess demand functions h^i. Given this information, then for any price vector p_t, the monopolist can determine the amounts of each good that the market (the competitive traders) wishes to sell or buy; and these amounts, in conjunction with his own initial holdings, enable him to determine his own final (after trade) bundle. The rule is, of course, that once the monopolist announces a set of prices, he must commit himself to carry out the trades offered by the competitive sector, and therefore he must be able to supply any amount demanded by the market. Put differently, since each choice of p_t implies a certain distribution of the available goods among all the traders, the monopolist is constrained to choose only from among those price vectors that yield a *feasible* distribution.

The monopolist's optimal set of prices may, therefore, be described as the solution to the problem of maximizing $\phi^1(x_t^{\cdot 1})$, subject to (14.35) and

(14.36) $\qquad \displaystyle\sum_{j=1}^{J} x_t^{ij} = \sum_{j=1}^{J} x_{t-1}^{ij}, \qquad i = 0, 1, ..., n.$

Combining (14.35) and (14.36), we can write

(14.37) $\qquad x_t^{i1} = x_{t-1}^{i1} - h^i(p_t; \; x_{t-1}^c), \qquad i = 0, 1, ..., n,$

and making use of the latter equations, we can write the monopolist's utility function as

$$u_t^1 = \phi^1[x_{t-1}^{01} - h^0(p_t; \; x_{t-1}^c), x_{t-1}^{11} - h^1(p_t; \; x_{t-1}^c), ..., x_{t-1}^{n1} - h^n(p_t; \; x_{t-1}^c)].$$

This function can now be maximized with respect to the p_t^i; and assuming an interior maximum, we see that the first-order conditions for this maximization problem are

$$(14.38) \qquad \sum_{i=0}^{n} \phi_i^1 h_r^i = 0, \qquad r = 1, 2, ..., n,$$

where $h_r^i = \partial h^i / \partial p_t^r$.

The fact that the optimal price vector [that is, the solution to the system of equations in (14.38)] satisfies condition (14.37) means, of course, that all markets are cleared in period t, so that p_t can be regarded as the final price vector for that period. For this reason, the present model is quite different from the tâtonnement process described by Eq. (13.7), in Section 13.1.2, inasmuch as, in the present scheme, goods are actually exchanged after the prices for the respective period are announced. However, we do assume that goods are not consumed until the entire process reaches a stationary state. In view of this assumption, it may perhaps be convenient to think of the x^{ij} as *claims* to goods (e.g., certificates) which are to be redeemed when prices reach their equilibrium levels.

But why should p_t not be regarded as an equilibrium price vector? Or, to put it differently, under what conditions will the monopolist find it beneficial to announce a different set of prices for period $t + 1$? To answer this question, let us consider the case in which the distribution that results from the exchange in period t is Pareto-optimal. Then it follows from the definition of Pareto-optimality that the monopolist could improve his position only if he succeeded in inducing some (at least one) competitive traders to accept bundles that are inferior to those which they held at the end of period t. But since no utility-maximizing trader will voluntarily engage in such a trade, it is clear that under these circumstances the monopolist will not be able to improve his position by trading with the competitive sector.

On the other hand, suppose that the distribution at the end of period t is not Pareto-optimal. Then there must exist at least one feasible distribution that is Pareto-superior to the former distribution; that is, at least one trader can be made better off without causing a deterioration in the positions of the remaining individuals. As a matter of fact, given appropriate convexity conditions, it will be possible to improve everybody's position, including that of the monopolist. In which case, the monopolist will, in general, be able to find a price vector such that the resulting trade will move every trader to a higher indifference curve. Thus, so long as the exchange of goods in any period yields a nonoptimal distribution, the monopolist will announce a new price vector in the succeeding period, and the trading process will go on. We will now formalize this process.

We write the solution to (14.38) as

$$(14.39) \qquad p_t^r = \theta^r(x_{t-1}), \qquad r = 1, 2, ..., n,$$

and substituting for p_t^r in (14.34) and (14.37), we get

$$(14.40a) \quad x_t^{ij} = x_{t-1}^{ij} + h^{ij}[\theta(x_{t-1}); \; x_{t-1}^j] = H^{ij}(x_{t-1}), \quad \left.\vphantom{\begin{matrix}1\\1\end{matrix}}\right\} \; i = 0, 1, \ldots, n,$$

$$(14.40b) \quad x_t^{i1} = x_{t-1}^{i1} - h^i[\theta(x_{t-1}); \; x_{t-1}^c] = H^{i1}(x_{t-1}), \quad \left.\vphantom{\begin{matrix}1\\1\end{matrix}}\right\} \; j = 2, 3, \ldots, J,$$

where $\theta(x_{t-1})$ is the vector of the $\theta^r(x_{t-1})$, and x_{t-1} denotes a distribution of the goods among all the J individuals. The equations in (14.40) may be recognized as a mapping, or system of first-order difference equations, in the $(n + 1)J$ variables x^{ij}. We will not investigate the dynamic properties of this process formally, but merely indicate informally why this process will be stable under quite general conditions. In the preceding paragraph, we saw that, so long as no Pareto-optimal distribution is reached, every trader becomes better off from one period to the next. This means that every individual's utility level is a monotonically increasing function of time. It is also clear, since the total amounts of the goods are fixed, that each utility level is bounded from above. Consequently, every trader's utility level is a bounded and increasing (infinite) sequence, and so a convergent sequence. Then it is not difficult to show that the x_t^{ij} must also converge. We shall simply assume, here, that the above process converges, and turn to an examination of the limit (equilibrium) distribution.

We rewrite (14.38) as

$$(14.41) \qquad \sum_{i=1}^n \Phi_i^1 h_r^i = -h_r^0, \qquad r = 1, 2, \ldots, n,$$

where $\Phi_i^1 = \phi_i^1/\phi_0^1$. If we regard (14.41) as a system of n linear equations in the unknowns Φ_i^1, then it may be represented more compactly by using the matrix notation

$$(14.42) \qquad\qquad h\Phi^1 = h^0,$$

where h is the $n \times n$ matrix $[h_r^i]$, Φ^1 is the column vector of the Φ_i^1, and h^0 is the column vector of the $-h_r^0$.

Next, we substitute the excess demand functions defined by (14.34) into the budget constraints in (14.32), and then sum over all competitive traders. This gives

$$(14.43) \qquad\qquad \sum_{i=0}^n p_t^i h^i(p_t; \; x_{t-1}^c) = 0.$$

Differentiating (14.43) with respect to each of the n prices, we get the system

$$(14.44) \qquad \sum_{i=1}^n p_t^i h_r^i = -h_r^0 - h^r(p_t; \; x_{t-1}^c), \qquad r = 1, 2, \ldots, n.$$

However, since in equilibrium (that is, when $x_t^{ij} = x_{t-1}^{ij}$ for all i, j, and t) we have $h'(p; x^c_{t-1}) = 0$, where p denotes the equilibrium price vector, we can represent (14.44) as

(14.45) $hp = h^0.$

The linear systems (14.42) and (14.45) being identical, it follows, if we assume a unique solution, that $p = \Phi^1$. Finally, in view of (14.33), and the definition of Φ^1, we have $\Phi^1_i = \phi^1_i/\phi^1_0 = \phi^j_i/\phi^j_0$ for all i and j, which are, of course, the conditions for a Pareto-optimal distribution.

We may now summarize the model as follows: Given an initial distribution that is nonoptimal, the monopolist selects a price vector that maximizes his own utility, and goods (or claims to goods) are exchanged accordingly. This exchange of goods makes every trader better off than he was before the trade. If the resulting distribution is not Pareto-optimal, the procedure is repeated, and everybody's utility level increases once more. As a result of this process, every trader's utility level becomes an increasing (and bounded) function of time. When nobody's utility can be increased further without causing somebody else a loss in utility, i.e., when a Pareto-optimal distribution is attained, the process reaches a stationary state. Thus, while the tâtonnement process of Chapter 13 can be thought of as a computational algorithm for finding a price vector that clears all markets simultaneously, the present process may be viewed as a market mechanism for achieving a Pareto-optimal distribution.

The two-good-two-individual case may be illustrated with the aid of a diagram. The initial distribution is represented by point D_0 in the Edgeworth box shown in Fig. 14.5, and the curve C is the "offer curve" of the competitive trader. The latter curve is the locus of all tangency points between any (negatively sloped) budget line through D_0, and an indifference curve of individual

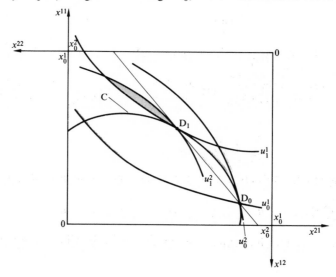

Figure 14.5

2; thus curve C indicates all the distributions that can be attained through trading. The initial distribution D_0 is assumed not to be optimal. Therefore, the monopolist (individual 1) can find at least one price vector such that the ensuing exchange will make both traders better off. The monopolist will, of course, choose that price vector which maximizes his utility. As the diagram shows, the highest level of utility that the monopolist can attain is given by the indifference curve that is tangent to the competitor's offer curve, and therefore the monopolist chooses the price vector which yields the budget line drawn in Fig. 14.5. As the diagram also shows, distribution D_1 is not Pareto-optimal, and hence the trading process will continue. To find the next distribution, that is, D_2, a new offer curve must be drawn, with D_1 as the initial distribution. Although the diagram does not show the new offer curve or the new distribution D_2, it is clear that the latter must lie somewhere inside the shaded region.

BIBLIOGRAPHICAL NOTES

Even though modern welfare economics is intimately associated with the name of V. Pareto, he did not carry out a rigorous mathematical analysis of the welfare problem. The first comprehensive mathematical treatment was undertaken by A. Bergson in "A Reformulation of Certain Aspects of Welfare Economics," *Quarterly Journal of Economics*, **52**, 310–334 (1938), and by O. Lange in "The Foundations of Welfare Economics," *Econometrica*, **10**, 215–228 (1942). Both articles are reprinted in K. J. Arrow and T. Scitovsky (eds.), *Readings in Welfare Economics*, Homewood, Ill.: Irwin, 1969, pp. 7–25, and 26–38, respectively. The former article is also reprinted in A. Bergson, *Essays in Normative Economics*, Cambridge: Harvard University Press, 1966, pp. 3–26. Generalizations of these initial results, as well as different formulations of the welfare problem, may be found in K. J. Arrow, "An Extension of the Basic Theorems of Classical Welfare Economics," in J. Neyman (ed.), *Proceedings of the Second Berkeley Symposium on Mathematical Statistics and Probability*, Berkeley: University of California Press, 1951, pp. 507–532, reprinted in P. Newman (ed.), *Readings in Mathematical Economics*, Volume 1, Baltimore: The Johns Hopkins Press, 1968, pp. 365–390; T. Koopmans, "Competitive Equilibrium and Pareto Optimality," in *Three Essays on the State of Economic Science*, New York: McGraw-Hill, 1957, Chapter 2 of Essay 1; G. Debreu, *Theory of Value* (Cowles Foundation Monograph No. 17), New York: Wiley, 1959, Chapter 6; and L. Hurwicz, "Optimality and Informational Efficiency in Resource Allocation," in K. J. Arrow, S. Karlin, and P. Suppes (eds.), *Mathematical Methods in the Social Sciences, 1959*, Stanford: Stanford University Press, 1960, pp. 27–46, reprinted in K. J. Arrow and T. Scitovsky (eds.), *Readings in Welfare Economics*, Homewood, Ill.: Irwin, 1969, pp. 61–80.

Over the years, a substantial number of books have been published in which various aspects of welfare economics, theoretical and others, are examined. Among these are the following: A. P. Lerner, *The Economics of Control*, New York: Macmillan, 1944; M. W. Reder, *Studies in the Theory of Welfare Economics*, New York: Columbia University Press, 1947; I. M. D. Little, *A Critique of Welfare Economics*, Oxford: Oxford University Press, 1950; K. J. Arrow, *Social Choice and Individual Values* (Cowles Foundation Monograph No. 12), New York: Wiley,

1951; W. J. Baumol, *Welfare Economics and the Theory of the State*, Cambridge: Harvard University Press, 1952; J. de V. Graaff, *Theoretical Welfare Economics*, Cambridge: Cambridge University Press, 1957; and J. Rothenberg, *The Measurement of Social Welfare*, Englewood Cliffs, N.J.: Prentice-Hall, 1961. A summary of the principal theorems of welfare economics may be found in J. Quirk and R. Saposnik, *Introduction to General Equilibrium Theory and Welfare Economics*, New York: McGraw-Hill, 1968, Chapter 4.

One of the important questions of welfare economics has to do with the behavioral rules that will ensure the attainment of a Pareto-optimal state, in particular under conditions of imperfect competition. Some aspects of this issue are reviewed and discussed in the following two articles by N. Ruggles: "The Welfare Basis of the Marginal Cost Pricing Principle," *Review of Economic Studies*, **17,** 29–46 (1949), and "Recent Developments in the Theory of Marginal Cost Pricing," *Review of Economic Studies*, **17,** 107–126 (1950). Two examples in which the optimality of imperfect markets is analyzed are K. J. Arrow and L. Hurwicz, "Decentralization and Computation in Resource Allocation," in R. W. Pfouts (ed.), *Essays in Economics and Econometrics*, Chapel Hill: University of North Carolina Press, 1960, pp. 34–104, and J. Hadar, "Optimality of Imperfectly Competitive Resource Allocation," *Western Economic Journal*, **7,** 51–56 (1969).

A more general framework for dealing with the implications of imperfections in an economic system is the *theory of the second best*. Some recent papers in this area are: R. G. Lipsey and K. Lancaster, "The General Theory of Second Best," *Review of Economic Studies*, **24,** 11–32 (1956); O. A. Davis and A. B. Whinston, "Welfare Economics and the Theory of Second Best," *Review of Economic Studies*, **32,** 1–14 (1965); P. Bohm, "On the Theory of 'Second Best'," *Review of Economic Studies*, **34,** 301–314 (1967); T. Negishi, "The Perceived Demand Curve in the Theory of Second Best," *Review of Economic Studies*, **34,** 315–316 (1967); M. McManus, "Private and Social Costs in the Theory of Second Best," *Review of Economic Studies*, **34,** 317–321 (1967); and O. A. Davis and A. B. Whinston, "Piecemeal Policy in the Theory of Second Best," *Review of Economic Studies*, **34,** 323–331 (1967).

A survey of welfare economics, including an extensive bibliography, can be found in E. J. Mishan, "A Survey of Welfare Economics, 1939–59," *Economic Journal*, **70,** 197–256 (1960). This survey is reprinted in E. J. Mishan, *Welfare Economics*, New York: Random House, 1964, pp. 3–94, and *Surveys of Economic Theory*, Volume 1, London: Macmillan, 1965, pp. 154–222.

CHAPTER 15

REVIEW OF MATHEMATICS

15.1 DIFFERENTIAL CALCULUS

15.1.1 General Concepts

One of the most frequently used concepts in mathematics is that of a *function*. In general, a function may be thought of as a rule of correspondence between the elements of two sets; one of these is called the *domain* of the function, the other is called the *range* of the function. With each element in the domain, the function associates a unique element in the range. An element in the domain of the function is called a *point*, while an element in the range is called the *value* of the function. In this review, we will be concerned only with functions whose domain and range contain real numbers. If the domain consists of the set of real numbers (also referred to as the *real line*) or a subset thereof (for example, the nonnegative *half-line*), the function is said to be *one-dimensional*; if the elements in the domain are points in a space of higher dimensions (such as points in a plane, a cube, and so on), the function is *multidimensional*.

A function is commonly represented symbolically by a letter such as f or g, or a Greek letter such as ϕ or ψ. The elements of the domain are usually denoted by x (or some other letter), and particular elements in the domain may be identified by subscripts attached to the letter denoting the elements of the domain; for example, x_0, x_1, and so on. The value of a function f at a point x is denoted by $f(x)$. When, to avoid confusion, one wishes to identify the elements of the domain on which a function f is defined, the notation $f(x)$ may also be used to denote the function f (rather than its value at a particular point). Sometimes, x is referred to as the *independent variable*, and y, where $y = f(x)$, as the *dependent variable*.

15.1.2 One-dimensional Functions

Monotonicity. If for all pairs of points x_0 and x_1 in some set S in the domain of the function it is true that, if $x_1 > x_0$, then $f(x_1) \geqslant f(x_0)$, then $f(x)$ is said to be an *increasing* function in S. If the preceding statement holds with a *strict* inequality between the functional values, $f(x)$ is said to be *strictly increasing* in S. If the inequality between the functional values is reversed, $f(x)$ is a *decreasing* (or strictly decreasing) function. If a function is either increasing or decreasing (but not both) in S, it is said to be *monotonic* (or strictly monotonic) in S. The set S may, of course, be the entire domain on which the function is defined.

Limits and Continuity. Frequently, it is of interest to know how the values of a function behave as the independent variable approaches some particular point; that is, one may ask: "What happens to $f(x)$ as x approaches x_0?" It will often be the case that as x approaches x_0, the value $f(x)$ will approach some number, say L. In that case, we say that as x approaches x_0, the function approaches the (finite) limit L. This statement is usually written in the short-hand notation

$$\lim_{x \to x_0} f(x) = L.$$

A formal way of *defining* the limit L is the following: For every positive number ε (no matter how small) there exists another positive number δ (which, in general, depends on ε) such that

$$\text{if } |x - x_0| < \delta, \text{ then } |f(x) - L| < \varepsilon.$$

The vertical bars in the above notation indicate absolute values.

Essentially, the existence of a limit value, such as L in the above example, means that the function $f(x)$ will take on a value which is as close to L as one may desire, provided the argument of the function (that is, the independent variable x) takes a value that is sufficiently close to x_0. Or, put differently, the functional value $f(x)$ can be made to lie in any prespecified neighborhood (interval) around L (no matter how small) if x is chosen from a sufficiently small neighborhood around x_0. It is important to note that the idea of a limit is concerned only with the behavior of a function as its argument *approaches* some point such as x_0, but not with the value of the function *at* the point x_0. Therefore, $\lim_{x \to x_0} f(x)$ may exist even if the function is itself not defined at x_0, that is, even if x_0 is not an element of the domain of definition. It is also possible that the limit may exist if the function is defined at x_0, but its value at x_0 is different from the limit as x approaches x_0.

Limits (whenever they exist) obey certain operational rules, as stated below:

a) The limit of a weighted sum (difference) of functions is equal to the weighted sum (difference) of the limits of the functions; that is, for any two real numbers a and b,

$$\lim_{x \to x_0} [af(x) + bg(x)] = a \lim_{x \to x_0} f(x) + b \lim_{x \to x_0} g(x).$$

b) The limit of the product of two functions is equal to the product of the limits of the functions, that is,

$$\lim_{x \to x_0} [f(x)g(x)] = \lim_{x \to x_0} f(x) \cdot \lim_{x \to x_0} g(x).$$

c) The limit of the quotient of two functions is equal to the quotient of the limits of the functions, provided the limit in the denominator is not zero; that is,

$$\lim_{x \to x_0} \frac{f(x)}{g(x)} = \frac{\lim_{x \to x_0} f(x)}{\lim_{x \to x_0} g(x)} \quad if \quad \lim_{x \to x_0} g(x) \neq 0.$$

For most functions in our analysis, it is true that as x approaches x_0, the function approaches a limit which is equal to the value of the function at x_0. In which case, the function $f(x)$ is said to be *continuous* at x_0. Formally, the function $f(x)$ is said to be continuous at x_0 if

i) $f(x)$ is defined at x_0,

ii) $\lim_{x \to x_0} f(x) = f(x_0)$.

Condition (ii) may also be stated in the following equivalent form:

ii′) $\lim_{x \to x_0} f(x) = f\left(\lim_{x \to x_0} x \right)$

In terms of neighborhoods, we can say that $f(x)$ is continuous at x_0 if it is defined at x_0, and if for each positive number ε there exists a positive number δ such that

$$if \quad |x - x_0| < \delta, \quad then \quad |f(x) - f(x_0)| < \varepsilon.$$

A function is said to be continuous in its domain of definition if it is continuous at every point in the domain. If a function is not continuous at some point in its domain, it is said to be *discontinuous* at that point.

The property of continuity is invariant to elementary operations, as stated in the rules below:

a) If the functions $f(x)$ and $g(x)$ are continuous at x_0, then the function $af(x) + bg(x)$ is also continuous at x_0, where a and b are real numbers.

b) If the functions $f(x)$ and $g(x)$ are continuous at x_0, then the function $f(x) \cdot g(x)$ is also continuous at x_0.

c) If the functions $f(x)$ and $g(x)$ are continuous at x_0, then the function $f(x)/g(x)$ is also continuous at x_0, provided $g(x_0) \neq 0$.

Continuous functions have certain properties, of which we shall state two. These properties hold for continuous functions defined on a (finite) *closed* interval, say $[x_0, x_1]$. (An interval is said to be closed if it contains its endpoints, and is sometimes denoted by $x_0 \leqslant x \leqslant x_1$.)

Proposition 15.1. *If the function $f(x)$ is continuous on the closed interval $[x_0, x_1]$, then it is bounded on that interval; that is, there exist two real numbers, say M and N, such that $M \leqslant f(x) \leqslant N$ for all x in the interval.*

Proposition 15.2. *If the function $f(x)$ is continuous on the closed interval* $[x_0, x_1]$, *then it attains an absolute maximum and an absolute minimum on that interval.*

Derivatives. For any two distinct points x and x_0 in the domain of a function $f(x)$, the ratio

$$\frac{f(x) - f(x_0)}{x - x_0}$$

is called the *difference quotient*. If we think of x_0 as a fixed point, and let x be a variable point, then the difference quotient is a function of x. If the latter function has a limit as x approaches x_0, this limit is called the *derivative of $f(x)$ at x_0*; that is, if

$$\lim_{x \to x_0} \left[\frac{f(x) - f(x_0)}{x - x_0} \right]$$

exists, then $f(x)$ has a derivative at x_0. In which case, the function $f(x)$ is said to be *differentiable* at x_0. The derivative of $f(x)$ is a function denoted by either f' of df/dx; the value of the derivative function at the point x_0 is denoted by $f'(x_0)$. If a function has a derivative at every point in its domain, it is said to be differentiable (or everywhere differentiable).

If in some interval of the domain of definition the derivative of a function $f(x)$ is always positive, it follows that $f(x)$ is strictly increasing in that interval; if the derivative is always negative, then the function is strictly decreasing; and if the derivative is always zero, then $f(x)$ is a constant function.

Like continuity, differentiability is invariant to elementary operations. If the functions $f(x)$ and $g(x)$ have a derivative at the point x_0, then the functions $af(x) + bg(x), g(x) \cdot f(x)$, and $f(x)/g(x)$ also have a derivative at x_0. The formulas for the derivatives of these latter functions are stated below:

a) $\dfrac{d[af(x) + bg(x)]}{dx} = af' + bg'.$

b) $\dfrac{d[f(x)g(x)]}{dx} = f(x)g' + f'g(x).$

c) $\dfrac{d[f(x)/g(x)]}{dx} = \dfrac{f'g(x) - f(x)g'}{[g(x)]^2}, \qquad provided\ g(x) \neq 0.$

Differentiability implies continuity as well as a stronger condition known as a *Lipschitz condition*. The latter is defined as follows:

If there exists a positive number k such that for all x in some neighborhood of the point x_0 it is true that

$$|f(x) - f(x_0)| \leqslant k|x - x_0|,$$

then the function $f(x)$ is said to satisfy a Lipschitz condition with constant k at x_0.

The relationship between differentiability, continuity, and the Lipschitz condition may be stated as follows:

Proposition 15.3. *If a function is differentiable at a point x_0, then it satisfies a Lipschitz condition at x_0.*

Proposition 15.4. *If a function satisfies a Lipschitz condition at x_0, then it is continuous at x_0.*

The two propositions taken together imply, of course, that if a function is differentiable at some point, then it is continuous at that point.

The Lipschitz condition, as defined above, is a local condition, inasmuch as it applies only in some neighborhood around a given point. It may also be defined as a global condition, in which case it holds for any two points in the domain of the function, or in a subset thereof. A sufficient condition for a global Lipschitz condition is given in the following proposition:

Proposition 15.5. *If there exists a positive constant k such that $|f'| \leqslant k$ in some interval, then for any two points x_1 and x_2 in that interval, the following inequality holds:*

$$|f(x_1) - f(x_2)| \leqslant k|x_1 - x_2|.$$

A derivative is a function of the same variable as the original function. Since it is a function, the derivative may also be differentiated. If $f'(x)$ is differentiable, its derivative is denoted by either $f''(x)$ or d^2f/dx^2, and is called the *second derivative* of $f(x)$. Similarly, the derivative of $f''(x)$ is denoted by $f'''(x)$, and is called the *third derivative* of $f(x)$, and so on. In general, a function may have derivatives of any order.

A frequently invoked mathematical result is the *Theorem of the Mean* (or Mean Value Theorem). It is stated in the following proposition:

Proposition 15.6. (*Theorem of the Mean.*) *If the function $f(x)$ is continuous on a closed interval $[x_0, x_1]$, and is differentiable everywhere in the interval (except possibly at the endpoints) then there exists a point in the interior of the interval, say ξ, such that*

$$f(x_1) = f(x_0) + f'(\xi)(x_1 - x_0),$$

or equivalently,

$$\frac{f(x_1) - f(x_0)}{x_1 - x_0} = f'(\xi).$$

What the theorem says, in effect, is that the difference quotient with respect to the endpoints of the interval is equal to the value of the derivative at some point in the interior of the interval.

A generalization of the Theorem of the Mean is *Taylor's formula with remainder*. According to this generalization, a function may be represented as a polynomial of degree n, provided it has derivatives up to order n. More precisely:

Proposition 15.7.   *(Taylor's formula with remainder.) If the function $f(x)$ has continuous derivatives up to order $n-1$ on some closed interval, and if the nth derivative exists and is finite at every point inside the interval, then for every variable point x and fixed point x_0, both in the interval, there exists a point ξ between x and x_0 such that*

$$f(x) = f(x_0) + f^1(x_0)(x - x_0) + \frac{f^2(x_0)(x - x_0)^2}{2!} + \frac{f^3(x_0)(x - x_0)^3}{3!}$$

$$+ \cdots + \frac{f^{n-1}(x_0)(x - x_0)^{n-1}}{(n-1)!} + \frac{f^n(\xi)(x - x_0)^n}{n!},$$

where f^i denotes the ith derivative of $f(x)$.

Since it is not usually possible (at best, very difficult) to find the point ξ, the remainder term will be unknown. In which case, the first n terms of the formula provide an approximation of the value of the function around the point x_0. It can be seen that the Theorem of the Mean is a special case of Taylor's formula with remainder obtained by letting $n = 1$.

A function may also be represented without a remainder term. Then the representation is an infinite series known as *Taylor's series*, and it takes the form

$$f(x) = f(x_0) + f^1(x_0)(x - x_0) + \frac{f^2(x_0)(x - x_0)^2}{2!}$$

$$+ \frac{f^3(x_0)(x - x_0)^3}{3!} + \cdots + \frac{f^n(x_0)(x - x_0)^n}{n!} + \cdots$$

Thus, if a function has only a finite number of nonvanishing derivatives at x_0, it may be correctly represented by a finite number of terms of the above sum. For example, a quadratic function is represented by the first three terms of the series. However, if a function has an infinite number of nonvanishing derivatives at x_0 (as in the case of an exponential function), then any finite number of terms of Taylor's series will yield only an approximation of the correct representation.

In the event that $x_0 = 0$, the above series is known as *Maclaurin's series*.

15.1.3 Extreme Points: One-dimensional Functions

Most problems in the context of microeconomic theory are concerned with some form of optimization (that is, maximization or minimization). This brings us to the problem of *extreme points*, that is, points at which a function has either a maximum or a minimum. In connection with this, we may raise two important questions.

    a) Under what conditions will a function possess an extreme point?

    b) If a function has an extreme point, how can one find it?

Suppose that the function $f(x)$ is defined on some interval $[x_0, x_1]$. Then the function is said to have a *relative* (or local) maximum at the point $\bar{x}$ (which is in the above interval) if there exists a neighborhood around $\bar{x}$, say $N(\bar{x})$, such that $f(\bar{x}) > f(x)$ for all x in $N(\bar{x})$, and $x \neq \bar{x}$. If $f(\bar{x}) > f(x)$ for all $x \neq \bar{x}$ in the entire interval $[x_0, x_1]$, then at $\bar{x}$ the function $f(x)$ has an *absolute* (or global) maximum. If, in the preceding statements, the inequalities are reversed, then $\bar{x}$ defines a minimum point. For simplicity, we exclude from the discussion so-called *weak* extreme points. These are defined by converting the strict inequalities in the above definitions into weak inequalities. (Examples of weak extreme points are the points on a horizontal line.)

It is convenient to separate the discussion into three different cases, depending on the nature of the domain of the function under consideration.

Compact Domain. We have earlier indicated (in Proposition 15.2) that if a function is continuous on a compact (that is, closed and bounded) interval, then it attains an absolute maximum and an absolute minimum on that interval. In which case, the existence of an extreme point is guaranteed. The problem of finding such a point, however, is not so simple; in fact, there exists no general rule that can be used for this purpose. We must again distinguish between different cases.

    a) Interior Extrema. If the extreme point $\bar{x}$ is located in the interior of the domain, then at $\bar{x}$ the first derivative of the function vanishes (assuming differentiability). The extreme point may be either a maximum or a minimum. If the second derivative at $\bar{x}$ is negative, the function has a maximum at $\bar{x}$; if the second derivative is positive, $\bar{x}$ furnishes a minimum. Of course, the second derivative may also be equal to zero at $\bar{x}$, in which case it is necessary to examine higher-order derivatives. The general rule is that, if the first non-vanishing derivative (at $\bar{x}$) is of even order (and at least of order two), then the function has a maximum at $\bar{x}$ if the nonvanishing derivative is negative, while a minimum is obtained if this derivative is positive. If the first nonvanishing derivative is odd, then at $\bar{x}$ the function has neither a maximum nor a minimum.

If at an interior extreme point the second derivative does not vanish, it is customary to refer to such a case as a *regular* maximum or minimum, as the case may be. For such cases, we may state the following:

> **Proposition 15.8.**   *The function $f(x)$ has a regular local maximum at the interior point $\bar{x}$ if and only if $f'(\bar{x}) = 0$, and $f''(\bar{x}) < 0$. For a regular local minimum the inequality is reversed.*

It may be noted that we have said nothing about the uniqueness of the point x. Clearly, the derivative conditions merely indicate whether a particular extreme point is a maximum or a minimum; they convey no information about whether the extreme point is an absolute or a relative extreme point. For instance, if there exists only one point x satisfying the conditions of the above proposition, then $\bar{x}$ furnishes an absolute maximum (or minimum). Of course, an absolute maximum (minimum) is also a relative maximum (minimum), but not vice versa. In general, the uniqueness of an extreme point must either be assumed, or guaranteed by imposing appropriate conditions on the function. Some possible cases are illustrated in Figs. 15.1 and 15.2.

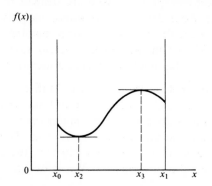

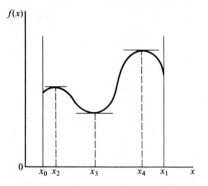

Fig. 15.1. $f(x_2)$ is an absolute minimum; $f(x_3)$ is an absolute maximum.

Fig. 15.2. $f(x_2)$ is a relative maximum; $f(x_3)$ is an absolute minimum; $f(x_4)$ is an absolute maximum.

b) Boundary Extrema.   If a boundary point of the domain of definition is an extreme point (and every boundary point is necessarily an extreme point), it is not necessary for the first derivative to vanish at that point. If x_0 and x_1 are the lower and upper boundary points, respectively, the following rules hold:

If point x_0 furnishes a relative maximum, then $f'(x_0) \leqslant 0$.

If point x_0 furnishes a relative minimum, then $f'(x_0) \geqslant 0$.

If point x_1 furnishes a relative maximum, then $f'(x_1) \geqslant 0$.

If point x_1 furnishes a relative minimum, then $f'(x_1) \leqslant 0$.

In these statements, however, the symbol $f'(x_0)$ represents a *right-hand* derivative, while $f'(x_1)$ is a *left-hand* derivative. (A right-hand derivative is the limit of the difference quotient as the variable point x approaches the fixed point x_0 *from the right*. A similar definition holds for a left-hand derivative.)

Unbounded Domain. If a function is defined on an unbounded domain (that is, the entire real line), and it has an extreme point, then such a point must necessarily be in the interior of the domain. In which case, the discussion in subsection (a) applies. Of course, a function defined on the entire real line may not have an extreme point. For example, the function $f(x) = x^3$ has neither a maximum nor a minimum.

Domain Bounded from Below. Many economic variables are nonnegative in nature, and so functions of such variables are defined on the nonnegative half-line; that is, for all $x \geqslant 0$. It is clear that, in this case, the origin (the point $x = 0$) is an extreme point. The nature of this point may, therefore, be determined by examining the right-hand derivative at that point. If the function also possesses interior extrema, then Proposition 15.8 applies. We emphasize again that there exists no simple rule for determining whether a particular extreme point is a relative or an absolute extreme point. Of course, by computing the value of the function at all its extreme points, one will be able to identify the relative and the absolute extreme points. A few examples are shown in Figs. 15.3 through 15.5.

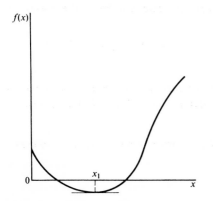
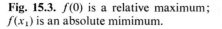
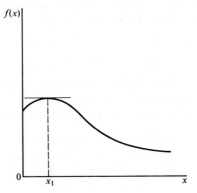

Fig. 15.3. $f(0)$ is a relative maximum; $f(x_1)$ is an absolute mimimum.

Fig. 15.4. $f(0)$ is a relative minimum; $f(x_1)$ is an absolute maximum.

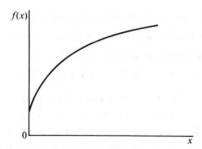

Fig. 15.5. $f(0)$ is an absolute minimum.

15.1.4   Multidimensional Functions

Let us now generalize the concepts and propositions discussed in Section 15.1.2 to functions of several variables. A function of n variables may be thought of as a mapping from points in an n-dimensional Euclidean space to points on the real line. Thus, the argument of an n-dimensional function is an n-dimensional vector $x = (x^1, x^2, ..., x^n)$, while the value of the function, $f(x)$, is a real number. Throughout this section we assume that $n \geqslant 2$.

Limits and Continuity.   We say that a function $f(x)$ has a limit as x approaches x_0, if the value of the function approaches a particular number. If such a limit exists, we write

$$\lim_{x \to x_0} f(x) = L.$$

Here, the notation $x \to x_0$ means $x^1 \to x_0^1$, $x^2 \to x_0^2$, ..., $x^n \to x_0^n$. In terms of neighborhoods, we may say that the value of the function will lie in any prespecified neighborhood around L if the point x is in a sufficiently small neighborhood around x_0. A neighborhood around a point such as x_0 may be defined in a number of different ways, one of which is as a "sphere." Thus, if the limit L exists, then for every positive number ε there exists a positive number δ such that

$$\text{if} \quad (x^1 - x_0^1)^2 + (x^2 - x_0^2)^2 + \cdots + (x^n - x_0^n)^2 < \delta^2,$$

$$\text{then} \quad |f(x) - L| < \varepsilon.$$

The algebra of limits is a straightforward generalization of the one-dimensional case. If the functions $f(x)$ and $g(x)$ have limits L and L', respectively, at the point x_0, then we have:

a) $\lim_{x \to x_0} [af(x) + bg(x)] = aL + bL'$,   *where a and b are real numbers.*

b) $\lim_{x \to x_0} [f(x)g(x)] = L \cdot L'$.

c) $\lim_{x \to x_0} \dfrac{f(x)}{g(x)} = \dfrac{L}{L'}$,   *provided* $L' \neq 0$.

If the function $f(x)$ is defined at the point x_0, and if its limit at that point is equal to $f(x_0)$, then the function is continuous at that point. In terms of neighborhoods, if the function is continuous at x_0, then for every positive number ε there exists a positive number δ such that

$$|f(x) - f(x_0)| < \varepsilon \qquad \text{whenever} \qquad \sum_{i=1}^{n} (x^i - x_0^i)^2 < \delta^2.$$

According to the algebra of continuous functions, if the functions $f(x)$ and $g(x)$ are continuous at the point x_0, then the functions $af(x) + bg(x)$, and $f(x)g(x)$ are also continuous at x_0, and so is the function $f(x)/g(x)$, provided $g(x_0) \neq 0$.

The generalization of Propositions 15.1 and 15.2 is as follows:

Proposition 15.9. *If a function is continuous over a compact region, then the value of the function is bounded in that region.*

Proposition 15.10. *If a function is continuous over a compact region, then it attains an absolute maximum and an absolute minimum in that region.*

Partial Derivatives. If we fix any $n - 1$ components of the vector x, and let the remaining, say ith, component vary, then if the function $f(x)$ has a derivative with respect to the variable x^i, the latter derivative is referred to as a *partial derivative*. The partial derivative may be denoted by $\partial f/\partial x^i$ or f_i. Like the derivative of a single-variable function, the partial derivative is defined as the limit of a difference quotient. Thus, if

$$\lim_{x^i \to x_0^i} \left[\frac{f(x_0^1, x_0^2, \ldots, x_0^{i-1}, x^i, x_0^{i+1}, \ldots, x_0^n) - f(x_0)}{x^i - x_0^i} \right]$$

exists, $f(x)$ has a first-order partial derivative f_i at the point x_0. The same definition applies to the other components of x.

Suppose now that, starting at the point x_0, each component x^i is given some increment Δx^i (positive, zero, or negative). Then the resulting increment in the value of the function $y = f(x)$ is denoted by Δy, and we have

$$\Delta y = f(x_0^1 + \Delta x^1, x_0^2 + \Delta x^2, \ldots, x_0^n + \Delta x^n) - f(x_0).$$

One may be interested in obtaining an approximation for Δy, at least when the Δx^i are relatively small. Such an approximation may be given by the function

$$dy = f_1 \Delta x^1 + f_2 \Delta x^2 + \cdots + f_n \Delta x^n,$$

where the functions f_i are evaluated at the point x_0. The function dy is an approximation of Δy, provided the difference $\Delta y - dy$ is sufficiently small relative to the Δx^i. More precisely, if

$$\lim_{\Delta x \to 0} \left[\frac{\Delta y - \sum_{i=1}^{n} f_i \Delta x^i}{\sum_{i=1}^{n} |\Delta x^i|} \right] = 0,$$

where $\Delta x = (\Delta x^1, \Delta x^2, ..., \Delta x^n)$, then dy is called the *differential* of $f(x)$, and the function $f(x)$ is said to be differentiable at the point x_0. The differential dy is sometimes written as

$$\sum_{i=1}^{n} f_i \, dx^i,$$

where the dx^i are considered as independent variables. As it turns out, the existence of the partial derivatives f_i does not necessarily imply the existence of a differential; but the converse is true. Two fundamental propositions concerning differentiability are stated below.

Proposition 15.11. *If a function has a differential at a point, then all its partial derivatives at that point exist.*

Proposition 15.12. *If all the partial derivatives of a function are continuous at a point, then the function has a differential at that point.*

Higher-order partial derivatives are defined in a similar fashion, and may be obtained by partially differentiating a partial derivative. Thus, differentiation of $f_i(x)$ with respect to x^j yields the second-order partial derivative $\partial^2 f / \partial x^i \, \partial x^j$, which may also be denoted by f_{ij}. If the first- and second-order partial derivatives are continuous, then to obtain the second-order cross derivative f_{ij}, it is immaterial in which order the differentiation is carried out; that is, one may first differentiate f with respect to x^i, and then differentiate the resulting first-order derivative with respect to x^j, or differentiate first with respect to x^j, and then with respect to x^i. Both procedures yield the same derivative, which means that, given the above continuity conditions, $f_{ij} = f_{ji}$.

We now introduce the concept of the *norm* (or length) of a vector. The norm of a vector x is denoted by $|x|$, and may be defined in several ways. Two frequently used definitions are

a) $|x| = \max |x^i|$,

b) $|x| = \sqrt{\sum_{i=1}^{n} (x^i)^2}.$

According to the first definition, the norm is simply equal to the magnitude of its largest component. According to the second, the norm is defined as the Euclidean distance of the vector from the origin. Fortunately, most theorems which make use of the norm of a vector hold for either definition.

We now make use of the norm in the definition of a Lipschitz condition for a function of several variables.

If there exists a positive number k such that for all x in some neighborhood of the point x_0 it is true that

$$|f(x) - f(x_0)| \leqslant k|x - x_0|,$$

then the function $f(x)$ is said to satisfy a Lipschitz condition with constant k at x_0.

Note that in this inequality, the vertical bars on the left-hand side indicate the absolute value of a real number, while on the right-hand side they indicate the norm of a vector (in this case, the difference between the vectors x and x_0).

As in the case of a single-variable function, differentiability implies a Lipschitz condition, which implies continuity. These relationships were already stated in Propositions 15.3 and 15.4 for single-variable functions; they are valid for multivariable functions, as stated. The global version of the Lipschitz condition is taken up in the next proposition.

Proposition 15.13. *If there exists a positive constant k such that*

$$\sum_{i=1}^{n} |f_i| \leqslant k$$

in some region, then for any two points x_1 and x_2 in that region, the following inequality holds:

$$|f(x_1) - f(x_2)| \leqslant k|x_1 - x_2|,$$

where $|x_1 - x_2| = \max |x_1^i - x_2^i|$.

If $f(x)$ is differentiable in some region, we can generalize the Theorem of the Mean (Proposition 15.6) to functions of several variables.

Proposition 15.14. (*Theorem of the Mean.*) *If $f(x)$ is differentiable in some region R, and if for any two points x_0 and x_1 in R the line segment between x_0 and x_1 is also in R, (that is, R is a convex region), then for any variable point x in R and any fixed point x_0 in R there exists a point ξ on the line segment between x_0 and x_1 such that*

$$f(x) = f(x_0) + \sum_{i=1}^{n} f_i(\xi)\,(x^i - x_0^i).$$

Implicit Functions. We frequently encounter functions of several variables which are of the general form $F(x^1, x^2, ..., x^n) = 0$. The question then arises as to whether this equation has an explicit "solution"; in other words, one wants to know whether it is possible to express one of the variables explicitly as some function of the remaining variables. The answer to this depends on the partial derivatives of the function $F(x)$. Thus, if $F(x)$ has continuous first-order partial derivatives at some point x_0 at which $F(x_0) = 0$, and also $F_i(x_0) \neq 0$, then for some values around the x_0^j, $j \neq i$, there exists a function f such that $x^i = f(x^{-i})$, where $x^{-i} = (x^1, x^2, ..., x^{i-1}, x^{i+1}, ..., x^n)$. The function $f(x^{-i})$ satisfies the equation

$$F[x^1, x^2, ..., x^{i-1}, f(x^{-i}), x^{i+1}, ..., x^n] = 0,$$

and it is differentiable; its partial derivatives in some neighborhood around x_0^{-i} are given by

$$f_j(x^{-i}) = \frac{-F_j[x^1, x^2, ..., x^{i-1}, f(x^{-i}), x^{i+1}, ..., x^n]}{F_i[x^1, x^2, ..., x^{i-1}, f(x^{-i}), x^{i+1}, ..., x^n]}.$$

The general case of implicit functions occurs when n variables are related by a set of m, $m < n$, implicit equations. To simplify the notation, we divide the n variables into two sets: one set of m variables will be represented by the vector $y = (y^1, y^2, ..., y^m)$, and the remaining $n - m$ variables are represented by the vector $x = (x^1, x^2, ..., x^{n-m})$. The system of implicit functions can then be written as

$$F^1(y^1, y^2, ..., y^m; \ x^1, x^2, ..., x^{n-m}) = 0,$$
$$F^2(y^1, y^2, ..., y^m; \ x^1, x^2, ..., x^{n-m}) = 0,$$
$$\vdots \qquad\qquad\qquad\qquad \vdots$$
$$F^m(y^1, y^2, ..., y^m; \ x^1, x^2, ..., x^{n-m}) = 0,$$

or, in vector notation, $F(y; x) = 0$.

In general, one may solve such a system for as many variables as there are equations; that is, for m variables as functions of the remaining $n - m$ variables. As in the one-equation case, the existence of an explicit solution depends on a condition involving the derivatives of the functions F^i. In the multiequation case, this condition involves a determinant of the partial derivatives of the m functions F^i with respect to the m variables that are to be solved for explicitly. (Determinants are defined in Section 15.2.2.) In the present example, the determinant may be denoted by

$$\frac{\partial(F^1, F^2, ..., F^m)}{\partial(y^1, y^2, ..., y^m)} = \begin{vmatrix} F_1^1 & F_2^1 & \cdots & F_m^1 \\ F_1^2 & F_2^2 & \cdots & F_m^2 \\ \vdots & & & \vdots \\ F_1^m & F_2^m & \cdots & F_m^m \end{vmatrix},$$

where $F_j^i = \partial F^i / \partial y^j$, $i, j = 1, 2, ..., m$. A still more compact notation for

submatrices of the Hessian matrix. In fact, it can be seen that each of the above determinants, up to order $(n - 1) \times (n - 1)$, is a *principal minor* of the Hessian matrix. (Principal minors are defined in Section 15.2.2.)

The point $\bar{x}$ is a relative minimum if the quadratic form is *positive definite*, which in turn is equivalent to the condition that the Hessian and all its principal minors are positive.

If $\bar{x}$ is a *regular* extreme point (that is, either a regular maximum or a regular minimum), then the vanishing of the first-order partial derivatives and the definiteness of the appropriate quadratic form together constitute a set of necessary and sufficient conditions. We emphasize again that these conditions do not guarantee the uniqueness of the extreme point $\bar{x}$, consequently, we cannot invoke these rules to determine whether $\bar{x}$ furnishes an absolute maximum (minimum).

Constrained Extrema. Suppose that the components of the vector x are restricted to values satisfying the side condition $g(x) = 0$, where $g(x)$ is assumed to be differentiable. We refer to the values of x satisfying the side condition as the *constraint set*, and denote it by C.

A convenient method for analyzing constrained optimization problems is to form the function

$$L(x, \lambda) = f(x) + \lambda g(x).$$

The function $L(x, \lambda)$ is called the *Lagrangian function*, and λ is called a *Lagrange multiplier*. Then, if $f(x)$ has an extreme point in the interior of the constraint set C, say at $\bar{x}$, there exists some value of λ, say $\bar{\lambda}$, such that the function $L(x, \lambda)$ has an extreme point with respect to x at the point $(\bar{x}, \bar{\lambda})$. Therefore, the first-order partial derivatives of $L(x, \lambda)$ with respect to x must vanish at $\bar{x}$. Hence, the first-order conditions for an interior extreme point are

$$f_i(\bar{x}) + \bar{\lambda} g(\bar{x}) = 0, \qquad i = 1, 2, ..., n,$$

and $$g(\bar{x}) = 0.$$

It is also assumed that $g_i(\bar{x}) \neq 0$ for some i.

The second-order conditions, as in the unconstrained problem, can be stated in terms of the associated quadratic form, except that the variables of the quadratic form are constrained by the side condition. Thus, the constrained extreme point $\bar{x}$ is a relative maximum if

$$\sum_{i=1}^{n} \sum_{j=1}^{n} [f_{ij}(\bar{x}) + \bar{\lambda} g_{ij}(\bar{x})] y^i y^j < 0$$

for all values of the ys satisfying

$$\sum_{i=1}^{n} g_i(\bar{x}) y^i = 0, \qquad \text{not all the } y^i = 0.$$

An equivalent statement of the above conditions is the following:

$$
\begin{vmatrix}
f_{11} + \lambda g_{11} & f_{12} + \lambda g_{12} & g_1 \\
f_{21} + \lambda g_{21} & f_{22} + \lambda g_{22} & g_2 \\
g_1 & g_2 & 0
\end{vmatrix} > 0,
$$

$$
\begin{vmatrix}
f_{11} + \lambda g_{11} & f_{12} + \lambda g_{12} & f_{13} + \lambda g_{13} & g_1 \\
f_{21} + \lambda g_{21} & f_{22} + \lambda g_{22} & f_{23} + \lambda g_{23} & g_2 \\
f_{31} + \lambda g_{31} & f_{32} + \lambda g_{32} & f_{33} + \lambda g_{33} & g_3 \\
g_1 & g_2 & g_3 & 0
\end{vmatrix} < 0,
$$

$$
\dots, (-1)^n
\begin{vmatrix}
f_{11} + \lambda g_{11} & f_{12} + \lambda g_{12} & \dots & f_{1n} + \lambda g_{1n} & g_1 \\
f_{21} + \lambda g_{21} & f_{22} + \lambda g_{22} & \dots & f_{2n} + \lambda g_{2n} & g_2 \\
\vdots & & & & \vdots \\
f_{n1} + \lambda g_{n1} & f_{n2} + \lambda g_{n2} & \dots & f_{nn} + \lambda g_{nn} & g_n \\
g_1 & g_2 & \dots & g_n & 0
\end{vmatrix} > 0.
$$

To simplify the notation, we have omitted the arguments of the functions f_{ij} and g_{ij}, but it should be clear that, in evaluating the above determinants, all the functions are to be evaluated at the extreme point $\bar{x}$; furthermore, the appropriate value for the Lagrange multiplier is that which satisfies the first-order conditions, namely, $\bar{\lambda}$. The $(n + 1) \times (n + 1)$ determinant is a *bordered Hessian*, while the determinants of order n and less are principal minors.

The point $\bar{x}$ is a relative minimum if the quadratic form is positive definite, subject to the constraint on the variables y^i. This condition is equivalent to requiring the bordered Hessian and its principal minors of order three and up to be negative. If $\bar{x}$ is a regular extreme point, then the vanishing of the first-order partial derivatives of the Lagrangian function and the definiteness of the associated quadratic form (subject to the appropriate side condition) are both necessary and sufficient conditions.

The function $f(x)$ may be subjected to more than just one side condition. If x has n components, then one may impose on them m, $m < n$, independent constraints, say, $g^k(x) = 0$, $k = 1, 2, \dots, m$. In which case, the first-order conditions for an extreme point $\bar{x}$ in the interior of the constraint set C are

$$
f_i(\bar{x}) + \sum_{k=1}^{m} \bar{\lambda}^k g_i^k(\bar{x}) = 0, \qquad i = 1, 2, \dots, n,
$$

and
$$
g^k(x) = 0, \qquad k = 1, 2, \dots, m.
$$

Here, an assumption is made about the $m \times m$ matrices that can be formed from the partial derivatives g_i^k. Since there are n variables, there exist

$n!/(n!(n - m)!)$ different $m \times m$ matrices $[g_i^k]$ that may be formed. The assumption is that the determinant of at least one of these matrices is not zero.

In the second-order conditions, the variables of the quadratic form are now constrained by m conditions. Thus, the extreme point $\bar{x}$ is a relative maximum if

$$\sum_{i=1}^{n} \sum_{j=1}^{n} \left[f_{ij}(\bar{x}) + \sum_{k=1}^{m} \bar{\lambda}^k g_{ij}^k(\bar{x}) \right] y^i y^j < 0$$

for all values of the ys satisfying

$$\sum_{i=1}^{n} g_i^k(\bar{x}) y^i = 0, \qquad k = 1, 2, \ldots, m, \qquad \text{not all the } y^i = 0.$$

To state equivalent conditions in terms of the bordered Hessian and its principal minors, we introduce a typical principal minor by using the following notation:

$$D^r =$$

$$
\begin{vmatrix}
f_{11} + \sum_{k=1}^{m} \lambda^k g_{11}^k & f_{12} + \sum_{k=1}^{m} \lambda^k g_{12}^k & \cdots & f_{1r} + \sum_{k=1}^{m} \lambda^k g_{1r}^k & g_1^1 & g_1^2 & \cdots & g_1^m \\
f_{21} + \sum_{k=1}^{m} \lambda^k g_{12}^k & f_{22} + \sum_{k=1}^{m} \lambda^k g_{22}^k & \cdots & f_{2r} + \sum_{k=1}^{m} \lambda^k g_{2r}^k & g_2^1 & g_2^2 & \cdots & g_2^m \\
\vdots & & & & & & & \vdots \\
f_{r1} + \sum_{k=1}^{m} \lambda^k g_{r1}^k & f_{r2} + \sum_{k=1}^{m} \lambda^k g_{r2}^k & \cdots & f_{rr} + \sum_{k=1}^{m} \lambda^k g_{rr}^k & g_r^1 & g_r^2 & \cdots & g_r^m \\
g_1^1 & g_2^1 & \cdots & g_r^1 & 0 & 0 & \cdots & 0 \\
g_1^2 & g_2^2 & \cdots & g_r^2 & 0 & 0 & \cdots & 0 \\
\vdots & & & & & & & \vdots \\
g_1^m & g_2^m & \cdots & g_r^m & 0 & 0 & \cdots & 0
\end{vmatrix}.
$$

Clearly, D^n represents the $(n + m) \times (n + m)$ bordered Hessian. Then the quadratic form will be negative definite subject to the constraints if and only if

$$(- 1)^r D^r > 0, \qquad r = m + 1, m + 2, \ldots, n.$$

The quadratic form will be positive definite (for a relative minimum at $\bar{x}$) if and only if

$$(-1)^m D^r > 0, \qquad r = m + 1, m + 2, ..., n.$$

Thus, we see that in the case of a maximum, the principal minors alternate in sign, the smallest being positive if the number of constraints is odd, negative if the number of constraints is even. For a minimum, all the principal minors and the bordered Hessian have the same sign: negative if the number of constraints is odd, positive if the number of constraints is even.

15.1.6 Infinite Sequences and Series

An infinite sequence is a sequence of numbers x_1, x_2, x_3, ..., in which the number of terms goes to infinity. Such a sequence may be thought of as a function defined on the set of positive integers, and whose functional value at the point (integer) n is denoted by x_n. The latter is called the nth, or *general*, term of the sequence, and sometimes the entire sequence is denoted by $\{x_n\}$.

One aspect of infinite sequences which is of special interest is the behavior of the nth term as n approaches infinity. Under certain circumstances, the nth term may approach a finite limit, say L, as n approaches infinity; that is, we may have

$$\lim_{n \to \infty} x_n = L.$$

If a limit such as L exists, we say that the sequence $\{x_n\}$ is *convergent*; if it is not convergent, then it is said to be *divergent*.

A special class of sequences is the set of monotonic sequences (that is, sequences that are either always increasing or always decreasing). For such a sequence, we state the following basic result:

Proposition 15.18. *A monotonic infinite sequence converges if and only if it is bounded.*

In general, of course, sequences may assume a variety of forms, so that the question of convergence must in each case be examined in the light of whatever information is known about the given sequence. Another example of a convergent sequence is one in which the difference between successive terms decreases steadily. Formally:

Proposition 15.19. *If there exists a number $k < 1$ such that for every integer n it is true that*

$$|x_{n+2} - x_{n+1}| \leqslant k|x_{n+1} - x_n|,$$

then the sequence $\{x_n\}$ converges to a finite limit.

This proposition may be applied to the case in which a sequence of numbers is generated by a recursive system such as $x_n = f(x_{n-1})$. It then follows that if the function $f(x)$ satisfies a global Lipschitz condition with constant $k < 1$ at every point in its domain, then the infinite sequence $\{x_n\}$ is convergent. In which case, the Lipschitz condition yields

$$|f(x_{n+1}) - f(x_n)| \leqslant k|x_{n+1} - x_n|,$$

and, by making use of the recursive formula $x_n = f(x_{n-1})$, we have

$$|x_{n+2} - x_{n+1}| \leqslant k|x_{n+1} - x_n|,$$

which satisfies the condition of the above proposition. These results also hold for a system of simultaneous sequences, that is, for the case in which x_n is a vector, and $f(x)$ is a vector-valued function. Of course, in that case the notation $|x_{n+1} - x_n|$ denotes the norm of the vector $x_{n+1} - x_n$.

Convergence of an infinite sequence may also be defined in terms of the distance between different terms of the sequence (rather than the distance between the general term and the limit of the sequence). This approach is particularly useful if the limit of the sequence is not known, and is difficult to compute.

Proposition 15.20. (*Cauchy condition.*) *The infinite sequence $\{x_n\}$ is convergent if and only if for every $\varepsilon > 0$ there exists on integer N such that*

$$|x_n - x_m| < \varepsilon \quad whenever \quad n \geqslant N \quad and \quad m \geqslant N.$$

If we sum the first n terms of an infinite sequence, we can write

$$s_n = \sum_{i=1}^{n} x_i.$$

The numbers s_n are also an infinite sequence denoted by $\{s_n\}$. Such a sequence is called an *infinite series*, and the term s_n is referred to as the nth *partial sum* of the series. An infinite series is said to be convergent if the sequence $\{s_n\}$ is convergent; it is divergent if $\{s_n\}$ is divergent. Thus, the convergence of an infinite series can be studied by means of the criteria and conditions that apply to the convergence of infinite sequences. We state a general relationship between the convergence of an infinite series and the general term x_n.

Proposition 15.21. *If the infinite series $\{s_n\}$ is convergent, then* $\lim_{n \to \infty} x_n = 0.$

We may point out that the converse of the above proposition is not true. For example, the sequence $x_n = 1/n$ is convergent, since $\lim_{n \to \infty} x_n = 0$; however, the series

$$\{s_n\} = \sum_{i=1}^{n} x_i = \sum_{i=1}^{n} \frac{1}{i}$$

diverges, since s_n tends to infinity as n approaches infinity.

The Cauchy condition may be applied to infinite series by direct translation (substitution).

Proposition 15.22. *The infinite series $\{s_n\}$ is convergent if and only if for every $\varepsilon > 0$ there exists an integer N such that*

$$|x_{m+1} + x_{m+2} + \cdots + x_n| < \varepsilon \quad \text{whenever} \quad n > m > N.$$

15.2 LINEAR ALGEBRA

15.2.1 Matrices

It is often convenient to arrange sets of numbers in the form of a rectangular array; such an array is called a *matrix*. A particular matrix, say A, may be represented in the following form:

$$A = \begin{bmatrix} a_{11} & a_{12} & \cdots & a_{1n} \\ a_{21} & a_{22} & \cdots & a_{2n} \\ \vdots & & & \vdots \\ a_{m1} & a_{m2} & \cdots & a_{mn} \end{bmatrix}.$$

The a_{ij}, which are numbers, are referred to as the *elements* of the matrix. Sometimes, the following abbreviated form of notation is used:

$$A = [a_{ij}], \quad i = 1, 2, \ldots, m, \quad j = 1, 2, \ldots, n,$$

where the first subscript denotes the row, the second subscript the column.

Matrix Operations.   Matrices may be operated on as defined by the rules given below.

a) *Scalar Multiplication.*   A matrix is said to be multiplied by a scalar (real number) if each of its elements is multiplied by the same scalar, that is,

$$kA = [ka_{ij}],$$

where k is a scalar.

b) *Matrix Addition.*   This operation can be performed only between *conformable* matrices. For the purpose of addition, conformability requires that the matrices to be added are of the same dimensions, that is, have the same number of rows and columns, respectively. To add two (conformable) matrices, we add their respective elements. Thus

$$A + B = C = [c_{ij}], \quad \text{where} \quad c_{ij} = a_{ij} + b_{ij}.$$

From the definition of this operation, it is clear that the order of the addition does not matter, that is,

$$A + B = B + A.$$

c) *Matrix Subtraction.* This operation is a combination of scalar multiplication and addition. Thus

$$A - B = A + (-1)B.$$

d) *Matrix Multiplication.* When two matrices A and B are such that one can be multiplied by the other, the product may be written as AB; in which case, we say that A is being multiplied (or postmultiplied) by B. Here, the matrix A is called the *premultiplier* and B the *postmultiplier*. The conformability rule for matrix multiplication requires that the number of columns in the premultiplier be equal to the number of rows in the postmultiplier. Thus, if A is of dimensions $m \times n$, and B is of dimensions $n \times r$, A may be postmultiplied by B (or B may be premultiplied by A). The product of this multiplication is a matrix C of dimensions $m \times r$; thus

$$\begin{matrix} m \times n & & n \times r & & m \times r \\ A & \cdot & B & = & C \end{matrix},$$

and a typical element of C is given by $c_{ij} = \sum\limits_{k=1}^{n} a_{ik} b_{kj}$.

The following example illustrates matrix multiplication. Let

$$\underset{3 \times 3}{A} = \begin{bmatrix} a_{11} & a_{12} & a_{13} \\ a_{21} & a_{22} & a_{23} \\ a_{31} & a_{32} & a_{33} \end{bmatrix} \quad \text{and} \quad \underset{3 \times 1}{B} = \begin{bmatrix} b_{11} \\ b_{21} \\ b_{31} \end{bmatrix}.$$

Then $A \cdot B = C$, where

$$\underset{3 \times 1}{C} = \begin{bmatrix} a_{11}b_{11} + a_{12}b_{21} + a_{13}b_{31} \\ a_{21}b_{11} + a_{22}b_{21} + a_{23}b_{31} \\ a_{31}b_{11} + a_{32}b_{21} + a_{33}b_{31} \end{bmatrix}.$$

Properties of Matrix Products. a) If the premultiplier and the postmultiplier are interchangeable, each of the two possible multiplications may yield a different product. Thus, in general

$$AB \neq BA,$$

as is illustrated by the following example. Let

$$A = \begin{bmatrix} 1 & 0 \\ 0 & 2 \end{bmatrix} \quad \text{and} \quad B = \begin{bmatrix} 1 & 1 \\ 0 & 0 \end{bmatrix}.$$

Then

$$AB = \begin{bmatrix} 1 & 1 \\ 0 & 0 \end{bmatrix} \neq BA = \begin{bmatrix} 1 & 2 \\ 0 & 0 \end{bmatrix}.$$

b) $A(BC) = (AB)C$,   associative law,

c) $A(B + C) = AB + AC, (B + C)A = BA + CA$,   distributive law.

Some Special Matrices

a) *Identity Matrix.*   The identity matrix is a square (that is, $n \times n$) matrix (of any order), with each element on the main diagonal (northwest-southeast diagonal) being equal to unity, all other elements being zero. It is denoted by I. Thus

$$I = \begin{bmatrix} 1 & 0 & \cdots & 0 \\ 0 & 1 & \cdots & 0 \\ \vdots & & & \vdots \\ 0 & 0 & \cdots & 1 \end{bmatrix}.$$

If A is any $n \times n$ matrix, and I is an $n \times n$ identity matrix, than $IA = AI = A$.

b) *Scalar Matrix.*   A scalar matrix is a square matrix with all elements on the main diagonal being equal to some scalar, all other elements being zero. If S is a scalar matrix, then

$$S = \begin{bmatrix} k & 0 & \cdots & 0 \\ 0 & k & \cdots & 0 \\ \vdots & & & \vdots \\ 0 & 0 & \cdots & k \end{bmatrix},$$

where k is a scalar. A scalar matrix can be thought of as the product of a scalar and an identity matrix; thus, $S = kI$. Of course, the identity matrix is itself a scalar matrix. Multiplying a scalar matrix by any other (conformable) matrix results in scalar multiplication; that is, $(kI)A = kA$.

c) *Diagonal Matrix.*   A diagonal matrix is a square matrix whose nonzero elements appear only on the main diagonal. If D denotes a diagonal matrix, then

$$D = \begin{bmatrix} k_1 & 0 & \cdots & 0 \\ 0 & k_2 & \cdots & 0 \\ \vdots & & & \vdots \\ 0 & 0 & \cdots & k_n \end{bmatrix},$$

where the k_i are scalars. Clearly, both identity and scalar matrices are special cases of diagonal matrices.

d) *Null Matrix.* A matrix (not necessarily square) all of whose elements are zero is called a *null matrix*, and is denoted by 0. When the conformability conditions for addition, subtraction, and multiplication, respectively, are satisfied, we have

$$A + 0 = 0 + A = A, \qquad A - A = 0, \qquad A0 = 0, \qquad 0A = 0.$$

If both A and 0 are $n \times n$, then $A0 = 0A = 0$.

It is interesting to point out that if the product of two matrices is a null matrix, then neither the premultiplier nor the postmultiplier need be a null matrix. That is, if $AB = 0$, then it does not follow that either $A = 0$, or $B = 0$. For example,

$$\text{if} \quad A = \begin{bmatrix} 1 & 1 \\ 1 & 1 \end{bmatrix} \neq 0, \quad \text{and} \quad B = \begin{bmatrix} -1 & 2 \\ 1 & -2 \end{bmatrix} \neq 0, \quad \text{then} \quad AB = 0.$$

e) *Transpose.* With each matrix, one can associate a transpose matrix. If A is any matrix, then the transpose of A is obtained by an interchange of columns and rows such that the ith row of A becomes the ith column of its transpose. The latter is denoted by A'. Thus, a typical element of A' is denoted by a'_{ij}, and $a'_{ij} = a_{ji}$. If a matrix A is identical to its transpose A', that is, $A = A'$, then A (and A') is said to be a *symmetric* matrix.

f) *Inverse.* Inverse matrices are associated only with square matrices; however, not every square matrix has an inverse. The inverse of a matrix A is denoted by A^{-1}, and it exists if and only if it satisfies the following equation:

$$A^{-1}A = AA^{-1} = I.$$

It is clear that A^{-1} must also be a square matrix. (Conditions for the existence of an inverse, and the representation of an inverse matrix, are discussed in Section 15.2.2.)

15.2.2 Determinants

With each square matrix, one can associate a number called the *determinant*. If A is a square matrix, its determinant is denoted by $|A|$. The basic rule for computing a determinant is quite complicated, and since it is hardly ever used in the context of mathematical economics, it is not stated here. A more indirect (but equivalent) form of representing (or computing) a determinant, which is more suitable for applications in economic models, will be given later in this section. In the meantime, we state a number of basic rules about determinants.

Basic Rules. We shall illustrate these rules with third-order determinants, which will be denoted by

$$\begin{vmatrix} a_{11} & a_{12} & a_{13} \\ a_{21} & a_{22} & a_{23} \\ a_{31} & a_{32} & a_{33} \end{vmatrix}.$$

a) When two rows or two columns of a square matrix are interchanged, the determinant is multiplied by -1. For example,

$$\begin{vmatrix} a_{11} & a_{12} & a_{13} \\ a_{21} & a_{22} & a_{23} \\ a_{31} & a_{32} & a_{33} \end{vmatrix} = - \begin{vmatrix} a_{11} & a_{13} & a_{12} \\ a_{21} & a_{23} & a_{22} \\ a_{31} & a_{33} & a_{32} \end{vmatrix},$$

$$\begin{vmatrix} a_{21} & a_{22} & a_{23} \\ a_{11} & a_{12} & a_{13} \\ a_{31} & a_{32} & a_{33} \end{vmatrix} = - \begin{vmatrix} a_{11} & a_{12} & a_{13} \\ a_{21} & a_{22} & a_{23} \\ a_{31} & a_{32} & a_{33} \end{vmatrix}.$$

b) The determinant of a matrix is equal to the determinant of its transpose; that is, $|A| = |A'|$. For example,

$$\begin{vmatrix} a_{11} & a_{12} & a_{13} \\ a_{21} & a_{22} & a_{23} \\ a_{31} & a_{32} & a_{33} \end{vmatrix} = \begin{vmatrix} a_{11} & a_{21} & a_{31} \\ a_{12} & a_{22} & a_{32} \\ a_{13} & a_{23} & a_{33} \end{vmatrix}.$$

c) If a square matrix has two identical rows or columns, then its determinant is zero. For example,

$$\begin{vmatrix} a_{11} & a_{12} & a_{13} \\ a_{21} & a_{22} & a_{23} \\ a_{11} & a_{12} & a_{13} \end{vmatrix} = \begin{vmatrix} a_{12} & a_{12} & a_{13} \\ a_{22} & a_{22} & a_{23} \\ a_{32} & a_{32} & a_{33} \end{vmatrix} = 0.$$

d) If each element in either a row or a column of a square matrix is multiplied by a scalar k, then the determinant is multiplied by k. For example

$$\begin{vmatrix} ka_{11} & a_{12} & a_{13} \\ ka_{21} & a_{22} & a_{23} \\ ka_{31} & a_{32} & a_{33} \end{vmatrix} = \begin{vmatrix} a_{11} & a_{12} & a_{13} \\ ka_{21} & ka_{22} & ka_{23} \\ a_{31} & a_{32} & a_{33} \end{vmatrix} = k \begin{vmatrix} a_{11} & a_{12} & a_{13} \\ a_{21} & a_{22} & a_{23} \\ a_{31} & a_{32} & a_{33} \end{vmatrix}.$$

An implication of this rule is that if every element of a $n \times n$ matrix A is multiplied by k, then the determinant is multiplied by k^n. Thus

$$|kA| = k^n|A|.$$

e) If each element in a row (column) of a square matrix is multiplied by a scalar, and then added to the corresponding element in another row (column), then the determinant remains unchanged. For example,

$$\begin{vmatrix} a_{11} & a_{12} + ka_{11} & a_{13} \\ a_{21} & a_{22} + ka_{21} & a_{23} \\ a_{31} & a_{32} + ka_{31} & a_{33} \end{vmatrix} = \begin{vmatrix} a_{11} & a_{12} & a_{13} \\ a_{21} & a_{22} & a_{23} \\ a_{31} & a_{32} & a_{33} \end{vmatrix},$$

and

$$\begin{vmatrix} a_{11} + ka_{31} & a_{12} + ka_{32} & a_{13} + ka_{33} \\ a_{21} & a_{22} & a_{23} \\ a_{31} & a_{32} & a_{33} \end{vmatrix} = \begin{vmatrix} a_{11} & a_{12} & a_{13} \\ a_{21} & a_{22} & a_{23} \\ a_{31} & a_{32} & a_{33} \end{vmatrix}.$$

Minors and Cofactors. A minor is the determinant of a square submatrix of some given matrix. Thus, if one deletes all but r rows and r columns of some matrix A, the remaining elements make up an $r \times r$ submatrix of A, say M, and its determinant, namely, $|M|$, is an rth order minor of A. For example,

if $\qquad A = \begin{bmatrix} a_{11} & a_{12} & a_{13} & a_{14} \\ a_{21} & a_{22} & a_{23} & a_{24} \end{bmatrix}, \qquad$ then $\qquad \begin{vmatrix} a_{12} & a_{14} \\ a_{22} & a_{24} \end{vmatrix}$

is a second-order minor of A. Minors of square matrices that are obtained by deleting a row and a column which intersect an element of the principal diagonal are called *principal minors*. For example,

if $\qquad A = \begin{bmatrix} a_{11} & a_{12} & a_{13} & a_{14} \\ a_{21} & a_{22} & a_{23} & a_{24} \\ a_{31} & a_{32} & a_{33} & a_{34} \\ a_{41} & a_{42} & a_{43} & a_{44} \end{bmatrix},$

then $\qquad \begin{vmatrix} a_{22} & a_{23} & a_{24} \\ a_{32} & a_{33} & a_{34} \\ a_{42} & a_{43} & a_{44} \end{vmatrix} \quad$ and $\quad \begin{vmatrix} a_{11} & a_{13} \\ a_{31} & a_{33} \end{vmatrix}.$

are principal minors of order three and two, respectively.

Every element a_{ij} of an $n \times n$ matrix A has associated with it a particular determinant called a *cofactor*, which will be denoted by A_{ij}. If we delete row i and column j of A, and multiply the determinant of the resulting $(n - 1) \times (n - 1)$ submatrix by $(- 1)^{i+j}$, then the number thus obtained is the cofactor of the element a_{ij}, that is, A_{ij}. It is clear that if $i + j$ is even, then the cofactor is equal to the corresponding minor. For example,

$$\text{if} \quad A = \begin{bmatrix} a_{11} & a_{12} & a_{13} \\ a_{21} & a_{22} & a_{23} \\ a_{31} & a_{32} & a_{33} \end{bmatrix},$$

$$\text{then} \quad A_{31} = \begin{vmatrix} a_{12} & a_{13} \\ a_{22} & a_{23} \end{vmatrix}, \quad \text{and} \quad A_{23} = - \begin{vmatrix} a_{11} & a_{12} \\ a_{31} & a_{32} \end{vmatrix}.$$

It may also be noted that the cofactors of elements on the principal diagonal are principal minors.

By means of cofactors, one can obtain a convenient representation of a determinant. This representation is called *expansion by cofactors*. According to this method, the determinant of any square matrix A is equal to the sum of the products of the elements in any row or column and their respective cofactors, that is,

$$|A| = \sum_{i=1}^{n} a_{ij} A_{ij} = \sum_{j=1}^{n} a_{ij} A_{ij} \qquad \text{for any } j \text{ and any } i.$$

This representation of a determinant is particularly useful in theoretical analysis, but it also yields a simple rule for evaluating the determinants of low-order matrices. For example, for a 2×2 matrix A, we get (expanding along the first column)

$$A_{11} = a_{22}, \quad A_{12} = -a_{21},$$

and hence $|A| = a_{11} a_{22} - a_{12} a_{21}$ (the product of the diagonal elements minus the product of the off-diagonal elements).

For a 3×3 matrix A, we have

$$|A| = a_{11} A_{11} + a_{21} A_{21} + a_{31} A_{31}.$$

Now, since in this case the A_{ij} are determinants of 2×2 matrices, we immediately find (by the above rule) that

$$A_{11} = a_{22} a_{33} - a_{23} a_{32}, \quad A_{21} = -(a_{12} a_{33} - a_{13} a_{32}),$$

and

$$A_{31} = a_{12} a_{23} - a_{13} a_{22}.$$

Hence,

$$|A| = a_{11}(a_{22} a_{33} - a_{23} a_{32}) - a_{21}(a_{12} a_{33} - a_{13} a_{32}) + a_{31}(a_{12} a_{23} - a_{13} a_{22})$$
$$= a_{11} a_{22} a_{33} - a_{11} a_{23} a_{32} - a_{21} a_{12} a_{33} + a_{21} a_{31} a_{32}$$
$$\quad + a_{31} a_{12} a_{23} - a_{31} a_{13} a_{22}.$$

If, in an expansion such as the above, the elements in a particular row (column) are multiplied by the cofactors of the corresponding elements of another row (column) the result is called *expansion by alien cofactors.* An expansion by alien cofactors always vanishes. Thus,

$$\sum_{i=1}^{n} a_{ij} A_{ik} = 0, \qquad j \neq k,$$

and

$$\sum_{j=1}^{n} a_{ij} A_{kj} = 0, \qquad i \neq k.$$

Adjoint and Inverse. Let us now construct a matrix by replacing each element a_{ij} of an $n \times n$ matrix A by its cofactor. Thus,

$$\begin{bmatrix} A_{11} & A_{12} & \cdots & A_{1n} \\ A_{21} & A_{22} & \cdots & A_{2n} \\ \vdots & & & \vdots \\ A_{n1} & A_{n2} & \cdots & A_{nn} \end{bmatrix}.$$

Forming the transpose of the above matrix, we get

$$\hat{A} = \begin{bmatrix} A_{11} & A_{21} & \cdots & A_{n1} \\ A_{12} & A_{22} & \cdots & A_{n2} \\ \vdots & & & \vdots \\ A_{1n} & A_{2n} & \cdots & A_{nn} \end{bmatrix},$$

where $\hat{A}$ is called the *adjoint matrix* of A. If we multiply the matrix A by its adjoint matrix, then, by virtue of the rule for expansion by cofactors, we get a scalar matrix, the scalar being the determinant of A; that is,

$$A \cdot \hat{A} = \begin{bmatrix} |A| & 0 & \cdots & 0 \\ 0 & |A| & \cdots & 0 \\ \vdots & & & \vdots \\ 0 & 0 & \cdots & |A| \end{bmatrix} = |A|I.$$

However, it then follows from the definition of the inverse matrix (Section 15.2.1.) that

$$A^{-1} = \frac{1}{|A|} \cdot \hat{A}.$$

Since the rhs of this equation is defined only if $|A| \neq 0$, we see that for a square matrix to have an inverse, its determinant must not vanish. If this condition holds, the matrix is said to be *nonsingular*; otherwise it is said to be *singular*. We can, therefore, restate the conclusion by saying that a matrix has an inverse if and only if it is nonsingular.

Except for some special cases, it is not immediately obvious whether a matrix is singular or not. A special class of nonsingular matrices are those having a *dominant diagonal*, which we define as follows:

An $n \times n$ matrix $[a_{ij}]$ is said to have a dominant diagonal if and only if there exists a vector of positive constants $(c_1, c_2, ..., c_n)$ such that either

$$c_i |a_{ii}| > \sum_{\substack{j=1 \\ j \neq i}}^{n} c_j |a_{ij}|, \qquad i = 1, 2, ..., n,$$

or

$$c_j |a_{jj}| > \sum_{\substack{i=1 \\ i \neq j}}^{n} c_i |a_{ij}|, \qquad j = 1, 2, ..., n.$$

Thus, a matrix has a dominant diagonal if there exists a set of weights such that the weighted magnitude (that is, absolute value) of the diagonal term is larger than the weighted sum of the magnitudes of the off-diagonal terms, either in the same row or in the same column. Hence, we may have row-wise dominance, or column-wise dominance. The following is a fundamental result concerning matrices with a dominant diagonal.

Proposition 15.23. *If a matrix has a dominant diagonal, then it is nonsingular.*

It follows immediately that if the matrix A has a dominant diagonal, then every principal submatrix of A (that is, the matrix associated with a principal minor of A) also has a dominant diagonal.

15.2.3 Vectors

A column vector may be defined as an $n \times 1$ matrix. Conversely, we may think of a matrix as an ordered set of column vectors, and it may be represented in the following form:

$$\underset{a_1}{\begin{bmatrix} a_{11} \\ a_{21} \\ \vdots \\ a_{n1} \end{bmatrix}} \quad \underset{a_2}{\begin{bmatrix} a_{12} \\ a_{22} \\ \vdots \\ a_{n2} \end{bmatrix}} \quad \cdots \quad \underset{a_m}{\begin{bmatrix} a_{1m} \\ a_{2m} \\ \vdots \\ a_{nm} \end{bmatrix}}.$$

Here, the first subscript of a typical element indicates the position of the element in the vector to which it belongs (counting from the top down), and the second subscript (which is the same for each element in the same vector) indicates the position of the vector in the particular set of vectors (counting from left to right). A matrix may, of course, also be thought of as a set of row vectors, but since all the fundamental theorems concerning vectors are invariant to a transposition from column to row vectors, and vice versa, we shall limit the discussion in this section to column vectors.

Linear Dependence. Given a set of vectors, it may be possible to write one of them as a linear combination of the remaining ones. For example, given three four-element vectors, one may find two numbers, say c_2 and c_3, such that

$$a_{11} = c_2 a_{12} + c_3 a_{13},$$

$$a_{21} = c_2 a_{22} + c_3 a_{23},$$

$$a_{31} = c_2 a_{32} + c_3 a_{33},$$

$$a_{41} = c_2 a_{42} + c_3 a_{43}.$$

Using vector notation, the above may also be written as

$$a_1 = c_2 a_2 + c_3 a_3,$$

where $c_j a_j$ denotes a scalar multiplication (as defined in Section 15.2.1). If this equation holds, we say that the above three vectors are *linearly dependent*. More formally, given any m vectors a_j, $j = 1, 2, ..., m$ (all having the same number of elements), then the set of vectors is said to be linearly dependent if and only if there exist m scalars c_j, $j = 1, 2, ..., m$, at least one of which is different from zero, such that $c_1 a_1 + c_2 a_2 + \cdots + c_m a_m = 0$. If the only set of scalars satisfying this equation is the set $c_1 = c_2 = \cdots = c_m = 0$, then we say that the set of vectors is *linearly independent*. If a set of vectors is linearly independent, the above definition implies that no vector in the set can be written as a linear combination of the remaining vectors.

The concept of linear independence plays a crucial role in an important property of matrices called the *rank* of a matrix. The rank of a matrix A, denoted by $R(A)$, is defined as the maximum number of linearly independent column vectors. There exists an important relationship between the rank of a matrix and certain properties of the minors of the matrix. This relationship is the subject of the following proposition.

Proposition 15.24. *Suppose that A is an $n \times m$ matrix. Then $R(A) = k$ if and only if every minor in A of order $k + 1$ vanishes, and at least one minor of order k does not vanish.*

In the case of square matrices, there also exists an important relationship between the rank and the determinant of a matrix.

Proposition 15.25. *If A is an $n \times n$ matrix, then $|A| \neq 0$ if and only if $R(A) = n$.*

Simultaneous Equations. In economic theory, we often encounter systems of simultaneous linear equations. Such a system may be written in the following way:

$$a_{11}x^1 + a_{12}x^2 + \cdots + a_{1n}x^n = b^1,$$
$$a_{21}x^1 + a_{22}x^2 + \cdots + a_{2n}x^n = b^2,$$
$$\vdots \qquad\qquad\qquad\qquad \vdots$$
$$a_{n1}x^1 + a_{n2}x^2 + \cdots + a_{nn}x^n = b^n,$$

where it is assumed that not all the *b*s are zero. Using matrix (and vector) notation, the above system may also be written as

$$Ax = b,$$

where A is the $n \times n$ matrix $[a_{ij}]$, x is the column vector (that is, $n \times 1$ matrix) of the x^j, and b is the column vector of the b^i. Note that the product Ax represents matrix multiplication. Two questions that we are most interested in are:

a) Does the above system have a solution? That is, does there exist a vector x satisfying the above equations simultaneously?

b) If the system has a solution, how can it be found?

The answer to the first question is very simple: If $R(A) = n$, then the system possesses a unique solution. This may be shown by the following argument. If $R(A) = n$, then we know that $|A| \neq 0$, hence the matrix A has an inverse A^{-1}. Premultiplying both sides of the above matrix equation by A^{-1}, we get

$$A^{-1}Ax = A^{-1}b.$$

But $A^{-1}Ax = Ix = x$, hence

$$x = A^{-1}b.$$

The last equation also indicates how the solution may be found; namely, by multiplying the inverse matrix by the column vector b. This method, however, is only of limited practical value, since, except for small matrices (say, of dimension 3×3 or smaller), the computation (by hand) of the inverse matrix may be a rather lengthy affair. For theoretical purposes, we may represent the solution vector x in a more convenient form.

Earlier (Section 15.2.2) it was shown that

$$A^{-1} = \frac{1}{|A|}\,\hat{A}.$$

Therefore, we can write

$$x = \frac{1}{|A|}\,\hat{A}b.$$

Then the jth component of x is given by

$$x^j = \frac{A_{1j}b^1 + A_{2j}b^2 + \cdots + A_{nj}b^n}{|A|}.$$

Recalling the formula for the expansion of a determinant by cofactors, we see that the numerator in the above equation is equal to the determinant of a matrix obtained as a result of replacing the jth column of A by the column vector b. We thus have the following rule for representing the jth component of the solution vector x:

To represent x^j, replace the jth column of A by the column vector b, and divide the determinant of the matrix thus obtained by $|A|$.

This method is called *Cramer's rule*, and it may be illustrated as follows:

$$x^j = \frac{1}{|A|} \begin{vmatrix} a_{11} & a_{12} & \cdots & a_{1,j-1} & b^1 & a_{1,j+1} & \cdots & a_{1n} \\ a_{21} & a_{22} & \cdots & a_{2,j-1} & b^2 & a_{2,j+1} & \cdots & a_{2n} \\ \vdots & & & & & & & \vdots \\ a_{n1} & a_{n2} & \cdots & a_{n,j-1} & b^n & a_{n,j+1} & \cdots & a_{nn} \end{vmatrix}.$$

Clearly, if $b^i = 0$ for all i, then $x^j = 0$ for all j.

15.3   INTEGRAL CALCULUS

15.3.1   Indefinite Integrals

An indefinite integral of some given function is a function which upon differentiation yields the original function. Thus, if for some given function $f(x)$ there exists a function, say $F(x)$, such that $F'(x) = f(x)$, then $F(x)$ is an indefinite integral of $f(x)$. As this definition suggests, the process of integration, that is, the derivation, or construction, of an indefinite integral, is the inverse of differentiation. The general form of an indefinite integral is obtained by adding to an indefinite integral an arbitrary constant c. This general form is called the *indefinite integral* of $f(x)$, and is denoted by $\int f(x)dx$. Hence

$$\int f(x)dx = F(x) + c.$$

Here, $f(x)$ is called the *integrand*, and the symbol $\int$ is the *integral sign*. The variable x is the *variable of integration*, that is, the variable with respect to which the process of integration is carried out. The constant c is the *constant of integration.*

If a function is continuous on some closed interval, then it possesses an indefinite integral over that interval.

15.3.2   Definite Integrals

Unlike an indefinite integral (which is a function), a definite integral is a number. To define a (Riemann) definite integral, let us consider a function $f(x)$ that is continuous over a closed interval $[a, b]$. We divide the interval $[a, b]$ into n subintervals, and denote the length of the ith subinterval by Δx_i, where $\Delta x_i = x_i - x_{i-1}$, $i = 1, 2, \ldots, n$, and $x_0 = a$, $x_n = b$. We then choose an arbitrary point in each of the n subintervals (not necessarily in the interior of the subinterval), and denote these points by ξ_i, where ξ_i is the point chosen in the ith subinterval, that is $x_{i-1} \leqslant \xi_i \leqslant x_i$. We can then form the following sum:

$$s_n = f(\xi_1)\,\Delta x_1 + f(\xi_2)\,\Delta x_2 + \cdots + f(\xi_n)\,\Delta x_n.$$

Geometrically speaking, the product $f(\xi_i)\Delta x_i$ represents the area of a certain rectangle, the height of which is given by the value of the function $f(x)$ at the point ξ_i, and the base of which is equal to the length of the ith subinterval. (See Fig. 15.6.) It is clear that the value of s_n depends [aside from the form of the function $f(x)$] on the number and sizes of the subdivisions, as well as on the points ξ_i.

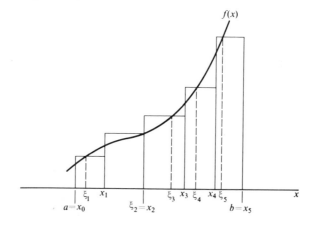

Figure 15.6

The interval $[a, b]$ may, of course, be divided into an arbitrarily large number of subdivisions, and one way of doing so is to let the largest subinterval, denoted by δ, approach zero as n (the number of subdivisions) is made to approach infinity. If the sum s_n has a limit as δ goes to zero, the limit being independent of the method of subdividing the interval and independent of the choice of the points ξ_i, then this limit is called the *definite integral* of $f(x)$ from point a to point b, and is denoted by

$$\int_a^b f(x)dx.$$

As in the case of an indefinite integral, in the above expression the function $f(x)$ is called the integrand. The numbers a and b are called the *lower limit of integration* and the *upper limit of integration*, respectively. We now state some basic properties of definite integrals.

a) *Reversing the limits of integration has the effect of multiplying the integral by* -1; *that is,*

$$\int_a^b f(x)dx = -\int_b^a f(x)dx.$$

b) $\int_a^a f(x)dx = 0.$

c) *A definite integral can always be written as a sum of integrals, that is,*

$$\int_a^b f(x)dx = \int_a^c f(x)dx + \int_c^b f(x)dx,$$

where the point c need not necessarily be in the interval $[a, b]$.

d) *For any constant k,*

$$\int_a^b kf(x)dx = k\int_a^b f(x)dx.$$

e) *The integral of a sum is a sum of integrals, that is,*

$$\int_a^b [f(x) + g(x)]\, dx = \int_a^b f(x)dx + \int_a^b g(x)dx.$$

f) *The value of an integral is independent of the notation used for the variable of integration; that is,*

$$\int_a^b f(x)dx = \int_a^b f(y)dy.$$

To evaluate a definite integral, one finds an indefinite integral of the integrand, and then computes the difference between the values of the indefinite integral at the lower and upper bound, respectively. Thus, if $F(x)$ is an indefinite integral of $f(x)$, then

$$\int_a^b f(x)dx = F(b) - F(a).$$

This equation is known as the *fundamental theorem of integral calculus*. It may be remarked, however, that it may be quite difficult, sometimes even impossible, to find an indefinite integral $F(x)$ for a given function $f(x)$.

For computational as well as analytical purposes, it is often helpful to replace the variable of integration by some function, say $x = g(t)$. This substitution is called *change of variable*. For example, suppose that the function $g(t)$ has a continuous derivative over an interval $[c, d]$, and let $a = g(c)$, $b = g(d)$. Then we have

$$\int_a^b f(x)dx = \int_c^d f[g(t)]\, g'(t)\, dt.$$

Another useful method for evaluating a definite integral is known as *integration by parts*. This method is particularly helpful if the integrand is a product of two functions. Thus, suppose that $G(x)$ is an indefinite integral of $g(x)$, that is, $G'(x) = g(x)$. Then the definite integral of the product $f(x)\, g(x)$ is given by

$$\int_a^b f(x)g(x)dx = f(b)\,G(b) - f(a)\,G(a) - \int_a^b f'(x)\,G(x)\,dx.$$

Frequently, the expression $f(b)\,G(b) = f(a)G(a)$ is denoted by $f(x)G(x)|_a^b$.

A definite integral may also be stated in a nonintegral form by means of the Mean Value Theorem for integrals. Suppose that $f(x)$ is continuous over the interval $[a, b]$. Then there exists a number ξ, $a < \xi < b$, such that

$$\int_a^b f(x)dx = f(\xi)(b - a).$$

Differentiation of Integrals. A definite integral may be thought of as a function (rather than a number) if one (or both) of the limits of integration is allowed to vary, or if the integrand depends (aside from the variable of integration) on another variable, or parameter.

If the upper limit of integration is variable, the integral is a function of the upper limit, and may be written as

$$\int_a^x f(t)dt = h(x).$$

Then we have

$$h'(x) = f(x).$$

It follows immediately (from the rule for the interchange of the limits of integration) that if we have

$$\int_x^b f(t)dt = h(x),$$

then

$$h'(x) = -f(x).$$

Suppose now that $f(x, y)$ is continuous with respect to x over the interval $[a, b]$, and that its partial derivative with respect to y is continuous. Then the integral with respect to x is a function of y, and may be written as

$$\int_a^b f(x, y)dx = h(y).$$

In that case,

$$h'(y) = \int_a^b f_y(x, y)dx,$$

where $f_y = \partial f/\partial y$.

Finally, suppose that both the integrand and the limits of integration depend on the variable y; that is,

$$\int_{\psi(y)}^{\phi(y)} f(x, y)dx = h(y),$$

where the functions ϕ and ψ have finite derivatives. Then

$$h'(y) = \int_{\psi(y)}^{\phi(y)} f_y(x, y)\,dx + f[\phi(y), y]\,\phi'(y) - f[\psi(y), y]\,\psi'(y).$$

BIBLIOGRAPHICAL NOTES

This chapter is designed strictly for purposes of review. For more comprehensive and rigorous expositions (including proofs of the various propositions), the reader is advised to consult appropriate works in mathematics. The tools most frequently used in this book are usually dealt with in texts in advanced calculus and linear algebra. Examples of these are: T. M. Apostol, *Mathematical Analysis*, Reading: Addison-Wesley, 1957; A. E. Taylor, *Advanced Calculus*, New York: Ginn, 1955; and G. Hadley, *Linear Algebra*, Reading: Addison-Wesley, 1961. A selected list of complementary texts dealing with more advanced mathematical topics relevant to microtheory is the following: J. La Salle and S. Lefschetz, *Stability by Liapunov's Direct Method*, New York: Academic Press, 1961; D. A. Sánchez, *Ordinary Differential Equations and Stability Theory: An Introduction*, San Francisco: Freeman, 1968; T. L. Saaty and J. Bram, *Nonlinear Mathematics*, New York: McGraw-Hill, 1964; and I. M. Gelfand and S. V. Fomin, *Calculus of Variations*, Englewood Cliffs, N.J.: Prentice-Hall, 1963.

There also are available several texts in mathematical economics which contain sections on pure mathematics. By and large, these are more selective in content, and are, of course, oriented primarily toward problems in economics. Among these are: R. G. D. Allen, *Mathematical Economics*, 2nd edition, London: Macmillan, 1959; W. J. Baumol, *Economic Dynamics*, 3rd edition, New York: Macmillan, 1970; A. C. Chiang, *Fundamental Methods of Mathematical Economics*, New York:

McGraw-Hill, 1967; R. Frisch, *Maxima and Minima*, Chicago: Rand McNally, 1966; and K. Lancaster, *Mathematical Economics*, New York: Macmillan, 1968.

For the study of stochastic models, a minimum background in probability theory is necessary. The following texts provide an introduction to this topic: J. Bass, *Elements of Probability Theory*, New York: Academic Press, 1966; H. Cramér, *The Elements of Probability Theory*, New York: Wiley, 1955; and P. L. Meyer, *Introductory Probability and Statistical Applications*, 2nd edition, Reading: Addison-Wesley, 1970.

AUTHOR INDEX

Allen, R. G. D., 207, 208, 365
Apostol, T. M., 365
Archibald, G. C., 143, 304
Arrow, K. J., 144, 208, 249, 283, 284, 303, 304, 327, 328

Bass, J., 366
Bassett, L., 304
Baumol, W. J., 328, 365
Bear, D. V. T., 75
Becker, G. S., 208
Bergson, A., 327
Bernoulli, D., 282, 283
Block, H. D., 304
Bohm, P., 328
Borch, K., 283
Borts, G. H., 44
Boulding, K. E., 23, 172, 207
Bram, J., 365
Brechling, F. P. R., 283
Brehm, C. T., 208
Breit, W., 8
Brumberg, R., 249

Carlson, S., 44
Chamberlin, E. H., 143
Champernowne, D. G., 7
Charnes, A., 284
Chiang, A. C., 365
Chipman, J. S., 7
Clower, R. W., 284
Cohan, A. B., 59
Cooper, G., 208
Cooper, W. W., 284
Cournot, A., 98, 143
Cramér, H., 366

Dantzig, G. B., 172
Davis, O. A., 328
Day, R. H., 284

Debreu, G., 207, 303, 327
Demsetz, H., 143
Diamond, P. A., 249
Dorfman, R., 7, 144, 172
Duesenberry, J. S., 7

Edwards, E. O., 98
Encarnación, J., 59
Euler, L., 343

Farrar, D. E., 283
Fellner, W., 283
Ferber, R., 249
Ferguson, C. E., 44, 75, 144
Fishburn, P. C., 207, 283
Fisher, F. M., 144
Foldes, L., 113
Folk, H. W., 208
Fomin, S. V., 365
Friedman, M., 8
Frisch, R., 44, 366

Gale, D., 172, 303
Gelfand, I. M., 365
Giffen, R., 186
Gorman, W. M., 208, 304
Gossen, H., 207
Gould, J. P., 249
Graaf, J. de V., 328

Habibagahi, H., 304
Hadar, J., 98, 144, 208, 249, 283, 284, 328
Hadley, G., 172, 365
Hahn, F. H., 144, 283
Hanoch, G., 283
Harris, T., 284
Hempel, C., 8
Henderson, J. M., 59, 75
Herstein, I. N., 283

SUBJECT INDEX

ABCDE7987654321